CORPUS LINGUISTICS AND LINGUISTICALLY ANNOTATED CORPORA

Also available from Bloomsbury

AN INTRODUCTION TO CORPUS LINGUISTICS
by David Oakey

COMPUTATIONAL AND QUANTITATIVE STUDIES
by M. A. K Halliday (edited by Jonathan J. Webster)

CONTEMPORARY CORPUS LINGUISTICS
edited by Paul Baker

CORPUS LINGUISTICS: A SHORT INTRODUCTION
by Wolfgang Teubert & Anna Cermáková

CORPUS LINGUISTICS: READINGS IN A WIDENING DISCIPLINE,
by Geoffrey Sampson & Diana McCarthy

LINGUISTICS: AN INTRODUCTION
by William McGregor

WEB AS CORPUS
by Maristella Gatto

WORKING WITH PORTUGUESE CORPORA
edited by Tony Berber Sardinha and Telma de Lurdes São Bento Ferreira

CORPUS LINGUISTICS AND LINGUISTICALLY ANNOTATED CORPORA

Sandra Kübler and Heike Zinsmeister

B L O O M S B U R Y

LONDON • NEW DELHI • NEW YORK • SYDNEY

Bloomsbury Academic

An imprint of Bloomsbury Publishing Plc

50 Bedford Square	1385 Broadway
London	New York
WC1B 3DP	NY 10018
UK	USA

www.bloomsbury.com

Bloomsbury is a registered trade mark of Bloomsbury Publishing Plc

First published 2015

© Sandra Kübler and Heike Zinsmeister 2015

British Library Cataloguing-in-Publication Data

A catalogue record for this book is available from the British Library.

ISBN: HB: 978-1-4411-6447-6
PB: 978-1-4411-1675-8
ePDF: 978-1-4411-1991-9
ePub: 978-1-4411-1980-3

Library of Congress Cataloging-in-Publication Data

Kuebler, Sandra.

Corpus Linguistics and Linguistically Annotated Corpora / Sandra Kuebler and Heike Zinsmeister.

p. cm

ISBN 978-1-4411-6447-6 (hardback) – ISBN 978-1-4411-6447-6 (paperback) 1. Corpora (Linguistics) 2. Compuational linguistics. I. Zinsmeister, Heike, 1967- author. II. Title.

P128.C68K84 2015

410.1'88–dc23

2014025488

Typeset by Fakenham Prepress Solutions, Fakenham, Norfolk NR21 8NN

CONTENTS

PREFACE

The idea for this textbook emerged when Sandra was teaching corpus linguistics to linguistics and computational linguistics students at Indiana University. One of the goals of this course was to demonstrate to her students how useful annotated corpora and tools established in computational linguistics are. She soon realized the two groups of students differed considerably with regard to prior knowledge. Many concepts that were familiar to her computational linguistics students were new to the linguists. She also found it necessary to introduce students to tools that allow easy access to corpora, especially those that go beyond pure text. Annotated corpora offer two types of challenges: On the one hand, they provide annotations that are often not familiar to linguists. Annotations need to cover complete texts, and thus many phenomena that are not well discussed in linguistic literature. For this reason, they tend to make fewer distinctions than linguistic analyses. On the other hand, the search in annotations requires specialized search tools, which are difficult to figure out on one's own. Additionally, the documentation of annotations and of tools often assumes knowledge that is not readily available to an uninitiated user. The goal of this book is to bridge the knowledge gap between linguistic users and the available documentation of the resources, as well as to promote the use of linguistically annotated corpora to the linguistic community in general.

This book has been a true collaboration between the two authors, with Sandra bringing her expertise in word-level and syntactic annotation to the project and Heike her expertise in semantic and dialogue annotation. But the final form was determined through dialogue. In the end, we both learned a lot about the topics covered in the book, and we also learned that the book is more than the sum of its parts.

We could not have completed this effort without the help of many colleagues in the field. We would like to thank Olga Babko-Malaya, Fabian Barteld, Kathrin Beck, Kelly Harper Berkson, Steven Bird, Donna Byron, Markus Dickinson, Stefanie Dipper, Kerstin Eckart, Johanna Flick, Steven Franks, Ulrich Heid, Erhard Hinrichs, Graeme Hirst, Varada Kolhatkar, Jonas Kuhn, Natalia Modjeska, Anna Nedoluzhko, Stella Neumann, Petya Osenova, Martha Palmer, Massimo Poesio, Arndt Riester, Sabine Schulte im Walde, Heike Telljohann, Yannick Versley, Bonnie Webber, and Tom Zastrow for sending examples, screenshots, and providing general support. Even if we could not integrate all material they provided, they contributed to the content of this book in a very substantial way.

Furthermore, we would like to thank the team at Bloomsbury Academic for their immense patience and support during the creation process. We would also like to thank Sandra's and Heike's families, colleagues, and students, who suffered along with us, especially during the final stages. Their patience was greatly appreciated.

Finally, our warmest thanks go to Olga Scrivner for help with proofreading and many useful suggestions that improved the text considerably. All remaining errors are, of course, ours.

Last but not least, we would like to thank all the linguists, annotators, and programmers who were involved in creating the resources and tools that we describe in this book. Without their work, this book would never have been written.

Sandra Kübler, Heike Zinsmeister
April 2014

PART I
INTRODUCTION

CHAPTER 1
CORPUS LINGUISTICS

1.1 Motivation

Corpus linguistics has a long tradition, especially in subdisciplines of linguistics that work with data for which it is hard or even impossible to gather native speakers' intuitions, such as historical linguistics, language acquisition, or phonetics. But the last two decades have witnessed a turn towards *empiricism* in linguistic subdisciplines, such as formal syntax. These subdisciplines of linguistics used to have a strong intuitionistic bias for many years and were traditionally based on introspective methods. Thus, linguists would use invented examples rather than attested language use. Such examples have the advantage that they concentrate on the phenomenon in question and abstract away from other types of complexities. Thus, if a linguist wants to study fronting, sentences like the ones listed in (1) clearly show which constituents can be fronted and which cannot. The sentence in (2) is an attested example[1] that shows the same type of fronting as the example in (1-a), but the sentence is more complicated and thus more difficult to analyze.

(1) a. In the morning, he read about linguistics.
     b. *The morning, he read about linguistics in.
(2) In the 1990s, spurred by rising labor costs and the strong yen, these companies will increasingly turn themselves into multinationals with plants around the world.

Nowadays, linguists of all schools consult linguistic corpora or use the world wide web as a corpus not only for collecting natural sounding examples, but also for testing their linguistic hypotheses against *quantitative* data of attested language use.

The amount of linguistically analyzed and publicly available corpora has also increased. Many of them had originally been created for computational linguistic purposes, to provide data that could be used for testing or developing automatic tools for analyzing language and other applications. In addition to their original purpose, many of the corpora have been made accessible, for example, in terms of online search interfaces to be readily used and explored by the linguistic community. But even if the resources are available, it is not always straightforward to determine how to use and interpret the available data. We can compare this to arriving in a foreign city. You can wander around on your own. But it is tremendously helpful to have a guide who shows you how to get around and explains how to profit from the characteristics of that particular city. And if you do not speak the local language, you need a translator or, even better, a guide, who introduces you to it.

This book is intended to guide the reader in a similar way. It guides the reader in how to find their way in the data by using appropriate query and visualization tools. It also introduces the reader to how to interpret annotation by explaining linguistic analyses and their encodings. The first part of the book gives an introduction on the general level, the second part deepens the understanding of these issues by presenting examples of major corpora and their linguistic annotations. The third part covers more practical issues, and the fourth part introduces search tools in more detail. The book has as its goal to make readers truly 'corpus-literate' by providing them with the specific knowledge that one needs to work with annotated corpora in a productive way.

This current chapter will motivate corpus linguistics per se and introduce important terminology. It will discuss introductory questions such as: What is a corpus and what makes a corpus different from an electronic collection of texts (section 1.2)? What kinds of corpora can be distinguished (section 1.3)? Is corpus linguistics a theory or a tool (section 1.4)? How does corpus linguistics differ from an intuitionistic approach to linguistics (section 1.5)? The chapter will end with an explanation of the structure of the book and a short synopsis of the following chapters (section 1.6). Finally, this chapter, like all chapters, will be complemented by a list of further reading (section 1.7).

1.2 Definition of Corpus

A modern *linguistic corpus* is an electronically available collection of texts or transcripts of audio recordings which is sampled to represent a certain language, language variety, or other linguistic domain. It is optionally enriched with levels of linguistic analysis, which we will call *linguistic annotation*. The origin of the text samples and other information regarding the sampling criteria are described in the *metadata* of the corpus.

The remainder of this section will motivate and explain different issues arising from this definition of corpus. For beginners in the field, we want to point out that the term corpus has its origin in Latin, meaning 'body'. For this reason, the plural of corpus is formed according to Latin morphology: one corpus, two *corpora*.

As indicated above, nowadays the term corpus is almost synonymous with *electronically available corpus*, but this is not necessarily so. Some linguistic subdisciplines have a long-standing tradition for working with corpora also in the pre-computer area, in particular historical linguistics, phonetics, and language acquisition. Pre-electronic corpora used in lexicography and grammar development often consisted of samples of short text snippets that illustrate the use of a particular word or grammar construction. But there were also some comprehensive quantitative evaluations of large text bodies. To showcase the characteristic properties of modern corpora, we will look back in time and consider an extreme example of quantitative evaluation in the pre-computer area in which relevant processing steps had to be performed manually.

At the end of the nineteenth century, before the invention of tape-recorders, there had been a strong interest in writing shorthand for documenting spoken language. Shorthand was intended as a system of symbols to represent letters, words, or even phrases, that allows the writer to optimize their speed of writing. The stenographer Friedrich Wilhelm Kaeding saw an opportunity for improving German shorthand by basing the system on solid statistics of word, syllable, and character distributions. In order to create an optimal shorthand system, words and phrases that occur very frequently should be represented by a short, simple symbol while less frequent words can be represented by longer symbols. To achieve such a system, Kaeding carried out a large-scale project in which hundreds of volunteers counted the frequencies of more than 250,000 words and their syllables in a text collection of almost 11 million words. It is obvious that it had been an enormous endeavor which took more than five years to complete.

To make the task of counting words and syllables feasible, it had to be split into different subtasks. The first, preparatory task was performed by 665 volunteers who simply copied all relevant word forms that occurred in the texts on index cards in a systematic way, including information about the source text. Subsequently, all index cards were sorted in alphabetical order for counting the frequencies of re-occurring words. Using one card for each instance made the counting *replicable* in the sense that other persons could also take the stack of cards, count the index cards themselves, and compare their findings with the original results. As we will see later, replicability is an important aspect of corpus linguistics.

The enormous manual effort described above points to a crucial property of modern linguistic corpora that we tend to take for granted as naïve corpus users: A corpus provides texts in form of *linguistically meaningful and retrievable units* in a reusable way.

Kaeding's helpers invested an enormous amount of time in identifying words, sorting, and counting them manually. The great merit of computers is that they perform exactly such tasks for us automatically, much more quickly, and more reliably: They can perform search, retrieval, sorting, calculations, and even visualization of linguistic information in a mechanic way. But it is a necessary prerequisite that relevant units are encoded as identifiable entities in the data representation. In Kaeding's approach, for example, he needed to define what a word is. This is a non-trivial decision, even in English if we consider expressions such as **don't**[2] or **in spite of**. How this is done will be introduced in the following section and, in more detail, in Chapter 3.

1.2.1 Electronic Processing

Making a corpus available electronically goes beyond putting a text file on a web page. At the very least, there are several technical steps involved in the creation of a corpus. The first step concerns making the text accessible in a corpus. If we already have our text in electronic form, this generally means that the file is in PDF format or it is a MS Word document, to name just the most common formats. As a consequence, such files can only be opened by specific, mostly proprietary applications, and searching in such files is restricted to the search options that the application provides. Thus, we can search for individual words in PDF files, but we cannot go beyond that. When creating a corpus, we need more flexibility. This means that we need to extract the text and only the text from these formatted files. If our original text is not available electronically, we need to use a scanner to create an electronic image of the text and then use an Optical Character Recognition (OCR) software that translates such an image to text. Figure 1.1 shows a scanned image of the beginning of the "Roman de Flamenca," a thirteenth-century novel written in Old Occitan, on the left and the results of using OCR on the image on the right. Generally, the OCR output is not free of errors; see for example the word **di[s]** in the image in Figure 1.1, which is recognized as **dies]**. Thus, if possible, the OCR output should be corrected manually.

We also need to decide how much of the original text formatting we need to represent in the corpus. Some corpus linguists are convinced that it is important to keep information about the number and type of white spaces or which words are written in bold face or in italics. However, if we want to perform linguistic annotations, then such formatting information is often more of a hindrance than an asset. Thus, if we want to keep such information, it would make sense to separate it from the text. Then, we have one file with pure text without any formatting and one file with the additional information.

The next problem that we need to solve is *character encoding*, i.e. the internal representation of characters on the computer. If our texts are in English, this is not a

Figure 1.1 An image of the first page of the "Roman de Flamenca" and the OCR output.

problem, but if we have additional characters, such as the accented characters in Figure 1.1, they have to be represented correctly; otherwise, they may be displayed as different characters if the text is opened in a different application. This problem becomes even more challenging for languages such as Arabic or Chinese, which are not based on a character set like English.

Character encodings are not corpus-specific but used for text representation in general. The most basic one is the ASCII format (American Standard Code for Information Interchange), which is a numeric encoding defined to represent the English alphabet, digits from 0 to 9, punctuation symbols, and some formatting-related commands such as space or line break. A more powerful encoding is Unicode, a comprehensive extension of ASCII that allows us to represent all kinds of scripts including Arabic, Cyrillic, or ancient scripts like Egyptian hieroglyphs, and also Chinese characters. A very common specification of Unicode is UTF-8. An important aspect here is that spaces or other empty text positions are also represented as atomic elements in character encoding.

The last problem concerns the *segmentation* of the text, which at this point is a long sequence of characters, into meaningful units, as mentioned above. The units that are generally used are sentences and words. The segmentation into word tokens is called *tokenization*. Non-word symbols can serve as word boundaries but this is not necessarily so. For example, **don't** is often tokenized into two tokens **do** and **not** as in (3-a), where || marks word boundaries. In contrast, multi-word expressions, such as **couch potato** or **in spite of**, are very often tokenized into their components defined by white space irrespective of their non-compositional semantics, cf. (3-b). Punctuation is stripped off the word string to which it is attached in the text and constitutes a token on its own, whereas abbreviations or ordinals are not segmented, as exemplified in (3-c).

(3) a. don't → ||do||not||
     b. in spite of → ||in||spite||of||
     c. Mr. Spielberg produced "Men in Black". →
         ||Mr.||Spielberg||produced||"||Men||in||Black||"||.||

The tokenization of corpus text can be done on the fly, for example, based on rules, such as: *Split at white-space and strip off punctuation*. Given the examples in (3), it is clear that there is still room for interpretation, which calls for more detailed rules about how contracted word forms, multi-word expressions, and punctuation are to be handled. In addition, there are scripts like Chinese that generally do not mark word boundaries by spaces. It is clear that tokenization is a much bigger challenge there.

The disambiguation of '.' as period versus other usages such as abbreviation marker plays a central role in automatic sentence segmentation. For human readers, this distinction is easy to make. But for computers, this disambiguation is not straightforward and requires rules or corpus-derived statistical evidence. Other phenomena in sentence segmentation are not as straightforward, even for the human reader. For example, does the colon in (4-a) mark a sentence boundary or not?[3] An argument against a boundary here is that **What's on the test** functions as the object of **know** hence the first part of the sentence would be an incomplete sentence without the second part after the colon. But should this decision hold even if there is a whole list of dependent sentences, for example, if the students wanted to know several things at the same time as in (4-b), or if the dependent sentence was presented as direct speech as in (4-c)? The way to deal with these cases has to be defined for corpus annotation. There is no predefined correct answer to this question. But it is important that these cases are handled consistently throughout the corpus.

(4)   a. ||Since chalk first touched slate, schoolchildren have wanted to know: What's on the test?||

        b. ||Since chalk first touched slate, schoolchildren have wanted to know:||What's on the test?||How many correct answers do I need to pass?||…

        c. ||Since chalk first touched slate, schoolchildren have wanted to know:||"What's on the test?"||

Hard-wiring tokenization and sentence segmentation by encoding it in the corpus itself is more replicable than doing it on the fly. This can be done implicitly by formatting the text, for example, in the *one-token-per-line format* as in (5-a) for the phrase **in spite of**.[4] Explicit marking involves markup that labels the word units. (5-b) exemplifies a simple markup which encloses each token by an opening tag (<token>) and a closing tag (</token>). For more on the encoding of tokenization, see section 2.2.1.

(5)   a. in
           spite
           of

        b. <token>in</token><token>spite</token><token>of</token>

The explicit encoding of tokenization can be seen as an electronic version of Kaeding's index cards with the advantage that the tokens are identified at their text position itself in a re-usable way.

For many corpora, corpus processing does not end with the encoding of tokens or sentences for that matter. These corpora comprise different types of linguistic analyses in terms of annotation. We will introduce the different types of annotation in greater detail in Part II of the book. The take-home message here is the following: A characteristic property of a corpus is that it encodes linguistic meaningful units and potentially other linguistic analyses in a way that they can be searched automatically.

1.2.2 Text Collection

Apart from the more technical issues in representing a corpus, there are also many decisions with regard to the content of a corpus. We will demonstrate these as far as possible using Kaeding's project described above. Kaeding planned to improve shorthand for German as a language as a whole and not just for a specific variety such as the language spoken in court sessions. To this end, he compiled his corpus from a whole range of genres including topics such as law, economics, theology, medicine, history, mixed newspapers and books, military, private letters, literature, etc. He tried to achieve a database that was *representative* for the use of German in a way that his frequency counts would generalize also to texts not included in his corpus.

This leads to the question of the criteria on which we should sample texts for a corpus. Here, expert opinions differ over whether it is a necessary condition that the collection has been sampled according to explicit sampling criteria or not. For some corpus linguists, there is no corpus without careful sampling. For many computational linguists, on the other hand, any text collection can be dubbed 'corpus' as long as the collection is used to gain some linguistic information from it, i.e. as long as the collection is used as a corpus, it can be called a corpus. Possible sampling criteria include the text type (used by Kaeding), the age of the speakers, or the time when a text was published, to name only a few.

As in Kaeding's early project, the motivation for sampling criteria is that the corpus is built to derive a representative sample for the language or language variety that is the object of investigation. A fundamental problem with this concept is that it is very hard, if not impossible, to define what a particular language or language variety is. For example, what is English? Is it all utterances and written texts produced by English native speakers? Produced today, in the last 20 years, or when? Produced by children and adults alike? Produced by dialect speakers, academics, or also people with little formal education? Produced in private settings or for official publication? It is clear, that we cannot answer the original question properly and, hence, we do not know how a representative sample should look, since we do not know the original object (or *population* in statistical terms). What we can do is *operationalize* the boundaries for the object under investigation.

Such an operationalized sampling strategy has been used, for example, in the BROWN Corpus, for which "English" is operationalized as all English texts published in the year 1961 in the United States—more precisely, as all English-language American publications of 1961 listed in two specific library catalogs. This *sampling frame* provides the population from which the actual corpus texts were randomly sampled, taking further *sampling criteria* into account. One of these criteria is the communicative purpose of a text in terms of its genre. The BROWN Corpus distinguishes 15 different genres such as press reportage or press editorials. For practical reasons, the BROWN Corpus consists of text samples of only 20,000 tokens each. Given that the limits of computer storage space are decreasing, it is no longer necessary to pose such restrictions on text samples. Another aspect of collecting samples of the same size is that it ensures a *balanced* collection.[5] As a consequence of the size restriction, frequency counts of different subcategories in the corpus can be more easily compared if the relevant reference sets have the same size. However, this consideration is no longer relevant if modern corpus statistical tests are used. Instead of comparing frequency counts, it is advisable to compare relative frequencies complemented with information about confidence intervals, i.e. the estimated range of values which are almost as likely to be observed as the observed values. If an observed value lies within a high confidence interval of another value, the two cannot be distinguished statistically. An alternative way is to test for statistically significant differences directly.

Another aspect to be considered in corpus sampling is that the texts sampled according to the same criteria should be *homogeneous* in the sense that there are no "rogue texts" that stand out in comparison to other texts of their category. An example of such a rogue text would be a listing of soccer results in a collection of newspaper texts. It is clear that homogeneity is not an objective criterion and that it has to be taken with a grain of salt. Too much homogeneity will fail to represent the full range of variation, which is a crucial property of language. In our example, soccer results are one type of newspaper text, and thus may have to be included to ensure that the full range of newspaper texts is covered.

In addition to carefully sampled corpora as described above, there are many resources which have been created following the doctrine that *more data are better data*. In the 1980s–90s, before the world wide web (WWW) became widespread, the amount of electronically available texts had been limited. This had the consequence that many projects had neither the financial means nor the time resources to sample different genres of text in a large-scale manner.

During this time, a turn towards empiricism occurred in computational approaches to linguistics, which then started developing linguistic grammars complemented by a probabilistic model of usage. Such a probabilistic model would state, for example, that the word sequence **we can sing** is more probable in English than **we can tuna**. For an automatic extraction of the probabilities, large amounts of manually annotated data were needed. Data that were easily available were newspaper data, for example, the American English Wall Street Journal or the German Frankfurter Rundschau. It is important to note that it is not just the sheer lack of electronic text but also copyright issues on existing texts that make corpus sampling according to fine-grained criteria difficult.

To conclude this section, we have investigated the question whether a corpus has to be representative, balanced, or both. Our answer is clearly: "Not in all cases—but they are helpful concepts when designing a corpus." We have already discussed that balance is not mandatory when appropriate statistical tests are applied. We have also discussed that it is hard to achieve representativeness because it is very hard to define the language object itself in the first place. However, there are corpora, called *reference corpora*, that are carefully sampled according to sampling criteria to be representative for a certain language. *Specialized corpora* are sampled to be representative for a certain domain, such as law text or car manuals, and are often used in lexicographic and terminology projects. Furthermore, there are corpora that are collected *opportunistically* using any data source of an appropriate type, such as newspaper text, that is available electronically, without applying further fine-grained sampling criteria. It is important to note that, independent of its sampling strategy, any corpus is representative for its language or variety to a certain extent. Even an opportunistically sampled English newspaper corpus represents the English language as a whole, just not as well as a carefully sampled one.

For keeping track of the representativeness of a particular corpus, it is crucial that information about the text sources is stored as part of the *metadata*. Metadata are data about the text; they can include information about the author, the publication venue, the data collection method, etc. The more fine-grained this documentation is, the better. The user is free to ignore any metadata; however, for many investigations it is relevant to take independent factors, such as text genre, into account because different genres, such as sports reportage and editorial letter, not only differ with respect to their vocabulary but also with respect to preferred grammatical structures and other linguistic phenomena. The necessity of taking metadata into account is probably more obvious when analyzing spoken data. Many studies differentiate, for example, between male and female speakers, or between speakers of different educational backgrounds. This is only possible when the information is available.

1.3 Types of Corpora

The last section gave a definition of characteristic properties of corpora in terms of corpus creation. This section will present corpora by highlighting characteristics that allow us to classify corpora into more specific subclasses. Being aware of these characteristics is relevant for deciding which corpus to use for a particular task, and also for designing a new corpus.

1.3.1 Choice of Language

Besides the actual language, such as English, corpora are distinguished by whether they comprise just one language—then they are called *monolingual*—or whether they comprise more than one language—if it is two languages we talk about *bilingual corpora*. Corpora with more than two languages are called *multilingual*. Note that we are talking about substantial subcorpora consisting of different languages or language varieties. A corpus would still be classified as monolingual if the text contains a small number of foreign sentences.

If a corpus comprises more than one language, it is important to specify the relation between the language-related subcorpora. If there are original texts and their translations, it is a *parallel corpus*. Parallel corpora often comprise alignments between paragraphs, sentences, or even words of the original texts and their translations in a way that allows the retrieval of all translations of a given word or phrase. The creation of such corpora has been motivated by translation studies, and more recently by statistical machine translation projects. The OPUS platform, for example, provides online access to a number of parallel corpora including the multilingual EUROPARL CORPUS of European Parliament debates and the OPENSUBTITLES Corpus of movie subtitles in various languages.

Another type of multilingual corpus is a *comparable corpus*. Its subcorpora all consist of original texts rather than translations. In a comparable corpus, all texts are similar in content, but they differ in the languages or language varieties in the sense that the texts of the same domain are aligned. For example, a comparable corpus could consist of all newspaper articles from one specific day, which would overlap in the stories covered in the different newspapers. In a comparable corpus, it is possible to compare the texts across languages with respect to vocabulary choice, preferred structures, and other text type-specific properties. It is not possible to have more specific alignments here. However, comparable corpora prove to be very useful, for example, for any contrastive language studies, and translation studies in particular, as well as for terminology extraction because, in contrast to parallel corpora with their translated texts, comparable corpora do not have the problem of "translationese." Translationese is used to describe expressions and structures in translated texts owing to the source language or the translation process, such as the German **macht Sinn**, which is a direct translation of the English **makes sense** and was originally not used in German. Wikipedia, for example, has been used as a source for comparable corpora. The OPUS platform contains an English-Swedish comparable corpus based on Wikipedia. The *International Corpus of English* (ICE) is a large corpus project that contains one-million-word subcorpora of English spoken in different regions of the world, such as British English, Australian English, or Indian English. It can be considered to be a comparable corpus because all the texts have been collected according to the same sampling frame.

There are two subtypes of comparable corpora which are not multilingual in the literal sense of the word. The first one is exemplified by the *International Corpus of Learner English* (ICLE), which is a *learner corpus*, i.e. a corpus that contains texts written by learners of English as a foreign language, complemented by similar texts of native speakers of English. Its subcorpora are comparable in the sense that the learners differ with respect to their first language and their proficiency levels but the texts were written in the same controlled setting and on a limited number of topics. The second type of comparable corpus which is not multilingual is used in particular for translation studies. It contains texts in only one language, either original texts in that language or translated into the language. This means that the translated texts are not translations of the original texts in the corpus. This kind of comparable corpus is used, for example, to study translation effects that result in "translationese."

1.3.2 Mode of the Primary Data

The primary source of a corpus is text either in spoken or written form. With respect to spoken data, we distinguish *spoken corpora* from *speech corpora*. The user of a spoken corpus will expect to find written representations of the spoken data. The corpus qualifies as spoken if there are transcriptions or transliterations of the speech events without any audio recordings. Speech corpora, on the other hand, always contain the recordings of their speech events, but not necessarily a written representation of them. In *multi-modal corpora*, in addition to audio data and/or transcripts, the primary data includes information on the communicative event, such as video documenting gestures and mimic (e.g. eyebrow movement) or eye-tracking data measuring the movement of the speaker's eyes.

In addition to the tangible realization of the primary data as sound recording or as graphic structure, it is often necessary to subclassify the mode of the primary data further. In example (6), copied from a chat conversation,[6] a classification into written language would overgeneralize.

(6)   night ya'all.
      'Good night to you all.'

Chat language and other user-generated content on the web often display strong characteristics of spoken language despite their written origin. In contrast, users of dictaphones, for example, produce spoken text which is intended to be finally realized as written reports. These examples show that we need to distinguish the materialization of text from its conceptual characteristics. For chat language, this means that it is materialized graphically because it is typed text, but that it is very often conceptually spoken since it has linguistic characteristics of spoken language such as abbreviations and elision.

1.3.3 Relation to Time

Data in *synchronic corpora* cover only language produced within a limited period of time, for example, close to the time of data collection. *Diachronic corpora*, in contrast, span a longer period of time; their data can provide evidence for different stages in the evolution of a language. One example for a diachronic corpus is the collection of *historical corpora* in the Penn Corpora of Historical English, which cover Middle English, Early Modern English, and Modern British English, thus covering English from 1150 until World War II.

1.3.4 Annotation Levels

Annotation can be a distinguishing property between different corpora. There are corpora that share the same primary data but differ with respect to their annotation levels, as we will see in the remainder of this book. At this point, we just want to point out that the most common type of linguistic annotation is part-of-speech annotation which can be applied automatically with high accuracy, and which is already very helpful for linguistic analysis despite its shallow character.

1.3.5 Persistency

Most linguistic corpora are *static corpora*, which means that the corpus is collected and released at a specific time point and does not change after the release. Such corpora have a fixed size and are conservative with respect to their content. The user can expect to find the same data in the corpus at different times. However, some corpora are released in stages; then the size and content may change from release to release. But they are still considered static. Sometimes, corpora are cleaned in the sense that textual duplicates and other dubious material are deleted. If so, this is documented in the metadata.

Monitor corpora, in contrast, either grow constantly (e.g. by adding each daily issue of a newspaper to an ever-growing corpus) or—in the original understanding of the term—expand because they are based on texts that are scanned on a continuing basis but not permanently archived. The reason for doing this can be copyright issues, for example, if certain online publications are scanned for lexical issues.

It is important to note here that *replicability* of corpus-based research requires the corpus to be frozen, or at least the corpus creation process to be documented in a thorough way so that it is possible to recreate the original text base.

1.4 Corpus Linguistics as Theory and as Tool

Linguists often pose the question whether corpus linguistics should be regarded as a tool or as a theory in its own right. This has consequences in how corpus linguistics is situated within linguistics, but also practical consequences for the corpus user, since tools often have to be justified. If corpus linguistics is regarded as a tool, it provides support in finding relevant information to answer questions that originate from a theory. If corpus linguistics is considered a theory, it should be able to pose questions and explain phenomena.

To answer the question whether corpus linguistics is a theory or a tool, we first need to have a closer look at the definitions of theory and tool. A theory explains observed evidence and allows the researcher to make predictions on unseen data. A theory can be falsified. It can guide the researcher by highlighting relevant aspects that need to be considered, and predict appropriate steps in an analysis. A tool, in contrast, helps to produce results, i.e. evidence. It is designed to perform an operation and needs to be handled in an appropriate way. A tool cannot be falsified. If a tool cannot be applied to relevant aspects, an alternative tool needs to be found.

Craftsmanship in handling a tool can be based on intuitive knowledge. If this knowledge is systematically collected in such a way that it allows us to induce optimizations for the tool and that we can predict its performance, we have created a new theory.

Now coming back to corpus linguistics: For the linguist proper, corpus linguistics can be used as a tool to collect relevant evidence by means of examples, frequency counts, or other statistical evidence. For the corpus linguist, however, corpus linguistics is a theory on its own—or, to be precise, many theories, such as the theory of what is a representative corpus or the theory concerning how to operationalize linguistic concepts for annotation. This also includes the theory concerning the reliability of annotation, and how it is measured.

In short, the answer to the question whether corpus linguistics is a theory or a tool is simply that it can be both. It depends on how corpus linguistics is applied. However, as corpus linguists, we need to be aware of these differences.

1.5 Corpus Linguistics and the Intuitionistic Approach

Independent of whether we use corpus linguistics as a tool or as a theory, the corpus-linguistic approach is clearly different from a traditional, intuitionistic approach. In this section, we describe the major differences between the two approaches and their consequences.

Imagine you are interested in double object structures in English such as in (7), where **gave** selects for a theme and a recipient, here **the CD** and **Brent** respectively, which can be realized either as a noun phrase (NP) and a prepositional phrase (PP) (7-a) or as two noun phrases (7-b) (for more information about double object structures see section 8.2).

(7) a. Leslie gave the CD to Brent.
     b. Leslie gave Brent the CD.

To learn more about this structure, for example, whether there is a subtle difference in meaning between the two alternatives, one would need more examples. Such examples one could either make up or look up in a corpus. The *intuitionistic approach*, on the one hand, is based on individual native speakers' judgments on the acceptability of individual examples. It often correlates with inventing appropriate examples from scratch, tailored to the question under investigation. The *corpus-linguistic approach*, on the other hand, is based on examples retrieved from corpora, which normally involves attested language use, that is, naturally occurring examples that were created without knowledge about the linguistic hypothesis they are used to be tested against. In addition, the corpus-linguistic approach has a quantitative dimension. It is not the individual example that is conclusive but many occurrences of competing realizations, the frequencies of which are counted and compared.

Thus, if we find 192 examples of the double NP construction but only 44 cases of the NP-PP construction for the verb **give** in 50,000 sentences of newspaper text,[7] we can conclude that newspaper writers prefer the double NP variant.

There are advantages and disadvantages to both approaches. Intuitionistic judgments are notoriously subjective, given that not only different speakers vary considerably in their judgments of the same examples but also one and the same speaker might give different judgments on the same structure at different points in time. This means that it is not necessarily possible to replicate findings based on the intuitionistic approach. Corpus frequency counts, in contrast, are objective in the sense that given the same data and tools, as well as the knowledge about how the relevant examples were identified in the corpus, we can replicate the findings—and identify misinterpretations or errors of previous approaches.

The subjectivity problem of intuitionistic judgments can be reduced by collecting a set of judgments under controlled conditions and taking the variation of the judgments into account in the analysis. This point relates to the questions of variability and grada-bility of language and how well these are captured by the two approaches.

If examples are invented, it is possible that the example inventor may not be aware of additional variants that are also possible in the language. For example, a prominent analysis for the examples in (7) suggested a difference in meaning between the two variants based on the judgements in (8). The conclusion was that the double noun phrase variant indicated a change in state whereas the noun phrase-prepositional phrase variant indicated a change in space.

(8) a. That movie gave me the creeps.   [NP-NP]
     b. *That movie gave the creeps to me.   *[NP-PP]

However, consulting a corpus provides a different picture as exemplified with example (9).[8]

(9) This story is designed to give the creeps to people who hate spiders, but is not true.
                                                           [NP-PP]

Apparently, there are other factors playing a role in determining the surface realization of the double object structure, such as the "weight" of the recipient constituent. Heavy recipients tend to be realized to the right end of the sentence, which means that they tend to be realized as prepositional phrase.

It is important to point out that the intuitionistic approach can avoid the criticism of not taking into account all variants. This can be achieved by consulting corpora when creating the set of examples. We also have to keep in mind that corpora are always limited in size, and we can only find in a corpus what is in there. That is, if a corpus only contains mono-transitive verbs you will have trouble finding evidence for double object structures at all (see the discussion of sampling and representativeness in section 1.2.2).

Another property of language, as mentioned above, is that the acceptability of structures is graded in the sense that a particular structure might sound odd without context but is completely fine if an appropriate context is provided. In other words, language is graded to a certain extent. The intuitionistic approach tries to capture this by allowing for graded judgements that include an intermediate label in addition to "acceptable" and "unacceptable," normally indicated by one or more question marks. It is an ongoing debate whether this gradedness can also be modeled in terms of corpus frequencies. In (10), we list standard tenets about the corpus-linguistic approach (see section 7.3 for a more extensive discussion). They show that there are only two correlations that robustly hold between corpus frequency and acceptability.

(10) (i)   If x occurs frequently in a corpus, x is very likely to be acceptable.
      (ii)   If x occurs infrequently in a corpus or does not occur at all, we cannot draw any conclusions about x's acceptability.
      (iii) If x is unacceptable, it is very likely that x occurs with very low frequency in a corpus or not at all.
      (iv)   If x is acceptable, we still do not know whether x will occur in a corpus or not.

Note that these (non-)correlations apply to individual frequencies. If we compare two close variants of the same phenomenon, and one occurs much less frequently than the other, as was the case for the double object construction given the verb **give**, we can still draw our conclusions.

A positive factor with regard to the corpus-linguistic approach is that it forces linguists to be very specific about their hypotheses. The linguistic research question needs to be *operationalized* in a way that the examples can be recovered from corpus data and their annotation. This means that linguistic concepts need to be translated into the syntax of the query tool by using the vocabulary provided by the annotation. If the positive examples are then annotated with the new analyses, the findings are even directly *reusable* by other researchers.

There are three shortcomings of corpus data that users need to be aware of (see section 7.3 for a more extensive discussion of the limitations of corpus linguistics). First, corpus data will never provide *negative evidence* in contrast to acceptability judgements—even if there are ungrammatical examples in corpora. This means that corpus data do not allow us to test the limits of what belongs to the language and what does not. As we saw above, we cannot draw an immediate conclusion from not observing an individual pattern at all. Second, corpus data are always *performance data* in the sense that they are potentially distorted by external factors such as incomplete sentences, repetitions, and corrections in conceptionally spoken language, or text-genre related properties in conceptionally written language such as nominalizations in law-related texts. Third—and this has been mentioned before—corpora are always *limited*; even web-based mega corpora comprise only a limited number of sentences. This means that there is a certain chance that the web pages with the linguistically interesting variant might just have been omitted by chance when the corpus was created.

Finally, we need to summarize the positive aspects of the corpus-based approach. It provides examples of attested language use and provides us with variants linguists tend to forget. It provides frequency counts. Additionally, corpus linguistics makes research falsifiable in that hypotheses can be disproved. And it ensures replicability and renders results reusable—if performed in an appropriate way.

To conclude this subsection, we want to emphasize that the corpus-linguistic approach and the intuitionistic approach can benefit from each other, by complementing each other's shortcomings: Corpora provide variants of structures that strengthen the empirical basis of intuitionistic judgements. Judgements, especially when collected as sets in controlled experiments, can be tested also on made-up negative evidence that is not attested in corpora.

1.6 Outline of the Book

This book is structured along four guiding questions concerning corpus linguistics and linguistically annotated corpora. The first part is concerned with the question of what corpus linguistics is and why linguistic annotation in corpora may provide useful information. The second part of the book is concerned with the question of what linguistic annotation is and what such annotations may look like. The third part considers how to use linguistic annotation as empirical evidence. The fourth part focuses on how to retrieve linguistic information from corpus annotation in practice.

The introductory first part, which also comprises the next chapter, provides the background to corpus linguistics and linguistic annotation, which will allow the reader to situate the work described in the rest of the book. The second part will familiarize the reader with linguistic annotation by introducing different levels of annotations in detail. It starts out from the word level and ends with discourse level phenomena that can span entire text paragraphs. It will give a comprehensive outline of what types of linguistic information can be found in state-of-the-art corpora. The reader will learn how linguistic phenomena are operationalized in terms of annotation schemes, and will also be introduced to corpora that provide these different types of annotation. The third part of the book will show the reader how annotation can be used in linguistic argumentation. Most notably, it will provide case studies. It will also give a detailed overview of the advantages and limitations of using corpus linguistics based on annotated corpora. It will show that it is possible to find a wider range of phenomena than when the search is based on a text corpus only. Finally, the fourth part will detail how to find the information encoded in annotated corpora by means of query tools and visualization.

This book is intended for readers with some background in linguistics. We assume that the reader is familiar with the linguistic subdisciplines of morphology, syntax, semantics, and pragmatics and with the most important terms used in these subdisciplines, as covered, for example, in an introduction to linguistics. We do not expect any specialized knowledge in any of the subdisciplines. Neither do we except any familiarity with corpora, corpus linguistics, or computational linguistics. However, while we will give a short introduction to corpus linguistics and provide an overview of the most important concepts in the following sections, this book focuses on corpus linguistics using linguistically annotated corpora, which at the same time provides different challenges and opportunities. The reader will become familiar with a range of corpora, linguistic annotations, and query tools. Every chapter will provide pointers to further reading and exercises. The further reading section below will also include pointers for introductions to corpus linguistics as it is generally defined, when based mostly on pure text, without annotation.

We want to point the reader to our companion webpage that provides lists of available linguistically annotated corpora and existing query tools. The lists concentrate on the most well-known and currently available resources with short descriptions of the type of annotation for the corpora and the coverage for the tools.

1.7 Further Reading

Many of the journal and conference papers cited in this book are available online from the *ACL Anthology* at http://aclweb.org/anthology/

Section 1.1

Corpus linguistics: For general introductions to corpus linguistics see Biber et al. (1998); McEnery and Hardie (2012); McEnery and Wilson (2001); McEnery et al. (2005); Teubert (2005); for an introduction in German see Lemnitzer and Zinsmeister (2010). A collection of 42 reprinted key articles on corpus-linguistic issues (with dates of first appearance ranging from 1952 to 2002) is provided by Sampson and McCarthy (2004).

Introduction to linguistics: For an introduction to linguistics, we recommend McGregor (2009); O'Grady et al. (2009); Fromkin et al. (2013).

Section 1.2

Brown Corpus: The sampling of the Brown Corpus is described in detail in Francis and Kučera (1967). The manual for the corpus is available online at http://icame.uib.no/brown/bcm.html.

Kaeding's corpus work: In addition to the description in McEnery and Wilson (2001), German readers can consult the original report (Kaeding, 1897).

Pre-electronic corpora: McEnery and Wilson (2001, Ch. 1) and Meyer (2008) describe pre-electronic corpora in more detail, Kaeding's work among others.

Roman de Flamenca Corpus: This corpus of Old Occitan was used as an example for encoding challenges. More details about the corpus can be found in Scrivner and Kübler (2012); Scrivner et al. (2013).

Sampling frames: Atkins et al. (1992) and Biber (1993) are two classic references for the discussion of sampling frames. Evert (2006) illustrates representativeness of corpus samples in terms of a library metaphor.

Statistics for linguists: There are three introductions to statistics for linguists, including statistical significance tests, all three using R: Baayen (2008); Johnson (2008), and Gries (2013).

Section 1.3

ICE: The *International Corpus of English* (ICE) is an international long-term project. The final aim is to produce up to 20 one-million-word corpora of international English varieties, each syntactically analyzed according to a common parsing scheme. A number of subcorpora are freely available from http://ice-corpora.net/ice/avail.htm. For more information on the project see http://www.ucl.ac.uk/english-usage/projects/ice.htm. The British component is documented by Nelson et al. (2002) and in Wallis and Nelson (2006).

ICLE: The *International Corpus of Learner English* (ICLE) contains argumentative essays written by intermediate and advanced learners of English from several mother tongues. All essays are annotated for lemmas and part-of-speech tags. The corpus is distributed on CD-ROM. For further information, see http://www.uclouvain.be/en-cecl-icle.html.

NLTK: The *Natural Language Toolkit* (NLTK)[9] is a platform for building Python programs to work with human language data. It includes the whole NPS Chat Corpus along with a large collection of corpus samples and lexical resources. It also provides a number of modules for working with the data. The NLTK is documented in Bird et al. (2009).

NPS Chat Corpus: The NPS Chat Corpus contains 706 posts from 20 different age-specific chat rooms. The posts are privacy masked, part-of-speech tagged with the Penn Treebank POS tagset (see section 3.3), and dialogue-act tagged. The corpus is described in Forsyth and Martell (2007). It is distributed as part of the NLTK distribution.

OPUS: More information about the OPEN PARALLEL CORPUS (OPUS) can be found in Tiedemann (2012) and at the webpage http://opus. lingfil.uu.se/, which also offers online search and a download option.

PENN CORPORA OF HISTORICAL ENGLISH: More information about the PENN CORPORA OF HISTORICAL ENGLISH can be found at http://www.ling.upenn.edu/hist-corpora/.

Section 1.5

Corpus frequency and acceptability: Bresnan (2006) relates frequency and acceptability of English dative alternations (see also section 8.2). Manning (2003) also discusses probabilistic properties of syntax. Bader and Häussler (2010) investigate the relationship between gradient and binary judgements of grammaticality (see also elicitation of judgements) and relate them to corpus frequencies. Sampson (2007) is a focus article on this topic and is accompanied by a number of commentary articles in the same journal issue.

Elicitation of judgements: Methods of eliciting native speaker judgements that account for the problems of subjectivity and gradedness are discussed by Sorace and Keller (2005) and Schütze (1996).

CHAPTER 2
CORPORA AND LINGUISTIC ANNOTATION

This chapter will give an introduction to linguistic annotation. We will discuss the following questions: What is linguistic annotation (section 2.1)? What types of annotation are available (section 2.2)? How does linguistic annotation help with corpus linguistic questions (section 2.3)? Which principles should corpus annotation follow (section 2.4)? How do we search for linguistic phenomena when annotation is present (section 2.5)? Which are the major annotation standards for linguistically annotated corpora (section 2.6)?

2.1 Linguistic Annotation

Corpora are generally electronic collections of text, as discussed in Chapter 1. In this section, we will show why adding linguistic information to such a corpus can be useful. Even though corpora are a useful tool for linguistic research, there are cases where access to electronic collections of texts is not sufficient. Imagine that you are looking for examples of reduced relative clauses such as in (1-a).

(1) a. The book I read yesterday was interesting.
     b. The book [$_{relRed}$ I read yesterday] was interesting.

Finding such constructions in a large text is difficult because they are characterized by a null element, i.e. an element that is absent, the missing relative pronoun. Thus, there is no indicator on the textual level that would allow us to search for those sentences. In such cases, we would need more linguistic information. In the ideal case, we would have an annotation telling us for each sentence whether it has a relative clause as well as the type of the relative clause (full or reduced)—for example, in the form of brackets plus label, as shown in (1-b). In this example, the square brackets delimit the relative clause, and the subscript gives additional information that it is a reduced one. However, this is very specific information, and it is very unlikely that someone has annotated the exact phenomenon in which we are interested, and only this. In the next best case, we have syntactic annotation available. Figure 2.1 shows an example of how such a clause is annotated in the PENN TREEBANK (cf. Chapter 4 for details on syntactic annotation and on the PENN TREEBANK). In this example, the nodes represent syntactic constituents, such as noun phrases (NP) or prepositional phrases (PP), and the arcs show information about syntactic groupings. This syntactic annotation is more general than what we need, which also means that it can be used for many different purposes. However, it

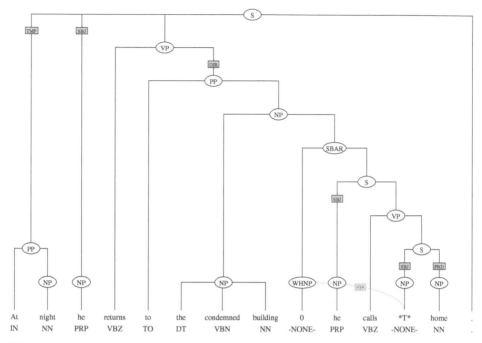

Figure 2.1 A syntactic tree from the PENN TREEBANK.

also means that the information for which we are searching is not directly represented in this annotation: There is no node saying this is a reduced relative clause, i.e. the reduced relative clause is represented as an SBAR with a null daughter WHNP. We can search for this combination of nodes, but then we need a fairly powerful query tool (see Chapter 12).

In more general terms, there are several advantages to having linguistic annotation available. Annotations increase the range of *linguistic phenomena* that can be found in a text collection. If we only have the text, we can only search for individual words or sequences of words. However, if we have linguistic information, we can often give a more specific description of what we want to find (e.g. the word **compromise**, but only used as a verb), and we can find phenomena which are not anchored in a specific word or phrase. Another advantage of annotations is that they are *reusable*. Some people may argue that annotations that can be performed automatically, such as part-of-speech (POS) annotation (see below), can be annotated on the fly and thus do not require a stable, manually annotated corpus. However, this is only true to a certain extent since manual annotation is more reliable than automatic ones. Additionally, manual annotation is time-consuming and expensive; thus, such an annotation should be preserved so that it does not have to be done again. A third, related advantage is that an annotated corpus can be used for many different, often non-obvious tasks. While linguistic search may be the obvious one, such corpora can also be used for training automatic methods, or they can be used for educational purposes, for example, to find authentic examples for learners of a language.

Linguistic annotation can be grouped along the standard *linguistic subdisciplines*, such as *morphology, syntax, semantics*, or *pragmatics*. We will see examples of these levels, and some more, in the next section. Since the linguistic annotation is information that is additional to the original sentence, we need to decide how to represent it. One major distinction here is concerned with whether the textual material is interleaved with the annotation or whether the two of them are kept separate. If we consider part-of-speech (POS) annotation, where each word is annotated with its word class, it is easy to insert the information into the sentence. This is called *inline annotation*. A typical format is shown in example (2-b), where we add the POS label to the word in (2-a),[1] separated by a '/'.

(2)   a. The inhabitants of Egypt were called mummies.
       b. The/Determiner inhabitants/Noun of/Preposition Egypt/Name were/Verb called/Participle mummies/Noun ./Punct
       c. w1:Det w2:Noun w3:Preposition w4:NE w5:Verb w6:Participle w7:Noun w8:Punct

Note that in this example, we split off the period from the last word in the sentence. This means that the text is irrevocably modified, and the original cannot be retrieved from the POS tagged version. For this reason, there is another approach that advocates keeping the original text and adding the linguistic annotation in a separate layer. This is called *stand-off annotation*. In many cases, the separate layers of text and annotation are stored in separate files. However, in this case, the annotation needs a way of referring back to the original text. A simplified version is shown in (2-c). There, the labels in front of the POS labels refer to the individual words, i.e. w1 refers to the first word, **The**, and w5 to the fifth one, **were**. The corpus would then consist of a combination of (2-a) and (2-c). Note that we keep the period attached in the original text, but it is assigned a separate label (w8). While this format has the advantage of preserving the original form of the text, searching for information becomes more difficult because the information may be distributed across different places.

Linguistic annotation covers any descriptive or analytic notations applied to raw language data.[2] However, while the analysis and description of language is the main goal, this process also involves an *interpretation* by the annotator. Thus while the word **were** in example (2-b) is annotated as a verb, one could just as easily interpret it more specifically as an auxiliary. Thus, the linguistic annotation may not always correspond to one's own intuitions or preferred linguistic theory. However, as long as we are able to express what we are looking for in terms of the annotations used in the corpus, we can search for it, i.e. even if I am convinced that the word **were** should be described as auxiliary rather than a verb, I can still find such occurrences as long as I know with which label they are annotated.

The entirety of decisions that are made during the annotations is often called an *annotation scheme*. An annotation scheme is normally documented in a *stylebook* or *annotation manual.* Such manuals are important for two different reasons. On the one hand, they are needed during the annotation process in order to ensure consistency in the annotations. For example, if we decide that nouns are also annotated for number (Noun_sg and Noun_pl), this decision should be documented in the manual so that annotators can look it up in case they are uncertain. The manual should also include recommendations on how to annotate difficult cases, such as the word **police** as used in sentence (3), where it is difficult to decide whether it is singular or plural.

(3)   We had to call the police last night.

Another important issue with regard to using linguistically annotated corpora concerns the question of how the annotation was performed. Typical approaches would be either *manual, automatic,* or *semi-automatic annotation.* For the manual annotation, we have human annotators; for the automatic one, we use automatic methods from computational linguistics (CL).[3] These methods will be described in the following section, and in more detail in the chapters in Part II. If a corpus is annotated semi-automatically, this means that the corpus is first annotated by an automatic method and then manually corrected, or the annotation is carried out in an interactive fashion between the human and the automatic methods. For syntactic annotation, for example, this could mean that the tool suggests a partial annotation, and the human can either accept or correct the suggestion before the tool suggests the next part.

The type of annotation also has an effect on the types of *errors* in the annotations one can expect: If the corpus is manually annotated, we would expect a high level of accuracy, and the errors in the annotations are either results of lapses in concentration, or they result from difficult phenomena. If the corpus is annotated automatically, in contrast, we expect a higher number of errors, and the errors are often less intuitive than the ones made by humans but also more consistent in their occurrence. In POS annotation, for example, distinguishing between a preposition **before** and a subordinating conjunction is relatively easy for humans but difficult for an automatic POS tagger. Thus, it is likely that the POS tagger will make the mistake not only once but for most or all occurrences of **before**. The individual error levels are dependent on the language, the task, the annotation scheme, and the tool used for annotation.

2.2 Levels of Linguistic Annotation

Linguistic annotation is a cover term for a multitude of different annotations. It can be as specific as marking only relative clauses, or it can be more general, such as annotating the syntax of a sentence in terms of constituent structure. We will concentrate on the latter type of annotations, mostly because annotations are very expensive in terms of effort and cost. As a consequence, normally annotations that can be used for different purposes are favored. Thus, they have to be general. However, there is often also a limit to how general the annotation can be, depending on the funding of an annotation project. It is intuitively clear that a complete syntactic annotation will require more effort than annotating only one specific phenomenon.

Linguistic annotation is available in many different forms, and on many different levels of linguistic information. However, there are differences between languages. The most resources, by far, exist for English. Then, there are a handful of languages, mostly Western European ones such as French, German, and Italian, for which a good range of resources exist. For most other languages, no resources, or only very rudimentary ones, exist.

In this section, we will concentrate on introducing the most important levels of linguistic annotation (more information will be provided in Part II): the word level, on which individual words are annotated, the syntactic, the semantic, and the discourse level. We will concentrate on the discourse level as the one area in pragmatics for which large-scale, annotated resources exist. On the discourse level, annotation generally goes beyond individual sentences as the basic units for annotation.

2.2.1 Word Level Annotation

By annotations on the word level, we mean annotations that are restricted to individual words, i.e. they do not cover more than one word. For this section, we will assume that we know what a word is, even though a definition is not as simple as it sounds. We will look into this in Chapter 3. Here, it will suffice to know that we consider words as parts of text, which means that we annotate them in context, as opposed to words as they occur in a dictionary. For some tasks, the context of the word in the sentence is important for the annotation, e.g. for POS labels or for word senses.

The first type of word level annotation is *lemma* information. A lemma is the basic form of a word, as it is represented in a dictionary. For example, (4)[4] shows a sentence and its lemma information.

(4)   One of their children , Cain , asked " Am I   my   brother 's
      one of POSS child   , Cain , ask   " be he POSS brother POSS
      son ? "
      son ? "

Note that in this example, our definition of a word does not fully coincide with English spelling. We split off punctuation as well as the possessive 's. Note also that for pronouns, the lemma is the masculine form he, and for the possessive forms, we used POSS instead of a word from the English lexicon since there is no real base form for these words.

Next, we look at *morphological information*. In English, a morphologically rather poor language, we can annotate nouns for number, verbs for number, person, tense, and mood, etc. Languages with more complex morphological systems generally make more distinctions, including gender and case for nouns, or aspect for verbs. The example in (5) shows a German sentence with its English translation and its morphological annotation.

(5) Die Köchin jagt den Hund .
     nsf nsf   3sis asm asm   .
     'The (female) chef chases the dog.'

For nouns (**Köchin, Hund**) and determiners (**Die, den**), this annotation presents information about case, number, and gender (nsf = nominative, singular, feminine; asm = accusative, singular, masculine). The verb **jagt** is annotated for person, number, mood, and tense (3sis = 3rd person, singular, indicative, present).

The next type of annotation on the word level is *part-of-speech* (POS) annotation. Parts of speech, as mentioned above, are word classes. The example in (6) gives an example of English POS annotation, this time using a standard POS tagset, the PENN TREEBANK tagset. We will provide more information on this tagset in section 3.3.

(6) The/DT inhabitants/NNS of/IN Egypt/NE were/VBD called/VBP mummies/NNS ./.

DT is short for determiner, NNS is a plural noun, IN a preposition, VBD a verb in past tense, VBP a past participle, and . sentence-final punctuation. A full list of the PENN TREEBANK tagset is shown in Appendix A. Note that this POS tagset also contains morphological information, such as number (NNS) or tense (VBD).

2.2.2 Syntactic Annotation

Syntactic annotation concerns the annotation of structural information, and is generally carried out on the sentence level. Currently, there are two major syntactic theories that are used for syntactic annotation: constituent-based and dependency-based annotations.

In constituent-based annotations, the goal is to identify groups of words that function as a unit. Smaller constituents are grouped into larger ones to build a hierarchical structure, also called a *syntax tree*. Figure 2.2 shows an example. In this tree, every round node, such as NP or VP, represents a constituent. The links between the nodes describe the hierarchical ordering. Thus, the noun phrase (NP) **A large number** is part of a larger NP, which also includes a prepositional phrase (PP), and which in turn is part of the clause (S). Note that this tree also contains square boxes, which indicate the grammatical function of a constituent. Thus, the NP **A large number of those leaving** is marked as the subject (SBJ), and the NP **managers and professionals** as the predicate of the clause (PRD).

Dependency annotation, in contrast, describes relations between pairs of words. The sentence that we showed with its constituent annotation in Figure 2.2 is shown with its dependency annotation in Figure 2.3. Note that the relationships between pairs of words, depicted as arcs, are directed. The word to which the arc is pointing is a dependant of the word it is related to, which is the head. Thus, **A** and **large** are dependent on **number**, and the latter, in turn, is dependent on **are**. The labels on the arcs describe the grammatical relations between the words, i.e. the label sbj states that

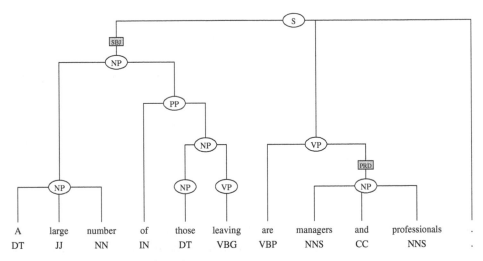

Figure 2.2 A syntactic tree from the PENN TREEBANK.

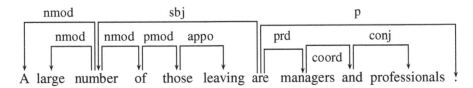

Figure 2.3 The dependency representation of the sentence in Figure 2.2.

number is the subject of **are**, nmod describes a nominal modifier, pmod a preposi-tional modifier, appo an apposition, prd a predicate, coord a conjunction, and conj the second conjunct in a coordination.

2.2.3 Semantic Annotation

Semantic annotation encompasses all forms of annotations that pertain to meaning in some way. It is less homogeneous than syntactic annotation. In this section, we will look at the annotation of word senses, which is annotated on the word level, of temporal information, which can cover individual words or larger chunks, and frame semantic annotations (see page 29), which are based on the clausal level.

Word senses describe the phenomenon that words can have different meanings, which can be activated by different contexts. In (7), we show different senses of the word **line**. The annotated senses are shown in curly braces at the end of the sentence.

(7) a. The cast stood in line for the curtain call. {line: a formation of people or things one beside another}

    b.   He drew a line on the chart. {line: a mark that is long relative to its width}

    c.   His face has many lines. {line: a slight depression or fold in the smoothness of a surface}

    d.   He called me on the phone, but the line was busy. {line: a telephone connection}

Word senses always refer to a sense inventory, i.e. a collection of words and their senses. In our case, we took the senses from Princeton WORDNET, a lexical resource that provides word senses for a wide range of words. We did not show every sense of **line** that is listed there; WORDNET lists 30 senses for the noun reading and another five for the verb reading. Note that in the examples in (7), we only gave the sense for our focus word, **line**. If we wanted to annotate a corpus for word senses, we would annotate all words, or at least all words that can be found in WORDNET. WORDNET only lists content words, i.e. nouns, adjectives, adverbs, and verbs; it does not list any function words such as prepositions or determiners, and it lists only a few names (of important people).

Temporal annotation generally focuses on identifying events and time expressions in language, as well as the relationship between events. Events are anchored in time with regard to the narrative and can thus provide information about what happened and in which order. Events can be either punctual, as the event, marked in square brackets, in (8-a), last for some time, as in (8-b), or they can be states or circumstances, as in (8-c).[5]

(8)   a.   Ferdinand Magellan, a Portuguese explorer, first [reached] the islands in search of spices.

    b.   11,024 people, including local Aeta aborigines, were [evacuated] to 18 disaster relief centers.

    c.   Israel has been scrambling to buy more masks abroad, after a [shortage] of several hundred thousand gas masks.

The most comprehensive temporal annotation scheme, TimeML, annotates four different types of information: events (as shown in (8)), time expressions, signals, and links. Events are annotated with regard to the minimal element that denotes the event (as shown in brackets in the examples above).

Time expressions are defined as explicit temporal expressions such as times, dates, etc. Examples for time expressions are shown in brackets in (9).[6]

(9)   a.   John left [30 minutes] before the show on [Monday].

    b.   He lived in Europe till [January 1990].

Note that in (9-a), the word **before** is not marked as a time expression. This is because **before** is not an explicit time, but rather indicates a temporal relation between the two events **left** and **show**. In TimeML, such words are called signals. They are also involved in links. Links are the connections between events: Events can happen simultaneously, one before or after the other, one can include the other, or one can be started or ended by another. However, not every link involves a signal. (10-a) shows an example of links without a signal, and (10-b) shows the sentence in (9-a) with its full annotation.[7]

(10) a. The [$_{E1}$ rains] [$_{E2}$ caused] the [$_{E3}$ flooding]. {link: E1→ E2, type: IDENTITY} {link: E2→ E3, type: BEFORE}

b. John [$_{E1}$ left] [$_T$ 30 minutes] [$_S$ before] the [$_{E2}$ show] on [$_T$ Monday]. {link: E1 → E2, S, type: BEFORE}

Another way of approaching the meaning of clauses is represented by *frame semantics*. In frame semantics, the meaning of what is called an event in TimeML is connected to encyclopedic knowledge. The underlying idea is that in order to understand the verb **sell**, for example, one needs to know more about what is involved in the process, i.e. that there is a buyer, a seller, an entity to be sold, a transfer of ownership from seller to buyer, and a transfer of money in the other direction. All this information is represented in a *semantic frame*. Additionally, the same semantic frame is also activated by the verb **sell**. (11)[8] shows the semantic frame annotations for two sentences whose verbs, **sell** and **purchase**, both activate the same semantic frame.

(11) a. [$_{buyer}$ The girl] bought [$_{goods}$ a car] [$_{seller}$ from her friend] [$_{money}$ for $5,000].

b. [$_{buyer}$ I] purchased [$_{goods}$ the calculator] [$_{purpose}$ for easier calculation of my debts].

Note that the verb is not marked here, it is the focal element in the semantic frame, the *frame-evoking element* in FRAMENET terminology. FRAMENET is a corpus annotated with frame semantics. Note that the frame elements are closer to syntactic phrases than the elements involved in TimeML annotation. Note also that a frame element is only typical for individual semantic frames, i.e. in another semantic frame, completely different frame elements can be present. (12)[9] shows examples of the hostile encounter frame.

(12) a. [$_{side1}$ Diana] confronted [$_{side2}$ her husband-to-be] [$_{issue}$ about his proposed gift].

b. [$_{side2}$ A tourist] is confronted [$_{side1}$ by a lion] [$_{place}$ on his home territory].

c. [$_{side1}$ He] fought four times [$_{purpose}$ for his seat on Southampton council] [$_{time}$ before winning it].

2.2.4 Discourse Annotation

Discourse annotation concentrates on linguistic phenomena that go beyond the sentence level. All these phenomena are based on the assumption of *coherence*. Coherence accounts for the observation that what people try to communicate in spoken or written form under normal circumstances is perceived as a coherent whole, rather than as a collection of isolated or unrelated sentences, phrases, or words. The short paragraphs in (13) show different degrees of coherence. While in (13-a), the two sentences are coherent, (13-b) contradicts our assumption that the pronoun in the second sentence should refer to a person mentioned in the previous text. Since the **businessman** is clearly male, the female pronoun has no clear referent. In (13-c), there is no coherence since there is no evident connection between the two sentences.

(13) a. Sipping the last of the bitter cordial, the businessman was presented with the cheque. A look of incredulity crept over his face.
  b. Sipping the last of the bitter cordial, the businessman was presented with the cheque. A look of incredulity crept over her face.
  c. Sipping the last of the bitter cordial, the businessman was presented with the cheque. This section is about discourse annotation.

In the following paragraphs, we look into two types of annotation, coreference and discourse annotation, which describe the phenomena violated in the two non-coherent sentences above.

Coreference describes the phenomenon that two expressions in a text refer to the same entity in the real world (see (14)). However, coreference annotation often unites reference proper with the annotation of *anaphoric relations*. In contrast to reference, anaphoric relations describe relations between two elements in the text that denote the same entity. This means that anaphoric relations can exist without coreference, as shown in (15) where the pronoun it refers back to the **donkey** in the relative clause, but there is no real-world donkey, i.e. there is no reference to a specific donkey.

(14) [William Jefferson "Bill" Clinton] is an American politician who served as [the 42nd President of the United States] from 1993 to 2001. Inaugurated at age 46, [he] was [the third-youngest president]. [Clinton] took office at the end of the Cold War, and was [the first president of the baby boomer generation].
(15) Every farmer who owns [a donkey] beats [it].

Coreference annotation often includes relations that go beyond the identity relation we have seen in (14). These types of reference are called *bridging*. Bridging relations can include part-whole (16-a), set-member (16-b), event-role (16-c), or more indirect, as in (16-d).

(16) a. Jason has bought [a new car]. Then [the front bumper] turned out to be dented.
  b. [The Portuguese team] didn't play well yesterday until [the center-forward] was replaced in the second half.
  c. Peter played in [a musical] last year. [The director] helped him understand [his character].
  d. Marie found [a new apartment] yesterday. She signed [the lease] right away.

Discourse annotation, in contrast to coreference annotation, focuses on annotating discourse relations in the text. Such discourse relations often manifest in the form of explicit discourse connectives. (17) gives examples with discourse connectives marked.

(17) a. The federal government suspended sales of U.S. savings bonds [because] Congress hasn't lifted the ceiling on government debt.

    b. The subject will be written into the plots of prime-time shows, [and] viewers will be given a 900 number to call.

    c. In the past, the socialist policies of the government strictly limited the size of industrial concerns to conserve resources and restrict the profits businessmen could make. [As a result], industry operated out of small, expensive, highly inefficient industrial units.

Not all connectives must be explicit, though. The *Penn Discourse Treebank* (PDTB), for example, also annotates implicit connectives, such as in (18).[10]

(18) But a few funds have taken other defensive steps. Some have raised their cash positions to record levels. {Implicit = BECAUSE} High cash positions help buffer a fund when the market falls.

2.3 Linguistic Annotation for Corpus Linguists

We have seen that linguistic annotations are available on different linguistic levels. But why would a corpus linguist care about linguistic annotations? In this section, we will explore various questions that can only be answered if linguistic annotation is available. All these questions will show that by accessing linguistic annotation, we can extend the range of phenomena that can be found with high precision (i.e. we do not get many irrelevant hits) and high recall (i.e. we find the whole range of phenomena and not only a potentially unintended subset).

In our first example, we want to search for *collocations*, i.e. words that have a tendency to appear together. More specifically, we are targeting patterns "the JJR the JJR," where JJR is an adjective in the comparative. Examples for this pattern are **the higher the mountain** or **the longer the break**. If we search in text corpora without annotation, we have to search for a sub-sequence of these words, for example, **the higher the**. If the search option of the corpus allows wildcards, i.e. symbols that can replace any words, we can search for **the * the**, assuming that * is the wildcard. For more details about complex searching involving regular expressions, see Chapter 10. The search with a wildcard would find all occurrences of the examples mentioned above, where the * would match **higher** and **longer**. Additionally, it would also find cases such as **the best the organizers could do**. But it would not find cases such as **the larger a group**. Ideally, we would like to restrict the search so that only comparative adjectives, such as **higher**, are allowed and that the second determiner must not be **the**. Since we cannot list all comparative adjectives, we need POS annotations. Then, we can search for the sequence **the JJR DT NN** directly. This means, the **the** is followed by an adjective in the comparative, a determiner (DT), and a noun (NN).

In our second example, we are interested in occurrences of the verb **book** in the sense of **recording a charge in a police register**. This leads to three complications: first, we need to make sure that we only find verb forms; second, that we find all inflected forms of the verb; and third, that we only find occurrences of that exact sense rather than occurrences such as **Their agent booked them for several concerts all over Europe** or **The agent booked tickets to the show for the whole family**. For this case, just searching for the word **book** and then manually extracting the correct senses would lead to an extremely low precision of the search, since we are very likely to find many more occurrences of **book** as a noun or in another verb sense. For such a search, we ideally need a corpus with POS, lemma, and sense annotations. In this case, we can search for **[lemma='book'; POS=VB; sense=v4]** where the sense would refer to the fourth verbal sense in WORDNET.

In our last example, we are interested in coordinations of unlikes such as in (19), i.e. coordinations where the conjuncts are of different syntactic types. In this case, we cannot list the types, the only restriction of which we know is that two of them are different. Luckily, the PENN TREEBANK has a special label for such cases: all the coordinations are grouped under a label UCP, for coordination of unlike conjuncts. Thus, if we have PENN TREEBANK-style syntactic annotation, finding such coordinations is simple. However, as (19-c) shows, we again have to accept the annotation decisions in the treebank, for example that **pressured** and **disappointed** are annotated as verb phrases (VP). If they were annotated as adjectives, there would be no coordination of unlikes.

(19) a. He was [$_{NP}$ a doctor of philosophy] and [$_{ADJP}$ proud of it].

b. Investors assume [$_{NP}$ reinvestment of dividends] and [$_{SBAR}$ that the current yield continues for a year].

c. I feel [$_{VP}$ pressured], [$_{VP}$ disappointed], [$_{ADJP}$ uncomfortable], and [$_{ADJP}$ quite angry with the government].

We are also restricted by the level of annotations that are present in a corpus. In the German treebank TÜBA-D/Z, for example, conjuncts in coordinations are specifically marked (in contrast to the PENN TREEBANK), but coordinations of unlikes are not. Thus, in this treebank, we would have to individually search for all combinations of syntactic constituents. Additional restrictions are imposed by the types of queries the query tool uses that we employ for searching in the corpus. One restriction that is often present in such tools, for example in TIGERSEARCH (see Chapter 12.3), is that we cannot search for things that are not there. This means that searching for subjectless sentences in German or Spanish, for example, is extremely difficult. In other words, we would like to have a query "give me all the sentences that do not have a subject," but this is something that cannot be searched for in TIGERSEARCH. In such cases, we need to find approximations, such as "search for all sentences in Spanish that start with a preposition in an oblique case." This would retrieve sentences such as in (20).

(20) Me   gusta   estudiar.
    To me pleases studying.
    I like studying.

Finding elliptical sentences, as in (21), is extremely difficult or almost impossible since we have flexibility in what we elide in a sentence. In this case, we would need annotations specifying that parts of the sentence are elided, and potentially information about what the elided part is. For example, in (21-a), we would have to specify that the verb **bought** is elided.

(21) a. Peter bought a book and Jane [] a CD.
    b. Peter bought a book and Mary [], too.
    c. Sam did it, not Fred [].
    d. When [] I don't know, but John will definitely call.

2.4 Principles of Corpus Annotation

Corpus annotation, no matter on which level, is a rather difficult time- and manpower-consuming enterprise. For this reason, there are best practices in the field that we need to be aware of before we start out with an annotation project. However, before we discuss these best practices, let us step back and look at arguments against annotation. Generally, there are the following arguments against annotation (McEnery et al., 2005):

1. The annotation is cluttered.
2. Annotation makes a corpus less accessible and expandable.
3. Annotation imposes one particular linguistic analysis.
4. Annotation cannot be done completely consistently.

All of these points of criticism are valid comments. Our answer to the first and second points is there are annotation formats, specifically stand-off annotation (see section 2.1 for an explanation), which allow the separation of the original text and the annotations. And even when both text and annotations are interleaved, there are often tools that allow the representation of only specific elements. Below, we will discuss an example in XML (short for Extensible Markup Language). In terms of expandability, we can often use automatic tools to annotate more text (with the risk that there may be errors in the automatic analyses). With regard to the third point, we have discussed previously that in many cases, even if we do not agree with the analysis, we can still find the phenomena in which we are interested, and we can create our own analyses once we do have the examples. Thus having analyses with which we do not agree allows us to find phenomena that we may not be able to find efficiently without the annotation. With regard to the last point, both human annotators and automatic methods do make mistakes, but there are ways to ensure a high quality of annotation (see below).

The annotation of a corpus is expensive in terms of time and funding. For example, Marcus et al. (1993) report that annotators correcting parser output for the PENN TREEBANK managed 475 words per hour after having been trained for six weeks. For this reason, annotations should be performed in a way that they can be reused. This means that standard data formats, for which annotation and/or query tools exist, should be used whenever possible. Also, the annotations should be as general as possible so that they can be used for as many uses as possible. However, this may not always be possible. If we want to find reduced relative clauses, for example, we may be able to hire an annotator to mark all relative clauses, but it may not be possible to have this annotator annotate the whole syntax of the sentences. The latter is a much more extensive task, which also requires more expertise as well as more time.

Leech (1997) cites seven principles of corpus annotation:

1. It should be possible to remove the annotation from an annotated corpus in order to revert to the raw corpus.

2. It should be possible to extract the annotations by themselves from the text.

3. The annotation scheme should be based on guidelines which are available to the end user.

4. It should be made clear how and by whom the annotation was carried out.

5. The end user should be made aware that the corpus annotation is not infallible, but simply a potentially useful tool.

6. Annotation schemes should be based as far as possible on widely agreed and theory-neutral principles.

7. No annotation scheme has the a priori right to be considered as a standard. Standards emerge through practical consensus.

Taking the first two principles together, the annotated corpus should allow maximum flexibility for manipulation by the user.

Principle 3 is important because annotations also have to be consistent in order to be useful. If we are looking, for example, for the reduced relative clauses, it would be difficult to find them if a part of such clauses were annotated in a different way from what we have seen in Figure 2.1. To reach consistency, explicit guidelines are very important. These guidelines describe the *annotation scheme*, i.e. the set of decisions that describe which phenomena to annotate in which way. They serve two purposes. On the one hand, they help annotators to decide for specific phenomena how to annotate them. In a way, guidelines are an external memory that stores decisions for phenomena that have occurred already. On the other hand, they are indispensable for the user to find out how a specific phenomenon has been marked.

The next two principles, 4 and 5, concern the authorship of the annotations and their quality. We already mentioned that it is important to know whether the annotations were carried out by a human annotator or automatically, which also allows conclusions about the quality of the annotations. Additionally, it is important to know more about the annotators. One way of ensuring quality is to have two (or more) annotators annotate each part of the corpus independently. Differences between these annotations can be discussed and corrected if necessary. Additionally, we can calculate *inter-annotator agreement*; this is a measure of how often annotators differ in their annotations of the same text. Inter-annotator agreement between a pair of annotators is generally calculated via *Cohen's kappa coefficient*. The kappa value ranges between 0 (no agreement between annotators) and 1 (full agreement). Generally, a kappa value higher than 0.8 indicates consistent annotations. However, note that the kappa value that can be reached depends on the difficulty of the annotation. If annotators have to decide between very similar senses in word sense disambiguation, for example, a high kappa may not be possible, even for highly trained annotators.

Principle 6 states that the annotation should also be based on an established linguistic theory. Having a linguistic theory in the background makes the decisions more accessible for users. Thus, if we develop our own sense inventory for the word **line**, which distinguishes where in the sentence it occurs, users as well as annotators may not be able to relate to those decisions. Linguistically motivated decisions also help consistency.

So far, we have talked mostly about the contents of the annotations. Another important point concerns the representation of these annotations: their *encoding*. We have already seen simple types of encoding for POS tags, such as in (22-a), where the POS tags are appended to the word, with / as a separator, and we have seen examples of bracketing, such as in (19), where syntactic constituents are shown by labeled brackets. Since the 1990s, efforts have been made to standardize annotation by use of *markup languages* such as XML (Extensible Markup Language). In XML, every type of information to be annotated is marked by tags.[11] The POS tagged sentence from (22-a) could be represented in XML as shown in (22-b).

(22) a.   The/DT inhabitants/NNS of/IN Egypt/NE were/VBD called/VBP mummies/ NNS ./.

  b.   <s><word pos = "DT">The</word> <word pos = "NNS"> inhabitants</word> <word pos = "IN">of</word> <word pos = "NE">Egypt</word> <word pos = "VBD">were</word> <word pos = "VBP">called</word> <word pos = "NNS"> mummies</word><word pos = ".">.</word></s>

In this annotation, every word has a beginning tag (<word>) and an end tag (</word>), characterized by the /. We also have a second type of annotated information: we mark the whole sentence with the tags <s> and </s>. Additionally, the word tag carries the POS information, in the attribute pos. Note than in the XML annotation, we can keep the information that **mummies** and the following period have no space between them; spaces are normally represented between the words, but the end tag of **mummies** is directly adjacent to the beginning tag of the period.

A well-formed XML document consists of two parts: one is the content part, which would contain, for example, the sentence in (22-b). The other part consists of a schema that describes the structure of the content part; in most cases, this is done by means of a *Document Type Description* (DTD). In our example, the DTD would contain the information that the text consists of sentences, that sentences consist of words, and that words have information about POS tags.

One advantage is that XML can represent many different types of information. It also does not use any predefined formatting that can only be interpreted by specific, and often proprietary, applications. Early corpora have often been annotated in typesetting applications such as MS Word or WordPerfect. Once the version of the application was obsolete, these corpora had turned into *data graveyards*, unusable or unreadable data collections. Since XML is an open standard that uses only simple characters, it should be readable even when there are no more XML readers, which allow a more user-friendly representation of the annotation.

A drawback of XML encoding is that it is rather verbose. This can easily be seen by comparing the length of (22-a) to (22-b). Another drawback is that information is often hidden deep within the XML structure, and thus it can become difficult to search for a combination of different types of information.

2.5 Searching in Annotated Corpora

Linguistically annotated corpora are only useful when they are searchable, i.e. when we can find the information that we are looking for. Plain text corpora, without annotations, are easy to use, even for the uninitiated user, since we can use standard text search. However, if we have annotations that intervene between the text, searching even for sequences of words becomes more complex. If we assume a POS annotated corpus, in the form shown in (22-a), we cannot simply search for the sequence **of Egypt**. We would either have to type the whole sequence including the POS tag, **of/IN Egypt**, or we have to use a query tool that allows us to specify which information we are looking for, for example [word="of"] . [word="Egypt"]. In this example, the square brackets represent entities, in our case words, and the period between them requires the two words to occur in sequence. This query language would also allow us to search for a sequence of words and POS tags, as in [pos="IN"] . [word="Egypt"], which would not only find **of Egypt** but any combination of a preposition followed by the word **Egypt**, such as **from Egypt** or **in Egypt**. This search can be made more powerful by using regular expressions (cf. Chapter 10). The types of information that can be used in such queries are dependent on the types of information annotated in the corpus, i.e. if we have word sense information, we can search for a combination of a word and its sense: **[word="line"; sense=4]**.

So far, we have looked at annotations on the word level. Searching for annotations that go beyond the word level is more complex. If we look at the coreference example in (14) again, we need to be able to search for identity relations as well as for bridging examples. Thus we need to allow sequences that are longer than one word and that are labeled. Even more complex are the cases of syntactic annotation. A constituent tree is a two-dimensional structure, and we would like to search in both dimensions: we need to be able to represent the order in which words occur, but we also need to be able to say that a word is part of a noun phrase, for example.

Query tools for searching in trees have a much larger search space since there are a huge number of relations in both dimensions to consider, even in a simple tree. For this reason, there are not many such tools. The most widely known ones are TGREP and TIGERSEARCH (cf. Chapter 12 for more information).

As mentioned before, we cannot search for phenomena that are not annotated. For example, we cannot know whether two noun phrases are coordinated or not if the annotation scheme does not mark coordination. We also cannot search for elliptical utterances since ellipsis is generally not annotated in treebanks. In many cases, however, approximations are possible. For example, we can search for coordination of unlikes by listing all the possible patterns, potentially with the help of regular expressions (see Chapter 10). The existing query tools also differ considerably in the types of negation they allow, i.e. whether it is possible to search for constituents that are not there.

2.6 Annotation Standards for Linguistically Annotated Corpora

In the previous section, we have seen that it is useful to have a standard encoding for the texts in our corpus, for example, in the form of XML. However, XML is basically just a format that offers us the syntax (the XML tags), and we can define our own semantics. For the example in (22-b), it was our decision to have sentence and word tags called <s> and <word> and to say that words are parts of sentences. We could have used other names in the tags, or completely different tags. However, in order to avoid reinventing the wheel every time we start a new corpus, there are standards available. These standards are important because they allow the exchange of annotated corpora so that different programs can be used to work with those corpora. If the data format is different for each corpus, integrating a new corpus into an annotation or query tool requires programming work.

One of the earliest standardization initiatives is the *Text Encoding Initiative* (TEI), which was founded in the late 1980s. This initiative created a standard, the TEI Guidelines, which define a format for coding and exchanging text corpora. The TEI Guidelines are constantly updated, and the latest versions are based on XML. The guidelines are organized in a modular fashion, each module providing a standard for specific applications in the digital humanities, such as for the annotation of poems, for literary criticism, or for the linguistic annotation of texts. Figure 2.4[12] shows an example of transcribed speech, in which individual utterances (<u>) are annotated as well as incidents and vocal but wordless phenomena. The XML tag <pause/> shows that there is a pause in the utterance. This tag collapses the beginning and end tag, marked by the / at the end.

Note that TEI only provides guidelines for basic text annotation, down to the sentence level. The *Corpus Encoding Standard* (CES), and more specifically, the XML-based XCES provides a standard for the annotation of text corpora, also including linguistic annotations. Figure 2.5[13] shows an example of an XCES conform sentence annotated with POS and lemma information.

```
<u who="#mar">you never <pause/> take this cat for show and tell
<pause/> meow meow</u>
<u who="#ros">yeah well I dont want to</u>
<incident>
    <desc>toy cat has bell in tail which continues to make a tinkling sound</desc>
</incident>
<vocal who="#mar">
    <desc>meows</desc>
</vocal>
<u who="#ros">because it is so old</u>
<u who="#mar">how <choice>
        <orig>bout</orig>
        <reg>about</reg>
    </choice>
    <emph>your</emph> cat <pause/>yours is <emph>new</emph>
    <kinesic>
        <desc>shows Father the cat</desc>
    </kinesic>
</u>
<u trans="pause" who="#fat">thats <pause/> darling</u>
<u who="#mar">
    <seg>no <emph>mine</emph> isnt old</seg>
    <seg>mine is just um a little dirty</seg>
</u>
```

Figure 2.4 A speech segment annotated in TEI.

There are also efforts to formalize the usage of linguistic terms, for example, in the *General Ontology for Linguistic Description* (GOLD). GOLD shows relationships between linguistic terms, with the goal of integrating different theories and terminologies. "For example, if one data set contains the term 'Class 1' and another uses the combination of terms 'Human' and 'Singular', both referring to a noun class representing human individuals, then these two data sets can be equated" via the ontology (Farrar and Langendoen, 2003). Figure 2.6[14] shows a part of the GOLD ontology for written linguistic expressions. The indentation here shows that for example, an affix is either a prefix, an infix, or a suffix.

```
<s>
    <w><orth>The</orth><pos>DET</pos><lem>the</lem></w>
    <w><orth>boat</orth><pos>NNS</pos><lem>boat</lem></w>
    <w><orth>sinks</orth><pos>VBZ</pos><lem>sink</lem></w>
    ...
</s>
```

Figure 2.5 A sentence in XCES.

WrittenLinguisticExpression
   WordPart
      SimpleWordPart
         Root
         Affix
            Prefix
            Infix
            Suffix
         Clitic
      Stem
Word
   SimpleWord
   ComplexWord
      Compound

Figure 2.6 Part of the GOLD ontology for written linguistic expressions.

While GOLD attempts to express (near-)synonymy between different linguistic terms, as exemplified above, the *ISO Data Category Registry* (ISOcat) has a slightly different goal: Here, each linguistic term is assigned a unique administrative identifier. This means that even synonymous terms are assigned different identifiers. The registry has a grass-roots approach in that linguists can add their data, but then a committee of experts decides which terms are admitted to standardized subsets. The goal of ISOcat is also the interoperability of linguistic data sources.

2.7 Summary

In this chapter, we have defined what we understand by linguistic annotation, and we have introduced different ways of representing annotations in section 2.1. In section 2.2, we gave a short overview of the major types of annotation on the word level, the syntactic, semantic, and discourse level. In section 2.3, we gave three examples where we searched for specific linguistic phenomena and explained what types of linguistic annotation are required to be able to find these phenomena. Then we looked at best practices in corpus annotations (section 2.4). In section 2.5, we had a closer look at how search for particular annotations can be carried out. We also discussed general limitations of searching based on linguistic annotation. In section 2.6, finally, we discussed annotation standards.

2.8 Further Reading

Section 2.1

Corpus annotation: There are two works that provide an overview of corpus annotation: The book by Garside et al. (1997) provides an extensive overview of corpus annotation; it discusses different levels of corpus annotation available in the 1990s as well as annotation methods. Wynne (2005) provides a collection of chapters by various authors that explain good practices in different areas relevant to the development of annotated corpora.

Section 2.2

Bridging: A good definition and description of the phenomena that fall under bridging can be found in Clark (1977).

FRAMENET: FRAMENET is documented in the following publications: Baker et al. (1998); Ruppenhofer et al. (2010). It is available from https://framenet.icsi.berkeley.edu/fndrupal/.

PENN DISCOURSE TREEBANK: The Penn Discourse Treebank is documented in Prasad et al. (2008). More information is available from http://www.seas.upenn.edu/~pdtb/.

TimeML: A description of TimeML can be found in Pustejovsky et al. (2003) and Saurí et al. (2006). More extensive information, including the TimeML specification, can be found at www.timeml.org/.

WORDNET: The Princeton WordNet (Fellbaum, 1998) is available from wordnet.princeton.edu/.

Section 2.4

Inter-annotator agreement: More information about inter-annotator agreement, including Cohen's kappa, can be found, for example, at http://www.john-uebersax.com/stat/agree.htm. Calculators for Cohen's kappa are available online, for example, at http://vassarstats.net/kappa.html. A related measure to Cohen's kappa is *Krippendorf's alpha*, which is discussed for usage in the annotation of coreference in Passonneau (2004).

Quality assurance: Zinsmeister et al. (2009) provide an overview with regard to questions concerning quality assurance, reusability, and sustainability.

XML: There are many introductions to XML. Those include the *IBM developer works* introduction at http://www.ibm.com/developerworks/xml/tutorials/xmlintro/ and the *w3schools* tutorial at http://www.w3schools.com/xml/.

XML formats for linguistic annotation: There are many different XML formats used for linguistic annotation. Influential ones include TigerXML (at http://www.ims.uni-stuttgart.de/forschung/ ressourcen/werkzeuge/TIGERSearch/doc/html/TigerXML.html), EXMARaLDA (at http://www.exmaralda.org/), and PAULA (at http://www.sfb632.uni-potsdam.de/d1/paula/doc/PAULA_intro. html).

Section 2.6

Corpus annotation standards: More information about TEI can be found at http://www.tei-c. org/index.xml. XCES is documented at http://www.xces.org/.

GOLD: The GOLD ontology is described in (Farrar and Langendoen, 2003); more information can be found at http://linguistics-ontology.org/.

ISOcat: ISOcat is documented at http://www.isocat.org/.

2.9 Exercises

1. **Uses of annotated corpora**: Find more examples for uses of linguistically annotated corpora. Consider dictionary making, computer programs that read text to the blind, and language teaching.

2. **Searching**: Which types of information would one need to find all forms of a word? Which would we need for finding the 100 most frequent words in English? Think about cases such as **leaves** as a form of **leaf** and of **leave**.

3. **XML**: In the example in Figure 2.4, the information who is talking is marked in the tag <u> in the attribute "who." Extract all utterances by the speaker "#mar."

PART II
LINGUISTIC ANNOTATION

CHAPTER 3
LINGUISTIC ANNOTATION ON THE WORD LEVEL

In this chapter, we will have a closer look at annotations on the word level. As introduced in section 2.2.1, we will look at lemma information, morphological information, and part-of-speech (POS) information. We will see such annotations for different languages, and we will discuss problems that occur in those languages. Finally, we will give an overview of how automatic annotation of these types of information can be performed, and what types of errors we can expect in automatically annotated texts. For a discussion of how to search in corpora with word level annotation, see Chapter 11.

Before we start looking at annotations, however, we have to define what we consider a word. Linguistically speaking, a word is the smallest element that we can use in language and that has meaning on its own. However, since this is rather vague, in computational linguistics (CL), a more pragmatic definition is used: a word is the sequence of characters between two spaces. However, there are problems with this approach, especially in languages where spaces are not usually written, such as in Arabic. The problems also occur, though to a lesser degree, in languages such as English: there are mergers, such as **don't**, which would count as one word if we use the CL definition (for more examples, cf. the next section).

There is another distinction that we need to make, namely the one between *type* and *token*. A token is the form of a word as it occurs in the text while a type is an abstraction, such as a lemma (cf. the next section). Thus, in the sentence in (1),[1] we have 14 tokens (also counting the period), but only 12 types. This is because the word **the** occurs three times, and thus counts three times towards the token count but only once towards the type count.

(1)   The Egyptians built the Pyramids in the shape of a huge triangular cube.

3.1 Lemma Annotation

A *lemma* is the basic form of a word, as it is represented in a lexicon. For English, this is the singular form for nouns (e.g. **tree, child**) and the infinitive for verbs (e.g. **deceive, run**). For languages that have grammatical gender, the lemma form for adjectives and nouns is the masculine form (e.g. **amigo** in Spanish), and in languages with a case system, the lemma form is in the nominative case (e.g. **amicus** in Latin). There are languages, such as Arabic, that do not have an infinitive form. In Arabic, the lemma form is typically the third person masculine singular perfective form for verbs. Note that in this case, the lemma is actually an inflected form.

Lemma information is useful in contexts where one needs to find all occurrences of a certain word. For example, if we are looking for the lemma **talk**, we would also want to find occurrences of the forms **talks**, **talked**, and **talking**. In the current example, this is easy to do because we can only look for the basic form and will get all other forms, since the basic form is a prefix of all other forms. However, this becomes more difficult when we look for the sequence **talk about**, since here the differences in the forms of **talk** are in the middle of the search string. Again, if we have lemma information, we can specify that we are looking for **lemma=talk + lemma=about**, which would find all forms. To demonstrate this, we will use the *Corpus of Contemporary American English* (COCA),[2] which has a web interface that allows us to search for lemmas. In this interface, we specify the lemma information in square brackets. Thus, the search term to look for **talk about** is as follows:

(2) [talk] about

This search term has to be entered in the field for "Word(s)." In COCA, this finds occurrences of **talking about, talk about, talked about, talks about**, and **talkin about**.

If we search for all forms of **be sorry**, the search term is:

(3) [be] [sorry]

This finds occurrences of **'m sorry, was sorry, am sorry, 're sorry, be sorry, 's sorry, is sorry, are sorry, were sorry, being sorry, been sorry, s sorry**, but also **am sorrier, 'm sorrier, are sorrier, 're sorrier**. If we had not used the square brackets around **sorry**, we would have found only the positives but not the comparative forms.

Determining what the lemma of a word is can be difficult when the language contains merged words, such as **don't** or **can't** in English. In such cases, the annotator has to decide whether to reduce the merged form to one word, e.g. **do** for **don't**, or to mark both forms, e.g. **do not**. In English, this also concerns possessives such as in **John's book**, or colloquialisms, such as **gonna** or **wanna**, which gain in popularity in social media texts. In other languages, mergers are more common: In German, for example, prepositions are merged with determiners, such as in **zum** (zu+dem, Eng. *to the$_{m/n}$*), **zur** (zu+der, Eng. *to the$_f$*), or **ins** (in+das, Eng. *into the$_n$*). In French, prepositions and determiners or relative pronouns are merged, too: **du** (de+le, Eng. *of the*), **aux** (a+les, Eng. *to the$_{pl}$*), or **duquel** (de+lequel, Eng. *of whom/which*).

Lemma information can be useful for English, but is more important for morphologically rich languages such as Arabic or Finnish, in which a word can have thousands of different forms, making it difficult to list all of them. In Arabic, for example, the lemma **ktb**[3] (Eng. **to write**) can be found in over 400 different forms. As a verb, **ktb** can be realized as **ktb, ktbt, ktbn, ktbnA, ktbA, ktbwA** in the past tense alone, and each of these forms can be preceded by proclitics and followed by pronouns, which are parts of the words. The same word can also be used as a plural noun, which can take similar prefixes and suffixes.

Lemma annotation can be performed automatically: there are tools, called *lemmatizers*, which perform automatic *lemmatization*. A lemmatizer generally requires a lexicon of lemmas as well as rules on how individual word forms are formed. For English, such rules would be fairly simple, stating that for nouns, we form the plural by adding an -**s**, and for verbs, we can add the following suffixes: -**s**, -**ing**, and -**ed**. However, we also would need to cover exceptions, such as the rule saying that if the word ends in **y**, and we add the suffix -**s**, we need to change the **y** into **ie**. This rule would convert the lemma **fly** into **flies**. For lemmatization, the lemmatizer applies these rules to the inflected form to reduce it to the lemma. Thus, the word **flies** would be converted to **fly**.

Since lemmatizers are generally rule-based, they are usually reliable. However, the exact reliability also depends on the coverage of the lemma lexicon integrated into the lemmatizer. If a word is not covered in the lexicon, the lemmatizer either leaves the word unchanged, or it has to guess the correct form. In order to guess the lemma, lemmatizers often look for typical suffixes. For example, if it cannot process the word **lemmatization**, it may know that -**ation** is a suffix. Then it could convert this word to **lemmatize**.

3.2 Morphological Annotation

Morphological annotation concentrates on annotating morphological information for words. This includes annotating nouns for number, gender, case, and definiteness, annotating adjectives for number, gender, case, and degree, and annotating verbs for person, number, mood, and tense, depending on which types of information are present in a language. Such features fall under *inflectional morphology*. Inflection refers to the changes to a word that model grammatical information such as case or tense. Inflectional morphological processes neither change the meaning of the word, nor do they change the POS of a word.

In addition to the inflectional features listed so far, words can also be annotated for word formation. This is called *derivational morphology*. Derivational morphology generally covers processes that change the POS of a word or that involve more than one meaning. The latter includes compounding. The English compound noun **greenhouse**, for example, would be annotated as **green=house**, where the = sign separates the two stems. However, in English, most compounds consist of individual words, which do not necessarily have to be annotated, for example, **computer system**, **football game**. In other languages, compounding leads to long, complex words. In German, noun compounding is extremely common, and compound nouns are spelled as single words, such as in **Donaudampfschifffahrtskapitänsmütze** (Eng. Danube steam shipping captain's hat). This word is analyzed as **Donau=Dampf=Schiff=Fahrt=Kapitän=Mütze**. Note that, for example, between **Kapitän** and **Mütze**, there is an -**s** in the compound, which disappears in the analysis. This is an infix that is inserted in order to make the word easier to pronounce. In German, there are cases where the segmentation of a word is genuinely ambiguous, even though those cases are exceedingly rare. One example is the word **Staubecken**, which can be analyzed as **Stau=Becken** (Eng. **water reservoir**) or as **Staub=Ecke** (Eng. **dust corner**). Such ambiguities in segmentation are more common in Arabic and Hebrew.

As mentioned above, derivational morphology also covers processes where words are changed into a different POS type. Thus, the English word **resocialization** can be analyzed as having the stem **social**, which is then changed into a verb, **socialize**, which is changed into a noun, **socialization**, which is then assigned an affix that shows a repeated action.

In general, morphological annotation concentrates on inflectional morphology. Since English has an impoverished morphology, this type of information is normally not annotated in corpora for English. For this reason, we will illustrate the morphological annotation of the German TiGer Corpus. TiGer is a syntactically annotated corpus (see also Chapter 4), but it also has annotation layers for lemmas, for morphology, and for POS (see next section).

An example for the first two types of annotation is shown in Figure 3.1 for the sentence in (4).

(4) Texaner gibt nur vage Auskunft   über seine Wirtschaftspolitik
     Texan   gives only vague information about his   economic policy

The example only shows the relevant information. It is organized in a column-based format, in which the first column shows the words of the sentence, the second column shows its lemma, the third its POS tag, and the last one the morphological annotation. The first line, starting with %%, contains a comment that explains the information in the columns. The lines starting with #BOS and #EOS are sentence markers, i.e. this is the third sentence of the corpus. The morphological annotation in the last column

%% word	lemma	tag	morph
#BOS 3			
Texaner	Texaner	NN	Nom.Sg.Masc
gibt	geben	VVFIN	3.Sg.Pres.Ind
nur	nur	ADV	--
vage	vage	ADJA	Pos.Acc.Sg.Fem
Auskunft	Auskunft	NN	Acc.Sg.Fem
über	über	APPR	--
seine	sein	PPOSAT	Acc.Sg.Fem
Wirtschaftspolitik	Wirtschaftspolitik	NN	Acc.Sg.Fem
#EOS 3			

Figure 3.1 The TiGer annotation for sentence (4).

Table 3.1 A morphological analysis for the sentence in (5).

Louis	Louis +Prop+Masc+Sg
	Louis +Prop+Fam+Sg
	Louis +Prop+Misc
Pastuer	Pastuer +open+NOUN
discovered	discover +Verb+PastBoth+123SP
	discover ed +Adj
a	a +Let
	a +Det+Indef+Sg
cure	cure +Noun+Sg
	cure +Verb+Pres+Non3sg
for	for +Prep
	for +Conj+Sub
rabbis	rabbi +Noun+Pl
.	. +SENT

specifies that **Texaner**, which is assigned Nom.Sg.Masc, is in the nominative case (Nom), singular (Sg), and masculine (Masc). The verb **gibt** is third person (3), singular, present (Pres), indicative (Ind). The adjective **vage** is positive (Pos), in accusative case (Acc), singular, feminine (Fem).

Morphological annotation can also be performed automatically. It generally falls into two steps: morphological analysis and morphological disambiguation. A *morphological analyzer* takes an inflected form of a word and produces all analyses that exist for this word. For example, the sentence in (5)[4] receives the analysis in Table 3.1, based on the *Xerox Finite-State Morphological Transducer* for English.

(5)   Louis Pastuer discovered a cure for rabbis.

In the analysis, the word **Louis** is three way ambiguous between a masculine first name (+Prop+Masc), a family name (+Prop+Fam), and some other type of name (+Prop+Misc). The misspelt **Pastuer** is an unknown word and the analyzer guesses that it is a noun (+open+NOUN). The next word, **discovered**, is ambiguous between a verb in the past tense (+Verb+PastBoth) and an adjective (ed +Adj), as in **the discovered solution**. Note that the analysis also has POS information since the morphological features depend on the word class, i.e. in English, verbs are annotated for tense and person, nouns are annotated for number and whether they are a proper noun. We also see that words can be ambiguous between different POS, as we have seen for

discovered. This example shows that generally few words receive wrong annotations. This only happens if the word is unknown and does not follow the standard regularities of the language. However, many words are ambiguous, which means that they have to be disambiguated before we can use the corpus. The disambiguation is performed by a *morphological disambiguator.* While morphological analysis is rule-based, the disambiguation module needs to be based on statistics. It generally looks at a local context of 2–3 words on either side of the ambiguous word and decides on the most likely analysis. For example, given that the word **cure**, which is ambiguous between a noun and a verb in present tense, follows a word that has a determiner reading (+DET+Indef), the noun reading for **cure** is much more likely.

While in many languages, morphological disambiguation is straightforward, German is an exception. This language combines relatively *free word order* with *case syncretism,* which means that a number of cases share the same suffix. The sentence in (6) is genuinely ambiguous between the meanings **The mouse chases the cat.** and **The cat chases the mouse.** The reason for the ambiguity is that both noun phrases can be either in nominative case, which marks the subject, or accusative, which marks the direct object. Morphological analyzers would generally make mistakes in such cases, especially when the order of the two noun phrases deviates from the *canonical word order.*

(6)   Die Maus jagt die Katze.
      The mouse chases the cat.

3.3 POS Annotation

The annotation of word classes, or parts of speech (POS) is closely combined with morphological annotation, as we have seen in the previous section. On the one hand, morphological analysis needs to determine the POS of a word before it can assign morphological features. On the other hand, POS tagging also annotates some morphological information, such as number in verbs or nouns. The amount of morphological information integrated into a POS tagset depends on the language as well as on the POS tagset. In the following, we will look at three different POS tagsets for English: the PENN TREEBANK tagset, the SUSANNE tagset, and the ICE tagset. All of these tagsets have been used for the POS annotation of corpora: the PENN TREEBANK tagset for the PENN TREEBANK, the SUSANNE tagset for the SUSANNE, CHRISTINE, and LUCY corpora, and the ICE tagset for different sections of the *International Corpus of English* (ICE), most notably the British one.

We will see that there is considerable variation in the granularity of these tagsets: the PENN TREEBANK tagset includes 36 tags for words and 9 tags for punctuation; the SUSANNE tagset comprises 406 distinct word tags and 20 punctuation tags; and the ICE tagset has 270. The PENN TREEBANK tagset is based on an extensive annotation manual (Santorini, 1990), the full list of POS tags is shown in Appendix A.; the SUSANNE tagset is described in Sampson (1995), and the ICE tagset in the manual at http://ice-corpora.

net/ice/manuals.htm. In Table 3.2, we show the annotation based on the three POS tagsets for the sentences in (7),[5] to the best of our knowledge.

(7) The sun never set on the British Empire because the British Empire is in the East and the sun sets in the West. Queen Victoria was the longest queen. She sat on a thorn for 63 years. Her reclining years and finally the end of her life were exemplatory of a great personality. Her death was the final event which ended her reign.

A comparison of the three POS annotations shows that the different POS tagsets provide different levels of information. The PENN TREEBANK tagset provides only rather coarse distinctions while the other two tagsets have more information. While the PENN TREEBANK and ICE tagsets only distinguish between common and proper nouns, singular and plural, SUSANNE distinguishes between common nouns, nouns of direction, preceding and following nouns of style or title, locative and numeral nouns, units of measurement, proper nouns, weekdays, and months, all in singular and plural, and, where applicable, in neutral form. For verbs, the PENN TREEBANK tagset distinguishes infinite/base forms, present tense third person and non-third person, past tense, **-ing** forms, and participles; SUSANNE has 31 separate POS tags that distinguish between auxiliary, modal, and lexical verbs, as well as between different forms of **be**, **do**, and **have**. The ICE tagset, in contrast, distinguishes between copulas,

Table 3.2 POS annotation using three different POS tagsets, the PENN TREEBANK, SUSANNE, and ICE tagset.

word	PENN	SUSANNE	ICE
Queen	NNP	NNS1c	N(prop,sing)
Victoria	NNP	NP1f	N(prop,sing)
was	VBD	VBDZ	AUX(pass,past)
the	DT	AT	ART(def)
longest	JJS	JJT	ADJ(sup)
queen	NN	NNS1c	N(com,sing)
.	.	YF	PUNC(per)
She	PRP	PPHS1f	PRON(pers,sing)
sat	VBD	VVDv	V(intr,past)
on	IN	II	PREP(ge)
a	DT	AT1	ART(indef)
thorn	NN	NN1c	N(com,sing)

word	PENN	SUSANNE	ICE
for	IN	IF	PREP(ge)
63	CD	MCn	NUM(card,sing)
years	NNS	NNT2	N(com,plu)
.	.	YF	PUNC(per)
Her	PRP$	APPGf	PRON(poss,sing)
reclining	VBG	VVGv	ADJ(ingp)
years	NNS	NN2	N(com,plu)
and	CC	CC	CONJUNC(coord)
finally	RB	RR	ADV(ge)
the	DT	AT	ART(def)
end	NN	NN1	N(com,sing)
of	IN	IO	PREP(ge)
her	PRP$	APPGf	PRON(poss,sing)
life	NN	NN1	N(com,sing)
were	VBD	VBDR	AUX(pass,past)
exemplatory	JJ	JJ	ADJ
of	IN	IO	PREP(ge)
a	DT	AT1	ART(indef)
great	JJ	JJ	ADJ
personality	NN	NN1	N(com,sing)
.	.	YT	PUNC(per)
Her	PRP$	APPGf	PRON(poss,sing)
death	NN	NN1	N(com,sing)
was	VBD	VBDZ	AUX(pass,past)
the	DT	AT	ART(def)
final	JJ	JJ	ADJ
event	NN	NN1	N(com,sing)
which	WP	DDQr	PRON(rel)
ended	VBD	VVDv	V(montr,past)
her	PRP$	APPGf	PRON(poss,sing)
reign	NN	NN1	N(com,sing)
.	.	YT	PUNC(per)

intransitives, monotransitives, transitives, ditransitives, complex-transitives, further split by their suffixes, as well as 55 different types of auxiliaries. We can also see that apart from notational differences, the tagsets do not always agree on the general POS of a word. One example is the word **reclining**, which is analyzed as gerund in the PENN TREEBANK and SUSANNE tagset, but as an adjective in **-ing** form in ICE. Another example can be found in the treatment of contracted negations, such as **weren't** or **didn't**. In the PENN TREEBANK, such contractions are separated into **were** and **n't**. Then each word is assigned a separate POS tag, VBD and RB respectively. SUSANNE also splits such words, but here, the second word is marked with a +: **were** and **+not**, and they are annotated as VBDR and XX. ICE, in contrast, keeps these words as contracted words and assigns the POS tag AUX(pass,past,neg) or AUX(prog,past,neg), depending on their usage. Note that this decision already needs to be considered on the tokenization level.

These differences in the annotation schemes have serious consequences for users of a corpus. One consequence is that when we work with different corpora, we may have to be fluent in different tagsets. Another consequence is that the different tagsets impose different restrictions on which phenomena can be looked up in corpora. If we have a corpus that is annotated with the PENN TREEBANK tagset, we find verbs in past tense, but we cannot find only transitive verbs in past tense. The valency of verbs is not explicitly marked in this tagset. We would need a corpus annotated in the ICE tagset to find verbs with a certain valency.

The differences between the tagsets also has consequences for the annotation of corpora. It is immediately obvious that using the PENN TREEBANK tagset is much easier than using the other two tagsets, simply because the annotator has to remember only a short list of tags. It may also lead to fewer mistakes in the annotation because annotators do not have to remember as many different verb cases, for example. However, the differences also have an influence on the quality of automatic POS annotation. This is performed by *POS taggers*. POS taggers generally use a statistical approach to decide on the best POS sequence for a sentence. For the individual decisions, they only look at the word to be tagged and two words to its left. For this reason, they are called *trigram POS taggers*, a trigram being a sequence of three words. Trigram POS taggers are generally very reliable. Their accuracy depends on the language to be tagged, the amount of training data, and the POS tagset. For English, such taggers reach accuracies of around 97 percent. This means that three out of 100 words are tagged with an erroneous tag. If we assume an average sentence length of 20 words, this means that we expect to find about three errors in any set of five sentences we pick from the corpus. These POS taggers often make mistakes when they have to consider *long-distance relationships*. For example, if the tagger looks at the word **parked** in the context **very recently parked**, it is impossible to decide whether the word is a verb in past tense, as in (8-a), or a past participle, as in (8-b).

(8) a. He very recently parked the car.
     b. We have very recently parked the car.

Problems are also caused by distinctions such as the valency information in the ICE tagset because these distinctions are lexical, and thus have to be known for every verb. In the design of the PENN TREEBANK tagset, decisions were made in such a way that a POS tagger has an optimal chance of assigning the correct tags. For this reason, prepositions and subordinating conjunctions share a single POS tag, IN, because it is often impossible to distinguish between the two based on local context, cf. the word **before** in (9).[6]

(9) a. King Harlod mustarded his troops before the Battle of Hastings.
     b. King Harlod mustarded his troops before the Battle of Hastings started.

3.4 Summary

In this chapter, we have looked at annotations on the word level; we considered lemma, morphological, and POS annotations. For each type of annotation, we showed examples, we gave ideas why these types of information can be useful for searching, and we discussed automatic annotation methods as well as potential errors that such automatic methods are likely to make. For the morphological annotation, we showed a German example, and for POS annotation, we compared three different annotation schemes for English. For more information on how to search for word level annotations, see Chapter 11.

3.5 Further Reading

Section 3.1

Buckwalter transliteration: The Buckwalter transliteration for Arabic is explained in detail by Habash (2010). The transliteration table can be found at http://www.qamus.org/transliteration.htm.

Lemmatizers: The POS tagger TREETAGGER (Schmid, 1994, 1995) (http://www.ims.uni-stuttgart.de/projekte/corplex/TreeTagger/) performs lemmatization as a first step. There are pre-existing language files available for English, German, Italian, Dutch, Spanish, Bulgarian, Russian, French, and Old French. There is also a lemmatizer for English called MORPHADORNER http://morphadorner.northwestern.edu/. This lemmatizer can also handle historical texts.

Section 3.2

Morphological analyzers: The most well-known morphological analyzer is the *Xerox Finite-State Morphological Transducer* (XFST) (Beesley and Karttunen, 2003; Karttunen and Beesley, 1992) for Czech, English, French, German, Spanish, Hungarian, Italian, Polish, and Russian, at http://open.xerox.com/Services/fst-nlp-tools/Pages/morphology. Lingsoft offers online demos for their English analyzer ENGTWOL (Tapanainen and Voutilainen, 1994) at http://www2.lingsoft.fi/cgi-bin/engtwol, a commercial product. They also have analyzers for Danish, Finnish, German, Norwegian, and Swedish.

Section 3.3

POS annotated corpora: There are many corpora with POS annotation, either as one annotation level in syntactically annotated treebanks or as sole layer of annotation. We concentrate here on the corpora mentioned in the chapter: the German TiGer Corpus (Brants et al., 2002, 2004) is available from http://www.ims.uni-stuttgart.de/forschung/ressourcen/korpora/tiger.en.html. Information about the Penn Treebank (Marcus et al., 1993) is available from http://www.cis.upenn.edu/~treebank/; the treebank is licensed by the Linguistic Data Consortium (LDC) at http://www.ldc.upenn.edu. Susanne (Sampson, 1993), Christine, and Lucy (Sampson, 2003) are available from http://www.grsampson.net/Resources.html, the annotation scheme is documented by Sampson (1995). Ice is available from http://ice-corpora.net/ice/, the British component is documented by Nelson et al. (2002) and in Wallis and Nelson (2006).

POS taggers: There are several implementations of POS taggers available. The most well-known one is TnT by Torsten Brants (Brants, 1998, 2000). This tagger has a very sophisticated module for guessing unknown words. It is available with a license. More information can be found at http://www.coli.uni-saarland.de/~thorsten/tnt/. There is also an open source trigram tagger called HunPOS. It is available from http://code.google.com/p/hunpos/.

More recent developments in POS tagging use machine learning approaches, such as MBT (Daelemans et al., 1996) at http://ilk.uvt.nl/mbt/, SMVTool (Giménez and Màrquez, 2004) at www.lsi.upc.edu/~nlp/SVMTool/, or the Stanford POS tagger (Toutanova et al., 2003; Toutanova and Manning, 2000) at http://nlp.stanford.edu/software/tagger.shtml. All of these POS taggers must be trained on pre-annotated data, but they generally come with pre-trained models for English and potentially other languages.

3.6 Exercises

1. **Lemmatization:** Lemmatize the following words:
   (a) shouldn't
   (b) gonna
   (c) won't
   (d) you're
   (e) dunno

2. **Lemmatization:** Describe one use case where the annotation of the individual lemmas in compounds such as **greenhouse** is necessary.

3. **Lemmatization + POS tagging:** Describe the changes to the Penn Treebank tagset if we decided to leave contracted words without splitting them up. Which different possibilities would we have?

4. **POS tagging:** POS tags the following text with the Penn Treebank and the Ice tagset. You can find the lists of POS tags in Appendices A and B respectively. Which tagset is easier to use? Are there distinctions that are clearer in one of the tagsets?

> During the Renaissance America began. Christopher Columbus was a great navigator who discovered America while cursing about the Atlantic. His ships were called the Nina, the Pinta, and the Santa Fe. Later the Pilgrims crossed the Ocean, and the was called the Pilgrim's Progress. When they landed at Plymouth Rock, they were greeted by Indians, who came down the hill rolling their was hoops before them. The Indian squabs carried porposies on their back. Many of the Indian heroes were killed, along with their cabooses, which proved very fatal to them. The winter of 1620 was a hard one for the settlers. Many people died and many babies were born. Captain John Smith was responsible for all this.[7]

CHAPTER 4
SYNTACTIC ANNOTATION

In this chapter, we will look at syntactic annotations. As we have seen in section 2.2.2, syntactic annotation is concerned with structural relationships of words in a sentence. Syntax can be described in different grammar formalisms. The most influential in terms of annotation are theories based on *constituent structure* and *dependency structure*. One of the earliest syntactically annotated corpora was the PENN TREEBANK, whose annotation is based on constituent structure, represented as a tree structure. For this reason, syntactically annotated corpora are also generally called *treebanks*. This chapter is structured as follows. After going over basic terminology in section 4.1, we will have a closer look at the three most important treebanks for English: the PENN TREEBANK (section 4.2), the SUSANNE/CHRISTINE corpora (section 4.3), and the International Corpus of English—Great Britain (ICE-GB; section 4.4), all of which are based on constituent structure. In section 4.5, we will look at two German treebanks, which also annotate *grammatical functions* (such as subject or direct object) on a large scale, and in section 4.6, we will look at dependency annotation. Finally, we will look at a more recent development, parallel treebanks (section 4.7), which are based on translated text in two languages.

4.1 Basic Terminology

As mentioned above, the two major syntactic formalisms with regard to syntactic annotation are constituent and dependency structure.

In constituent structure, the basic notion is that words are grouped into *phrases*, such as noun phrases, verb phrases, or adverbial phrases. For each phrase, one word serves as the *head*, which determines the syntactic category of the phrase. Phrases in a sentence are hierarchically grouped into larger phrases and finally clauses. The example in (1)[1] shows a constituent analysis in which the phrases are marked as square brackets, and the phrase types are marked as subscripts.

(1) $[_S [_{NP}$ A myth$] [_{VP}$ is $[_{NP}$ a $[_{ADJP}$ female$]$ moth$]]]$.

The brackets state that **A myth** and **a female moth** are both noun phrases (NPs). The second NP has an embedded adjectival phrase (ADJP) **female**, and it forms a verbal phrase (VP) in combination with the verb **is**. The first NP and the VP together constitute the final constituent, the clause (S). If we visualize this bracketed annotation as a graph, in which the constituents are represented as nodes, we have the tree structure shown in Figure 4.1.

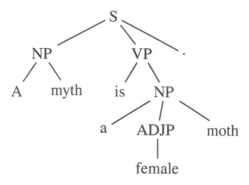

Figure 4.1 The constituent structure for sentence (1).

In the tree structure in Figure 4.1, the S node is also the *root node* of the tree. In addition to the syntactic constituents, we could also annotate the *grammatical functions* of the maximal phrases with regard to the clause: the first NP is the *subject* of the clause, and the second one the predicate. However, since English has a fixed word order, many of the grammatical functions can be inferred from the position of a phrase within the clause and thus do not need to be annotated. For languages with a freer word order, the annotation of the grammatical functions is of extreme importance since otherwise it is impossible to determine the subject of a clause.

While constituent structure models the hierarchical ordering of phrases, dependency structure is concerned with the relationships between pairs of words. Such relationships are called *dependencies*. A dependency is a directed relation from a *head* to a *dependent*. Other names used for the pair are *governor/modifier* or *regent/subordinate*. Most syntactic annotations assign labels such as *subject* or *nominal modifier* to the dependencies. Figure 4.2 shows a dependency graph for the sentence in (1).

In the dependency annotation in Figure 4.2, there is a dependency from the word **myth** to **A**, which means that **A** is a dependent of the head **myth**, and the dependency is of type *nominal modifier* (nmod). The word **myth**, in turn, is a dependent of type *subject*

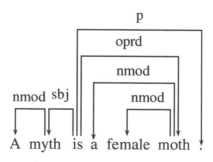

Figure 4.2 The dependency representation of the sentence in (1).

(sbj) of the verb **is**. Note that the latter has no head since it is the head of the whole sentence. We also see that many types of information are present in the constituent and the dependency annotations, just in a different form. If we assume that **myth** is the head of the NP, then we conclude from both syntactic structures that the determiner **A** in some form depends on it. In general, constituent structure and dependency are equivalent, constituent annotation providing more information about phrase types, and dependency annotations providing more information about direct relationships between words. For example, the constituent tree in Figure 4.1 provides the information that the sequences **A myth** and **a female moth** are of the same type, NP, which is not present in the dependency annotation. The latter, in contrast, provides direct information in sentence (2)[2] that the preposition **into their own hands** depends on the verb **took** (cf. Figure 4.3) while the constituent annotation attaches the PP to the VP.

(2)   [$_S$ [$_{NP}$ The people] [$_{VP}$ took [$_{NP}$ the law] [$_{PP}$ into [$_{NP}$ their own hands]]]].

So far, we talked about constituent and dependency annotation as if those were clearly defined linguistic theories. However, this is not the case: These terms cover many different variants of constituent and dependency theory (cf. section 4.9 for examples). The theories differ in many respects: For constituent grammars, for example, a main difference concerns the treatment of long-distance relationships. Here, theories may assume crossing branches (cf. the TiGER treebank in section 4.5), use null words and traces (cf. the PENN TREEBANK in section 4.2) or use specific labels (cf. the TüBA-D/Z treebank for German in section 4.5). They also differ in how many layers of phrases they assume, and which labels they use. Additionally, there are higher order grammar formalisms, such as *Head-Driven Phrase Structure Grammar* (HPSG), *Lexical-Functional Grammar* (LFG), *Combinatory Categorial Grammar* (CCG), and *Tree-Adjoining Grammar* (TAG), which propose additions to the standard phrase structure that make them more powerful than standard tree structures, but are less useable for direct annotation. Since these formalisms require considerable information beyond pure phrase structure, they are difficult to present in a readable format without

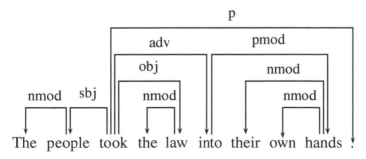

Figure 4.3 The dependency representation of the sentence in (2).

leaving out the information going beyond phrase structures. For this reason, we refrain from presenting them here in more detail.

In dependency grammar, one main difference between theories concerns the number of different levels they assume. There are dependency theories that assume only one level of annotation (cf. the dependency version of the PENN TREEBANK in section 4.6), others assume a separate level for coordination phenomena, and others have more than one level, e.g. for morphological information, for analytical, and for tectogrammatical information (cf. the PRAGUE DEPENDENCY TREEBANK in section 4.6).

4.2 The PENN TREEBANK

The PENN TREEBANK is the main syntactically annotated corpus for English. Version 3, from 1999, consists of several parts: one million words of the *Wall Street Journal* (WSJ), a small sample of the ATIS-3 corpus, the re-annotated BROWN CORPUS, and the SWITCHBOARD section. ATIS contains airline travel information dialogues, the BROWN CORPUS is a balanced corpus of American English, and the SWITCHBOARD section is a corpus containing telephone conversations as its textual basis. However, when the PENN TREEBANK is mentioned, people generally refer to the WSJ section of the treebank. The one million words correspond to roughly 50,000 sentences.

The PENN TREEBANK contains POS annotations (see section 3.3) as well as syntactic annotations, including some predicate-argument structure. Both types of information can be accessed separately, or in a merged version. The syntactic annotation is based on X-bar theory. Figure 4.4 shows an example sentence from the PENN TREEBANK in the original bracketed annotation, often called the "Penn Treebank format." A graphical representation of this syntax tree is shown in Figure 4.5.[3] In the bracketed version, each opening parenthesis starts a new constituent, the following label describes the syntactic category

```
( (S
    (NP-SBJ
      (NP (NNP GTE) (NNP Corp.) )
      (CC and)
      (NP (NNP MCI) (NNP Communications) (NNP Corp.) ))
    (VP (VBD reported)
      (NP
        (NP (JJ strong) (NNS earnings) (NNS gains) )
        (PP (TO to)
          (NP (JJ record) (NNS levels) )))
      (PP (IN for)
        (NP (DT the) (JJ third) (NN quarter) )))
    (. .) ))
```

Figure 4.4 A tree from the WSJ section of the PENN TREEBANK.

of the constituent, a closing bracket finishes the respective constituent, and daughters are embedded. Leaf nodes consist of the POS tag and the word. For example, the last PP has two daughters, the preposition **for** (POS tag: IN) and the NP **the third quarter**. The indentation of daughters is purely to increase readability for the human reader.

The annotation shows that on the constituent level, phrases are annotated with a rather flat structure. Thus, the noun phrase **strong earnings gains** does not have any internal structure. Postmodifications, in contrast, are attached on the next higher level, as is the case for the prepositional phrase **to record levels**. Figure 4.6 shows an example with a complex verb phrase (VP) structure involving the control verb **try**.[4]

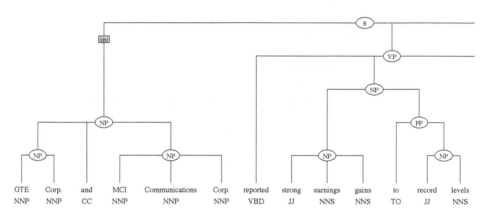

Figure 4.5 The tree from Figure 4.4 in graphical form.

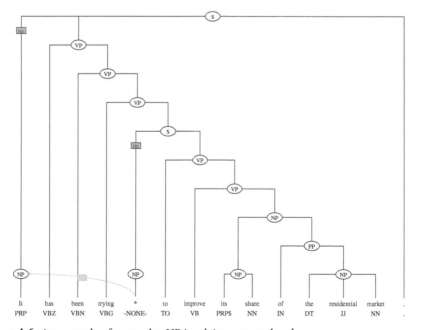

Figure 4.6 An example of a complex VP involving a control verb.

```
( (S
  (NP-SBJ (CD Three) (VBG leading) (NN drug) (NNS companies) )
  (VP (VBD reported)
    (NP
    (NP (JJ robust) (NN third-quarter) (NNS earnings) )
    (, ,)
    (VP (VBN bolstered)
      (NP (-NONE- *) )
      (PP (IN by)
        (NP-LGS
          (NP (JJ strong) (NNS sales) )
          (PP (IN of)
            (NP
              (NP (JJR newer)
              (, ,)
              (JJ big-selling) (NNS prescriptions) (NNS drugs) )
              (SBAR
                (WHNP-1 (WDT that) )
                (S
                  (NP-SBJ (-NONE- *T*-1) )
                  (VP (VBP provide)
                    (NP (JJ hefty) (NN profit) (NNS margins) )))))))))))))
  (. .) ))
```

Figure 4.7 An example with null elements from the PENN TREEBANK.

We can also see that the subject **GTE Corp. and MCI Communications Corp.** is explicitly marked via the label SBJ, which is attached to the noun phrase in the bracketed structure in Figure 4.4 and represented as a gray box between the noun phrase and its mother node in the graphical representation in Figure 4.5. However, note that the direct object **strong earnings gains to record level** does not have a grammatical function. The reasoning is that direct objects can be recognized from the tree structure without annotation: The direct object is always the first noun phrase after the verb.

The PENN TREEBANK uses null elements for a number of cases, such as to mark a deep subject in passive constructions. Figure 4.7 shows a sentence that has two different null elements. The first null element, *, marks a null subject of a non-finite clause. The second null element, *T*, indicates a trace, and the attached number refers to the moved element, in our example the WHNP **that**. The numbers by themselves are meaningless, they are only used as an indexing mechanism. The example in Figure 4.6 shows that the indices are translated into arcs in the graphical representation.

Figure 4.8, finally, shows a sentence with more grammatical functions marked. SBJ marks subjects, LOC locatives, PRD predicates, and TMP temporal modifiers. Note that the PP **in Tokyo** has been assigned two grammatical functions: LOC and PRD. This means it is ambiguous between locative and predicate.

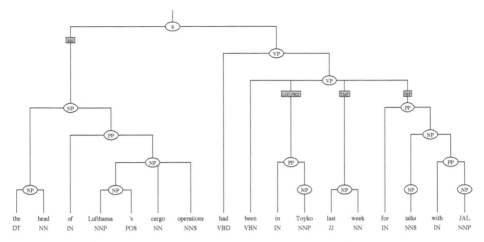

Figure 4.8 A sentence fragment with a range of grammatical functions.

4.3 The SUSANNE/CHRISTINE Corpus

The SUSANNE Corpus is a corpus with POS and syntactic annotation, developed under the leadership of Sampson (1993). The corpus contains approximately 156,000 words of the following text genres: press reportage; belles lettres, biography, memoirs; learned (mainly scientific and technical) writing; and adventure and Western fiction. The texts were taken from the BROWN Corpus (Francis and Kučera, 1979), and each selected text contains 2,000 words. The corpus is annotated with POS tags from the SUSANNE tagset (cf. section 3.3) and with syntactic annotation documented in Sampson (1995). The annotations are in a column-based format, as shown in an example in the original format in Figure 4.9 and in a graphical format in Figure 4.10.

While SUSANNE is based on written texts, the CHRISTINE Corpus serves as its spoken language counterpart. CHRISTINE is based on the demographic section of the *British National Corpus*. It contains approximately 112,000 words of transcriptions of recordings, in which individuals recorded all their speech events in two days of their lives. The CHRISTINE Corpus is annotated for POS tags and syntax based on the SUSANNE annotation scheme.[5]

The annotation format consists of six columns, shown in Table 4.1. The first column contains a unique identifier for each word, which encodes the genre, the text number, the line in the text, and a word number. For example, an explanation of the identifier "A02:0010.18" is shown in Table 4.2. It specifies that this is text no. 2 of the press genre (A), line 10 in the Brown Corpus, and word 18 in the given text in SUSANNE. The second column gives information about the status of the word, whether it is an abbreviation (A), a symbol (S), a misprint (E), or a normal word (-). The third column contains the POS tag (cf. section 3.3), the fourth one the word, and the fifth column the lemma (cf. section 3.1). In the word column, special characters, such as quotes, are written as SGML entities. For example, <apos> is an apostrophe. The final column contains the syntactic constituent

A02:0010.18	-	YD	<mdash>	-	[O.
A02:0010.21	-	NNJ1c	Committee	committee	[S[Ns:s.
A02:0010.24	-	NN1u	approval	approval	.
A02:0010.27	-	IO	of	of	[Po.
A02:0010.30	A	NNS	Gov.	-	[Ns[G[Nns.
A02:0010.33	-	NP1m	Price	Price	.
A02:0010.39	-	NP1s	Daniel	Daniel	.Nns]
A02:0010.42	-	GG	+<apos>s	-	.G]
A02:0020.03	-	YIL	<ldquo>	-	.
A02:0020.06	-	JJ	+abandoned	abandoned	[Ns.
A02:0020.09	-	NN1n	property	property	.Ns]
A02:0020.12	-	YIR	+<rdquo>	-	.
A02:0020.15	-	NN1c	act	act	.Ns]Po]Ns:s]
A02:0020.18	-	VVDi	seemed	seem	[Vd.Vd]
A02:0020.21	-	JJ	certain	certain	[J:e.J:e]
A02:0020.24	-	NPD1	Thursday	Thursday	[Nns:t.Nns:t]
A02:0020.27	-	II	despite	despite	[P:c.
A02:0020.30	-	AT	the	the	[Np.
A02:0020.33	-	JJ	adamant	adamant	.
A02:0030.03	-	NN2	protests	protest	.
A02:0030.06	-	IO	of	of	[Po.
A02:0030.09	-	NP1p	Texas	Texas	[Np[Nns.Nns]
A02:0030.12	-	NN2	bankers	banker	.Np]Po]Np]P:c]S]
A02:0030.15	-	YF	+.	-	.O]

Figure 4.9 An example of a sentence from the SUSANNE Corpus.

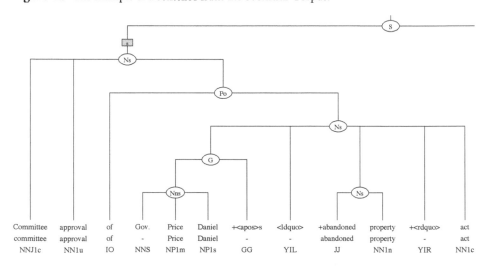

Figure 4.10 The example from Figure 4.9 in graphical form (detail).

Table 4.1 The column format in SUSANNE.	
column	description
1	unique identifier
2	word status
3	POS tag
4	word
5	lemma
6	syntactic annotation

Table 4.2 Example for a unique identifier in SUSANNE.	
A	genre: press
02	text in Brown: 2
0010	line in Brown: 10
18	word in Brown text: 18

annotation. Since the corpus has adopted a one-word-per-line format, the tree structure needs to be split based on the words. In the syntactic annotation, the word is replaced by a period. This means that the word **Committee** in Figure 4.9, which has the syntactic annotation "[S[Ns:s." has mother node Ns:s, which, in turn, has the mother node S. If a word forms a constituent on its own, the period is followed by the closing bracket. The word **Texas**, for example, is a noun phrase of its own ([Nns.Nns]), but it also starts a larger NP (**Texas bankers**). Note that the closing bracket also gives the syntactic category. Similar to the PENN TREEBANK annotation, the SUSANNE Corpus also marks grammatical functions. Grammatical functions are separated from the constituent label by a colon. The noun phrase **Thursday**, for example, is marked as "NNs:t," i.e. it is a temporal constituent (:t), and the label for **Committee** shows that this word starts a (surface) subject (:s). A full inventory of the label set can be found at http://www.grsampson.net/SueDoc.html.

Similar to the PENN TREEBANK, the SUSANNE Corpus also marks null words, called ghosts. They mark words that have been shifted or deleted in the surface representation of the sentence, and they receive the POS tag YG. Figure 4.11 shows an example in which the direct object of the subordinate clause **I had with him** is extracted and serves as the subject of the main clause. The trace is indicated by the number 111. The number itself, again, is meaningless, but every occurrence of the number denotes the occurrence of the trace.

4.4 The ICE-GB Corpus

The *International Corpus of English* (ICE)[6] is a corpus designed to document different national and regional varieties of English. It currently consists of 12 subcorpora, covering, for example, Great Britain, East Africa, the Philippines, and Jamaica. Each subcorpus has a size of 1 million words. Some of those subcorpora are annotated for POS using the ICE-GB tagset (see section 3.3), but only the British subcorpus (ICE-GB) is also annotated for syntax. ICE-GB is a mix of spoken and written English. The syntactic

N18:0100.48	-	AT	The	the	[S[Ns:s111.
N18:0110.03	-	NN1n	arrangement	arrangement	.
N18:0110.06	-	PPIS1	I	I	[Fr[Nea:s.Nea:s]
N18:0110.09	-	VHD	had	have	[Vd.Vd]
N18:0110.12	-	YG	-	-	[o111.o111]
N18:0110.15	-	IW	with	with	[P:w.
N18:0110.18	-	PPHO1m	him	he	.P:w]Fr]Ns:s111]
N18:0110.21	-	VBDZ	was	be	[Vsb.Vsb]
N18:0110.24	-	TO	to	to	[Ti:e[Vi.
N18:0110.27	-	VV0v	work	work	.Vi]
N18:0110.30	-	MC	four	four	[Np:t.
N18:0110.33	-	NNT2	hours	hour	.
N18:0110.39	-	AT1	a	a	[Ns.
N18:0110.42	-	NNT1c	day	day	.Ns]Np:t]Ti:e]S]
N18:0110.48	-	YF	+.	-	.

Figure 4.11 An example of a sentence from the SUSANNE Corpus with a ghost word.

annotation scheme is based on the grammar by Quirk et al. (1985). For each node in the syntactic tree, three types of information are encoded: the syntactic category, its grammatical function, and its features. A full list of all labels can be found at http://www. ucl.ac.uk/english-usage/resources/grammar/index.htm.

Figure 4.12 shows an example of an annotated sentence in the original ICE-GB data format.[7] Elements in square brackets, such as in the first line, show meta information, such as a sentence identifier, and formatting information. The words of the sentence are marked in curly braces, the syntactic annotation is displayed in an indented format similar to the one of the PENN TREEBANK in section 4.2. Each line contains one syntactic node. The first type of information is the grammatical function, followed by the syntactic category and its features in parentheses. For example, the node "PU,CL(main,intr,pres)" represents the information that the node is a clause with function parsing unit and features main clause, intransitive, and present. The daughters of the clause are shown on the lines with indentation level 1. For readability, we show the same sentence in the Penn bracketing format in Figure 4.13, minus the features. Note that the ICE-GB Corpus has multi-word lexemes, such as **George_Farquhar**. This lemmatization decision also has influence on the syntactic annotation since, in contrast to the PENN TREEBANK and the SUSANNE annotation schemes, no node is necessary to group names.

```
[<#7:1> <sent>]
PU,CL(main,intr,pres)
   SU,NP
      DT,DTP
         DTCE,ART(def) {The}
      NPHD,N(com,sing) {term}
   VB,VP(intr,pres)
      MVB,V(intr,pres) {comes}
   A,PP
      P,PREP(phras) {from}
      PC,NP
         DT,DTP
            DTCE,ART(def) {the}
         NPHD,N(com,sing) {name}
         NPPO,PP
            P,PREP(ge) {of}
            PC,NP
               DT,DTP
                  DTCE,ART(indef) {a}
               NPHD,N(com,sing) {character}
               NPPO,PP
                  P,PREP(ge) {in}
                  PC,NP
                     DT,DTP
                        DTCE,NP(genv)
                           NPHD,N(prop,sing) {George [<w>] Farquhar}
                           GENF,GENM {'s}
[</w> <it>]
                     NPHD,N(prop,sing) {The [<w>] Beaux ' [</w>] Stratagem}
[</it>]
                     PUNC,PUNC(comma) {,}
                     NPPO,NP
                        NPHD,NUM(card,sing) {1707}
   PUNC,PUNC(per) {.}
[</p>]
```

Figure 4.12 An example from THE ICE-GB Corpus.

Also in contrast to the PENN TREEBANK and the SUSANNE Corpus, ICE-GB does not have null categories or traces. Instead, null categories are marked as features. Figure 4.14 shows an example of a reduced relative clause with a null relative pronoun. Here, we have an NP that consists of the NP **coffee** and the reduced relative clause **laced with brandy**, which has the function "noun phrase postmodifier" and features dependent clause, zero relative pronoun, monotransitive, passive, **-ed** participle, and without subject.

```
( ((CL-PU
    (NP-SU
      (DTP-DT (ART-DTCE The))
      (N-NPHD term))
    (VP-VB (V-MVB comes))
    (PP-A (PREP-P from)
      (NP-PC
        (DTP-DT (ART-DTCE the))
        (N-NPHD name)
        (PP-NPPO (PREP-P of)
          (NP-PC
            (DTP-DT (ART-DTCE a))
            (N-NPHD character)
            (PP-NPPO (PREP-P in)
              (NP-PC
                (DTP-DT
                  (NP-DTCE (N-NPHD George_Farquhar) (GENM-GENF 's)
                  (N-NPHD The_Beaux_'_Stratagem) (PUNC-PUNC -)
                  (NP-NPPO (NUM-NPHD 1707)))))))))
    (PUNC-PUNC .)) )
```

Figure 4.13 Penn bracketing of the example in Figure 4.12.

Since part of the ICE-GB Corpus is based on spoken language, it has to model typical speech phenomena in the syntactic annotation. Figure 4.15 shows an example of a correction. Here, the speaker interrupts after **But they would** and corrects to **they were...** The utterance also shows a short pause after the last word.

4.5 The German Treebanks

German is an interesting language with regard to treebanks because typologically, it is similar to English, but because of its richer morphology it has freer word order, as discussed in section 3.2. On the level of syntactic annotation, this means that the annotation of grammatical functions is obligatory since the functions are not determined by the configuration of the tree. While in English, the direct object is generally the noun phrase following the verbs in a clause, this is not necessarily the case for German. In German, the direct object can be placed in different positions in the clause. Another consequence of the freer word order is that German has a significant number of long-distance phenomena. Such phenomena are difficult to integrate into a pure tree structure, as we have seen for English. In this section, we will present two of the four German treebanks, TIGER and TÜBA-D/Z. Both treebanks show different decisions, especially with regard to the treatment of long-distance phenomena. While TIGER uses

```
[<p> <#13:1> <sent>]
PU,CL(main,ditr,past)
   A,NP
      DT,DTP
         DTPE,PRON(univ) {All}
         DTCE,ART(def) {the}
      NPHD,N(com,sing) {way}
      NPPO,PP
         PMOD,AVP(ge)
            AVHD,ADV(ge) {back}
         P,PREP(ge) {from}
         PC,NP
            NPHD,N(prop,sing) {Birmingham}
      SU,NP
   [<w>]
      NPHD,PRON(pers,sing) {she}
VB,VP(ditr,past,perf)
      OP,AUX(perf,past,encl) {'d}
   [</w>]
      AVB,AUX(prog,edp) {been}
      MVB,V(ditr,ingp) {promising}
OI,NP
      NPHD,PRON(ref,sing) {herself}
OD,NP
      NPHD,N(com,sing) {coffee}
      NPPO,CL(depend,zrel,montr,pass,edp,-su)
         VB,VP(montr,edp,pass)
            MVB,V(montr,edp) {laced}
         A,PP
            P,PREP(ge) {with}
            PC,NP
               NPHD,N(com,sing) {brandy}
PUNC,PUNC(scol) {&semi;}
```

Figure 4.14 An example from the ICE-GB Corpus with a reduced relative clause.

crossing branches to annotate these phenomena, TüBa-D/Z uses an extended set of function labels in combination with *secondary edges*, i.e. edges that are not part of the tree, but rather annotate additional information.

The TiGER treebank is based on texts from a regional German newspaper, the Frankfurter Rundschau. It comprises 50,000 sentences. Apart from the POS and syntactic annotation, TiGER has lemma and morphological information on the word level. For the POS annotation, TiGER uses the *Stuttgart-Tübingen Tagset* (STTS), the quasi-standard for German. Figure 4.16 shows an example of the syntactic annotation

```
[<#6:1:B> <sent>]
PU,CL(main,cop,past,supersede)
    DISMK,CONNEC(ge) {But}
[<}> <->]
    NPHD,PRON(pers,plu,ignore) {they}
    OP,AUX(modal,past,ignore) {would}
    SU,NP
[</-> <=>]
        NPHD,PRON(pers,plu) {they}
    VB,VP(cop,past)
        MVB,V(cop,past) {were}
    A,AVP
        AVPR,AVP(inten)
[</=> </}>]
            AVHD,ADV(inten) {very}
            AVHD,ADV(inten) {much}
CS,PP
    P,PREP(ge) {in}
    PC,NP
        DT,DTP
            DTCE,ART(def) {the}
        NPHD,N(com,plu) {shadows}
        PAUSE,PAUSE(short) {<,>}
```

Figure 4.15 An example from the spoken part of the ICE-GB Corpus.

in TIGER for the sentence in (3). For readability, we only show the words, POS tags, and the syntax tree, but not the lemma and morphological annotation.

(3) Als größte Schwäche des   Texaners nennen die Befragten
     As greatest weakness of the Texan   name   the interviewees
     seinen Mangel an Erfahrung auf dem politischen Parkett.
     his   lack   of experience on the political   parquet.
     'The interviewees list his lack of political experience as the greatest weakness of the Texan.'

The syntax tree in Figure 4.16 shows that TIGER annotates grammatical functions on every level, on the phrase level as well as on the clausal level. On the phrase level, the initial prepositional phrase **Als größte Schwäche des Texaners** has the preposition **Als** marked as adpositional case marker (AC), the next two words are marked as nominal elements (NK), and the postmodifying NP **des Texaners** is marked as genitive argument (AG). On the clausal level, we find the grammatical functions: the first PP is marked as a modifier (MO), the finite verb **nennen** is the head, the NP **die Befragten** the subject (SB), and the final NP is marked as direct, accusative object

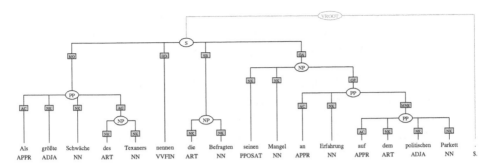

Figure 4.16 An example from the TiGER Treebank.

(OA). Note that the PPs do not contain explicitly marked NPs; the TiGER annotation scheme uses an extremely flat annotation within phrases, which also refrains from marking phrases with only one daughter (cf. the first three words in Figure 4.17).

(4) Wie könnte sich unsere Gesellschaft ein solches
     How could   itself our   society   a   such
     Reifezeugnis   ausstellen?
     certificate of maturity issue?
     'How could our society issue such a certificate of maturity to itself?'

As mentioned above, TiGER annotates long-distance relationships via crossing branches. We show an example of a non-canonical word order in Figure 4.17 for the sentence in (4). In this sentence, the reflexive dative object **sich** precedes the subject **unsere Gesellschaft**. Since the subject is grouped on the clause (S) level, and the dative object on the VP level, this leads to a crossing branch on the VP level.

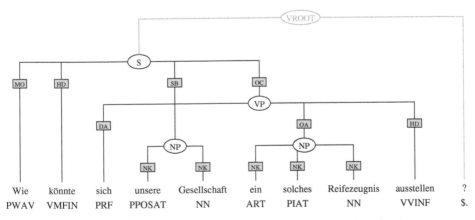

Figure 4.17 An example from the TiGER Treebank with non-canonical word order.

Another reason for crossing branches are extraposed constituents, such as relative clauses. Figure 4.18 shows the annotation for sentence (5). Here, the relative clause (grammatical function: RC) is extraposed past the past participle **angekündigt**.

(5)   Möllemann hat ein Gesetz angekündigt, das   in   notleidenden
      Möllemann has a   law   announced, which in   financially suffering
      Betrieben   eine   niedrigere   Bezahlung   erlauben   soll.
      companies   a   lower   payment   allow   should.
      'Möllemann announced a law which would allow lower payment for companies in
      default.'

The TüBa-d/z treebank is based on the German newspaper taz, and currently covers approximately 75,000 sentence in release 8.0. The syntactic annotation is a pure tree structure, in contrast to TiGer. While TüBa-d/z significantly differs from the TiGer Corpus, they both use the same POS tagset, the STTS. An example of the syntactic annotation for sentence (6), similar in structure to TiGer example (3), is shown in Figure 4.19.

(6)   Als Grund für diese Befürchtung nannte Schreiber die
      As reason for this fear   named Schreiber the
      Gesundheitspolitik der   rot-grünen Bundesregierung.
      health policy   of the red-green federal government.
      'Schreiber listed the health policy of the red-green federal government as reason
      for this fear.'

The TüBa-d/z annotation scheme shows noticeable differences to TiGer. On the one

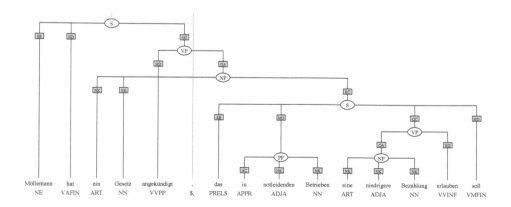

Figure 4.18 An example from the TiGer Treebank with an extraposed relative clause.

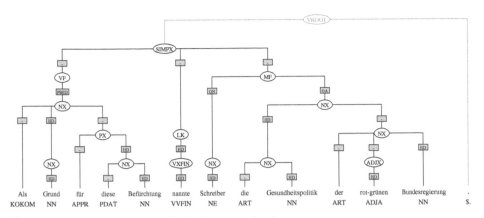

Figure 4.19: An example from the TüBa-D/z treebank.

hand, TüBa-D/z has more internal structure within phrases. This is obvious in the noun phrase (NX) **die Gesundheitspolitik der rot-grünen Bundesregierung**, which has two internal noun phrases, and the second one integrates the explicitly annotated adjectival phrase (ADJX) **rot-grünen**. On the phrasal level, TüBa-D/z annotates head (HD) and non-head (-) information. Maximal phrases are annotated for grammatical functions, which are based on case information: the first noun phrase is annotated as a predicate (PRED), the subject **Schreiber** is marked as nominative object (ON), and the direct object as accusative (OA). Between the phrasal and the clausal level, TüBa-D/z annotates topological fields, which structure a German clause. In the present examples, these are the initial field (VF), the left verb bracket (LK), and the middle field (MF). Topological fields are based on the fact that in German clauses, the position of the verb is fixed: the finite verb in a declarative clause is always in second position, i.e. it is preceded by exactly one constituent—in our case, the predicative NX. All other verbal elements, such as infinitives, participles, or verbal prefixes, are positioned at the end of the clause, in the final field (VC), if present. The two verbal fields are separated by the middle field. Note also that while TiGer annotated the **als** phrase as a prepositional phrase, TüBa-D/z interprets it as a noun phrase.

As mentioned above, TüBa-D/z annotates long-distance relationships via specific labels, in combination with secondary edges. Figure 4.20 shows the annotation for sentence (7).

(7) Ein Museum wurde errichtet, das   als solches nicht zu nutzen ist.
    A   museum was   erected, which as such   not to use   is.
    'A museum was erected, which cannot be used as such.'

In this example, the relative clause (R-SIMPX) modifies the subject of the main clause, **Ein Museum**. This is shown by the grammatical function ON-MOD, which states that the relative clause modifies the ON, i.e. the subject. In cases where the extraposed

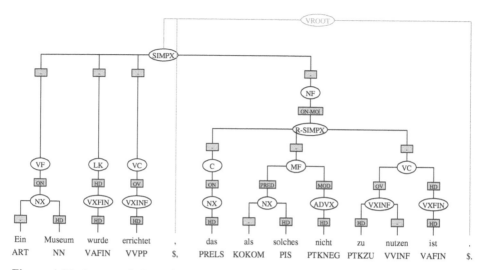

Figure 4.20 An example from the TüBa-D/z treebank with an extraposed relative clause.

element modifies only part of a maximal phrase, TüBa-D/z uses secondary edges, as shown in Figure 4.21 for sentence (8). Here, the relative clause (R-SIMPX) modifies the noun phrase **den** "**Großflächen**, rather than the whole prepositional phrase. This is marked by the secondary edge from the NX to the R-SIMPX.

(8) Scherf redet nicht von Großflächen-Plakaten der   SPD, sondern
     Scherf talks not   of   large-scale posters   of the SPD, but
     von den "Großflächen, die   Karin Jöns gebucht hat."
     of the "large areas,   which Karin Jöns booked has."
     'Scherf does not talk about large-scale posters by the SPD, but rather
     of the "large areas, which Karin Jöns booked."'

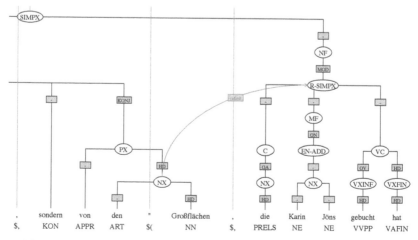

Figure 4.21 An example from the TüBa-D/z treebank with a secondary edge (detail).

4.6 Dependency Treebanks

The second major syntactic paradigm used for annotating treebanks is dependency grammar, as described in section 4.1. However, dependency grammar has been neglected for several decades; only recently has it received renewed attention. For this reason, many treebanks were annotated in a constituent framework, and then converted to dependencies. One example for such a conversion is the PENN TREEBANK, for which several converters exist. The dependency version of the sentence in Figure 4.4, using PENNCONVERTER, is shown in Figure 4.22; a graphical representation of the dependencies is shown in Figure 4.23.

The dependency representation in Figure 4.22 is in the CoNLL column format,[8] which has become a standard for dependency annotations in recent years. In this format, every word is displayed in a separate line, and the annotations are split into columns, as described in the comment in the first line. The first column shows the number of the

%no.	word	lemma	POS	FinePOS	feat	head	label		
1	GTE	_	NNP	_	_	7	SBJ	_	_
2	Corp.	_	NNP	_	_	1	POSTHON	_	_
3	and	_	CC	_	_	1	COORD	_	_
4	MCI	_	NNP	_	_	5	NAME	_	_
5	Communications	_	NNP	_	_	3	CONJ	_	_
6	Corp.	_	NNP	_	_	5	POSTHON	_	_
7	reported	_	VBD	_	_	0	ROOT	_	_
8	strong	_	JJ	_	_	10	NMOD	_	_
9	earnings	_	NNS	_	_	10	NMOD	_	_
10	gains	_	NNS	_	_	7	OBJ	_	_
11	to	_	TO	_	_	10	NMOD	_	_
12	record	_	JJ	_	_	13	NMOD	_	_
13	levels	_	NNS	_	_	11	PMOD	_	_
14	for	_	IN	_	_	7	ADV	_	_
15	the	_	DT	_	_	17	NMOD	_	_
16	third	_	JJ	_	_	17	NMOD	_	_
17	quarter	_	NN	_	_	14	PMOD	_	_
18	.	_	.	_	_	7	P	_	_

Figure 4.22 The sentence from Figure 4.4 with its dependency annotation.

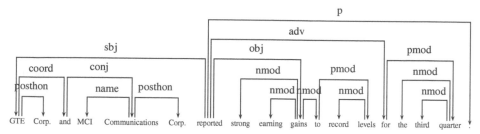

Figure 4.23 A graphical representation of the dependency annotation from Figure 4.22.

word in the sentence; the second column shows the words, the third the lemma. The fourth and fifth columns show coarse- and fine-grained POS tags, followed by a column for additional features such as morphology. The last two columns show the dependency annotation, the head of a word (i.e. its number) and the label of the dependency. Missing values are marked with a _. In the PENN TREEBANK example, there are no lemmas, no fine-grained POS labels, and no additional features. The head information refers back to the numbers from column 1—i.e. the head of the first word in Figure 4.22, **GTE**, is word 7, **reported**.

Null elements are discarded during the conversion to dependencies. This is shown for the sentence in Figure 4.24, and the dependency version in Figure 4.25. The constituent tree shows two null words, one for the null subject of the **to**-clause, the other for the subject of the S inside the relative clause. In the dependency conversion, both null elements disappear, and in the relative clause, the relative pronoun, **that**, is considered the subject.

In the conversion, extraposed elements are attached directly to the words from which they are dependent. This leads to *non-projective* dependencies, i.e. dependencies that cross. The sentence in Figure 4.26 has an extraposed relative clause, which, in the constituent annotation, is grouped under the VP, and which has a trace to a null element in the NP **roughly 310 million bushels of U.S. corn**. In the dependency version, shown in Figure 4.27, the relative clause is a dependent of the noun **bushels**, which results in the dashed non-projective dependency.

An example for a genuine dependency treebank is the *Prague Dependency Treebank* (PDT) for Czech. It is also the largest treebank at present, with almost 90,000 sentences that are syntactically annotated. The annotation of the PDT consists of three levels: the *morphological layer*, the *analytical layer*, and the *tectogrammatical layer*. We will focus here on the analytical layer, which contains the dependency annotation. The tectogrammatical layer represents the deep structure, in which prepositions have been converted into dependencies, and omitted elements such as null subjects have been restored. Figure 4.28 shows the analytical annotation for the sentence in (9).[9] In this representation, the root node of the dependency graph is a virtual node, shown as #. The other words in the sentence are shown as nodes in the graph, and the edges between a higher

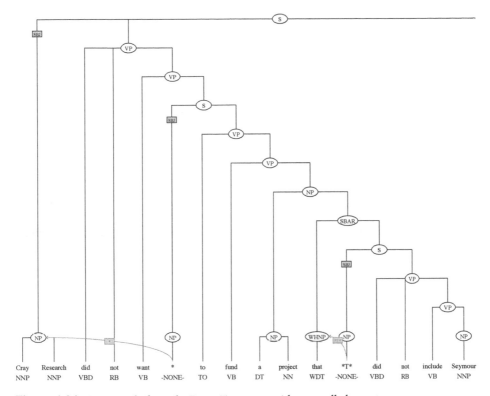

Figure 4.24 An example from the PENN TREEBANK with two null elements.

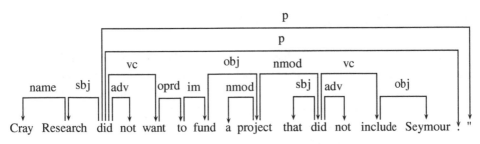

Figure 4.25 The sentence from Figure 4.24 with its dependency annotation.

word and a lower one show head-dependent relations, and the dependency labels are annotated under the words. For example, the word **Karel** is a dependent of **sedával**, and it is the subject (Sb). Word order is represented by the direction of the edges.

(9) Karel by   byl   sedával   na své židli.
     Karel would be-Past used-to-sit on his chair.
     'Charles would have used to sit in his chair.'

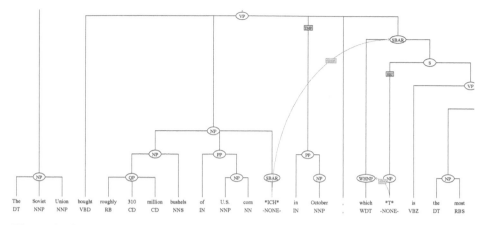

Figure 4.26 An example from the Penn Treebank with an extraposed relative clause (detail).

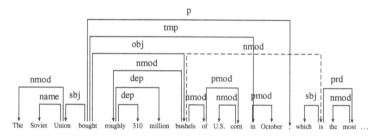

Figure 4.27 The sentence from Figure 4.26 with its dependency annotation.

4.7 Multilingual, Parallel Treebanks

In more recent years, research has started on *multilingual, parallel treebanks*, i.e. treebanks which comprise more than one language. In general, such treebanks start with an existing treebank, such as the PENN TREEBANK for English, and then translate the underlying text into one or more languages. These target languages are then annotated syntactically. Such treebanks are of interest not only for linguists who work on multiple languages, but also for researchers in machine translation.

An additional type of information in multilingual treebanks is alignment information. Alignment annotates correspondences between the different languages, generally on the word level—i.e. for the German sentence in (10), the word alignment is as follows: {Sofie, Sofie}, {Amundsen, Amundsen}, {war, was}, {auf, on}, {dem, her}, {Heimweg, way home}, {von, from}, {der, }, {Schule, school}. Note that the German word **Heimweg** is translated into two words, and the word **der** does not have a translation.

(10) Sofie Amundsen war auf dem Heimweg von der Schule.
Sofie Amundsen was on the home way from the school.
'Sophie Amundsen was on her way home from school.'

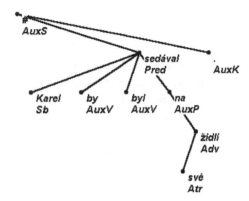

Figure 4.28 An example from the *Prague Dependency Treebank*.

While most parallel treebanks are aligned only on the textual basis, there is one treebank, the *Stockholm Multilingual Treebank* (SMULTRON), which also aligns phrase nodes between languages. SMULTRON is a treebank that covers several text types: an excerpt from the novel *Sophie's World*; economics texts, both of them in English, German, and Swedish; and mountaineering texts in German and French.

Figure 4.29 shows an example for the syntactic alignment. In this example, two German sentences (on top) are aligned with two Swedish sentences, but there is no 1:1 correspondence between the sentences.

Since the annotation of the alignment has to be performed manually, this treebank is considerably smaller than the other treebanks described in this chapter.

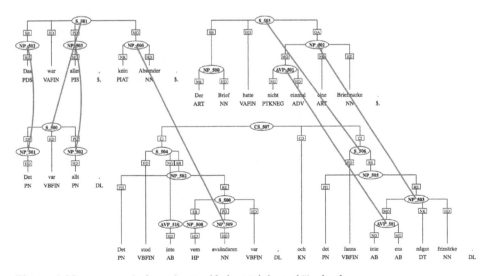

Figure 4.29 An example from the *Stockholm Multilingual Treebank*.

4.8 Summary

In this chapter, we introduced treebanks, i.e. syntactically annotated corpora. We concentrated on the two major annotation schemes: constituent annotation, in combination with grammatical functions, and dependency annotation. We introduced the most important English treebanks: the PENN TREEBANK, the SUSANNE/CHRISTINE corpora, and the ICE-GB Corpus. Then we introduced two major German treebanks, the TIGER and TÜBA-D/Z treebanks, to show how the freer word order affects annotation schemes. For dependency annotations, we looked at a conversion of the PENN TREEBANK and at a genuine dependency treebank, the *Prague Dependency Treebank* for Czech. Finally, we also had a look at a parallel treebank, SMULTRON, which contains aligned texts in more than one language. Additionally, SMULTRON also has an explicit alignment of syntactic nodes.

4.9 Further Reading

Section 4.1

Dependency theory: For dependency theory, the first work was by Tesnière (1959). Other influential theories in the dependency grammar tradition include *Functional Generative Description* (Sgall et al., 1986); *Meaning-Text Theory* (Mel'čuk, 1988); *Word Grammar* (Hudson, 1990, 2007); and *Dependency Unification Grammar* (Hellwig, 2003). There are also constraint-based theories of dependency grammar such as *Constraint Dependency Grammar*, originally proposed by Maruyama (1990), which was converted into *Weighted Constraint Dependency Grammar* (Menzel and Schröder, 1998; Schröder, 2002); *Functional Dependency Grammar* (Tapanainen and Järvinen, 1997; Järvinen and Tapanainen, 1998), largely developed from *Constraint Grammar* (Karlsson, 1990; Karlsson et al., 1995); and finally *Topological Dependency Grammar* (Duchier and Debusmann, 2001), which later evolved into *Extensible Dependency Grammar* (Debusmann et al., 2004).

Higher order grammar formalisms: There are higher order grammar formalisms, i.e. formalisms that go beyond simple phrase structure grammars. The following belong in the category of higher order formalisms: *Head-Driven Phrase Structure Grammar* (HPSG) (Pollard and Sag, 1994); *Lexical-Functional Grammar* (LFG) (Bresnan, 2000); *Combinatory Categorial Grammar* (CCG) (Steedman, 2000); and *Tree-Adjoining Grammar* (TAG) (Joshi, 1987).

There exist several treebanks using HPSG as the underlying theoretical framework: the REDWOODS TREEBANK (English) http://moin.delph-in.net/RedwoodsTop; BULTREEBANK (Bulgarian) http://www.bultreebank.org/ (Chanev et al., 2007); and the HPSG Treebank for Polish http://nlp.ipipan.waw.pl/CRIT2/.

Phrase structure grammar (PSG): There are many introductions to the different variants of Phrase Structure Theory, such as X-bar theory (Santorini and Kroch, 2007), Government & Binding (GB) (Carnie, 2002), minimalism (Adger, 2003; Radford, 2004).

Section 4.2

ATIS Corpus: The ATIS Corpus is a corpus of transliterations of dialogues in which a user requests information from a database. The corpus is documented by Hemphill et al. (1990).

Brown Corpus: More information about the Brown Corpus can be found in (Francis and Kučera, 1967). The manual for the corpus can be found at http://icame.uib.no/brown/bcm.html.

Penn Treebank: For the Penn Treebank there is an early overview paper (Marcus et al., 1993) and a paper on predicate argument structure (Marcus et al., 1994). The bracketing guidelines (Santorini, 1991) are also freely available. The treebank is available from the Linguistic Data Consortium (LDC) at http://www.ldc.upenn.edu/.

Switchboard: The Switchboard Corpus (Godfrey et al., 1992) was published in two releases. It is available from the LDC.

masc: This is a 500,000 word subset of the Open American National Corpus (see below), which has been annotated for lemma and POS labels, for noun and verb chunks, named entities, syntax, and coreference (Ide et al., 2008, 2010). masc is an open language data resource and sustained by community contributions. It can be browsed or downloaded from http://www.anc.org/data/masc/.

Open American National Corpus (oanc): The oanc is a balanced corpus of approximately 15 million words of American English, including transcripts of spoken data. More information about oanc can be found in Ide and Suderman (2004), Ide et al. (2010), and at http://www.americannationalcorpus.org/.

Section 4.3

susanne (Sampson, 1993), christine, and lucy (Sampson, 2003) are available from http://www.grsampson.net/Resources.html, the annotation scheme is documented by Sampson (1995).

Section 4.4

International Corpus of English (ice): The *International Corpus of English* (ice) is an international long-term project. The final aim is to produce up to 20 one-million-word corpora of international English varieties, each syntactically analyzed according to a common parsing scheme. A number of subcorpora are freely available from http://ice-corpora.net/ice/avail.htm. For more information on the project see http://www.ucl.ac.uk/english-usage/projects/ice.htm. The British component is documented by Nelson et al. (2002) and in Wallis and Nelson (2006).

Section 4.5

German treebanks: For German, there are mainly four treebanks: TiGer (Brants et al., 2002, 2004), TüBa-D/z (Hinrichs et al., 2004; Telljohann et al., 2004, 2012), negra (Skut et al., 1998, 1997), and TüBa-D/s (Hinrichs et al., 2000a, b; Stegmann et al., 2000). The latter is based on spontaneous dialogues, and originated in the project *Verbmobil* (Wahlster, 2000). negra and TiGer are based on the same annotation scheme, with minor differences. More information about negra is available from http://www.coli.uni-saarland.de/projects/sfb378/negra-corpus/negra-corpus.html and about TiGer from http://www.ims.uni-stuttgart.de/forschung/ressourcen/korpora/tiger.html. TüBa-D/z and TüBa-D/s also share a common syntactic annotation scheme with only minor differences. Information about TüBa-D/z is available from http://www.sfs.uni-tuebingen.de/en/ascl/resources/corpora/tueba-dz.html; information about TüBa-D/s from http://www.sfs.uni-tuebingen.de/en/ascl/resources/corpora/tueba-ds.html.

Section 4.6

Dependency converters: There are several converters that convert the Penn Treebank into dependencies; the most well-known ones are PENNCONVERTER (Johansson and Nugues, 2007) and PENN2MALT http://w3.msi.vxu.se/~nivre/research/Penn2Malt.html.

Prague Dependency Treebank (PDT): The *Prague Dependency Treebank* is described by Hajič et al. (2000). Information about the PDT can be found at http://ufal.mff.cuni.cz/pdt2.0/.

Section 4.7

Parallel treebanks: Examples for parallel treebanks are the Prague Czech-English Dependency Treebank (Čmejrek et al., 2004) and SMULTRON (Samuelsson and Volk, 2005, 2006).

4.10 Exercises

1. **Penn Treebank**: We have seen the bracketed format of the Penn Treebank and a graphical representation of this structure, e.g. in Figures 4.4 and 4.5. Take the bracketed structure in Figure 4.7 and draw the graphical tree structure. Leave the null elements in place, but convert the trace "-1" into a crossing branch.

2. **Punctuation**: You may have noticed that the English treebanks group punctuation signs into the tree structure while the German treebanks do not annotate punctuation at all. One reason for the latter is that it is often difficult to decide on which level to attach commas. In many cases, they perform multiple functions. Take the following sentences and decide on which levels the punctuation should be attached.
   (11)   a. Pierre Vinken, 61 years old, will join the board as a non-executive director Nov. 29.
          b. Japan's reserves of gold, convertible foreign currencies, and special drawing rights fell by a hefty $1.82 billion in October.
          c. United Illuminating is based in New Haven, Conn., and Northeast is based in Hartford, Conn.
          d. Slower growth countries included Greece, at 2.5 per cent, the U.K., at 2.25 per cent, and Denmark, at 1.75 per cent.

3. **SUSANNE**: In the conversion from the original format of the SUSANNE example in Figure 4.9 to the graphical form in Figure 4.10, the grammatical functions were removed from the syntax labels and added as arc labels. Locate all grammatical functions in both figures, and discuss advantages and disadvantages of both representations.

4. **PDT**: The Prague Dependency Treebank uses a dependency representation that is different from our representation for the English dependencies. Convert the dependency graph in Figure 4.28 into the format used for the English dependencies.

5. **Parallel treebanks**: One of the problems in annotating parallel treebanks concerns translations where there is no 1:1 correspondence between the languages. Have a look at the German sentence in (12) and its English translation. Discuss possible consequences of aligning the German dative NP **mir** to the English subject I.
   (12)   [S [NPdat Mir] [VP ist [ADJP kalt]]].
                     To me   is   cold.
          'I am cold.'

CHAPTER 5
SEMANTIC ANNOTATION

In this chapter, we will look at semantic annotations. Semantics is concerned with the literal meaning of language, as opposed to pragmatics, which looks at the meaning in context. Linguists traditionally distinguish between lexical semantics, which deals with the meaning of words, and compositional semantics, which computes the meaning of phrases and whole sentences in terms of truth-based interpretations based on the meanings of their words and the way they are combined. Most semantic annotation projects do not cover the whole range of semantic analysis but are concerned with individual phenomena only, most of which belong to the area of lexical semantics. This is why semantic annotation in corpora often seems to be shallow to the theoretical linguist. But even shallow semantic annotation is helpful in approximating the meaning of a sentence in terms of "*Who did what to whom, when and where?*". Semantic annotation abstracts away from syntactic and lexical variation found in natural language and thus supports semantically motivated search in corpora. Furthermore, annotation of semantic concepts in authentic texts helps to better understand the concepts themselves by testing them against the variety, gradedness, and contextual influences that are always an issue when analyzing actual language use instead of designed examples. Finally, we can use a semantically annotated corpus to obtain frequency information, which is useful for determining semantic preferences. For example, a corpus annotated for word senses allows us to count frequencies of these senses and thus to determine the most frequent senses, which should be presented first in a lexicon.

This chapter starts out by looking at semantic annotation on the word level. One existing type of annotation is concerned with broad types of *named entities*, such as persons or locations (section 5.1). The annotation of such broad semantic classes is similar to part-of-speech tagging in that it disambiguates words by assigning them a tag from a well-defined set of named entity classes. Another type of annotation, still at the word level, is concerned with *word senses*, such as distinguishing between **bank** as in the financial institution as opposed to the river bank (section 5.2). In a way, this is still a classification task, assigning sense labels to all occurrences of the word **bank**. However, since there are many words to be annotated, a simple list of sense labels is not sufficient. This kind of annotation relies on complex knowledge bases that organize word senses in fine-grained hierarchies, in which words are related to more general and more specific meanings. In such a knowledge base, we find information that "a dog is a kind of mammal" or that "a bank can be a credit union, a commercial bank, a state bank, etc.".

The next level of semantic annotation goes beyond the level of individual words and adds semantic relations between words and phrases. For instance, in example (1), someone named John sold cars, i.e. the phrase **John** represents the *seller* and the phrase **sold a lot of cars** represents the selling events. More generally, **John** is the *agent* of **sold**.

(1)   John sold a lot of cars.

As we will see in section 5.3, the annotation of semantic roles is closely related to the annotation of syntactic functions on the predicate-argument level, such as *subject* or *object*, as introduced in Chapter 4. A further well-studied type of semantic annotation is the annotation of temporal information, which requires both the classification of individual words and phrases and the annotation of relations between the words as well as relations between whole sentences (see section 5.4). Finally, section 5.5 will introduce a recent project that embraces the annotation of compositional semantic analyses on the sentence level and beyond, in terms of logical form.

5.1 Named Entity Class Annotation

The idea of categorizing the world into semantic classes has a very long tradition, going back to the ancient Greek philosophers. Aristotle (384–322 BCE) defined ten categories with the intention to classify everything there is in the world. Starting out with substance, which is related to the question "What is it?," he defined categories such as quantity ("How much?"), quality ("What sort?"), and location ("Where?"), among others. In modern corpora, variants of the Aristotelian categories are often used for the type of semantic annotation discussed here. In general, this annotation concentrates on subsets of words, namely those referring to named entities, which can be loosely defined as entities that are distinguished from other entities of the same kind by their name, such as **Lottie** or **Lisa** for persons, and **New York** or **Berlin** for cities. Frequently used categories include person, location (for sights, mountains, and other geographical areas), and geopolitical entity (e.g. for countries, states, and cities).

Table 5.1 Named entity classes in the TÜBA-D/Z treebank and samples of defining subclasses.

Class		*Common subclasses*
PER	*person*	persons, surnames, names of animals (personified)
ORG	*organization*	organizations, companies, museums, newspapers, clubs, theaters …
LOC	*location*	districts, sights, churches, planets, geographical areas …
GPE	*geopolitical entity*	countries, states (incl. historical), cities (incl. historical)
OTH	*other*	operating systems, titles of books, movies …

For example, the German TüBa-d/z treebank, whose syntactic annotations were discussed in section 4.5, also marks the reference to named entities on the phrase level.[1] It distinguishes the following five classes of named entities: person (PER), organization (ORG), location (LOC), geopolitical entity (GPE), and other (OTH), the latter comprising all remaining named entities that do not fit into the first four classes. Instead of specifying properties that define different classes, the TüBa-d/z guidelines provide lists of more specific named entity subclasses (Table 5.1). This is in line with the fact that the annotation of such named entity classes is often performed automatically based on *gazetteers*, i.e. lists of geographical entities, collections of names, etc.

Sentence (2) from TüBa-d/z states that the German play "Bis Denver" (lit. 'until Denver')[2] by Oliver Bukowski had its opening in a particular theatre. The named entity is integrated into the syntactic annotation, as shown in Figure 5.1 for the sentence in (2): **Oliver Bukowski** is the name of a person (PER), and **Bis Denver** is the name of an entity of category OTH, which contains the name of the geopolitical entity (GPE) **Denver**. In addition, the sequence **Altonaer Theater** is marked as an organization (ORG). The adjective **Altonaer** itself is derived from the town Altona but since it is a morphological derivation it is not classified as a named entity in TüBa-d/z.

(2) Oliver Bukowskis derbes "Bis   Denver" feierte   im   Altonaer
     Oliver Bukowski's bawdy "until Denver" celebrated in the Altona
     Theater Premiere.
     Theater premiere.
     'Oliver Bukowski's bawdy "Bis Denver" had its opening in the Altona Theater.'

The way the named entity tags are added can be interpreted as *typing* in the sense that the named entity labels group the syntactic categories into subtypes: In addition to the annotation of the syntactic phrase, NX, we now have the subclassification

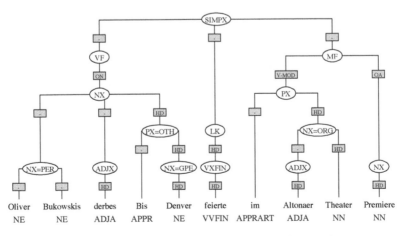

Figure 5.1 An example from the TüBa-d/z treebank with named entity class annotation on the phrase level (**NX=PER, PX=OTH, NX=GPE, NX=ORG**).

into person (NX=PER) or organization (NX=ORG). It is important to note that in TüBa-d/z, part of the identification of named entities is already carried out at the level of POS annotation via the *Stuttgart-Tübingen Tagset* (STTS), in which common nouns (NN) are separated from proper names (NE). In Figure 5.1, both words in the name **Oliver Bukowskis** are tagged as NE, identifying them as proper names. However, it is easy to see that the annotation on the POS level alone is not suffcient. The first word in the name of the play **Bis Denver** in Figure 5.1 is the preposition **Bis**, which is tagged as an ordinary preposition on the POS level (APPR). The fact that it belongs to a name is encoded only at the phrase level by marking the prepositional phrase as OTH.

A linguistically interesting observation that can be derived from the annotation in Figure 5.1 is that an entity of the class OTH can feature as subject (grammatical function: ON) of the verb **feiern**. More indirectly, the sentence also shows evidence that an entity of the type organization (ORG) can be interpreted as being a location in certain contexts—a phenomenon that is described as a systematic polysemy in lexical semantics.

Since the annotation of named entities in TüBa-d/z is performed by typing the phrase (see above), this annotation is based on the inherent assumption that named entities always correspond to phrases. Unfortunately, this is not always the case. Such mismatches between phrase boundaries and named entity boundaries often concern the use of determiners, which are not considered to be part of the name, or even further pre-modification of the noun phrase. An example of the latter case occurs in (3) and its annotation in Figure 5.2.

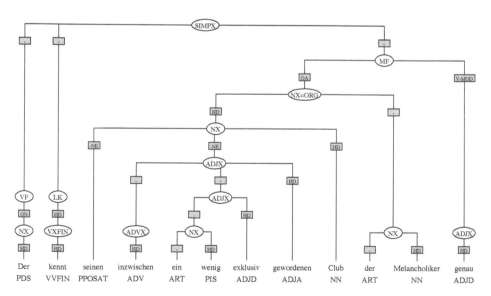

Figure 5.2 An example from the TüBa-d/z treebank with a named entity that does not correspond completely to a syntactic phrase (non-NE material marked).

Table 5.2 Named entity classes (and some temporal and numerical ones) in the ONTONOTES corpus and samples of defining subclasses.

Class	Common subclasses
PERSON	People, including fictional
NORP	Nationalities or religious or political groups
FACILITY	Buildings, airports, highways, bridges, [...]
ORGANIZATION	Companies, agencies, institutions, [...]
GPE	Countries, cities, states
LOCATION	Non-GPE locations, mountain ranges, bodies of water
PRODUCT	Vehicles, weapons, foods, [...] (not services)
EVENT	Named hurricanes, battles, wars, sports events, [...]
WORK OF ART	Titles of books, songs, [...]
LAW	Named documents made into laws
LANGUAGE	Any named language

The following values are also annotated similarly to names:

DATE	Absolute or relative dates or periods
TIME	Times smaller than a day
PERCENT	Percentage (including "%")
MONEY	Monetary values, including unit
QUANTITY	Measurements, as of weight or distance
ORDINAL	**first, second**
CARDINAL	Numerals that do not fall under another type

(3)   Der kennt seinen inzwischen ein wenig exklusiv gewordenen "Club
       He knows his meanwhile a little exclusive become "Club
       der Melancholiker" genau.
       of the Melancholics" well.
       'He has come to know his "Club of Melancholics", which in the meantime has become somewhat exclusive, rather well.'

In this example, we have a named entity **Club der Melancholiker**, which is pre-modified by the possessive pronoun **seinen** and a complex adjectival phrase (ADJX). The situation is complicated further by the fact that according to the guidelines for syntactic annotation, pre-modifiers attach low while postmodifiers attach high. This means that the base NP **seinen inzwischen ein wenig exklusiv gewordenen "Club** is grouped first to a noun phrase (NX) level, and the genitive noun phrase **der Melancholiker** is attached high, thus making the higher NP the recipient of the named entity annotation (NX=ORG). Thus, while the determiner and the adjectival phrase belong to the noun phrase, they are not part of the named entity. To make this fact explicit, these pre-modifiers receive a special edge label, -NE (instead of the normal -), which specifies that they are *not* part of the named entity. This is one of the examples where a seemingly straightforward decision to combine two types of annotation leads to difficult follow-up decisions, which may compromise the modularity in the annotation of the two types of information.

The second corpus with named entity annotation that we consider here is the ONTONOTES Corpus. ONTONOTES is a corpus of English, Chinese, and Arabic. The corpus contains annotations on different levels, including syntax, named entities, and coreference (see section 6.1 for details on the latter type of annotations). The textual basis of the corpus covers a wide range of text genres, including the texts from the Wall Street Journal that are incorporated in the PENN TREEBANK (see section 4.2), dialogue data, as well as the Bible. ONTONOTES is annotated with eleven classes of named entities, including the types used in TÜBA-D/Z. In addition, it provides annotation of seven numerical and temporal classes, which are marked in a similar vein (see Table 5.2).

Example (4) shows a sentence from the named entity annotation layer of ONTONOTES called NAMEBANK along with its inline markup for named entities.[4] The markup is based on XML elements called ENAMEX, which have an attribute TYPE that specifies the named entity class. The label NORP is the label for *nationalities or religious or political groups*.

(4) a. Perhaps without realizing it, Mr. Taffner simultaneously has put his finger on the problem and an ideal solution: "Capital City" should have been a comedy, a worthy sequel to the screwball British "Carry On" movies of the 1960s.

   b. Perhaps without realizing it, Mr. <ENAMEX TYPE="PERSON">Taffner</ ENAMEX> simultaneously has put his finger on the problem and an ideal solution: <ENAMEX TYPE="WORK_OF_ART" >"Capital City"</ENAMEX> should have been a comedy, a worthy sequel to the screwball <ENAMEX TYPE="NORP">British</ENAMEX> "<ENAMEX TYPE="WORK_OF_ ART" >Carry On</ENAMEX>" movies of <ENAMEX TYPE="DATE">the 1960s</ENAMEX>.

A remark on the markup terminology: ENAMEX is one of three labels defined for the coding of automatic named entity tagging in a series of open competitions organized by the *Message Understanding Conference* (MUC) in the 1990s. The original MUC definition distinguished between ENAMEX, TIMEX, and NUMEX elements to mark named entity, temporal, and number expressions respectively. Example (4) shows that this distinction is not maintained in ONTONOTES, where only the first category is used.

In addition to the inline annotation shown above, ONTONOTES provides a more readable version of the annotations that merges all levels of syntactic, semantic, and pragmatic annotation. It is called the ONTONOTES Normal Form View (ONF).[5] Figure 5.3 illustrates a part of example (4) in ONF.[6] Named entity tags are added to the vertical list of terminal syntax leaves together with a numerical code that indicates the yield of the named entity. **British**, for example, begins at leaf 3[7] and also ends there since it is a one-word named entity. **Carry On**, in contrast, has a yield of two words, spanning #39 and #40.

Treebank tree:

    (NP (NP (DT the)

                    (JJ screwball)

                    (JJ British)

                    (" ")

                    (NML-TTL (NNP Carry)

                      (NNP On))

                    (" ")

                    (NNS movies))

  Leaves:

(...)

    35 the

    36 screwball

    37 British

        name: NORP   37-37 British

    38 "

    39 Carry

        name: WORK_OF_ART   39-40 Carry On

    40 On

    41 "

    42 movies

Figure 5.3 Sample annotation of ex. (4) displayed in ONTONOTES Normal Form View.

Named entity annotation does not have to be restricted to the coarse categories described above, it can also be performed on a more fine-grained level. The annotation of such more fine-grained classes is normally based on a structured representation of the concepts. A simple way of extending the categories is to specify a hierarchy of more general classes that are split into more specific subclasses. One such detailed hierarchy is the *BBN hierarchy* of named entities, which consists of 29 types and 64 subtypes. Figure 5.4 shows the subclassification of work-of-art entities according to the BBN hierarchy.

The annotation of the expression **Carry On** in example (4) would then be refined to WORK_OF_ART:OTHER, see (5), given that movies belong to the class OTHER:

Figure 5.4 BBN hierarchy of the named entity class WORK_OF_ART.

(5)   <ENAMEX TYPE="WORK_OF_ART:OTHER" >Carry On</ENAMEX>

The relation that is encoded in Figure 5.4 can be paraphrased as: *A book is a work of art; A play is a work of art;* etc. The is_a relation—or simply ISA—is the most basic relation for creating an ontology. It is important to point out that this relation is not symmetric but directed: It is true that every book is a work of art (in some broad sense), but not every work of art is a book. Given that the named entity classes themselves are generalizations of the actual words in the text, the hierarchy allows for additional generalizations on top of the named entity classes.

However, even in the case of the more fine-grained annotation, we need to keep in mind that the named entity annotation is restricted to a very specific type of words. In the next section, we will introduce large-scale hierarchical inventories that are used for corpus annotation on a more general basis. These word sense annotations can cover all words, and thus have a wider coverage, but at the same time, they are much more specific in that they model more fine-grained senses than even the fine-grained annotation scheme for named entities.

5.2 Semantic Word Sense Annotation

The annotation of named entities specifies only a small part of the meaning of a text because only a subset of words is annotated. For linguistic tasks, it is more interesting to be able to distinguish senses of all types of words, especially those of *open class* words, i.e. common nouns, verbs, adjectives, and adverbs. This type of annotation is generally called *word sense annotation*. In Chapter 6, we will also introduce a type of sense annotation for *closed class* words in terms of discourse connectives.

The English SEMCOR Corpus is an example for word sense annotation for open class words. It is a subset of the English BROWN Corpus (see sections 1.2.2 and 4.2) and consists of almost 700,000 running words. The corpus is composed of two parts: One part in which all nouns, verbs, adjectives, and adverbs are annotated for parts of speech, lemma, and sense (186 texts), and a second part in which only verbs are annotated for lemma and sense (166 texts).

If we annotate word senses, we need to know what the set of senses is. Thus, we need something like a tagset for POS tagging, except that the situation in word sense annotation is more complicated because we have different sets of senses for each word. For this reason, the annotation is based on a lexical resource that provides such *sense inventories* for words.

In SEMCOR, the sense inventory is based on WORDNET, a large lexical database for English. Since it is important to understand the structure of WORDNET in order to understand the SEMCOR annotations, we will provide a quick overview here. WORDNET is not a dictionary in the standard sense because the main ordering principle in the database is *synsets*, i.e. sets of (quasi-)synonymous words. In WORDNET, synonymy means that words are interchangeable in *some* contexts without changing the overall meaning in terms of truth conditions. In other contexts, they can cause different readings. For the user, this organization means that we do not search in an alphabetical list—rather, we look up individual words, and are provided with the different senses and with the synset to which the word in a specific sense belongs. As an additional ordering principle, WORDNET defines hierarchical and other semantic relations between its synsets (see below).

The word senses in WORDNET are often rather fine-grained. The word **line**, for example, has 30 different senses, two of which are shown in (6), and an example for the second sense is shown in (7).[7]

(6)   a.   a telephone connection
      b.   (often plural) a means of communication or access
(7)   lines of communication were set up between the two firms

Synsets are chosen in a way that each sense of a word is expressed by a different synset, which means that synsets are often highly specific. Examples (8)–(11) illustrate the four different senses of the verb **remain**. Each entry starts with a unique identifier for this sense, a so-called *sense key*. For sense 1 of **remain**, for example, the sense key is [remain%2:30:00::]. This is followed by a list of all members of the synset, followed by a paraphrase of the concept in parenthesis. Finally, sample sentences illustrate the meaning of the concept and show the syntactic distributions of synset members. The numerical encoding of the sense key is explained below.

(8)   [remain%2:30:00::]: **stay, remain, rest**
      (stay the same; remain in a certain state)
      a.   The dress remained wet after repeated attempts to dry it.
      b.   rest assured
      c.   stay alone
      d.   He remained unmoved by her tears.
      e.   The bad weather continued for another week.
(9)   [remain%2:42:03::]: **stay, stay on, continue, remain**
      (continue in a place, position, or situation)
      a.   After graduation, she stayed on in Cambridge as a student adviser.
      b.   Stay with me, please.
      c.   despite student protests, he remained Dean for another year
      d.   She continued as deputy mayor for another year.
(10) [remain%2:42:05::]: **remain**
      (be left; of persons, questions, problems, results, evidence, etc.)
      a.   There remains the question of who pulled the trigger.
      b.   Carter remains the only President in recent history under whose Presidency
           the U.S. did not fight a war
(11) [remain%2:42:01::]: **persist, remain, stay**
      (stay behind)

a. The smell stayed in the room.
b. The hostility remained long after they made up.

If WordNet is used to annotate word senses in a corpus, using inline annotation, as we have seen for POS tagging, is not feasible. Instead, the annotation refers back to WordNet directly by using the sense key of the word's sense. Note that this means that the annotation can only be interpreted with reference to WordNet.

Figure 5.5 shows the SemCor annotation for the sentence in (12).[8] The sentence belongs to the fully annotated part of the corpus and exemplifies an occurrence of the verb **remain** in the sense of **stay the same; remain in a certain state** (sense key: remain%2:30:00::).

(12) Mike remained in trance; there was much to grok, loose ends to puzzle over and fit into his growing …

Figure 5.5 shows the annotation of example (12) in a slightly simplified manner. Each word is embedded in its own word form (wf) element. In addition to part of speech and lemma annotations, nouns, verbs, adjectives, and adverbs are annotated for word sense (wnsn and lexsn). The only content word that is not semantically tagged is the word **grok**, which is manually marked as being a nonce word.

```
<wf pos="NNP" lemma="person" wnsn="1" lexsn="1:03:00::"
   pn="person">Mike<wf>
<wf pos="VB" lemma="remain" wnsn="1" lexsn="2:30:00::">remained<wf>
<wf pos="IN">in<wf>
<wf pos="NN" lemma="trance" wnsn="1" lexsn="1:26:00::">trance<wf>
<punc>;<punc>
<wf pos="EX">there<wf>
<wf pos="VB" lemma="be" wnsn="5" lexsn="2:42:04::">was<wf>
<wf pos="JJ" lemma="much" wnsn="1" lexsn="3:00:00::">much<wf>
<wf pos="TO">to<wf>
<wf pos="VB" ot="nonceword">grok<wf>
<punc>,<punc>
<wf pos="NN" lemma="loose_end" wnsn="1" lexsn="1:04:00::"> loose_ends<wf>
<wf pos="TO">to<wf>
<wf pos="VB" lemma="puzzle_over" wnsn="1" lexsn="2:31:00::"> puzzle_over<wf>
<wf pos="CC">and<wf>
<wf pos="VB" lemma="fit" wnsn="1" lexsn="2:42:05::">fit<wf>
<wf pos="IN">into<wf>
<wf pos="PRP">his<wf>
<wf pos="NN" lemma="growing" wnsn="1" lexsn="1:22:00::">growing<wf>
```

Figure 5.5 SemCor Corpus annotation of example (12) (simplified).

To understand the meaning of the semantic tags, it is necessary to have a closer look at WORDNET again. In WORDNET, senses are identified by *sense keys*, which consist of the lemma and a numerical *lexical sense* (lexsn), which, in turn, consists of the parts shown in Table 5.3.

Example (13) breaks down the sense key schema of **remain** in the meaning of **stay the same; remain in a certain state** as shown in (8) above.

(13) remain%2:30:00::
     remain% 2 (=VERB) 30 (=verb.change) 00 (=sense #00)

The main purpose of the lexsn annotation is to allow automatic tools to access the folder structure of WORDNET directly for identifying particular senses. It is also optionally displayed for manual inspection in the WORDNET browser window. In addition to this rather cryptic number, SEMCOR offers a second semantic tag, the *WordNet sense* (wnsn), which is more easily interpretable by the human reader. The *WordNet sense* indicates at which rank a sense is displayed in the WORDNET browser display. Example (14) decodes the sense positions for two words of the synset shown in (11). This synset includes the first sense of the verb **remain**, as it is displayed in WORDNET, and the seventh sense of the verb **stay**. Note that the numbering of senses is based on the frequency of this sense in SEMCOR. As a consequence, we know that the synset shown in (14) is the most frequent sense of **remain** in the corpus.

Table 5.3 The different parts of a lexical sense in WORDNET.

Lexsn part	Explanation
ss_type	Each synset belongs to a type in terms of its syntactic category, as listed in Table 5.4
lex_filenum	Lexicographer files group the synsets of related senses, for examples see Table 5.5.
lex_id	Unique identifier for the sense of a lemma within a lexicographer file.
head_word	Only relevant for adjectives, see example (15).
head_id	Only relevant for *head_word*.

Table 5.4 Numerical encoding of the syntactic category (ss_type).

Code	Type
1	NOUN
2	VERB
3	ADJECTIVE
4	ADVERB

Table 5.5 Sample encoding of lexicographer files (lex_filenum).

Code	Label	Explanation
00	adj.all	all adjective clusters
01	adj.pert	relational adjectives (pertainyms)
03	noun.Tops	unique beginner for nouns
26	noun.state	nouns denoting stable states of affairs
30	verb.change	verbs of size, temperature change, intensifying, etc.
42	verb.stative	verbs of being, having, spatial relations

(14) a. lemma="remain" wnsn="1" lexsn="2:30:00::"
    b. lemma="stay" wnsn="7" lexsn="2:42:04::"

Let us return to the sense key schema itself. The numerical code in (13) offers two additional, empty positions marked by colons (::): *head_word* and *head_id* (15) have not been introduced so far. Both positions are used exclusively for adjective clusters, which are organized in a slightly different manner than the other syntactic categories. The sense key for adjectives is described in (15).

(15) lexsn = ss_type:lex_filenum:lex_id:head_word:head_id

In addition to semantic similarity, the main organization principle in adjective clusters is *antonymy*—pairs of adjectives that denote a strong semantic contrast like **wet** and **dry**. Not all adjectives have direct antonyms themselves, but if they are semantically similar to one that has an antonym, then this adjective features as their head_word and the head_id identifies its sense in the lexicographer file. The other adjectives are called satellites of the head word. Example (16) illustrates the head word wet together with some of its satellites (**bedewed, besprent, clammy**) and its direct antonym **dry**.

(16) [wet%3:00:01::] **wet**
    (covered or soaked with a liquid such as water)
    examples: **a wet bathing suit; wet sidewalks; wet weather**
    a. similar to:
        1. **bedewed**   [bedewed%3:00:00:wet:01] (wet with dew)
        2. **besprent**   [besprent%3:00:00:wet:01] (sprinkled over)
        3. **clammy**   [clammy%3:00:00:wet:01] (unpleasantly cool and humid)
    b. antonym:
        1. **dry** [dry%3:00:01::] (free from liquid or moisture; lacking natural or normal moisture or depleted of water; or no longer wet)

The adjectives **bedewed, besprent**, and **clammy** do not have direct antonyms themselves. Their sense keys point to lemma **wet**, which functions as their head word that has a direct antonym.

At this point, we should add a brief remark on the history of the SEMCOR Corpus. The Princeton team that created WORDNET was also responsible for the annotation of the corpus. The motivation behind this effort was to evaluate and extend the coverage of WORDNET. The SEMCOR Corpus is thus not just an annotated corpus but contributed directly to the lexical resource. The corpus was created in close combination with an early version of WORDNET. Subsequently, it has been automatically mapped and updated to new versions of WORDNET. As a consequence, there exist several versions of the corpus, which correspond to the different releases of WORDNET. SEMCOR is also a part of the MULTISEMCOR Corpus, in which the English texts are aligned with their Italian translations—and more recently also with Romanian ones. The parallel texts are aligned on the sentence and, if possible, also on the word level. Thus, the sense inventory can automatically be transferred from English to the aligned translated words. The resulting Italian and Romanian sense inventories are collected in the multilingual MULTIWORDNET, which also includes resources from other languages.

As we have seen above, WORDNET serves as the sense inventory for the annotation in the SEMCOR corpus. This is necessary to handle the large number of senses and the fact that every word has its own set of senses. However, this combination of annotated corpus and lexical hierarchy also offers added potential for users of the corpus: Since we have the WORDNET hierarchy in the background, we can generalize over individual senses via the lexical relations between the synsets. In WORDNET, these lexical relations are *hyponymy* and *hyperonymy*.

Example (17) shows the entry for the sense of the word **trance** that is shown in Figure 5.5 (**trance%1:26:00::**). Its direct hyponyms (**possession** and **fascination**) are more specific facets of **trance** while its direct hypernym (**psychological state**) is a more general term.

(17) [trance%1:26:00::] **enchantment, spell, trance**
 (a psychological state induced by [or as if induced by] a magical incantation)
 a. direct hyponym
 − **possession** (being controlled by passion or the supernatural)
 − **fascination, captivation** (the state of being intensely interested [as by awe or terror])
 b. direct hypernym
 − **psychological state, psychological condition, mental state, mental condition** ([psychology] a mental condition in which the qualities of a state are relatively constant even though the state itself may be dynamic), **a manic state**

The hyponyms, in turn, may have their own hyponyms although **possession** and **fascination** do not have any, being the most specific terms in WORDNET. The hypernym does have its own hypernym, etc. If we follow the line of hypernyms, at some point we reach the most general term, called *upper level concept*. This results in a tree-like structure in which all concepts ultimately are grouped under a small number of upper level concepts, such as **entity** for our example **trance**. The tree for the word **trance** in the sense in (17) is shown in Figure 5.6. Note that there does not always exist a proper tree structure in the mathematical sense because some concepts relate to more than one hypernym, which means that some concepts have more than one immediate parent concept. For example, **milk** has two hypernyms, being a dairy product and also a liquid. It does not hold that all dairy products are liquids and neither are all liquids dairy products. Hence, the two concepts do not stand in a hyperonymy relation to each other, and **milk** has a hyponymy relation to both concepts.

As mentioned above, this hierarchy of senses can be utilized in the use of SEMCOR to extend the set of examples. Let us say that we are looking for all occurrences of the verb **devour** in the sense of **eat greedily**. Then, by looking up this sense, [devour%2:34:00::] in WORDNET, we can find all its synonyms, **guttle**, **raven**, and **pig**, and look up their occurrences, too, since they have a very similar meaning to **devour**. We can also look at the hypernym of **devour**, which is **eat** in the sense **take in solid food** (sense key: [eat%2:34:00::]). Note that such extensions of the search are much more focused than just looking for all these words, since all of them have other meanings that are not as closely related to **devour**.

Coverage is a serious issue when we apply a lexical resource to new data. It is easy to imagine that WORDNET originally had to overcome lexical restrictions given that it

Figure 5.6 WORDNET tree for the word **trance** from the example in (17).

had originally been based on samples of the BROWN Corpus (see section 1.2.2 for more information about the corpus), which were all published in 1961—i.e. no later development is recorded. For example, the relatively new usage of **friend** as a verb as in (18)[9] is not documented in either SEMCOR or WORDNET.

(18) Call me a faddy daddy, but there's no way I'm going to friend or tweet or do anything else that compromises the privacy I had fought hard to maintain.

Additionally, certain types of words, such as proper names, are not covered in WORDNET—with the exception of famous people. Thus, in a way, word sense annotation as presented in this section and named entity annotation in section 5.1 are complementary.

5.3 Semantic Role Annotation

As we saw in the last section, word senses in WORDNET are determined on the basis of clustering (quasi-)synonymous words into fine-grained synsets. Polysemous words are then linked to more than one concept in terms of a sense key. Another way of grouping words into meaning classes, which holds in particular for verbs, is to classify them according to *semantic frames* with which they are associated. A frame is a recurring situation that is characterized by certain facts. The commercial transaction frame, for example, is characterized by involving a buyer, a seller, goods, and money, as well as by certain interactions between these participants and objects. Verbs that are associated with the same frame can take different perspectives on the situation: For example, **sell** takes a different perspective on a commercial transaction than **buy**.

Semantic frames characterize the meaning of predicates in terms of the semantic roles with which they are associated. The commercial transaction frame, as described above, is characterized by the semantic roles *buyer, seller, goods/thing sold*, and so forth. For a particular predicate, these frame-specific roles can be mapped onto more general semantic roles, also known as *theta roles*. The characterization of **sell**, for example, would map seller to the theta role *agent* and buyer to *recipient* whereas the characterization of **buy** would map buyer to agent, instead, and seller to *source*, reflecting the different views that these verbs take on the transaction.

In WORDNET, different senses of a word are separated into different synsets. Similarly, different readings of polysemous verbs are distinguished by being assigned to different frames. Example (19) shows this separation for two readings of the verb **draw**.[10]

(19) a. *Semantic roles*: artist, art, beneficiary
          example: He was drawing diagrams and sketches for his patron.
      b. *Semantic roles*: puller, thing pulled, source
          example: The campaign is drawing fire from anti-smoking advocates.

There are two influential projects that performed corpus annotation of semantic roles on the basis of frames: FRAMENET and PROPBANK, both of which we will introduce in the following sections. These projects have in common that both created annotated corpora along with the computational lexicons. Sense distinctions based on frames are normally much more coarse-grained than sense distinctions based on synonymy. This means that sense distinctions provided in FRAMENET and PROPBANK normally correspond to a set of several senses in WORDNET.

5.3.1 PROPBANK

Since the PROPBANK project had as its goal to annotate a corpus with semantic interpretation of predicate-argument structure, it makes sense to start the semantic annotation based on a syntactically annotated corpus. The PROPBANK project used the syntactic annotations of the Wall Street Journal section of the PENN TREEBANK[11] (for more information about the PENN TREEBANK, see section 4.2) and added a semantic layer on top. This project was motivated by the results of a series of semantic tagging workshops in the late 1990s (SENSEVAL), which had the goal of annotating running text with word senses in a reliable way, indicated by high inter-annotator agreement (see section 2.4).

Influenced by the idea of semantic frames, PROPBANK aimed at labeling arguments of a predicate in a consistent way independent of their syntactic realization. The sentences in (20)[12] show an example of a *causative alternation*, which relates pairs of transitive and intransitive verbs.

(20) a. [$_{\text{Arg0}}$ John] broke [$_{\text{Arg1}}$ the window].
    b. [$_{\text{Arg1}}$ The window] broke.

In the transitive sentence in (20-a), an agent (**John**) causes a patient (**the window**) to break. The intransitive sentence in (20-b) describes the same situation, except that the agent remains implicit and the patient is now realized as syntactic subject of the intransitive sentence. The annotation captures the correspondence between the two sentences of this alternation by assigning the same semantic label to the patient in both sentences, independent of its syntactic status. To capture cross-predicate generalizations without being forced to subscribe to a universal set of roles, the semantic arguments of an individual verb are numbered, beginning with zero (Arg0, Arg1, etc.; see below).

Based on the annotations of a sample of occurrences of the same predicate, it is possible to induce a semantic frame description for this predicate from the corpus. Continuing the toy example in (20), example (21) sketches such a description, a *Frameset* for the predicate **break**.

(21) Roles:
       Arg0
       Arg1

Note that a collection of such Framesets is a lexical resource in its own right since it documents the different semantic roles that different senses of a predicate can take.

The argument label inventory is based on a rather restrictive set of labels. Table 5.6 summarizes this set (including syntactic modifiers) used in PROPBANK along with their most common interpretation. Arg0 is generally the argument exhibiting features of a prototypical agent while Arg1 is a prototypical patient or theme. Higher numbered arguments are less predictable. In addition, there is a label for modifiers and a particular label for agents of induced actions as **Mr. Dinkins** in (22).[13]

(22) Mr. Dinkins would march his staff out of board meetings and into his private office …

However, these labels are convenient generalizations, which are interpreted individually per predicate. Thus, let us first consider the Frameset for the first sense of the verb **break**, break.01.[14] We show its Frameset in (23).

(23) Roles:
      Arg0-pag: breaker
      Arg1-ppt: thing broken
      Arg2-mnr: instrument
      Arg3-prd: pieces

This entry shows that this sense of the verb **break** selects for all four major roles, and Arg0 is interpreted for this verb as breaker; Arg1 is the thing broken, etc. In addition to ordered argument roles, the Frameset integrates the thematic interpretation of the arguments. The suffix -pag is short for Proto-Agent and identifies the argument which realizes typical agentive properties such as that it acts volitionally, is sentient, or perceives, causes a change of state, or moves. -ppt stands for Proto-Patient, which, in a way, is a counterpart to Proto-Agent agent. The other two suffixes are used to label modifiers, in

Table 5.6 Common argument interpretation in PROPBANK.

Argument	Common semantics
Arg0	prototypical agent
Arg1	prototypical patient
Arg2	instrument, benefactive, attribute
Arg3	starting point, benefactive, attribute
Arg4	ending point
ArgM	modifier
ArgA	agent of induced action

particular, manner (-mnr) and secondary predication (-pred). In a second example, we look at **remain**, the Frameset of which is shown in (24). This verb has three semantic roles, Arg1, Arg2, and Arg3. For this verb in this specific sense, Arg1 is defined as thing remaining, Arg2 as benefactive, and Arg3 as attribute of Arg1. -gol stands for goal.

(24) Roleset id: remain.01
    Roles:
        Arg1-ppt: Thing remaining (proto-agent)
        Arg2-gol: benefactive, entity who gets the remainder (goal)
        Arg3-prd: attribute of Arg1 (secondary predication)

All Framesets of PROPBANK are linked to the fine-grained semantic sense lexicon VERBNET and also to FRAMENET frames. *SemLink* is a project for linking these kinds of lexical resources and making them interoperable. See the Further Reading section for details.

Figure 5.7 shows the annotation of the sentence in (25), in which the predicate **remain** is annotated with sense remain.01.[15]

```
Tree:
-----
        (TOP (S (S-TPC-1    (ADVP (RB However))
                            (, ,)
                            (NP-SBJ (NP    (CD five)
                                           (JJ other)
                                           (NNS countries)) ...
Leaves:
-------
        0 However
        1 ,
        2 five
        3 other
        4 countries
...
        16 will
        17 remain
...
            prop:   remain.01
              v * -> 17:0, remain
              ARGM-DIS * ->        0:1,     However
              ARG1 * ->     2:2,    five other countries -- China, Thailand, (...)
              ARGM-MOD * -> 16:0, will
              ARG3 * -> 18:1, on that so – called priority watch list
              ARGM-CAU * ->        26:1, as a result of an interim review
```

Figure 5.7 PROPBANK-style sense annotation in the ONTONOTES Corpus.

(25) However, five other countries—China, Thailand, India, Brazil and Mexico—will remain on that so-called priority watch list as a result of an interim review, ...

The figure includes part of the syntactic bracketing structure and a fraction of the PROPBANK-style sense annotation of the syntactic leaves. Only Arg1 and Arg3 are realized in this example, Arg2 is left implicit. In addition, there are three different modifiers ArgM of the types discourse (DIS), modals (MOD), and causal (CAU), which are not specific for this frame, and are therefore not listed in the Frameset in (24).

To understand the annotation fully, we need to consider the syntax tree in combination with the frame annotations: The information following ARGM-DIS, for example, indicates the location and yield of the discourse modifier ARGM-DIS. The notation 0:1 corresponds to *word:hight*, in which the value of word indicates the starting point of the modifier in terms of leaf id—here, it starts at the leaf #0, i.e. **However**. The value of *hight* indicates the number of nodes we have to go up in the tree to find the appropriate phrasal node for the argument. For ARGM-DIS, we have to go up one level—the relevant phrasal node is ADVP. For ARG1, we start at leaf #2 and go up two nodes, which leaves us at the NP-SUBJ level.

As shown in the last example, PROPBANK annotation relies strongly on the syntactic annotation. However, there are cases in which the semantic predicate-argument structure does not correspond to the syntactic phrase structure segmentation. For the sentence in (26), we show a fragment of the annotation in Figure 5.8.

Tree:
...
```
   (NP (DT a)
           (ADJP (RB widely)
                           (VBN employed))
           (JJ anti-takeover)
           (NN defense))
```
Leaves:
...
```
   15   a
   16   widely
   17   employed
           prop:  employ.02
           v                   * -> 17:0, employed
           ARGM-MNR            * -> 16:0, widely
           ARG1               * -> 18:0, anti-takeover
                                   -> 19:0, defense
   18   anti-takeover
   19   defense
```

Figure 5.8 Non-isomorphic PROPBANK-style sense annotation in the ONTONOTES Corpus (Normal Form (ONF) View).

(26) The West German retailer ASKO Deutsche Kaufhaus AG plans to challenge the legality of a widely employed anti-takeover defense of companies in the Netherlands.

Here, the predicate **employ** is syntactically realized as an adjective modifying a noun. The adjective itself has two semantic arguments, ARG1 and ARGM-MNR, corresponding to its syntactic head noun and its adverbial modifier. There is no syntactic node that dominates all tokens of ARG1 **anti-takeover defense** without also dominating **employed** itself and **widely**. In cases like this, the semantic annotation is based on discontinuous elements. In other words, all elements belonging to this role are listed. In the case of ARG1, these are the adjective **anti-takeover** and the noun **defense**.

5.3.2 FrameNet

FRAMENET is an ongoing project, in which semantic frames are annotated. It has mainly been a lexicographic endeavor involving authentic corpus examples. Thus, the annotation of the corpus is of secondary importance in this project. The annotation of running text has actually been motivated by PROPBANK, in order to allow a comparison of FRAMENET and PROPBANK-style annotations. The annotation in FRAMENET proceeds by semantic frame and by predicate, i.e. all occurrences of a specific predicate in a specific sense are annotated at the same time. This means that, at current, there are certain predicates annotated, others are not. Meanwhile, FRAMENET offers a collection of different subcorpora for online browsing and also for download. FRAMENET DATA (release 1.5) contains a collection of 78 texts, most of which are fully annotated with frames. Six of them are Wall Street Journal articles on a wide variety of topics provided by the PROPBANK project, another substantial part of the texts has its origin in the Nuclear Threat Initiative. The texts deal with weapon programs of many nations. They have been used before in computational linguistics programs on question answering.[16] Other texts originate from the AMERICAN NATIONAL CORPUS MASC project, and finally the LUCORPUS, a collection of extremely varied documents, including transcripts of phone conversations, e-mails, and other miscellaneous texts ("LU" refers to FrameNet's concept of *lexical unit*). The texts are annotated on several linguistic levels such as part of speech and syntax, but we will concentrate on the frame semantic annotation in the following.

In FRAMENET, the concept of frames is linguistically instantiated by a frame evoking element and its *frame elements* (FE), i.e. the predicate and frame-specific defined semantic roles. Consequently, the basic units of a frame are its frame elements. A frame evoking element is labeled as *target* with respect to the lemma under consideration. This means, if a sentence has more than one predicate, there are two targets, and consequently two different frames to be annotated. Example (27) is annotated in the FRAMENET corpus with respect to two targets: **remained** and **another**.[17]

(27) ..., but the Cyclades remained in Venetian hands for another generation or more

    a. ..., but [$_{Entity}$ the Cyclades] remained^{Target} [$_{State}$ in Venetian hands] [$_{Duration}$ for another generation or more]

    b. ..., but the Cyclades remained in Venetian hands for another^{Target} [$_{Class}$ generation] or more

The annotation of **remained** in (27-a) introduces three frame elements of the semantic types Entity, State, and Duration. This corresponds to the frame of State_continue which is defined as: "Despite some implication that a State would be interrupted, the Entity remains in the specified State. Note that State includes locative relations."[18] Other lexical units of State_continue, apart from remain.v, are rest.v and stay.v. The frame of State_continue is characterized by two core frame elements and a number of non-core elements; see Table 5.7 for a description of these frame elements. Non-core elements are always optional. Additionally, core elements may be omitted in two cases, either because the sentence allows or requires an omission (e.g. the subject of an imperative, the agent of a passive verb) or because its identity is understood from the context. These cases are marked in the full text annotation as *constructional null instantiation* (CNI) and *definite null instantiation* (DNI) respectively. An example of a CNI is shown in (28),[19] the empty CNI element is added at the end of the sentence.

(28) It hopes to speak to students at theological colleges about the joys of [$_{Sound\_maker}$ bell] ringing^{Target} and will shortly publish a booklet for every vicar in the country entitled, "The Bells in Your Care. [$_{Agent}$ CNI]

Other frames in which remain.v participates are: Remainder, Left_to_do, and Existence. (29)–(32) show examples for all readings in FRAMENET with only core elements marked for comparison.

Table 5.7 Core and non-core frame elements of State_continue.

Frame element	Definition
Entity	Concrete or abstract *Entity*.
State	*State* of an *Entity*.
Circumstances	The circumstances under which the *State* continues.
Depictive	This FE describes a participant of the state of affairs introduced by the target as being in some state during the action.
Duration	The time period over which the *State* continues to hold of the *Entity*.
Explanation	The reason why the *State* continues.
Place	The location where the *Entity* is in the *State*.
Reason	The state of affairs that explains why the State persists.
Time	The time when the *State* is found to still persist.

(29) State_continue

..., but [$_{Entity}$ the Cyclades] remained^{Target} [$_{State}$ in Venetian hands] for another generation or more

(30) Remainder

[$_{Remainder}$ What] there truly remains^{Target} [$_{Resource}$ of me]

(31) Left_to_do

But [$_{Remainder}$ it] remains^{Target} [$_{Process}$ to be seen whether that will prove a significant omission].

(32) Existence

[$_{Entity}$ the often-restored complex] has remained^{Target} a focus of local Buddhist activities.

In addition to verbs, nominalizations and other nouns denoting events or states evoke their own frames. Common nouns are also annotated with a sense similar to WORDNET hypernyms, for example, *artefact*, and sometimes even evoke their own frame. The Clothing frame is an example for this, which is illustrated in (33) and (34).[20]

(33) He took a packet of Woodbines out of the breast pocket of [$_{Wearer}$ his] [$_{Material}$ cotton] [$_{Garment}$ shirt^{Target}] and lit one.

(34) The well-known Stanley Market (see page 55) is a major source for [$_{Descriptor}$ bargain] [$_{Garment}$ clothing^{Target}] and other merchandise.

Similar to the relations between WORDNET synsets, there are relations between FRAMENET frames, which, for example, relate more specific to more general frames that share relevant frame elements. These relations can be looked up in the Frame Index.

As we can see in the examples in (29) and (31), the set of frame elements includes semantic roles like State and Process. These frames are also annotated for semantic roles like Date and Time to mark temporal expressions, for example in the case of **for another generation or more** in (29). These annotations are not shown above to increase readability. However, note that such temporal annotations are similar to the temporal named entities in section 5.1. In the next section, we will introduce TIMEBANK, a resource in which the annotation of temporal expressions, temporal signals, events, and links between them is performed in a comprehensive way, subsuming the limited temporal annotation of the other types of semantic annotations.

5.4 TIMEBANK

The TIMEBANK Corpus (version 1.2) contains 183 news articles from newswire and transcribed broadcast news. News text in general is rich in temporal information, both in the form of temporal expressions and of events that can be anchored or ordered in time. Furthermore, the creation time of the text is generally part of the document and offers an additional reference point for temporal deixis, such as **late yesterday** in

(35),[21] which deicticly refers to 29 October 1989, the day before the article was originally published. To relate events to a general timeline, it is often necessary to resolve such deictic references.

(35) Rally officials weren't available to comment late yesterday.

In terms of coverage, the TIMEBANK Corpus includes 134 Wall Street Journal newswire texts from the PROPBANK Corpus, mostly texts published in 1989.[22] Furthermore, it contains 49 texts from the *Automatic Content Extraction* (ACE) program, about half of which are transcribed broadcast news (ABC, CNN, Public Radio International, Voice of America), the other half is from newswire (Associated Press and New York Times), all of which were published in the first half of 1998. The annotation is based on an extensive annotation scheme called *TimeML*. The corpus is annotated in XML (see section 2.4). However, for the sake of readability, we will present most examples as pure text with minimal annotation, focussing on the phenomena in question.

The TIMEBANK Corpus (version 1.2) has been annotated semi-automatically based on *TimeML* version 1.2.1. The scheme specifies four primary elements that are annotated: TIMEX3 for explicit temporal expressions; EVENT for event denoting expressions, typically verbs; SIGNAL for expressions like prepositions or conjunctions, which signal temporal relationships; and three different LINK elements for representing relationships between elements.

We will now discuss the annotation of TIMEBANK in more detail. Examples (36) and (38) show TIMEX3 elements, which mark temporal expressions, such as times, dates, durations, etc. These are shown as underlined expressions. The annotation of additional information for each TIMEX3 element is shown in (37) and (39) respectively.[23]

(36) NEWS STORY 02/13/1998 14:26:00
... Prime Minister John Howard, a monarchist himself, promised to put the question to a national referendum next year after convention delegates voted 89–52 for a republic, with 11 abstentions.

(37) a. **02/13/1998 14:26:00**
tid: t109
type: TIME
value: 1998-02-13T14:26:00 (format: ISO 8601)
temporalFunction: false
functionInDocument: CREATION_TIME

b. **next year**
tid: t112
type: DATE
value: 1999
temporalFunction: true
functionInDocument: NONE
anchorTimeID: t109 (= document creation time)

(38) Mr. Antar is being investigated by a federal grand jury in Newark, where prosecutors have told him that they may <u>soon</u> seek an indictment on racketeering and
securities fraud charges.

... In that suit, the SEC accused Mr. Antar of engaging in a "massive financial
fraud" to overstate the earnings of Crazy Eddie, Edison, N.J., over <u>a three-year
period</u>.

(39) a. **soon**
tid: t234
type: DATE
value: FUTURE_REF
temporalFunction: true
functionInDocument: NONE
anchorTimeID: t232 (= document creation time)

 b. **a three-year period**
tid: t238
type: DURATION
value: P3Y
temporalFunction: false
functionInDocument: NONE

In TIMEX3 annotations, the type of the temporal expression is encoded in the type
attribute (see, for example, (37)), which corresponds to the ENAMEX encoding of temporal
expressions introduced in section 5.1. However, TIMEX3 elements are designed to provide
more detailed information on the temporal expression than just its type. The attribute
value provides the actual meaning of the temporal expression in the text, which is either
a particular date or time, as in (37), or an abstraction of the temporal expressions such
as FUTURE_REF for **soon** or P3Y for **a three-year period** in (39). TemporalFunction
indicates whether value is derived by means of a rule, for example, in relation to the
creation time of the document, which is then explicitly referenced in anchorTime.

The second type of annotation in TIMEBANK concerns the annotation of events. The
tag EVENT identifies all classes of event expressions independent of their syntactic realization, i.e. this annotation covers tensed verbs as well as event nominals. It is also used
to annotate a subset of states or circumstances, namely those that are either transient or
explicitly marked as participating in a temporal relation. Besides a numerical identifier,
EVENT has two attributes: An obligatory class (see Table 5.8) and an optional stem
attribute for providing a base form of the token. Examples (40) and (41) are copies of
examples (36) and (38), but this time with events underlined instead of temporal expressions. Their event classes are resolved in Table 5.8.

(40) NEWS STORY 02/13/1998 14:26:00
... Prime Minister John Howard, a monarchist himself, <u>promised</u> to <u>put</u> the
<u>question</u> to a national <u>referendum</u> next year after convention delegates <u>voted</u>
89–52 for a republic, with 11 abstentions.

Table 5.8 EVENT classes in TimeBank.

Class	Event description
PERCEPTION	Physical perception of another event Example: **seen** in **was seen as inevitable**
REPORTING	Action of a person or an organization declaring something, narrating an event, informing about an event, etc. Example: **told** in example (41)
ASPECTUAL	Focus on different facets of event history like initiation, culmination, continuation Example: **continue, completed** in **regulations ... that would allow thrifts to continue ..., haven't yet been completed**
STATE	Circumstances in which something obtains or holds true Example: **inevitable** in **was seen as inevitable**
I_STATE	Intensional State, which introduces another event argument referring to alternative or possible worlds Example: **expected** in **results were ... worse than expected**
I_ACTION	Intensional Action, which introduces another event argument Example: **promised** in example (40); **investigated, seek, accused, engaging** in example (41)
OCCURRENCE	Something that happens or occurs in the world (= default) Example: **put, question, referendum, voted** in example (40); **indictment, suit, fraud, overstate** in example (41)

(41) Mr. Antar is being <u>investigated</u> by a federal grand jury in Newark, where prosecutors have <u>told</u> him that they may soon <u>seek</u> an <u>indictment</u> on racketeering and securities fraud charges.

... In that <u>suit</u>, the SEC <u>accused</u> Mr. Antar of <u>engaging</u> in a "massive financial <u>fraud</u>" to <u>overstate</u> the earnings of Crazy Eddie, Edison, N.J., over a three-year period.

The EVENT tag is assigned only to the head of the event expression. This decision was made to avoid problems with identifying the yield of the event expression, which is particularly difficult in cases that involve discontinuous realizations of events, as in (42).[24] In this example, the event expression is underlined, the head is marked in bold, and the event is discontinuous because of the adverb **fully**, which intervenes between the two verbal elements of the event expression.

(42) There is no reason why we would not <u>be</u> fully **<u>prepared</u>**.

Additional linguistic information about an event expression is provided in an additional tag MAKEINSTANCE. It includes information about parts of speech and polarity (e.g. neg in **was not elected**). For verbal events, it also contains information about its tense (future, past, etc.) and aspect (progressive, perfective, etc.). The decision to split

Table 5.9 LINK types in TimeBank.

Link	Description
TLINK	A temporal link between EVENTs and TIMEX3s (or EVENT-EVENT etc.)
SLINK	Subordination relationships that involve modality, evidentiality, and factuality
ALINK	Aspectual connection between two event instances

the representation of the event from its instantiations was motivated by examples like (43),[25] in which one event expression, **taught**, represents two event instantiations, one for **on Monday** and one for **(on) Tuesday**. However, in more recent specifications of TimeML, this decision has been revised, and all information is to be provided in the EVENT element itself.

(43) John taught on Monday and Tuesday.

The tag SIGNAL is used to annotate temporal function words, such as **after, during, when,** and **if,** which are then used in the representation of temporal relations, see below. Example (44) repeats a part of example (41) with its two signals, **in** and **over**, underlined.

(44) In that suit, the SEC accused Mr. Antar of engaging in a "massive financial fraud" to overstate the earnings of Crazy Eddie, Edison, N.J., over a three-year period.

The fourth major type of annotation is represented by LINK elements. There are three subtypes of links, as listed in Table 5.9. TLINK is used for temporal links that relate two temporal expressions, two event instances, or a temporal expression and an event instance. It encodes the temporal relation between the two linked expressions, i.e, whether one precedes the other (BEFORE), succeeds it (AFTER), includes it (INCLUDES), etc. For example, the event introduced by the head **investigated** in (41), for convenience repeated here as (45), is related to the document creation time by a TLINK of type INCLUDES, whereas the event introduced by **told** is linked to it by a TLINK of type BEFORE since the telling event took place before the document was published. Finally, the event of **seek** is linked to the time indicated by **soon** in terms of an IS_INCLUDED TLINK because it may take place in the future. If a relation is explicitly marked by a signal, this is recognized in the TLINK too. For example, the preposition **in** signals the IS_INCLUDED relation between the event triggered by the head suit and the event denoted by **accused** in (45). In this case, the TLINK does not only connect the two events but also the prepositional signal **in**.

(45) Mr. Antar is being investigated by a federal grand jury in Newark, where prosecutors have told him that they may soon seek an indictment on racketeering and securities fraud charges.

… In that <u>suit</u>, the SEC <u>accused</u> Mr. Antar of engaging in a "massive financial fraud" to overstate the earnings of Crazy Eddie, Edison, N.J., over a three-year period.

The other two links mark subordination relations. The more general one is called SLINK, which is used for marking subordinating relations that involve modal aspects, evidentiality, or factivity. Its types are MODAL, EVIDENTIAL, NEG_EVIDENTIAL, FACTIVE, COUNTER_FACTIVE, and CONDITIONAL accordingly. In contrast to TLINK, an SLINK only interacts with specific event classes, namely those that introduce another event, which is to a certain degree dependent on the first one: REPORTING, I_STATE, and I_ACTION. We will illustrate this with two SLINKs from (45), part of the example is repeated here as (46) with relevant elements underlined and event types added as subscripts. There is an SLINK of type EVIDENTIAL that links **told** to its dependent **seek**. The second SLINK, this time of type MODAL, links **seek** to its dependent **indictment**.

(46) Mr. Antar is being investigated by a federal grand jury in Newark, where prosecutors have $_{REPORTING}$<u>told</u> him that they may soon $_{I\_ACTION}$<u>seek</u> an <u>indictment</u> on racketeering and securities fraud charges.

The third link type is ALINK, which marks an aspectual connection between two event instances. It is similar to SLINK but the introducing event has to be of the class ASPECTUAL. For an example see (47).

(47) Analysts said Mr. Stronach wants to $_{ASPECTUAL}$<u>resume</u> a more influential role in <u>running</u> the company.

Inter-annotator agreement studies that were performed in the course of creating the TIMEBANK annotation show that assigning LINK relations was the task that resulted in the lowest agreement between the annotators. More specifically, it turned out that TLINK was the most difficult type.

To conclude this section, we provide a fully annotated XML version of the text in (38) and (41) above in Figure 5.9, including MAKEINSTANCE and LINK annotation.

5.5 Annotation of Formal Semantics

The corpora introduced in this chapter so far are annotated with shallow semantic information and have been in existence for several years so that they are well established in the (computational) linguistic community. In this section, we will introduce the GRONINGEN MEANING BANK (GMB), which is a very recent corpus project that had its first release in 2012. It differs from the other corpora in that it provides formal semantic analyses in addition to shallow layers. The analysis goes beyond the meaning of individual sentences

Mr. Antar is being <EVENT eid="e73" class="I_ACTION">investigated</EVENT> by a federal grand jury in Newark, where prosecutors have <EVENT eid="e74" class="REPORTING">told</EVENT> him that they may <TIMEX3 tid="t234" type="DATE" value="FUTURE_REF" temporalFunction="true" functionInDocument="NONE" anchorTimeID="t232">soon</TIMEX3> <EVENT eid="e75" class="I_ACTION">seek</EVENT> an <EVENT eid="e77" class="OCCURRENCE">indictment</EVENT> on racketeering and securities fraud charges.

<MAKEINSTANCE eventID="e73" eiid="ei2020" tense="PRESENT" aspect="PROGRESSIVE" polarity="POS" pos="VERB"/>
<MAKEINSTANCE eventID="e74" eiid="ei2021" tense="PRESENT" aspect="PERFECTIVE" polarity="POS" pos="VERB"/>
<MAKEINSTANCE eventID="e75" eiid="ei2022" tense="NONE" aspect="NONE" polarity="POS" pos="VERB" modality="may"/>
<MAKEINSTANCE eventID="e77" eiid="ei2023" tense="NONE" aspect="NONE" polarity="POS" pos="NOUN"/>

<TLINK lid="126" relType="INCLUDES" eventInstanceID="ei2020" relatedToTime="t232"/>
<TLINK lid="128" relType="BEFORE" eventInstanceID="ei2021" relatedToTime="t232"/>
<TLINK lid="129" relType="IS_INCLUDED" eventInstanceID="ei2022" relatedToTime="t234"/>

<SLINK lid="196" relType="EVIDENTIAL" eventInstanceID="ei2021" subordinatedEventInstance="ei2022"/>
<SLINK lid="197" relType="MODAL" eventInstanceID="ei2022" subordinatedEventInstance="ei2023"/>

Figure 5.9 Fully annotated TIMEBANK example.

in a more comprehensive way than temporal linking in the TIMEBANK Corpus. In addition to the annotation of semantic phenomena like scope, tense, and presuppositions, it includes an analysis of elements that are coreferent across sentences and also logical linking of sentences or other parts of the text, thus going beyond pure semantics and approaching the area of discourse analysis (see Chapter 6 for details).

The motivation for creating GMB with regard to a deep semantic analysis of full texts was to provide an empirical basis for data-driven semantic analysis and future developments in computational semantics, which provide means to deal with ambiguities on the sentence level that require discourse context for resolving them.

Version 2.1 of GMB contains 8,000 documents (about 1 million tokens), most of which are newswire texts from Voice of America (7,609 texts, published between 2004 and 2011), Aesop's fables (199 texts), country descriptions from The World Factbook by the CIA (178 texts), a collection of texts from the *Open American National Corpus* (MASC Full, 11 texts published since 1990), and a few legal texts (3 texts). All texts are open domain and not subject to copyright restrictions.

The semantic annotation starts out at the word level. Each token is annotated with a representation of its meaning in terms of a *lambda* Discourse Representation Structure (λ-DRS). The λ-DRSs of the words in a sentence are combined into a *Discourse Representation Structure* (DRS) representing the meaning of the text. Figure 5.10 illustrates the meaning composition of **remains under arrest** in example (48).

(48) This means Mr. Fujimori remains under arrest.

Informally speaking, the meaning is represented in two-partite boxes. The lower box contains the predicate-logic predicates like arrest(x). The upper box is called the *discourse universe* and collects variables for discourse referents that are accessible for further predications. There are three types of variables: events (e), times (t), and other referents (x). For example, the plain DRS for **arrest** is combined with a discourse referent x2, which is the referent for **under arrest** in the discourse universe of the combined DRS.

The meaning of verbal predicates like **remain** in Figure 5.10 is represented in a compositional way in the lower box of its λ-DRS.[26] The meaning of **remain** is decomposed into the verbal predicate proper, remain(e4), and its arguments, realized as predicates in terms of thematic roles like THEME, here THEME(e4, v3). The verbal meaning is re-composed in that all parts predicate over a (so-called neo-Davidsonian) event argument, here e4. The predicate THEME(e4, v3) has a second argument in addition to the event argument. The additional variable v3 needs to be instantiated by the actual theme element in the clause. In the further derivation of the example

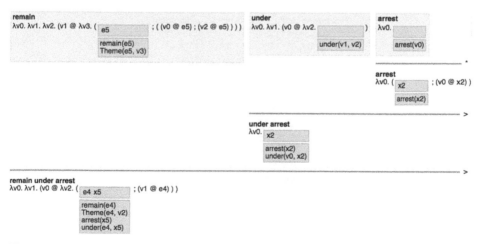

Figure 5.10 Meaning composition of **remain under arrest** in terms of λ-DRSs in the GRONINGEN MEANING BANK.

sentence, v3 will be instantiated by the syntactic subject **Mr. Fujimori** (x11). For the DRS of the whole sentence, see Figure 5.11.

The box in Figure 5.11 is, in fact, a box-in-box structure. The outer box represents the matrix clause **This means**, and the inner box the subordinate clause **Mr. Fujimori remains under arrest**. At the bottom of the outer box, there is a predication now(t7) that indicates that the time t7 refers to the present. It furthermore specifies that the event e4 related to the matrix predicate **mean** is included in or equal to time t8 (e4 $\subseteq$ t8). t8 itself is then set to t7 (t8=t7), i.e. to the present. In short, the event specified by **means** takes place in the present.

Our example represents the meaning of a complex sentence. It is important to mention that GMB provides DRSs for the meaning of whole texts. This means that the box in Figure 5.11 will ultimately be part of a much larger box representing the complete text. However, getting deeper into Discourse Representation Theory and its combinatorial variant applied in GMB is beyond the scope of this book. We refer the interested reader to the Further Reading section and will return to the corpus as such instead. Table 5.10 summarizes the layers of annotation included in the GMB, combined with examples of how they are integrated into a DRS if applicable.

In the course of creating an annotated corpus, there is always a trade-off between effort in time (and money) and reliability of annotation. The GMB was created in a semi-automatic way, combining a natural language processing pipeline with manual post-correction. The post-correction is partly carried out by experts and partly collected by crowdsourcing. For the latter, instead of collecting annotations via a micro worker platform like Amazon's Mechanical Turk,[27] the creators of GMB designed *Wordrobe*,[28] a game designed for the purpose of collecting judgements on questions that originate from the automatic annotation. The gamers' judgements as well as the expert annotations

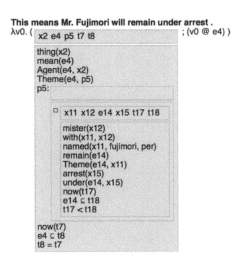

Figure 5.11 Full sentence λ-DRS for example (48) from the GRONINGEN MEANING BANK

Table 5.10 Annotation layers in the GRONINGEN MEANING BANK.

Level	Source	DRS encoding example
POS tag	PENN TREEBANK	
named entity	EXTENDED NAMED ENTITY	named(X,'John','Person')
word senses	WORDNET	pred(X,loon,n,2)
thematic roles	VERBNET	rel(E,X,'Agent')
syntax	Combinatory Categorial Grammar (CCG)	
semantics	Discourse Representation Theory (DRT)	drs(Referents,Conditions)
rhetorical relations	Segmented Discourse Representation Theory (SDRT)	rel(DRS1,DRS2,because)

are then re-integrated into the database as stand-off annotation layers, called *Bits of Wisdom*. In sum, the GRONINGEN MEANING BANK is a special corpus, both in the sense of its compositional semantic annotation and with respect to its method of creation by collaborative crowdsourced annotation.

5.6 Summary

In this chapter, we have looked at semantic annotation, i.e. annotation that is concerned with meaning on the word and on the sentence level. The first type of semantic annotation we considered pertains to the annotation of named entities. Then, we looked at more general annotation in terms of lexical semantics, word sense annotation. This is the first type of annotation that we have seen that requires separate resources in which the inventory of the annotation is based. The same also holds true for the annotation of semantic roles, both in PROPBANK and in FRAMENET. After that, we had a closer look at temporal information in TIMEBANK, which extends temporal annotation that has also been integrated in the other semantic annotations to a fully specified annotation of temporal relations in text. Finally, we have looked at a recently started project that annotates semantics in terms of formal semantics. This type of annotation goes beyond the sentence level and includes phenomena such as coreference, which will be discussed in the following chapter.

5.7 Further Reading

Section 5.1

BBN HIERARCHY of named entities: This is a hierarchical sense inventory for named entities that is used for the BBN PRONOUN COREFERENCE AND ENTITY TYPE CORPUS, a supplement to the Wall Street Journal part of the PENN TREEBANK. The corpus is available from the Linguistic Data Consortium (LDC) at http://www.ldc.upenn.edu/. The named entity guidelines are provided online (http://catalog. ldc.upenn.edu/docs/LDC2005T33/BBN-Types-Subtypes.html).

Message Understanding Conferences (MUC): A short overview of MUC-1 through MUC-6 can be found in Grishman and Sundheim (1996). More information about MUC-6 and MUC-7 can be found at http://www.cs.nyu.edu/cs/faculty/grishman/muc6.html and http://www.itl.nist.gov/iaui/894.02/related_projects/muc/proceedings/muc_7_toc.html respectively.

ONTONOTES DB TOOL: This is a Python-based tool for building and accessing the ONTONOTES MySQL database on the basis of SQL queries. It is part of the corpus release; a description is provided in Pradhan and Kaufman (2012).

ONTONOTES: This corpus was published in five releases, covering the languages English, Chinese, and Arabic. It is available free of charge from the LDC. The corpus is documented in a conference paper (Hovy et al., 2006). The annotation of named entities, word senses and PROBANK frames is described in the annotation guidelines (Weischedel et al., 2012).

ONTONOTES Normal Form View (ONF): This is a reader-friendly textual format that integrates all annotation layers of ONTONOTES, which are otherwise stored in separate stand-off files. The format of ONF is explained in the annotation guidelines (Weischedel et al., 2012).

PENN TREEBANK: For the PENN TREEBANK there is an early overview paper (Marcus et al., 1993) and a paper on predicate argument structure (Marcus et al., 1994). The bracketing guidelines (Santorini, 1991) are also freely available. The treebank is available from the LDC at http://www.ldc.upenn.edu/.

Sekine's EXTENDED NAMED ENTITY Hierarchy: The extended hierarchy, which is used in the GRONINGEN MEANING Bank (see below), subsumes about 150 named entity types. It is described at http://nlp.cs.nyu.edu/ene/.

TÜBA-D/Z TREEBANK: This treebank for German was discussed extensively in Chapter 4. Since version 7, the treebank has a new representation of named entities, integrated into the syntactic nodes. The annotation of named entities is documented in the stylebook (Telljohann et al., 2012).

Section 5.2

BABELNET is an automatic derivative of WORDNET (see below). It is a free multilingual resource that combines WORDNET with WIKIPEDIA and automatically translated it into about 50 languages (Navigli and Ponzetto, 2010).

BROWN Corpus: More information about the BROWN CORPUS can be found in Francis and Kučera (1967). The manual for the corpus can be found at http://icame.uib.no/brown/bcm.html. The data has been used in many projects, for example, in PENN TREEBANK and SEMCOR.

MULTISEMCOR: This is a parallel corpus on the basis of SEMCOR and professional translations of its English texts into Italian, and recently into Romanian. The project is described by Bentivogli and Pianta (2005). The parallel corpus and its sense annotations can be searched online and is available for download at http://multisemcor.fbk.eu. The sense inventories are collected in MULTIWORDNET.

MULTIWORDNET: This is a multilingual collection of word sense inventories, which are inspired by the English WORDNET. A description of the project is published by Pianta et al. (2002). The data can be browsed and downloaded from http://multiwordnet.fbk.eu/english/home.php.

SEMCOR Corpus: Short descriptions of the SEMCOR Corpus can be found in Miller et al. (1993, 1994). Versions 1.6 through 3.0 are freely available from Rada Mihalcea's website: http://

www.cse.unt.edu/~rada/downloads.html#semcor. The version numbers correspond to the version numbers of WORDNET, on which the annotation was based.

WORDNET: WORDNET is documented in a journal paper (Miller, 1995) and in a book (Fellbaum, 1998). It can be searched online at http://wordnetweb.princeton.edu/perl/webwn or downloaded from http://wordnet.princeton.edu/wordnet/download/. There is also an online reference manual available at http://wordnet.princeton.edu/wordnet/documentation/. The Global WordNet Association promotes the standardization of wordnets across languages (http://globalwordnet.org/).

Section 5.3

FRAMENET: The project is concerned with building a lexical database of English that is both human- and machine-readable. Extensive documentation is provided at https://framenet. icsi.berkeley.edu including a thorough description of the annotation (Ruppenhofer et al., 2010). You can browse the FRAMENET corpus, which can also be ordered from the project for download free of charge. There are also German and Japanese frame-annotated corpora (Burchardt et al., 2006; Ohara, 2012).

OPEN AMERICAN NATIONAL CORPUS (OANC): The OANC is a balanced corpus of approximately 15 million words of American English, including transcripts of spoken data. More information about OANC can be found in Ide et al. (2010) and at http://www. americannationalcorpus.org/.

PROPBANK: An overview of the PROPBANK project can be found in Palmer et al. (2005). The corpus is available from the LDC at http://www.ldc.upenn.edu/ as a stand-off layer complementing the syntactic annotation of the PENN TREEBANK. There is also an annotation manual by Babko-Malaya (2005). NOMBANK (Meyers et al., 2004) is a closely related project focussing on the annotation of nominals (http://nlp.cs.nyu.edu/meyers/NomBank.html).

Proto-roles: Dowty (1991) introduced the concept of proto-roles as a collection of prototypical properties of agents or themes which can be instantiated by arguments of particular verbs to a greater or lesser degree.

Semantic frames: The idea of semantic frames was first introduced in a conference talk by Fillmore (1976), who had earlier established the concept of thematic roles.

SemLink: This is a project that attempts to link different lexical resources via mappings. More information can be found in Palmer (2009) and at https://verbs.colorado.edu/semlink/.

SensEval: This was a series of conferences for automatic word sense disambiguation. For the first conference, there is an introduction by Kilgarriff (1998). More information, including the data sets, is available at http://www.senseval.org/.

VERBNET: This is a fine-grained verb lexicon relating PROPBANK framesets to more fine-grained verb senses, which are organized according to distributional classes (called Levin classes because they are based on Levin (1993)): see http://verbs.colorado.edu/~mpalmer/projects/verbnet.html. It is described in a conference paper (Kipper et al., 2000) and a PhD thesis (Kipper Schuler, 2005). The VerbNet annotation guidelines are available online (http://verbs. colorado.edu/verb-index/VerbNet_Guidelines.pdf). The lexicon can be downloaded and is also accessible online via the UNIFIED VERB INDEX (http://verbs.colorado.edu/verb-index/), which merges sense descriptions from several resources.

Section 5.4

Automatic Content Extraction (ACE): ACE was a program for developing automatic methods for named entity detection, coreference resolution, and event extraction. The ACE corpora from 2004 and 2005 are available from the Linguistic Data Consortium at http://www. ldc. upenn.edu/. The annotation is documented by Doddington et al. (2004).

TimeBank: The corpus is distributed by the LDC free of charge including its annotation guidelines (Saurí et al., 2006). A brief version of those is available online at http://www. timeml.org/site/timebank/documentation-1.2.html. A description of the annotation and the project history is provided by Pustejovsky and Stubbs (2013, Ch. 10).

TimeML: A description of TimeML can be found in Pustejovsky et al. (2003) and Saurí et al. (2006). More extensive information, including the TimeML specification can be found at www.timeml.org/. Further resources annotated with TimeML are listed at http://www. timeml.org/site/timebank/timebank.html.

Section 5.5

Combinatory Categorial Grammar (CCG): An introduction to CCG can be found in Steedman (2000).

Discourse Representation Theory (DRT): DRT is a comprehensive semantic framework for modeling the meaning of sentences and also longer stretches of text. The classic reading is Kamp and Reyle (1993). See also the entry in the Stanford Encyclopedia of Philosophy (http://plato.stanford.edu/entries/discourse-representation-theory/).

Groningen Meaning Bank (GMB): This conference paper describes the annotation project (Basile et al., 2012). Further information and online access to the data can be found at http:// gmb.let.rug. nl/.

5.8 Exercises

1. **WordNet**: Go to the online search for WordNet at http://wordnetweb.princeton.edu/ perl/webwn and look up the following words. How many different meanings do the verbal readings of these words have? Are they related via the hypernymy relation? To look at hypernyms of word senses, click on the S link at the beginning of a sense definition and select *inherited hypernym*.
   (a) kill
   (b) murder
   (c) assassinate

2. **More WordNet**: Look up the word line in WordNet (see above). Then select the option *Show Frequency Counts*. Which are the most frequent non senses? Why are there senses that do not have any frequency information?

3. **FrameNet**: Go to the online search for lexical units in FrameNet at https://framenet.icsi. berkeley.edu/fndrupal/index.php?q=luIndex. Look up the words from exercise 1 in the frame **Killing**. Which roles do they have? If you look at the annotations, which roles are realized most often? Does that differ between the verbs?

4. **MASC**: Go to http://www.anc.org/data/masc/downloads/data-download/ and download the MASC-CoNLL version. Open file 110CYL067.conll in the written section in an editor (e.g. MS Word). How many occurrences of the verb **have** in the sense have.04 are there? How many different types of ArgM (here: AM) can you find?

5. **TimeBank:** Go to the TimeBank browser at http://www.timeml.org/site/timebank/ browser_1.2/index.php, click on signals, and then select during. With which TIMEXes does it occur? Can you group them with regard to the length of the TIMEX?

6. **WordRobe**: Play WordRobe at www.wordrobe.org.

CHAPTER 6
DISCOURSE ANNOTATION

This chapter is concerned with the annotation of meaning, as was the last chapter. In contrast to the last chapter, which looked at the literal meaning of words, phrases, and sentences, this chapter focuses on meaning of language in larger contexts. We can also call this *meaning of language in use*, or *discourse meaning*. As discussed in section 2.2.4, all phenomena described in the current chapter are related to the phenomenon of *coherence*, which describes how language users perceive communication or text as a coherent whole. This means that we have to give up the sentence as our basic linguistic unit since information usually is not conveyed in just one sentence, but related bits and pieces of information are distributed across different sentences and need to be integrated into a joint representation in the minds of the language users. Thus, the sentence in (1-b) is difficult to understand if we do not have the sentence in (1-a) as context.

(1) a. Our Spanish teacher thinks, we are bilingual.
     b. He makes us translate sentences that have words I have never heard before.

In linguistics, these phenomena fall under the area of *pragmatics*. A core property of pragmatics is that it goes beyond the sentence in two ways. First, it takes larger linguistic units than the sentence into account. And second, it includes the language user, who processes the meaning of text (including spoken communications) in terms of a *discourse model*. This discourse model is not just based on the literal meaning provided in text, but is enriched by general knowledge and unconscious inference processes by the language user.

Pragmatic concepts are often harder to specify than syntactic or semantic ones due to the fact that many of them are not fixed, hard-coded rules, but are rather guidelines of how to convey and interpret language to achieve mutual understanding in a cooperative way. This may explain why pragmatic annotation is much more limited than, for example, syntactic annotation. This chapter focuses on the annotation of three pragmatic phenomena related to discourse: First, in section 6.1, we look at the annotation of entities across text, such as the pronoun used in (1-b). Such references can only be interpreted if they can be related to other mentions of their entities. Second, we look at the annotation of information structure in sentences in section 6.2. Information structure is strongly related to the way language users build up their discourse model to understand text—for example, how they relate back to information that has been mentioned before. And third, we look at the annotation of discourse relations that encode logical relations between sentences or larger stretches of text, and which again provide a significant contribution to the perception of text as a coherent whole (section 6.3).

6.1 Anaphora and Coreference

6.1.1 Basic Concepts

Anaphora and coreference are concerned with relations of expressions in the text to each other and to entities in the real world. When we write a text, it is likely that we will mention certain persons or objects several times. In the excerpt in (2),[1] for example, all the expressions that refer to **Michael Jackson** and **a juror** are marked with subscripts [1] and [2] respectively.[2] Note that it is possible to refer to them in different ways, as shown by the forms **Michael Jackson** and **Jackson.**

(2) New York Daily News today reports that jurors are saying there were all sorts of shannanigans going on in the jury room at the [₁ Michael Jackson] case, that [₂ a juror] wanted to convict [₁ Jackson] smuggled in a medical dictionary to prove [₁ Jackson] fits the definition of a pedophile. [₂ She] was later [₂ she] says intimidated into changing [₂ her] vote to not guilty.

Coreference is defined in linguistics as the relationship between different expressions in texts that refer to the same entity in the discourse. Thus, all marked occurrences of the juror in example (2) refer to the same person in the real world. *Anaphora*, in contrast, describes the relation of a referring expression back to the expression in the text to which it refers. Note that anaphora is the term for the phenomenon; an expression that shows an anaphoric relation to a preceding expression in the text is called an *anaphor*. The preceding expression is called *antecedent*. Thus, the antecedent of **She** in example (2) is **a juror.**

The difference between coreference and anaphora is a subtle one: Coreference involves relations between expressions in the text and persons, object, or states in the real world, while anaphora is a relation between elements of the text. In many cases, both relations hold for the same expressions. Thus, in the example in (2), all the marked expressions are coreferent as well as anaphoric. These relations are based on the assumption of a discourse model that participants in a conversation share. In this discourse model, discourse entities exist, which can potentially refer to entities in the real world. These discourse entities, often called *mentions* or *markables*, are generally expressed as noun phrases (NPs). Thus, the annotation of such mentions needs to be based on syntactic notions, either explicitly by using NPs annotated in a treebank (for example in the German TüBa-d/z treebank, which has also been annotated for coreference) or automatically by a parser (for example in the ONTONOTES Corpus). All mentions referring to one referent in the real world constitute a *coreference chain*. For example, all mentions of the **juror** in (2) constitute a coreference chain.

One of the difficult questions in the annotation of coreference and anaphora is the question whether maximal noun phrases should be used as mentions or smaller NPs. For example, the sentence in (3) consists of a long, complex noun phrase, and the shortest possible mention would be **Same juror**, the longest one would consist of the whole sentence. Different annotation schemes for coreference adopt different strategies. The ONTONOTES Corpus, for example, uses the maximal projection of the phrase.

(3)   Same juror we told you about yesterday Eleanor Cook who's reportedly writing a tell-all book titled Guilty as Sin Free as a Bird.

A related question concerns the annotation of *singleton mentions*. Singletons are mentions that do not enter into any referential relations. Note that in the previous two examples from the ONTONOTES Corpus, we have shown only partial coreferential annotation. Example (4) repeats the example from (2) with a full annotation, including singletons.[3]

(4)   [$_3$ New York Daily News] today reports that [jurors] are saying there were all sorts of [shannanigans] going on in [$_4$ the jury room] at [the [$_1$ Michael Jackson] case], that [$_2$ a juror] wanted to convict [$_1$ Jackson] smuggled in [a medical dictionary] to prove [$_1$ Jackson] fits the definition of [a pedophile]. [$_2$ She] was later [$_2$ she] says intimidated into changing [[$_2$ her] vote] to not guilty.

Singleton mentions are marked by square brackets without subscript. Note that mentions can be embedded into other mentions, as shown in the case of **the Michael Jackson case** where the whole phrase is a mention referring to the court case and the subsequence **Michael Jackson** is a separate mention referring to the person. There are several reasons why mentions are singletons. The mention **the Michael Jackson case** is a singleton because it is mentioned in the text only once—i.e. if it were mentioned in the article again later, it would enter into a coreferential relation. Another type of singletons consists of noun phrases that are never coreferent, such as **general** in the collocation **in general**. In some corpora, such as in ONTONOTES, such singletons are not annotated, mostly to minimize annotation efforts.

Coreference relations can be of different types. The examples that we have seen so far all fall under *identity* relations, i.e. the mentions connected in a coreference chain refer to the same entity. However, there are other types of relations. Note, for example, that in example (4), the noun phrase **jurors** consists of a set of people, and that the later mentioned NP **a juror** is one of those persons. This constitutes the *subset* relation, sometimes also called *element* relation. This is a case of *bridging* (see next section). Another type of relation occurs if the annotation does not consider maximal NPs as mentions but smaller NPs. If this is the case, then we can find *appositive* relations, such as shown in (5). In these cases, two or more appositives are annotated as separate mentions, and are thus coreferent.

(5)   a.   [$_1$ Mary], [$_1$ a well known scientist],
      b.   [$_2$ a dangerous bacteria], [$_2$ bacillium],
      c.   [$_3$ a trade deficit], [$_3$ the third setback this year],

Anaphora can occur without coreference. This is the case, for example, with *bound anaphora*. Bound anaphora cover cases in which there is a relation between a definite pronoun and a quantified noun phrase/pronoun as its antecedent. Examples of bound anaphora are shown in (6).

(6)   a.   [$_1$ Most linguists] prefer to use [$_1$ their] own examples.
      b.   [$_2$ Every student] should bring [$_2$ his] computer.

Another question concerns the types of mentions that are annotated. If we restrict ourselves to NPs as mentions, as many annotation projects have done, we ignore more complicated types of relations such as *event anaphora*. For a discussion of these phenomena, see section 6.1.3.

Now that we have introduced the most important terminology, in the next section, we will focus on the annotated corpora and their annotation schemes.

6.1.2 Annotated Corpora

The first corpora annotated for anaphora and coreference were annotated in settings related to information retrieval. The first corpora were provided as evaluation data for the *Message Understanding Conference* (MUC). The second set of corpora consists of the ACE Corpora, created within the program on *Automatic Content Extraction*. Both sets of corpora were annotated with a focus on the automatic extraction of knowledge from text, which means that many decisions were taken that do not necessarily agree with linguistic theory. We will focus on the MUC annotation scheme. We will then look at a corpus for Bulgarian in which the annotation of coreference is restricted to intra-sentential phenomena, at a German corpus that annotates a wide range of phenomena on top of a treebank, at ONTONOTES again, and at a small corpus with very fine-grained annotation, GNOME. Another corpus with coreference annotation for English is MASC. This corpus covers a wide range of genres.

In the MUC corpora, coreference is restricted to noun phrases. The annotation uses maximal NPs for mentions, but if necessary, the minimal phrase is listed as additional information in the SGML markup. SGML is a predecessor of the markup language XML (cf. section 2.4). An example is shown in (7),[4] where the minimal phrase is listed under MIN.

(7)   <COREF ID="100" MIN="Haden MacLellan PLC">Haden MacLellan PLC of Surrey, England</COREF>

The MUC annotation scheme identifies the following phenomena: identity relations, bound anaphora, appositions, and predicated relations, such as the ones in (8-a). However, it is a matter of debate whether predicates are referential and hence eligible mentions or whether they are just denoting properties without being referential. Since in MUC, they are considered referential, this decision results in annotations in which values change over time and in which the changing values are annotated as coreferent, as shown in (8-b).

(8) a. [₁ ARPA program managers] are [₁ nice people].
     b. [₂ Henry Higgins, who was formerly [₂ sales director for Sudsy Soaps]], became [₂ president of Dreamy Detergents].

Other corpora, mostly treebanks whose annotations also cover anaphora and coreference, use a syntactic definition of these phenomena. This means that they restrict the annotation to anaphora and coreference within sentences. Examples for such annotations can be found in the BULTREEBANK for Bulgarian.

The BULTREEBANK is a treebank whose syntactic annotation is based on the syntactic theory of *Head-Driven Phrase Structure Grammar* (HPSG). The annotation of anaphora concentrates on pronominal anaphora. Figure 6.1 shows an example of the annotation of subject control for the sentence in (9). In the figure, the arc from the syntactic node Prn* to the empty pronoun **pro-ss** shows subject-control from the matrix clause to the embedded one. Since Bulgarian is a pro-drop language, such phenomena are systematic.

(9) Аз обичах да разговарям с   него.
     I   liked   to talk   with him.
     'I used to talk to him.'

The BULTREEBANK annotation scheme also covers subset relations, as shown in the sentence in (10) and the annotation in Figure 6.2. Here, the first person singular personal pronoun and the possessive pronoun are coreferent. At the same time, they are a subset of the first person plural pronoun. This relation is shown in the horizontal links between the **pro-ss** nodes and between the **pro-ss** and Prn* node.

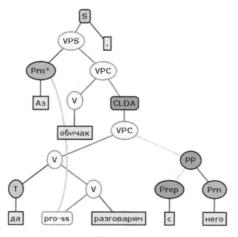

Figure 6.1 The BULTREEBANK annotation for the sentence in (9).

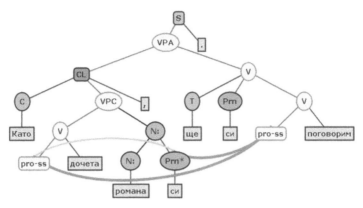

Figure 6.2 The BULTREEBANK annotation for the sentence in (10).

(10) Като дочета романа си,   ще си   поговорим.
   When read-I   novel-the my-REFL, will PRON-REFL talk-we.
   'As soon as I read my novel through, we will talk to each other.'

Coreference across sentences is not annotated in the BULTREEBANK.

Another treebank that annotates anaphora and coreference information is the German TüBA-D/Z treebank. In this treebank, the syntactic annotation provides the basis for further annotation steps. For anaphora and coreference annotation, this means that the mentions are extracted from the treebank, thus ensuring absolute consistency between the syntactic annotation of NPs and mentions. TüBA-D/Z also restricts this level of annotation to NPs, but it annotates a wide range of coreference and anaphoric relations: The identity relation is split into an anaphoric relation, which covers pronoun anaphors, a coreferential relation for definite NP anaphors, and a cataphoric relation for cases in which the antecedent follows the anaphor, as, for example, in (11).

(11) "Bei bedeutenden Bau- und Verkehrsplanungen müssen [₁ unsere] Einflußmöglichkeiten gestärkt werden," fordern [₁ die Behindertenverbände].
   "For major building and traffic planning, [₁ our] political leverage needs to be strengthened," [₁ the disability associations] demand.'

Additionally, split antecedent, bound, and instance relations are annotated, and expletive pronouns are marked as such. *Split antecedent* relations occur between coordinate or plural NPs and NPs referring to one member of the plural expression. An example is shown in (12). Here, the two mentions, no. 1 and 2, are subsumed in the plural pronoun in mention no. 3.

(12) "Vor allem die letzten Stunden waren fürchterlich," sagt [₁ eine junge Frau], die [₂ ihre gebrechliche Mutter und vier Kinder] über die Grenze führt. Sie sind zu

Fuß gekommen, denn das Auto wurde [₃ ihnen] von serbischen Freischärlern abgenommen.

"'Especially the last hours were terrible," said [₁ a young woman], who is leading [₂ her invalid mother and four children] across the border. [₃ They] have arrived on foot because the car was taken from [₃ them] by Serbian irregulars.'

Bound anaphors cover anaphora to quantified antecedents (including certain indefinite antecedents). Examples for this case are shown in (13).

(13) a. [₁ Kein Tag] vergeht, an [₁ dem] das no longer amused Kollegium nicht auf den Bellizisten und mutierten Friedensbewegten herumdrischt.
'[₁ No day] passes, on [₁ which] the no longer amused council does not thresh the warmongers and mutated followers of the peace movement.'

   b. Im Mai wird er in Hamburg zwei ungewöhnliche Seminare geben: für Schauspieler, Regisseure, Sänger, Tänzer und [₂ alle Menschen], [₂ die] mehr über den schöpferischen Prozeß erfahren möchten.
'In May, he will give two unusual seminars in Hamburg: for actors, directors, singers, dancers, and [₂ all people] [₂ who] want to learn more about the creative process.'

The subset relation is called *instance* relation in TüBA-D/Z; an example for such a relation is shown in (14). Here, mention no. 2 constitutes one of the two instances of the set in mention no. 1.

(14) Bonn (taz) – Von [₁ den zwei Deutschland zustehenden Posten eines EU-Kommissars] werden SPD und Grüne [₂ je einen] besetzen.
'Bonn (taz) – Of [₁ the two appointments of an EU commissioner] to which Germany is entitled, the SPD and the Green Party will fill [₂ one each].'

Expletive pronouns, also called *pleonastic pronouns*, are cases in which a pronoun has no meaning per se but is required by the syntax. Consequently, expletive pronouns are never anaphoric. The sentence in (15) shows examples from TüBA-D/Z, the expletive pronouns are marked by brackets.

(15) a. Vor der dritten Verhandlungsrunde im Tarifstreit der Druckindustrie ist [es] in der Nacht zum Donnerstag auch in Bremen zu Warnstreiks gekommen.
'Before the third round of negotiations in the trade dispute of the printing industry, [it] also has come to deterrent strikes in Bremen in the night of Thursday.'

   b. [Es] soll zum Wochenende sogar teilweise Schauer geben.
'On the weekend, [there] may even be showers in parts.'

While for the German corpus, the treebank existed first and the coreference annotations were added later, the ONTONOTES Corpus was designed to have annotations on the morpho-syntactic, syntactic, semantic, and dialogue level from the very beginning, for the languages English, Arabic, and Chinese (see section 5.1 for information about the named entity annotation in this corpus). An example of the annotation (in text form) is shown in (16). Note that the mention no. 4 is marked because it appears again later in the text.

(16) Although [₁ [₂ his] team] lost the World Series, [₂ [₁ [₅ San Francisco] Giants] owner Bob Lurie] hopes to have [₃ a new home for [₁ them]]. [₂ He] is an avid fan of a proposition on next week's ballot to help build [₃ a replacement for [₄ Candlestick Park]]. Small wonder, since [₂ he]'s asking [₅ San Francisco] taxpayers to sink up to $100 million into [₃ the new stadium]. As [₅ San Francisco] digs out from The Pretty Big One, opponents say the last thing [₅ the city] can afford is an expensive new stadium …

The annotation of anaphora and coreference concentrates on identity and appositive relations. As mentioned above, no singleton mentions are annotated, thus only expressions are annotated that enter into a referential relation. This means that expletive pronouns are not marked at all. Since no bound relation is annotated, such cases have to be treated within the identity relation. Here, the decision was made that generics are anaphoric to referring pronouns and other definite mentions, but not to generic nominals. Thus, we have an annotated relation in (17-a), but not in (17-b).[5] In the second example, the non-annotated relations are marked as starred to highlight potential relations, but in the corpus, there would be no marking.

(17) a. [₁ Meetings] are most productive when [₁ they] are held in the morning. [₁ Those meetings], however, generally have the worst attendance.
    b. Allergan Inc. said it received approval to sell the PhacoFlex intraocular lens, the first foldable silicone lens available for *[cataract surgery]. The lens' foldability enables it to be inserted in smaller incisions than are now possible for *[cataract surgery].

The restriction to identity and appositive relations also means that subset relations are not marked.

ONTONOTES is a large corpus that was created mainly as a resource for training computational linguistic analysis programs, such as for coreference resolution. For this reason, the annotations had to be economical, which generally means that the annotations are surface-oriented. This shows in the decisions not to mark singleton mentions and in the small set of relation types. There is another corpus, which is the opposite with regard to these design decisions: GNOME. The GNOME Corpus was created for the investigation into how discourse entities (such as mentions) are realized. For this goal, a very detailed annotation is required. Therefore, this corpus is small and covers only approximately 3,000 NPs. The coreference annotation in GNOME is based on the *MATE* scheme, a very broad annotation scheme designed to cover a wide range of languages.

Example (18) shows two sentences from the GNOME Corpus with the mentions marked in (18-a) and three relations in these sentences in (18-b)–(18-d). GNOME is annotated in stand-off XML, so this is how we also represent the relations. The first relation, shown in (18-b), relates mention 48, **Two of them**, to its antecedent, mention 46 **they**, and this relation is annotated as a subset. The second relation is an identity relation between **them** and **they**, and the third one is an element relation between **the third** and **them**. The latter is a case of *bridging* (see the next section for details).

(18) a. [$_{43}$ These three pieces] are [$_{44}$ examples of [$_{45}$ costume jewelry]], and [$_{46}$ they] come from [$_{47}$ the 1930's]. [$_{48}$ Two of [$_{49}$ them]] are [$_{50}$ buttons], and [$_{51}$ the third] is a [$_{52}$ dress clip, [$_{53}$ which] was used to fasten [$_{54}$ the straps of [$_{55}$ a dress]] at [$_{56}$ the neckline]].

   b. <!– ne48 subset ne46 –> <ante current='ne48' rel='subset'> <anchor antecedent='ne46'> </anchor> </ante>

   c. <!– ne49 ident ne46 –> <ante current='ne49' rel='ident'> <anchor antecedent='ne46'> </anchor> </ante>

   d. <!– Massimo: added bridge from 'the third' to 'them' –> <!– ne51 element ne49 –> <ante current='ne51' rel='element'> <anchor antecedent='ne49'> </anchor> </ante>

In addition to the coreference annotation, the GNOME Corpus contains a considerable amount of information about the mentions. Example (19) shows the information for mention 55 from the example in (18).

(19) <ne id="ne55" cat="a-np" per="per3" num="sing" gen="neut" gf="np-compl" deix="deix-no" lftype="term" onto="concrete" ani="inanimate" count="count-yes" generic="generic-yes" structure="atom" reference="quantified" loeb="sort"> a dress </ne>

In this example, cat describes the coarse category of the noun phrase, specifying the type of determiner and whether it contains a noun or a proper noun. This is followed by information about person, number, gender, grammatical function, deixis, the semantic type of the NP (lftype, here: the default value term vs quantifier or predicates), taxonomic type (onto), animacy, countability, genericity, structure (atomic or set), and the Löbner (loeb) category (here: sortal).

Note also that this annotation scheme is less well defined than other annotation schemes, for example for syntactic annotation. This is obvious from the comments in the annotations. One such comment is shown in (18-d), another comment is shown in (20).

(20) <!– Interesting here – the complementizer seems to behave more like the referent than like the predicate (but I annotated according the instructions anyway) –>

In sum, in this section, we introduced corpora annotated for the standard anaphora and coreference types. All the corpora discussed in this section annotate NP coreference, and most of them are restricted to identity relations. However, there are other, more complex types of coreference relations, and there are more general types of anaphora, namely event anaphora and abstract anaphora. These types will be discussed in the following section.

6.1.3 More Complex Types of Anaphora

The annotation of noun phrase anaphora and coreference, as shown in the previous section, can be performed reliably. However, there are other types of anaphora/coreference, which are much more difficult to define, and thus to annotate. In this section, we will discuss bridging phenomena and event anaphora before we approach abstract anaphora more generally.

6.1.3.1 Bridging Anaphora

One of these more complex types of anaphoric relations has already been mentioned in the previous section, *bridging anaphora* or simply *bridging*. In bridging, the anaphor and the antecedent are not related by an identity relation but rather more indirectly by different contiguity relations. These relations include set-element, part-of, and converse relations. An example of each of these relations respectively is given in (21).

(21) a. The [soccer team] left by bus, but [one player] came later. {set/element}
    b. [The protesters] brought posters and chanted slogans. [Some of them] even performed a dance routine. {part-of}
    c. Of our budget, we spent approximately [$85] on paint. [The remaining 15%] were used for pictures. {converse set}

Apart from the relations mentioned so far, which have a predefined semantic definition, there is another type that is more ad hoc, namely *other-anaphora*. By ad hoc, we mean that the relation is dependent on the context, for example, in **painting and his other hobbies**. Here, **hobbies** is not a pre-defined class, but rather a set that is defined by the interests of the person in question. Other-anaphora have an anaphor that starts with a lexical item such as **other**, which creates an ad hoc set-complement. The sets that are created by this type of anaphor are not generally recognized but rather introduced by the context. We show examples for other-anaphora in (22).[6] Unfortunately the only annotated data set (Markert and Nissim, 2005) does not seem to be available any more.

(22) a. In addition to [increasing costs] as a result of greater financial exposure for members, these measures could have [other, far-reaching repercussions].
    b. The ordinance, in Moon Township, prohibits locating [a group home for the handicapped] within a mile of [another such facility].

Bridging anaphora are often not annotated at all in corpora annotated for anaphora and coreference. If bridging is considered, it is restricted to a subset of phenomena. As mentioned above, TüBa-d/z annotates the subset relation. In the GNOME Corpus, we find set-element, set-subset, and generalized possession—for examples see (23). The annotators found that restricting the annotation greatly increased the consistency of the annotation in terms of the type of anaphora to which an example belongs.

(23) a. Dermovate Cream is a strong and rapidly effective treatment for [inflamed skin conditions] such as [exzema], [psoriasis], and [dermatitis]. {set-element}
      b. One or two times a day, after washing your hands, gently rub [the correct amount of cream] into the skin until it has all disappeared. For an adult: You should find that [two fingertips of cream] will treat both hands or one foot, … {set-subset}
      c. Remove one sachet from the box and tear [it] open at [the notch]. {generalized possession}

Another corpus that is annotated for bridging anaphora is ISNOTES. This corpus consists of 50 documents of the ONTONOTES Corpus and inherits all the annotations of the original corpus. It extends the annotations by a fine-grained annotation of information status and bridging relations. *Information status* is a concept that is closely related to anaphora. It describes to what degree a discourse entity has already been introduced into the discourse. ISNOTES distinguishes between *discourse-old*, *discourse-new*, and *mediated* entities or mentions (cf. section 6.2.1). A mention is discourse-old when it has been mentioned in discourse before, i.e. it is coreferent with a previous mention. Mediated mentions have not been introduced before but can be inferred from other entities or from world knowledge. All other entities are considered discourse-new. Mediated entities can be split into different categories, bridging anaphora being one of them. Examples of such bridging relations are shown in (24).[7]

(24) a. [Oranjemund, the mine headquarters], is a lonely corporate oasis of 9,000 residents. Jackals roam [the streets] at night.
      b. Initial steps were taken at [Poland's first environmental conference, which I attended last month]. … it was no accident that [participants] urged the free flow of information

Note that ISNOTES does not distinguish between different types of bridging relations, thus the two different underlying relations in the examples in (24) are not marked explicitly.

The PRAGUE DEPENDENCY TREEBANK (PDT) for Czech, whose syntactic annotation was introduced in section 4.6, is a dependency treebank with an additional layer of coreference annotations, similar to the German TüBa-d/z treebank. In contrast to the German treebank, however, the PDT annotates a wider range of bridging phenomena, including part-of and set-element relations. Additional relations are the object-individual function, contrast (which is not a bridging relation in the narrow sense), non-cospecifying explicit anaphora, and a category for the remainder of the phenomena (rest). Examples for the additional types are shown in (25).[8] As usual, the annotation is restricted to NP antecedents.

(25) a. Na přímou podporu podnikání vydá letos [stát] přibližně 1,8 procenta hrubého dom]ácího produktu. Tuto skutečnost jednoznačně konstatuje ministr hospodářství Karel Dyba v analýze, kterou předložil [vládě]. {object/individual}
The [state] will give about 1.8 percent of gross domestic product to direct business support this year. This fact is clearly stated by Economy Minister Karel Dyba in his analysis which he presented to the [government].

   b. Dnes, po rozdělení ČSFR, je jasné, že [osud ČR] bude stále více spojený s Německem a přes něj s Evropskou unií a [osud Slovenska] s Ruskem. {contrast}
Nowadays, after the split of Czechoslovakia, it is clear that [the fortune of the Czech Republic] will become more associated with Germany, further with the European Union, while the [fortune of Slovakia] will be more associated with Russia.

   c. "[Duha]?" Kněz přiložil prst [k tomu slovu], aby nezapomněl, kde skončil. {non-cospecifying explicit anaphora}
"[Rainbow]?" The priest put the finger [on this word] so that he didn't forget, where he stopped.

   d. V ČR bývají [prostitutky] zadržovány zpravidla jenom kvůli ověření totožnosti. Zákon o [prostituci] se u nás teprve připravuje. {rest}
In Czech Republic, [prostitutes] are usually controlled just for verification of identity. The law on [prostitution] is still being prepared.

There is another German corpus, the DIRNDL Corpus, which annotates bridging. DIRNDL is short for *Discourse Information Radio News Database for Linguistic Analysis*. As indicated by the name, the corpus is based on German radio news broadcasts, and the main level of analysis is information status, in terms of *discourse-new* and *given entities*. In addition to information status, the corpus also includes annotations for syntax and prosody for the transliterations of the approximately 3,000 sentences. In the corpus, there are also annotations of terms with regard to whether they are anaphoric, inferable, deictic, or discourse-new. Examples are shown in (26)–(28), the first two showing examples of the given relation, and the last one an example of three bridging relations. Figure 6.3 shows the bridging relations when integrated into the syntactic trees.

(26) [₁ Im Irak sind erneut fünf US-Soldaten durch Bomben getötet worden.] [₁ Die Anschläge] hätten sich in der Provinz Dijala sowie im Nordwesten Bagdads ereignet, gab die US-Armee bekannt. {R-GIVEN}
'[₁ In Iraq, five more US soldiers have been killed by bombs.] [₁ The assaults] happened in the province Dijala as well as in the north of Baghdad, the US Army disclosed.'

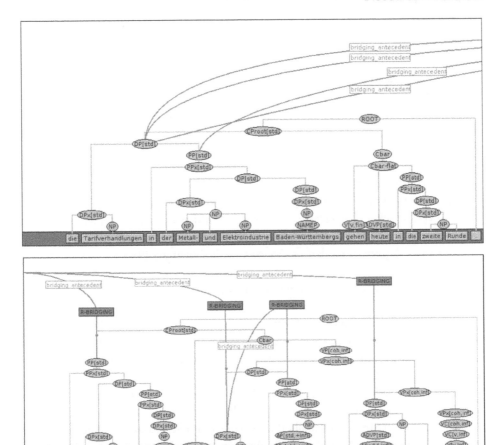

Figure 6.3 The annotation of bridging relations and syntactic structure in DIRNDL.

(27) Der UNO-Generalsekretär kam aus Ramallah, wo [₁ er gestern mit Palästinenserpräsident Abbas konferiert hatte]. [₁ Dabei] hatte Ban die neue Einheitsregierung unter Ministerpräsident Hanija von der Hamas aufgerufen, das Existenzrecht Israels anzuerkennen. {R-GIVEN}

'The UN general secretary came from Ramallah, where [₁ he had conferred with Palestinian president Abbas yesterday]. [₁ During that], Ban had appealed to the new unity government under president Hanjia from Hamas to recognize Israel's very right of existence.'

(28) [₁ Die Tarifverhandlungen [₂ in der Metall- und Elektroindustrie Baden-Württembergs]] gehen heute in die zweite Runde. [₁ Bei den Gesprächen in Sindelfingen] wollen [₂ die Arbeitgeber] [₂ nach eigenem Bekunden] [₁ das bundesweit erste Angebot] vorlegen. {R-BRIDGING}

'[₁ The collective negotiations in [₂ the metal and electrical industries of Baden-Württemberg]] are starting the second round today. [₁ At the talks in Sindelfingen,]

[$_2$ the entrepreneurs] will, [$_2$ by their own account], provide [$_1$ the first offer nationwide].'

One interesting factor of the DIRNDL Corpus is that the antecedents are not necessarily always noun phrases. The examples in (26) and (27) show a clause and prepositional phrases as antecedents. To our knowledge, this makes this corpus the most general in terms of the type of antecedents. ONTONOTES, as described above, also goes beyond noun phrase antecedents, but it is restricted to verbal antecedents.

6.1.3.2 Event Anaphora

So far, we have concentrated on types of anaphora for which the antecedent is a noun phrase. *Event anaphora* is concerned with cases in which an anaphor refers to an event rather than an entity previously mentioned in the text. Such antecedents are generally expressed as verb phrases or clauses. An example is shown in (29).

(29) He [went to the movies] yesterday and enjoyed [it] immensely.

Event anaphora are difficult to annotate because annotators find it difficult to decide on the exact bounds of the event. For example, in example (29), it would be possible to include **yesterday** into the event. For this reason, annotations for event anaphora are rare, and mostly restricted.

One way of restricting this type of annotation is to annotate only the *event triggers* instead of the whole event. An event trigger is the lexical element in a sentence that best describes the event. This is normally the verb, for example, **go** in (29), but the trigger can also be realized as a gerund, a nominalization, or an adjective, as shown in (30).[9]

(30) a. A bomb [exploded], [killing] 14 passengers.
     b. [The bombing] lasted for five minutes.
     c. [Panic-stricken] residents were seen running for cover.

The ONTONOTES Corpus is one corpus in which a subset of event anaphora are annotated. In addition to NPs, the annotation in ONTONOTES is restricted to single verbs, which corresponds to a subset of the event triggers discussed above. Note that the nominal event triggers are also captured via the standard NP annotation, but they are not marked specifically as events. We show two examples from the corpus in (31).

(31) a. so he [$_{118}$ had] a good smile nice teeth. Yes I would have to say [$_{118}$ that] yes.
     b. The judge scheduled to preside over his trial was [$_{160}$ removed] from the case today. DeLay's attorney heads off [$_{160}$ the recusal] because they questioned the judge's impartiality since he had contributed to Democratic causes.

There is another corpus, NP4E, which was annotated in a project that had as its goal to develop methodology for NP and event anaphora within and across documents. For this reason, the corpus is small, consisting of 16 texts that have been annotated for events (for NP coreference, there are more texts). However, four of these texts have been annotated by two annotators, and both versions are available. In order to make the annotation of events feasible, event triggers are annotated. In contrast to ONTONOTES, all event triggers described above are marked. However, the annotation is restricted to a set of specific event types related to the domain of terrorism and security: ATTACK, DEFEND, INJURE, DIE, and CONTACT. An example from the corpus for the type CONTACT is shown in (32).

(32) Talks to end Peru's three-month hostage standoff appeared to be moving forward again on Sunday after two neutral mediators [$_1$ met] with the Marxist rebels holding 72 people at the Japanese ambassador's home. Members of an independent guarantor's commission, Archbishop Juan Luis Cipriani and Canadian ambassador Anthony Vincent, [$_2$ met] the hostage-takers inside the besieged residence for about 90 minutes.

For all event types, *event arguments* are specified in NP4E. Thus, the event ATTACK has 3 participant slots (attacker, target, means) and 2 attribute slots (time, place). The annotation guidelines specify a two-stage annotation process. In the first pass through a text, triggers are marked and annotated with information about trigger type, polarity, modality, and tense. In the second pass, event categories, arguments, and coreference are annotated.

6.1.3.3 Abstract Anaphora

Abstract anaphora, also called *indirect anaphora* or *discourse deixis*, is concerned with cases of anaphora in which the antecedent is an abstract entity. In case this abstract entity is an event, we speak of event anaphora, as discussed above. However, there are other possible types of antecedents, including processes, states, facts, and propositions. Anaphors are generally either demonstrative pronouns, such as **this** and **that**, or the third person personal pronoun **it**. Since the type of the antecedent is somewhat difficult to determine, there is a test: The annotator checks whether these pronouns can be replaced by complete noun phrases, such as **this situation**.

The first annotation effort with regard to abstract anaphora is work by Donna Byron, who looked at (third person) personal pronouns and demonstrative pronouns. In this project, two small corpora were annotated, parts of the TRAINS93 Corpus and the *Boston University News Corpus* (BUR). The first corpus consists of transcriptions of spontaneous dialogues in a collaborative problem-solving setting; the second corpus contains transcripts of news items transmitted by a radio station. For ease of reference, we will refer to the whole set of annotations as the BYRON CORPUS.

The BYRON Corpus is annotated in the *SGML* markup language. The two sub-corpora differ somewhat in their annotation schemes since they have different characteristics and were annotated in sequence. In the transition from the TRAINS93 Corpus to the BUR Corpus, the lessons learned from the first set of annotations were integrated into the second set of guidelines. Additionally, the guidelines had to be adapted to phenomena that occurred in the news monologues but not in the dialogues. An example of the annotations in TRAINS93 is shown in (33-a), with only the text repeated in (33-b).

(33) a. <UTT> <UTTNUM> utt73 </UTTNUM> <SPEAKER> s </SPEAKER> <TEXT> okay/AC so/CC_D that/DP was/BED so/CC_D we'll/PRP^MD get/VB to/PREP Dansville/NNP about/PREP four/CD_LOW a.m./NN now/RB_D the/DT other/JJ problem/NN is/BEZ is/BEZ that/SC if/SC we/PRP have/HAVEP this/DT train/NN so/CC_D we/PRP also/RB have/HAVE <LA PronID="3341"> engine/NN E/NNP one/CD_LOW that's/WP^BEZ going/VBG back/RB and/CC forth/RB</LA> right/AC</TEXT> </UTT> <UTT> <UTTNUM> utt74 </UTTNUM> <SPEAKER> u </SPEAKER> <TEXT> oh/UH_D right/AC <PRON ID="3341" ref="the fact the engine e1 is going back and forth" level="m" syntax="s" LAform="non-np" LAlevel="m" LAsyntax="n" LAdistance="a"> **that**'s/DP^BEZ </PRON> true/JJ</TEXT> </UTT>

   b. okay so that was so we'll get to Dansville about four a.m. now the other problem is is that if we have this train so we also have engine one that's going back and forth right
      oh right that's true

Annotations delineate individual utterances (<UTT>), give them a unique identifier (e.g. <UTTNUM> utt73 </UTTNUM>) and record the identity of the speaker (e.g. <SPEAKER> s </SPEAKER>). All words are annotated with fine-grained part-of-speech (POS) tags, and anaphors are marked via the <PRON... > tag. They receive an ID, which links them to the antecedent (called *linguistic antecedent*). Thus, the anaphor **that**, marked in bold in (33-a), is linked via the ID 3341 to its antecedent **engine one that's going back and forth**, which is marked with the <LA... > tag. The annotation of the anaphor includes a description of the real world referent (REF), information about the level of embedding of the anaphor (level), its syntax, as well as information about the antecedent. Unfortunately, no information about the relation between anaphor and antecedent exists in this corpus.

In the BUR Corpus, one of the major changes is that relations between antecedent (called *linguistic anchor*, LA) and the referent are annotated. Byron (2003) reports that these relations were not predetermined before the annotation started, but were determined based on the phenomena encountered in the text and based on the discussions between annotators. The following relations were used in the end: coreference, inferable, subset, pronouns refer to the KIND of the LA, conclusion supported by the LA, metonymy, complement set, outcome of the situation described in LA, and no LA. Examples of anaphors are shown in (34). Note that the corpus does not contain the complete text but rather only the anaphors and their antecedents. However, the offset marked in the XML tags allows users with access to the full corpus to locate the mentions.

(34) a. <PRON OFFSET="434" Ref="the fact that public transportation is not a high priority" Rel="inf" level="m" syntax="do" LA="public transportation is still not a high priority" reasonForNoLA="0" LAform="non-NP" LAlevel="d" LAsyntax="do" LAdistance="p">that </PRON>

b. <PRON OFFSET="203" Ref="moving the votes" Rel="action" level="m" syntax="s" LA="move the few votes" reasonForNoLA="0" LAform="non-NP" LAlevel="d" LAsyntax="oth" LAdistance="a">That </PRON>

c. <PRON OFFSET="243" Ref="The uncertainity of how Volk feels about the tax" Rel="conclusion which has been supported by several events listed in previous discourse" level="m" syntax="s" LA="none" reasonForNoLA="0" LAform="none" LAlevel="none" LAsyntax="none" LAdistance="none">this </PRON>

d. <PRON OFFSET="195" Ref="the increase in state funding necessary to qualify for federal funds" Rel="outcome" level="m" syntax="s" LA="states … treatment" reasonForNoLA="0" LAform="non-NP" LAlevel="m" LAsyntax="oth" LAdistance="a">that </PRON>

Another corpus in which such abstract anaphora are annotated consists of a subset of the EUROPARL Corpus. EUROPARL is a parallel corpus (see section 1.3) which provides translations from transcriptions of the debates of the European Parliament. The subset used for annotating abstract anaphora contains texts from the language pairs German-English and English-German, currently 100 texts per language pair. For ease of reference, we will call this corpus the EUROPARL-PRON Corpus. This corpus is annotated for the German demonstrative pronouns **dies**, **das**, and the personal pronoun **es** as well as their translations into English, **this**, **that**, **it**, **so**, and **as**. In (35), we show examples from the English-German language pair. For readability, we only show the English original.

(35) a. There will also be evidence of the fact that [we have taken heed of the representations made in this House particularly in the Committee on Budgetary Control], and [that] is significant in the use of ex ante visas in Directorates-General.

b. [Content issues will affect infrastructure regulation]. Where [this] occurs, the Member State should be free to set its own priorities.

c. It is also important to try to [correct the situation where things have gone wrong], but in [so] doing not to exaggerate [it] in such a way that …

Note that since the corpus contains annotations for language pairs, it also allows investigations into how such abstract anaphors are treated in translations, for example, whether the translation also contains abstract anaphora. For example, the **so** in (35-c) is translated as **dabei** in German, as shown in (36). However, currently the annotation of the translations is restricted to annotations of the anaphors and their aligned word in the source language.

(36) Es ist auch wichtig, korrigierend und verbessernd einzugreifen, aber [es] darf [dabei] nicht in einer Weise übertrieben werden, die …

As we have seen in this section, anaphora and coreference are mostly well-understood phenomena, but the question of how to annotate them is far from solved. While we have standards for the annotation of definite noun phrases, the situation is less clear for more complex phenomena, such as event anaphora. In the next section, we will look at information structure, where the situation is even less clear, even in linguistic terms.

6.2 Information Structure

Information structure is concerned with the way in which a sentence is presented to the recipient. Thus, once we know the content of a sentence, we need to decide in which way we want to structure it. This structure depends on the previous context. Important considerations are which part of the information is new to the recipient, but also which elements serve as the relation to the previous content because coherent texts tend to not switch topics in every sentence, but rather add more information to the established topic in the course of the text. This is also called *information packaging*.

Example (37) describes the same situation in five different ways; capitalized words are stressed. The first sentence, which is in canonical word order, could be part of an account of what happened during a day. The second sentence contradicts a previous assumption that the speaker's computer was working fine, etc.

(37) a. My computer stopped working.
    b. My computer STOPPED working.
    c. It was my computer that stopped working.
    d. It was MY computer that stopped working.
    e. What happened was that my computer stopped working.

In each sentence, another part of the information is highlighted, i.e. every sentence has a different syntactic structure and a different information structure. Thus, it becomes clear that information structure is related to syntactic structure on the one hand and to the communicative side of language on the other hand. An important concept in information structure is *presupposition*, which is concerned with implicit assumptions that are part of the common knowledge of participants in discourse. Thus, the sentence in (37-a) has the presupposition that the speaker owns a computer. This sentence would be considered strange if it was known that the speaker does not have a computer. Other important concepts are the contrasts of *focus/ground*, *givenness/newness*, and *topic/comment*. Focus is concerned with the part of the information that is especially interesting in the sentence, givenness indicates that the information was mentioned before, and topic is the part about which the information is given. Another contrast that is often used is *theme/rheme*, which is also related to the given/new contrast.

However, there are many different interpretations of information structure in linguistics. As a consequence, it is very difficult to operationalize the concepts used in linguistic analysis to devise an annotation scheme. For this reason, many annotation projects resort to the annotation of information status instead, which is better defined. Below, we will look at annotation effort in both areas.

6.2.1 Annotation of Information Status

Information status is an approximation of information structure. It focuses on referential expressions in terms of whether they are old or new. As a consequence, the annotation of information status is directly related to annotation of anaphora and coreference, as already shown in section 6.1.3 with regard to the German DIRNDL Corpus. The most well-known annotation scheme distinguishes between discourse-old, mediated, and discourse-new entities/information. When an entity is introduced into the discourse, it is discourse-new. Thus, it also does not have an antecedent. An entity is discourse-old if it is definite and has an antecedent in the preceding discourse. Such entities are also sometimes called evoked. Mediated entities have not been introduced in discourse before but can be inferred from other entities or from world knowledge. Such entities are also sometimes called inferable. Examples are shown in (38).

(38) a. My brother bought [$_{new}$ a new car].
   b. She brought [$_{new}$ a chicken dish] to the party.
   c. I met my new student yesterday. [$_{old}$ This bright kid] is taking the most challenging classes.
   d. [$_{old}$ Stupid me] bought a book I already own.
   e. I went to work in my car, and [$_{mediated}$ the front left tire] had a slow leak.

One corpus that annotates discourse status is the NXT SWITCHBOARD Corpus. The original SWITCHBOARD Corpus is a collection of spontaneous telephone conversations of speakers of American English. The NXT SWITCHBOARD Corpus is an effort to integrate different annotations of the SWITCHBOARD Corpus into a unified XML representation, including annotations of syntax, information structure, dialogue acts, and prosody. The corpus uses three labels for the annotation of information status: old, med, and new. For old and mediated categories, there is a further split into more specific categories, indicating whether the entity is a pronoun, a bound pronoun, etc. A full list of these labels is shown in table 6.1.[10] An example of the whole annotation is shown in figure 6.4.[11] In this figure, there are two entities that are annotated for information status: the noun phrases **the government** and **it**. The former is annotated as mediated-general, meaning that it is generally known. The latter entity is annotated as discourse-old, which means it has an antecedent in the preceding context.

We have already mentioned above that the German DIRNDL Corpus has mainly been annotated for information status; the bridging annotations described in section 6.1.3 were secondary to the information status annotation. In short, DIRNDL is a corpus of German radio news broadcasts. The annotation of information status is based on a hierarchical annotation scheme, which first distinguishes between two different levels

Table 6.1: The information status annotation in NXT SWITCHBOARD.

Type	Value	Description
old	ident	anaphoric reference to a previously mentioned entity
	relative	relative pronoun
	generic	generic pronoun
	ident_generic	generic possessive pronoun
	general	I and **you**
	event	reference to a previously mentioned VP
	none	not specified
med	bound	bound pronoun
	general	generally known, e.g. **the sun**
	event	relates to a previously mentioned VP
	aggregation	reference to previously mentioned co-ordinated NPs
	func_value	refers to the values of a previously mentioned function, e.g. **centigrade**
	set	subset, superset or member of the same set as a previously mentioned entity
	part	part-whole relation for physical objects
	poss	intra-phrasal possessive relation (pre- and post-nominal) that is not part
	situation	part of a situation set up by a previous entity
	none	not specified

of givenness (or novelty), *lexical givenness* (L-given) and *referential givenness* (R-given). The R-level characterizes referential nouns or prepositional phrases. For instance, a phrase is R-given if it refers to the same referent as some antecedent in the text. In the same vein, a phrase is R-new if it introduces a new referent, which cannot be related to the previous context. R-new categories are normally realized by indefinite phrases. In contrast to the R-level, the L-level is not concerned with referents but with lexical items. The target instances of this annotation level are content words and other non-referential (parts of) phrases. An L-given element is basically a word (or *lexeme*) that has occurred in the previous text. Figure 6.5 is an English example to illustrate the two different levels.[12] The second mention of **man** is L-given but R-new, because it repeats the lexeme **man** but refers to a different referent than the first mention.

Additionally, the annotation scheme is recursive in that it starts by annotating the smallest categories, i.e. words, and then increasingly larger syntactic constituents. Figure 6.6 shows an example of this recursive annotation.[13] In addition to the already

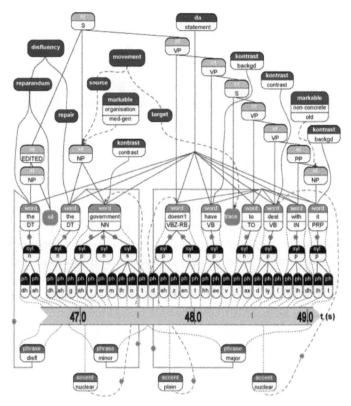

Figure 6.4 An example from the NXT SWITCHBOARD Corpus.

A	man	came in.	Another	man	left.
	L-NEW			L-GIVEN	
R-NEW			R-NEW		

Figure 6.5 Two levels of givenness/novelty: lexical and referential.

Ein	starkes	Erdbeben	hat	Zentral-Japan	erschüttert.
a	strong	earthquake	has	central Japan	shaken
	(AP) L-NEW	(N) L-NEW		(NP) L-NEW	(V) L-NEW
	(NP) L-NEW			(DP) R-UNUSED	
(DP) R-NEW			(VP) L-NEW		
(IP) L-NEW					

Figure 6.6 An example for the annotation of information status in DIRNDL.

familiar labels new and old, the annotation scheme uses a third label, *unused* to mark uniquely identifiable, definite entities when they are used for the first time in a text. Thus, **Zentral-Japan** is annotated as an entity that is known to all discourse participants without having to be introduced.

As mentioned above, the recursive annotation follows the syntactic annotation. Figure 6.7 shows the sentence from Figure 6.6 with the syntactic and the information status annotation.[14]

6.2.2 Annotation of Information Structure

In this section, we review corpora with annotations that go beyond information status. First, we return to the NXT SWITCHBOARD Corpus. While the annotation mostly focuses on information status, there is one type of annotation in this corpus that falls within the area of information structure proper: NXT SWITCHBOARD annotates for *kontrast/ background*. Kontrast marks salient words in a sentence; it is further divided into the categories listed in Table 6.2.[15] The annotation in Figure 6.4 also shows examples of the contrast annotation, the words **government** and **deal** are assigned a contrastive label while **have** and **it** are assigned the label for background information.

There is also a German corpus that is annotated for information structure: the POTSDAM COMMENTARY CORPUS (PCC). The PCC is a collection of 220 German newspaper commentaries from the online version of the German newspaper Märkische Allgemeine Zeitung. The corpus is annotated for POS tagging, morphology, and syntax

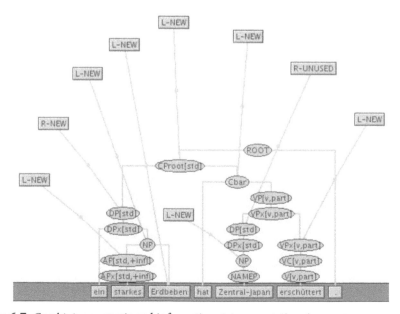

Figure 6.7 Combining syntactic and information status annotations in DIRNDL.

Table 6.2 The kontrast annotation in NXT SWITCHBOARD.

Type	Value	Description
kontrast	correction	corrects or clarifies another word or NP just used by the other speaker
	contrastive	contrasts with another word or NP used in the discourse that is semantically related to the current word, such that they could both belong to a plausible set
	subset	a member of a more general set mentioned in the context
	adverbial	the focus of a focus-sensitive adverb, i.e. **only, even, always, especially, just, also, too**
	answer	fills an open proposition (such as wh-focus) set up by the context (no explicit question required)
	other	salient in comparison or contrast to another element evoked by the context, but not explicitly mentioned (only used if no other categories apply)
background		not kontrastive, word either not salient, or no implication of alternative sets
nonapplic		not marked for kontrast status

Table 6.3 The information structure annotation in PCC.

Layer	Tag	Description
information status	giv	given
	acc	accessible
	new	new
	idiom	idiomatic expression
topic	ab	aboutness topic
	fs	frame setting topic
focus	nf	new-information-focus
	cf	contrastive focus

following the annotation scheme of the TIGER Corpus (see section 4.5). It is further annotated for coreference, information structure, discourse structure, discourse connectives, and illocutions. We will focus on the annotation of information structure here.

On the information structure level, PCC annotates topic and focus in addition to information status. The annotation distinguishes between the categories shown in Table 6.3.[16] We show an excerpt from a news commentary including its annotation in (39).

(39) [$_{Topic\_fs}$ Als 1999] [$_{Topic\_ab\ IS\_new}$ die im Rahmen der Dorferneuerung neu gestaltete Radeweger Ablage inklusive [$_{IS\_acc}$ Seebrücke]] [$_{IS\_nf}$ mit [$_{IS\_idiom}$ viel Pomp] einge-weiht wurde, war klar: Da fehlt noch was]. Wer [$_{IS\_new}$ die Infrastruktur] für [$_{IS\_new}$ den Wassertourismus] vorantreiben will, darf nicht nur bis zum [$_{IS\_idiom}$ nächsten Steg] denken. [$_{Topic\_ab\ IS\_acc}$ Sanitäre Anlagen] [$_{IS\_nf}$ gehören heute zum Standard [$_{IS\_acc}$ großer Liegeplätze]].

'[$_{Topic\_fs}$ When in 1999], [$_{IS\_new}$ the Radeweger Ablage, which was refashioned as part of the program for rural renewal, including the [$_{IS\_acc}$ Seebrücke]], was inaugurated [$_{IS\_nf}$ with [$_{IS\_idiom}$ lots of pomp], it was obvious: something is missing]. Whoever wants to promote [$_{IS\_new}$ the infrastructure] for [$_{IS\_new}$ water tourism], cannot stop the process at [$_{IS\_idiom}$ the next jetty]. [$_{Topic\_ab\ IS\_acc}$ Sanitary facilities] [$_{IS\_nf}$ are part of today's standard of [$_{IS\_acc}$ large moorings]].'

We have already discussed the categories for information status previously. But we need to add that PCC has an additional label for idiomatic expressions, which do not have a clearly defined information status. The annotation scheme additionally distinguishes between two types of topic: The *aboutness topic* specifies the focused entity—typically these entities are fronted in sentences; the *frame setting topic* defines the time or the location of an event. An example for an aboutness topic is the subject **Sanitäre Anlagen** in (39). An example for a frame setting topic is the temporal phrase **Als 1999**. On the focus layer, the annotation scheme distinguishes between a *new information focus* and a *contrastive focus*.

As we have seen in this section, the annotation of information structure is carried out on the sentence level. In the next section, we will look at annotations that go beyond the sentence level: discourse relations.

6.3 Discourse Relations

In the preceding sections of this chapter we saw that we often need context for fully understanding the meaning of a sentence. In this section, we will go one step further and look at the meaning of textual units that are themselves larger than just one clause or sentence. There are two important concepts for the analysis of such larger units: *discourse relations*, which can be signaled in the text by means of *discourse connectives*. A discourse relation is an abstract concept. It is an interpretation of how two or more propositions are related to each other. For example, two propositions can be related to each other in terms of temporal sequencing, such that we understand that one event took place after the other one. We show examples in (40-a) and (41-a). Another common interpretation is that two propositions are related by a cause-effect relation, as in (40-b) and (41-b). The examples show that the concept of discourse connectives denotes a pragmatic function that can be realized by different types of parts of speech with different syntactic functions. The underlined connectives in (40) are subordinating conjunctions, the ones in (41) adverbs with adverbial functions.

(40) a. Meryl went rock climbing in the mountains, after she had taken a couple of indoor lessons.

    b. Theo was exhausted because he had run to the university.

(41) a. Meryl went rock climbing in the mountains. She had taken a couple of indoor lessons before.

    b. Theo had run to the university. Therefore, he was exhausted.

It is important to note that there is no one-to-one mapping from discourse connectives to discourse relations and vice versa. For example, **since** is ambiguous between a temporal and a causal interpretation, among others. We also know that causal relations are not only signaled by **since**, but also by other conjunctions, such as **because** and **therefore**, as shown in (40-b) and (41-b) above.

In the literature, there is no consensus about the actual set of discourse relations and how many of them are needed. Similarly, there is some discussion about the nature of units that are related by them. However, a quasi-standard has been established, referring to these units as *elementary discourse units* (EDUs).

Below, we will introduce two corpus-related efforts of analyzing discourse relations, which have influenced many other projects, also for other languages.

6.3.1 Penn Discourse TreeBank

The annotation of the *Penn Discourse Treebank* (PDTB) adds a pragmatic layer to the syntactically annotated Wall Street Journal section of the PENN TREEBANK. The current release, PDTB-2.0, comprises 40,600 tokens of pragmatically motivated relations in 2,177 files of the WSJ corpus.

The underlying idea of the annotation is to treat discourse connectives as discourse-level predicates, similar to the way in which verbs are treated as clause-level predicates. Also, in the same way in which verbs generally take noun phrases or prepositional phrases as arguments, discourse connectives take clauses or sentences as their arguments (see (42)).[17] The formatting of the examples follows the way in which examples are presented in the PDTB guidelines: The connective is underlined, the argument that appears in the clause that is syntactically bound to the connective is labeled Arg2 and set in bold, and the other argument is labeled Arg1 and printed in italics.

(42) <u>Since</u> [$_{Arg2}$ **McDonald's menu prices rose this year**], [$_{Arg1}$*the actual decline may have been more*].

In the annotation of discourse connectives, we distinguish between *explicit* and *implicit connectives*. Explicit connectives are realized in the sentence while implicit connectives are not (see below). In PDTB-2.0, only a well-defined set of parts of speech is annotated as explicit connectives. In particular, these are subordinating conjunctions (e.g. **since, because, when, although**—for an example see (42)); coordinating conjunctions (e.g. **but, and, or, nor**—see (43)); and adverbial phrases and prepositional phrases functioning as adverbials (e.g. **as a result, for example, however, otherwise, then**—see (44)).

(43) [$_{Arg1}$ *The House has voted to raise the ceiling to $3.1 trillion,*] <u>but</u> [$_{Arg2}$ **the Senate isn't expected to act until next week at the earliest.**]

(44) [$_{Arg1}$ *In the past, the socialist policies of the government strictly limited the size of new steel mills, petrochemical plants, car factories and other industrial concerns to conserve resources and restrict the profits businessmen could make.*] <u>As a result,</u> [$_{Arg2}$ **industry operated out of small, expensive, highly inefficient industrial units.**]

Elementary discourse units mostly consist of clauses. If necessary, an argument can also span multiple sentences or discontinuous strings. However, the annotation of PDTB is guided by a Minimality Principle, according to which only as many clauses and/ or sentences should be included in an argument selection as are minimally required and sufficient for the interpretation of the relation. Other text that seems relevant but not necessary for the interpretation is annotated as *supplementary information* (Sup1, Sup2)—see (45). In PDTB-2.0, each connective is related to maximally two arguments.

(45) ($_{Sup1}$ Workers described "clouds of blue dust") *that hung over parts of the factory,* <u>even though</u> **exhaust fans ventilated the area.**

So far, we have looked at the annotation units consisting of connectives and their arguments; now we want to look at the interpretation of these units. Similar to the annotation of word senses or other semantic classes that have been introduced in Chapter 5, connectives are labeled with a pragmatic sense. Figure 6.8 gives a taxonomic overview over the discourse relations annotated in PDTB.[18] There are four major classes of relations: TEMPORAL, CONTINGENCY, COMPARISON, and EXPANSION, which are further subclassified into more specific types and subtypes. The annotation manual reports that in PDTB-2.0, 111 distinct senses are recorded for explicit connectives if all sub-distinctions are taken into account.

We use the class of TEMPORAL relations to illustrate the annotation. It is realized by two types: Synchronous, which means that Arg1 and Arg2 are not temporally ordered but overlapping as in (46), and Asynchronous, which indicates a temporal ordering between Arg1 and Arg2. The latter is further subclassified into two subtypes: Precedence, which is used when the situation in Arg1 precedes the situation described in Arg2 (see (47)), and Succession, which is assigned otherwise (see (48)).

(46) *Most oil companies,* <u>when</u> **they set exploration and production budgets for this year,** *forecast revenue of $15 for each barrel of crude produced.* {TEMPORAL:Synchrony}

(47) But a Soviet bank here would be crippled unless Moscow found a way to settle the $188 million debt, *which was lent to the country's short-lived democratic Kerensky government* <u>before</u> **the Communists seized power in 1917.** {TEMPORAL:Asynchronous:precedence}

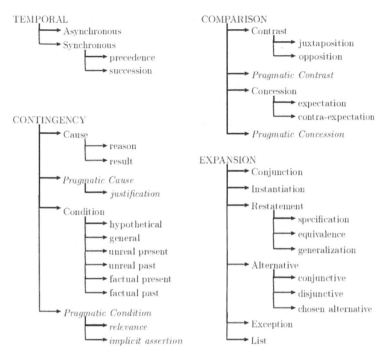

Figure 6.8 Discourse relations in the *Penn Discourse Treebank*: CLASS–Type–subtype. Pragmatic types are set in italics.

(48) No matter who owns PS of New Hampshire, <u>after</u> **it emerges from bankruptcy proceedings** *its rates will be among the highest in the nation,* he said. {TEMPORAL: Asynchronous:succession}

The hierarchical organization of the sense relations allows the annotators to choose an annotation level with which they are comfortable. If they cannot disambiguate a sense into its subsenses, then they assign the more general sense. An example of such an ambiguous case is given in (49). Since the annotators could not derive from the context (or their world knowledge) whether the events described in Arg1 and Arg2 are ordered or overlapping, they only assigned the class label TEMPORAL without type information.[19]

(49) *Fujitsu Ltd.'s top executive took the unusual step of publicly apologizing for his company's making bids of just one yen for several local government projects,* <u>while</u> **computer rival NEC Corp. made a written apology for indulging in the same practice.** {TEMPORAL}

The same method was applied in consolidating the final annotation based on annotations by two annotators: if the two annotators disagreed on the type/subtype, the more general sense was assigned, assuming that the instance is in fact ambiguous between the two interpretations. In cases of ambiguity between types of different classes, mixed labels were assigned—for example, the label reason/TEMPORAL was assigned to one instance of **as**.

To illustrate the annotation with a second sense relation, we will have a look at the type Concession of the class COMPARISON. Concession is defined as a relation between two arguments, when one argument describes a situation that causes another situation, and the other argument asserts or implies that this situation does not hold. For example, in (50), Arg2 (in bold) asserts that the index was indicating a slowing economy. Slowing economies normally cause recessions. This is why the reader expects that there is a recession. However, Arg1 (in italics) denies this expectation by asserting that the index does not signal an imminent recession. PDTB specifies two subtypes of Concession depending on whether it is Arg1 or Arg2 that creates the expectation or denies it respectively. If it is Arg2 that creates the expectation, as in (50), the subtype is expectation, otherwise it is called contra-expectation, as in (51).

(50) <u>Although</u> **the purchasing managers' index continues to indicate a slowing economy**, *it isn't signaling an imminent recession*, said Robert Bretz, chairman of the association's survey committee and director of materials management at Pitney Bowes Inc., Stamford, Conn. {COMPARISON:Concession:expectation}

(51) *The Texas oilman has acquired a 26.2% stake valued at more than $1.2 billion in an automotive-lighting company, Koito Manufacturing Co.* <u>But</u> **he has failed to gain any influence at the company**. {COMPARISON:Concession:contra-expectation}

When looking at Figure 6.8, we observe that some of the relations are set in italics. These are pragmatic relations in the sense that at least for one of the arguments, it is not its literal meaning that is relevant for the interpretation but its pragmatic use. Example (52-b) shows this. It is a variant of (40) (here repeated as (52-a)).[20] While in (52-a), it is the running that causes Theo to be exhausted, in (52-b) it is not the breath grasping that causes Theo to be exhausted. Instead, the author takes it as evidence for her reasoning about Theo's state. In other words, the fact that Theo is grasping for breath causes her to think that Theo is in a state of exhaustion.

(52) a. Theo was exhausted <u>because</u> he had run to the university.
     b. Theo was exhausted <u>because</u> he was grasping for breath.

Discourse relations do not always need to be signaled by an explicit discourse connective. For example, causal relations can be understood implicitly, as in (53), where the second sentence gives an explanation for why the first sentence should hold true. Note that this is another case of a pragmatic reasoning, similar to (52-b) above.

(53) Mrs Yeargin is lying. They found students in an advanced class a year earlier who said she gave them similar help.

Corpus studies show that in running text, in fact, only a fraction of the relations is expressed overtly by discourse connectives. For example, in the RST DISCOURSE TREEBANK, a selection of 385 Wall Street Journal articles from the PENN TREEBANK (see section 6.3.2), only about 26 percent (61 out of 238) Contrast relations between adjacent sentences are signaled by explicit connectives. This is why the annotation of PDTB also includes marking implicit discourse connectives, based on the same set of discourse relations as for explicit connectives. In addition to providing the discourse relations, the annotators are asked to fill in an appropriate connective. For example, the annotation of (53) is shown in (54). The subtype justification is used since Arg1 expresses a claim and Arg2 provides justification for this claim and there is no causal influence between the two situations.

(54) *Mrs Yeargin is lying.* <u>Implicit</u> = BECAUSE **They found students in an advanced class a year earlier who said she gave them similar help.** {CONTINGENCY:Pragmatic Cause:justification}

There is one exception to the annotation of implicit connectives: Sometimes, a discourse relation is signaled by "non-connective" expressions, such as a major reason in Arg2 of (55).[21] Such alternative lexicalizations are marked in terms of an AltLex relation in PDTB.

(55) *But a strong level of investor withdrawals is much more unlikely this time around,* fund managers said. <u>ALTLEX</u>= **A major reason is that investors already have sharply scaled back their purchases of stock funds since Black Monday.** (CONTINGENCY:Cause:reason)

An additional type of relation in PDTB is entity-based coherence, EntRel, which involves anaphoric and coreference relations between Arg1 and Arg2, as described in section 6.1. In this case, there is a coreference relation between **Hale Milgrim** and **Mr. Milgrim**, which also marks the discourse relation between the two sentences. EntRel is a sort of last-resort annotation in the treebank because it is only annotated if there is no explicit connective, and no implicit connective can be inserted either.

(56) *Hale Milgrim, 41 years old, senior vice president, marketing at Elecktra Entertainment Inc., was named president of Capitol Records Inc., a unit of this entertainment concern.* <u>EntRel</u> **Mr. Milgrim succeeds David Berman, who resigned last month.**

Finally, there is a label noRel, which is used if establishing a discourse relation between two adjacent sentences within a paragraph in terms of explicit or implicit connectives or alternative lexicalization is not possible, and if there is no entity relation between the two sentences.

Table 6.4 Distribution of relation types in PDTB-2.0

PDTB Relation	Explanation	Frequency
Explicit	(explicit connective)	18,459
Implicit	(implicit connective)	16,224
AltLex	(alternative lexicalization)	624
EntRel	(entity-based relation)	5,210
NoRel	(no pragmatic relation)	254
Total		**40,600**

To sum up this subsection, Table 6.4 summarizes the distribution of label types in PDTB-2.0.[22] The PDTB-style of annotating discourse connectives as discourse predicates has been adopted by several other projects, for example, the TURKISH DISCOURSE BANK and the GERMAN POTSDAM COMMENTARY CORPUS (see section 6.3.2).

6.3.2 Discourse Relations Reference Corpus

The DISCOURSE RELATIONS REFERENCE CORPUS is a collection of texts annotated according to the framework of *Rhetorical Structure Theory* (RST). The corpus comprises 2,451 instances of relations in 65 texts.

The analyses were originally created in three different projects and differ with respect to their tagsets and partly their annotation approach. The corpus is organized in three subcorpora accordingly, which are described in greater detail below.

The reference corpus had been compiled for corpus linguistic purposes, more specifically for the study of RST relations, and not for computational applications in the first place. So it was more important to provide user-friendly visualizations of the analyses instead of large amounts of data. The analyses are available as a PDF file or can be individually browsed by means of the RSTTOOL, which will be introduced in Chapter 13. In contrast to the annotation method applied in the PENN DISCOURSE TREEBANK that was introduced in the last section, RST does not focus on discourse connectives, but attempts to capture the intended meaning of a text by creating a hierarchical tree of discourse relations with the final goal of having a single relation spanning the whole text. Note that in the RST literature, discourse relations are referred to as *rhetorical relations*. However, for reasons of comparability with the last section, we will continue to call them discourse relations.

Figure 6.9 gives a first impression of the hierarchical RST approach. The short text in (57) is analyzed as consisting of six elementary discourse units (EDUs), which are combined by one Concession relation (creating the complex span 1–2) and three Elaboration relations (creating the complex span 1–5). The top level of this discourse tree consists of two spans (1–5 and 6) which are not further related.[23]

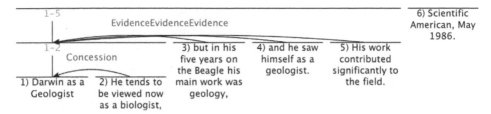

Figure 6.9 Rhetorical Structure Theory analysis in the DISCOURSE RELATIONS REFERENCE CORPUS (visualized by RSTTOOL).

(57) Darwin as a Geologist
      He tends to be viewed now as a biologist, but in his five years on the Beagle his main work was geology, and he saw himself as a geologist. His work contributed significantly to the field.
      Scientific American, May 1986.

Before we explain the annotation in more detail, we will briefly introduce the three subcorpora of the DISCOURSE RELATIONS REFERENCE CORPUS. The first one is the RST WEBSITE CORPUS. It consists of 14 texts created by the developers of RST, William Mann, Sandra Thompson, and Christian Matthiessen.[24] Five of these texts were used in publications by the developers. The other nine texts are called "unpublished analyses," among them the Darwin text in Figure 6.9. These texts were used to exemplify specific properties or problems of RST. For one of the texts ("Mother Teresa"), the corpus even provides three alternative analyses, which shows the subjectivity of this type of annotation. The texts come from various written genres and vary in text length (between 4 to 43 EDUs). The analyses conform to a classic version of RST, consisting of a set of 32 discourse relations.

The second subcorpus is a random sample of 21 texts from the much larger RST DISCOURSE TREEBANK, which had originally been created by Daniel Marcu, who was interested in developing computational applications for discourse analysis and text summarization. The original corpus comprises 385 articles from the Wall Street Journal section of the PENN TREEBANK. Note that these texts are also annotated in the PENN DISCOURSE TREEBANK described in the previous section. The WSJ texts mostly belong to the genre of news texts and are much longer than the RST website texts. Marcu applied an extended set of 78 fine-grained discourse relations to these texts.

Finally, the last subcorpus consists of 30 texts sampled from the SFU REVIEW CORPUS compiled by Maite Taboada, which had originally been created for the computational analysis of text sentiment. The texts are all reviews, half of them of movies, the other half of books. This subcorpus differs from the other two in that only intra-sentential relations were annotated. This means that there are no text-spanning hierarchical trees but only a few relations annotated per text. The set of relations used in this subcorpus conforms to the classical set which was applied to the RST WEBSITE CORPUS, extended by general relations for Result and Cause.

As mentioned at the beginning of this section, the annotation of discourse relations on the basis of RST does not start out from discourse connectives; instead, all elementary discourse units (mainly clauses) are seen as leaves in a discourse tree, which are recursively combined into larger units. Each node in this tree represents such a unit, which corresponds to a continuous span of text. Nodes are complex in the sense that they are built up from at least two adjacent, non-overlapping daughter units. The daughter units are not necessarily equally important. RST distinguishes two types of daughter units: nucleus, which is the more essential unit, and satellite, which is the supporting unit. Each node can be characterized by this nuclearity and the type of discourse relation that holds between its daughter units. There are five nuclearity types, which are called schema in RST. Figure 6.10 illustrates these schemas with five different discourse relations.[25]

The straight vertical lines in the schemas identify nuclear span(s), and the arcs represent relations. Most relations annotated in the texts correspond to the simple nucleus-satellite schema exemplified by Circumstance in Figure 6.10. Here, the first span is the less important satellite unit, and the second span is the nucleus (see also example (58) and the left subtree in 6.11). The motivation-enablement schema in figure 6.10 is more complex since two satellites point to one nucleus (see (59) and the right subtree in 6.11 for a similar scheme with two elaboration relations).[26]

(58) CIRCUMSTANCE: [$_{Satellite}$ When we released the results of ZPG's 1985 Urban Stress Test], [$_{Nucleus}$ we had no idea we'd get such an overwhelming response].

(59) ELABORATION: [$_{Satellite}$ In the case of the Whydah, a pirate ship discovered off Wellfleet, Massachusetts, by treasure hunter Barry Clifford, the objects have been kept together, at least for the time being.] [$_{Nucleus}$ They are now on view at the National Geographic Society in Washington, D.C.,] [$_{Satellite}$ which agreed to display them after other museums refused to do so out of concern that doing so would encourage commercial exploitation of other wrecks.]

In multi-nuclear schemas like Contrast, Joint, or Sequence in Figure 6.10, all units are equally important. While in a Sequence relation, there needs to be a succession

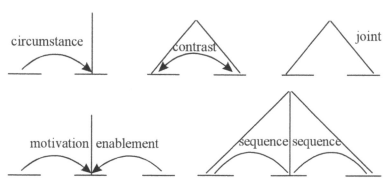

Figure 6.10 Examples of the five schema types in RST.

relationship between the situations in the nuclei (see (60) and the left subtree in Figure 6.12), there is no such constraint on the nuclei of Joint. In fact, Joint represents the lack of a discourse relation between the nuclei (see (61) and the right subtree in Figure 6.12).

(60) SEQUENCE: [$_{Nucleus}$ one agent pointed to a massive chandelier and asked,] [$_{Nucleus}$ "What would you call that in England?"]

(61) JOINT: [$_{Nucleus}$ Interest in underwater archeology is on the rise,] [$_{Nucleus}$ while those exploring the seabed are going ever deeper to recover objects from shipwrecks.]

Figure 6.13 is an example from the RST DISCOURSE TREEBANK based on WSJ texts. It shows the hierarchical character of RST analyses. For example, the first Attribution relation combines the satellite EDU **Mr. Henderson said** with a complex nucleus (span 11–12) that consists of two EDUs, which are related by a Contrast relation

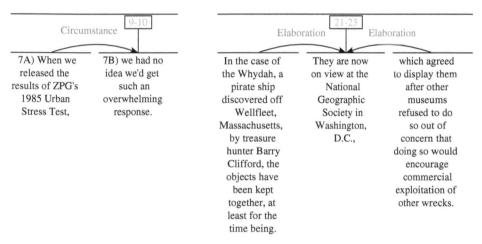

Figure 6.11 Examples for schemas in RST, realized by Circumstance (left) and Elaboration (right).

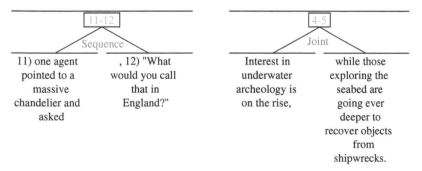

Figure 6.12 Examples for schemas in RST, realized by Sequence (left) and Joint (right).

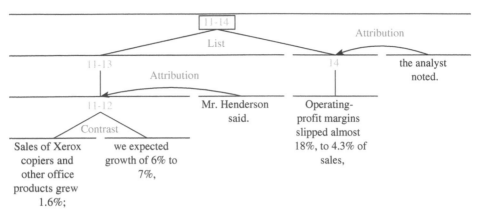

Figure 6.13 Example discourse subtree in the RST DISCOURSE CORPUS.

themselves. Attribution is one of the refinements that distinguishes Marcu's corpus from the classical RST relations. It marks complements of attribution verbs (speech acts and other cognitive acts).

We mentioned in the last section that only a fraction of discourse relations is signaled by explicit connectives. Even when alternative realizations are taken into account, there is still a large number of discourse relations that are not explicitly marked in the text. Because of this fact and also because of the ambiguity of connectives, the developers of RST refrain from directly relating their discourse relations to explicit signals in the text.

Table 6.5 summarizes the list of 23 discourse relations which have been suggested by the developers of RST. The relations are not defined hierarchically as in the PENN DISCOURSE TREEBANK, but they can be grouped into subclasses of similar relations. It is important to note that this is not an ultimately fixed list. As the three subcorpora of the DISCOURSE RELATIONS REFERENCE CORPUS show, other classifications are possible, and longer (and shorter) lists have been proposed.

The developers of RST further distinguish relations of two different types. *Subject matter* relations, on the one hand, relate the content of the text spans like Cause, Purpose, Condition, and Summary. *Presentational* relations, on the other hand, are more pragmatic in nature. They are meant to achieve some effect on the reader like Motivation, Antithesis, Background, and Evidence.

This distinction is reminiscent of the distinction between pragmatic and non-pragmatic relations in the PENN DISCOURSE TREEBANK as introduced in the last section. However, PDTB defines discourse relations on the basis of relations between the (literal or derived) meaning of Arg1 and Arg2 and not with respect to effects on the reader. Rhetorical Structure Theory as annotated in the DISCOURSE RELATIONS REFERENCE CORPUS takes a different approach. It defines a discourse relation (rhetorical relation) in terms of the stance or belief states of the reader and the writer. In particular, it defines constraints on how the reader and/or writer relate to the content of the

Table 6.5 Grouped discourse relations in RST.

Circumstance	Antithesis and Concession
Solutionhood	Antithesis
Elaboration	Concession
Background	Condition and Otherwise
Enablement and Motivation	Condition
Enablement	Otherwise
Motivation	Interpretation and Evaluation
Evidence and Justify	Interpretation
Evidence	Evaluation
Justify	Restatement and Summary
Relations of Cause	Restatement
Volitional Cause	Summary
Non-Volitional Cause	Other Relations
Volitional Result	Sequence
Non-Volitional Result	Contrast
Purpose	

units that take part in the relation and also their combination. In addition, it takes the intended effect on the reader into account.

Consequently, the definition of a discourse relation in RST consists of four fields, which have to be tested in the course of the annotation: (i) Constraints on the Nucleus; (ii) Constraints on the Satellite; (iii) Constraints on the combination of Nucleus and Satellite (or the Nuclei); and (iv) Effect (on the reader).

Table 6.6 describes how relations for Concession, Non-volitional Cause, and Sequence are defined in RST. Concession is a presentational relation, Non-volitional Cause is a subject matter relation, and lastly, Sequence is a multi-nuclear relation.

The analysis of text in terms of Rhetorical Structure Theory has been very influential both in linguistics as well as in computational linguistics. Here, we restrict ourselves to listing some more corpus projects. RST SPANISH TREEBANK is a Spanish corpus that adapts RST to Spanish. This corpus is accompanied by an easy-to-use online search tool. The German POTSDAM COMMENTARY CORPUS (PCC) has been described already, among others in combination with the PENN DISCOURSE TREEBANK. It contains both an annotation layer of connectives and their arguments (but without relations) and a layer of hierarchical discourse relations annotated according to RST. More generally, it is a multi-level annotated corpus that makes use of an XML stand-off representation such that annotations from all annotations layers can be related to each other—for

Table 6.6 Definitions of Concession, Non-volitional Cause, and Sequence in RST.

Relation	Constraints on either S or N	Constraints on combination N+S / N+N	Intended Effect
Concession	on N: W has positive regard for N; on S: W is not claiming that S does not hold;	W acknowledges a potential or apparent incompatibility between N and S; recognizing the compatibility between N and S increases R's positive regard for N	R's positive regard for N is increased
Non-volitional Cause	on N: N is not a volitional action	S, by means other than motivating a volitional action, caused N; without the presentation of S, R might not know the particular cause of the situation; a presentation of N is more central than S to W's purposes in putting forth the N-S combination	R recognizes S as a cause of N
Sequence	none	there is a succession relationship between the situations in the nuclei	R recognizes the succession relationships among the nuclei

example, discourse relations and syntax or information structure. The CorpusTCC and the Rhetalho Corpus are two RST-annotated resources for Brazilian Portuguese. They inspired the creation of the RST Spanish Treebank in the first place. The annotation in the Discourse Graphbank is strongly inspired by RST but goes beyond the tree-structure approach of RST, applying more flexible graph-like analyses in which one unit can take part in several relations creating circular structures.

6.4 Summary

In this chapter, we looked at different types of pragmatic or discourse annotation. We first looked at anaphora and coreference annotation, including relations that go beyond the standard identity relation, such as bridging, and types of anaphora that go beyond an NP antecedent, such as event anaphora and, more generally, abstract anaphora. A second type of discourse annotation is concerned with the annotation of information structure and information status. This annotation uses sentences as the basic units of annotation and distinguishes discourse entities based on whether they are new or old in discourse. The last area of annotation that we looked at concerns discourse relations. This type of annotation uses texts as their underlying units, and it annotates how sentences are connected into coherent texts. As we went from smaller to larger annotation units, we also saw that the level of difficulty and of subjectivity in annotation increased significantly. While we have good annotation schemes for noun phrase coreference, linguists are still working on good inventories to describe how coherence is reached on the textual level.

6.5 Further Reading

Section 6.1

ACE Corpora: These corpora, the 2004 and 2005 data sets, are available from the Linguistic Data Consortium (LDC) at http://www.ldc.upenn.edu/. The annotation was documented by Doddington et al. (2004).

Additional corpora and data sets for abstract anaphora: There is a Danish/Italian set of corpora annotated for abstract anaphora; more information can be found at http://www.cst.dk/dad/ and in Navaretta (2008); Navaretta and Olsen (2008).

BULTREEBANK: More information about the BULTREEBANK for Bulgarian can be found at http://www.bultreebank.org/indexBTB.html and in Chanev et al. (2007).

BYRON Corpus: The annotation of the BYRON Corpus is documented in a technical report (Byron, 2003). An approach to resolving abstract pronouns can be found in Byron (2002). The two sub-corpora are available from the following sites: TRAINS93: ftp://ftp.cs.rochester.edu/pub/papers/ai/03.TR703-TRAINS93-pron-annotation.sgml and BUR: ftp://ftp.cs.rochester.edu/pub/papers/ai/03.TR703-BUR-pron-annotation.sgml. The original corpora that serve as the textual basis for the BYRON Corpus are available from the Linguistic Data Consortium at http://www.ldc.upenn.edu/.

DIRNDL Corpus: The DIRNDL Corpus for German is described in Eckart et al. (2012). A detailed introduction to the information status and coreferential annotation scheme is given in Baumann and Riester (2012). In order to obtain the corpus, contact dirndl@ims.uni-stuttgart.de.

EUROPARL: The EUROPARL Corpus is available at http://www.statmt.org/europarl/. It is described in Koehn (2005).

EUROPARL-PRON: The EUROPARL-PRON Corpus is available upon request. Please contact Heike Zinsmeister.

GNOME: Those texts of the GNOME Corpus that are not subject to copyright are available from the University of Essex. More information about the corpus and the annotation manual (Poesio, 2000) can be found at http://cswww.essex.ac.uk/Research/nle/corpora/GNOME/. In order to obtain the corpus, contact Massimo Poesio at massimo.poesio@unitn.it.

ISNOTES Corpus: More information about the ISNOTES Corpus and the files to download can be found at http://www.h-its.org/nlp/download/isnotes. The corpus is described in Hou et al. (2013); Markert et al. (2012). Note that in order to access the annotations with their textual basis, one needs to have access to the ONTONOTES Corpus (see below).

Löbner categories: Löbner (1985) introduced a theory of definiteness in which he distinguished four conceptually different types of nouns. A generalization of this theory is provided in Löbner (2011).

MASC: This is a 500,000-word subset of the OPEN AMERICAN NATIONAL CORPUS (see below), which has been annotated for lemma and POS labels, for noun and verb chunks, named entities, syntax, and coreference. MASC is an open language data resource and sustained by community contributions. It can be browsed or downloaded from http://www.anc.org/data/masc/.

MATE: The MATE meta-annotation scheme is documented by Poesio et al. (1999).

MUC Corpora: The MUC Corpora, namely MUC-6 and MUC-7, are available from the Linguistic Data Consortium at http://www.ldc.upenn.edu/. The annotation was documented by Hirschman and Chinchor (1997).

NP4E Corpus: More information about the NP4E Corpus as well as the annotated files can be found at http://clg.wlv.ac.uk/projects/NP4E/. There are annotation manuals for the NP coreference annotation (Hasler, Naumann, and Orăsan, 2006b) and the event annotation (Hasler, Naumann, and Orăsan, 2006a) as well as a conference paper describing the annotation scheme (Hasler, Orăsan, and Naumann, 2006).

ONTONOTES Corpus: This corpus was published in five releases, covering the languages English, Chinese, and Arabic. It is available free of charge from the Linguistic Data Consortium at http://www.ldc.upenn.edu/. The corpus is documented in a conference paper (Hovy et al., 2006). There is also an annotation manual for the English coreference annotation (BBN Technologies, 2004).

OPEN AMERICAN NATIONAL CORPUS (OANC): The OANC is a balanced corpus of approximately 15 million words of American English, including transcripts of spoken data. More information about OANC can be found in Ide et al. (2010) and at http://www.americannationalcorpus.org/.

PRAGUE DEPENDENCY TREEBANK: Information about the Prague Dependency Treebank for Czech can be found in section 4.6 and at http://ufal.mff.cuni.cz/pdt2.0/. The coreference annotation is described in Nedoluzhko et al. (2009); Nedoluzhko and Mírovský (2011).

TÜBA-D/Z TREEBANK: This German treebank was discussed extensively in Chapter 4. Since version 3, the treebank also contains anaphora and coreference annotations. These are documented in a separate stylebook (Naumann, 2007). Since version 7, it also includes the annotation of selected discourse connectives (Versley and Gastel, 2013), cf. section 6.3.

Section 6.2

Information status annotation: The classic reading is Prince (1981). Prince (1992) presents an early corpus-based study. Nissim et al. (2004) developed an annotation scheme for spoken dialogues. Götze et al. (2007) present a comprehensive annotation scheme for information status, topic, and focus. Baumann and Riester (2012) give a detailed introduction to the information status annotation of the DIRNDL Corpus.

Information structure: The term was introduced by Halliday (1967). Information structure is the packaging of information within a sentence—see Chafe (1994); Vallduví and Engdahl (1996). Krifka (2008) provides the theoretical basis for Götze et al. (2007) (see above). Hajičová (2009) gives an overview of information structure annotation from a perspective of the PRAGUE DEPENDENCY TREEBANK.

NXT SWITCHBOARD Corpus: The NXT SWITCHBOARD Corpus is documented in Calhoun et al. (2010). It is available from the LDC for a small fee.

POTSDAM COMMENTARY CORPUS (PCC): This is a German corpus of 176 newspaper texts annotated with multiple layers including connectives and their arguments in the spirit of the PENN DISCOURSE TREEBANK and relations according to Rhetorical Structure Theory (Stede, 2004). Stede (2008) discusses problems that arise in the annotation of hierarchical discourse relations. The PCC is available upon request from Manfred Stede at the University of Potsdam, Germany http://www.ling.uni-potsdam.de/acl-lab/Forsch/pcc/pcc.html

SWITCHBOARD: The original SWITCHBOARD Corpus (Godfrey et al., 1992) was published in two releases. It is available from the LDC.

TiGer: The TiGer Corpus is a treebank for German; it is documented in Brants et al. (2002, 2004) and is available from http://www.ims.uni-stuttgart.de/forschung/ressourcen/korpora/ tiger.html.

Section 6.3

Corpus studies about implicit discourse connectives: Marcu and Echihabi (2002) discuss whether information from explicitly marked relations can be used to automatically identify implicit relations in texts. Sporleder and Lascarides (2008); Blair-Goldensohn et al. (2007) challenge their findings. Torabi Asr and Demberg (2012) discuss hypotheses on continuity and causality-by-default on the basis of the PENN DISCOURSE TREEBANK (see below). Taboada (2009) summarizes studies based on RST annotations.

CorpusTCC: This is a corpus of 100 Brazilian Portuguese scientific texts annotated with RST described by Salgueiro Pardo and Marques Seno (2005). The corpus is available from http:// www.icmc.usp.br/pessoas/taspardo/Projects.htm, along with the list of relations used in the annotation.

DISCOURSE GRAPHBANK: The data consist of 135 English texts from AP Newswire and the *Wall Street Journal*, annotated with coherence relations (Wolf et al., 2004), available via the LDC. The corpus creation motivated the authors to question the tree-structure approach of RST and argue for a more flexible graph-like analysis (Wolf and Gibson, 2006).

DISCOURSE RELATIONS REFERENCE CORPUS: This corpus consists of a collection of 65 English texts annotated with RST discourse relations (Taboada and Renkema, 2008): 14 texts from the RST development team, which are further described at http://www.sfu.ca/ rst/02analyses/; 21 texts from the RST DISCOURSE TREEBANK (see below); and 30 texts from the SFU REVIEW CORPUS (Taboada et al., 2006). The corpus is available from http://www.sfu. ca/rst/06tools/discourse_relations_corpus.html.

Discourse theory: We refer the reader to handbook articles by Andrew Kehler for a summary and links to further literature (Kehler, 2004, 2012). Renkema (2004) is an introductory textbook on discourse analysis in general, with a linguistic, descriptive focus. Different definitions of the concept of an elementary discourse unit are summarized by Carlson and Marcu (2001, sec. 2.0). Rösner and Stede (1992); Schauer (2000) argue for including prepositional phrases.

GRONINGEN MEANING BANK (GMB): The semantically annotated corpus (Basile et al., 2012), which was discussed extensively in Chapter 5, also includes the annotation of discourse relations in terms of Segmented Discourse Representation Theory (SDRT) (see below).

PENN DISCOURSE TREEBANK (PDTB): Webber (2004) motivates the creation of the PDTB. The discourse annotation is a stand-off extension of the 1 million Wall Street Journal section of the PENN TREEBANK (version 2.0) and is available via the LDC. The annotation of PDTB-0.2 is described in detail by Prasad et al. (2008); annotation guidelines are also available (Prasad et al., 2007). For the annotation of alternative means signaling discourse relations, see Prasad et al. (2010). Further information can be found at http://www.seas.upenn.edu/~pdtb/.

RHETALHO: This is another RST corpus of Brazilian Portuguese of 40 texts from two different text genres, all texts doubly annotated. The corpus and further information are available from http://www.icmc.usp.br/pessoas/taspardo/Projects.htm.

Rhetorical Structure Theory (RST): A framework for analyzing texts as hierarchical structures of logical relations (Mann and Thompson, 1988; Taboada and Mann, 2006).

RST DISCOURSE TREEBANK: This is another discourse annotation of the PENN TREEBANK (version 2.0). 385 articles from the Wall Street Journal are annotated according to RST. The guidelines are by Carlson and Marcu (2001); see also http://www.isi.edu/~marcu/discourse/ for further information. The RST DISCOURSE TREEBANK is available from the LDC.

RST SPANISH TREEBANK: The corpus compilation method and annotation are described in a conference paper (da Cunha et al., 2011), which also gives an overview of the other RST corpora in other languages. The corpus annotation is ongoing. As of March 2014, the corpus consists of 264 texts from different genres, a considerable part of them doubly annotated. The corpus is available for online-querying and browsing, as well as for download at http://corpus.iingen.unam.mx/rst/, along with the annotation guidelines.

Segmented Discourse Representation Theory (SDRT): This is an extension of the semantic Discourse Representation Theory (Kamp and Reyle, 1993; Geurts and Beaver, 2011), which also includes logical/rhetorical relations between discourse units (Asher and Lascarides, 2003).

TURKISH DISCOURSE BANK (TDB): This corpus consists of 197 texts from different genres annotated according to the guidelines of the English PDTB. Annotation details are described in Zeyrek et al. (2013). It is available upon request from www.medid.ii.metu.edu.tr.

6.6 Exercises

1. **Information structure**: Table 6.3 gives a description of layers and tags for the annotation of information structure. Assign a layer and a tag to the underlined NPs:
   (a) Peter went into the garden. He was happy.
   (b) Could you pass the sugar, please?

2. **RST SPANISH TREEBANK**: Go to http://corpus.iingen.unam.mx/rst/, select your preferred language, and click on the Corpus tab. Compare texts from Astrofísica and from Derecho. Which type of texts has more Causa relations?

PART III
USING LINGUISTIC ANNOTATION IN CORPUS LINGUISTICS

CHAPTER 7
ADVANTAGES AND LIMITATIONS OF USING LINGUISTICALLY ANNOTATED CORPORA

In Part II of this book, we have mostly discussed the types of linguistic annotation that are currently available. While this gave us some insights into why we need linguistic annotation, we will come back to this issue and discuss it in more depth in section 7.1. We will use the annotations introduced in Part II of the book to motivate the use of these annotations in corpus linguistics. Following this discussion, in section 7.2, we will have a closer look at annotations, manual or automatic, and show how errors or inconsistencies in the annotations can have an effect on search results. Then, we will discuss the limitations of corpus linguistics in section 7.3, with a focus on research questions where we need other types of methodology than corpus linguistics to approach a problem. There, we will discuss types of phenomena that cannot reliably be found in corpora. In Chapter 8, we will have a closer look at case studies that used corpus linguistic concepts in linguistic research and show how linguistic questions can be answered with the help of annotated corpora.

7.1 Relating Linguistic Annotation and Search

We already mentioned in section 2.3 that the range of phenomena which we can find is dependent on the types of available annotations. Or viewed from the other side: depending on the type of phenomenon that we want to investigate, we need to choose our corpus so that the relevant annotation is available. In this section, we will discuss two phenomena, one syntactic and one on the interface between syntax and semantics. We will concentrate on which types of annotation will help us to find examples of these phenomena.

In syntax, there is one type of noun phrases that is semantically restricted and distributionally different from other noun phrases: temporal NPs. Such NPs generally fill adjunct positions, either on the level of the verb phrase (VP) or on the clausal level (S). However, they can also occur as postmodifiers in complex NPs. We show examples in (1), from the Penn Treebank (Marcus et al., 1993).

(1) a. The economic and foreign ministers ... will meet in Australia next week ...
     b. The exact amount of the refund will be determined next year based on actual collections made until December 31 of this year.
     c. The next morning, with a police escort, busloads of executives and their wives raced to the Indianapolis Speedway, ...

    d.   Earlier this year, Japanese investors snapped up a similar fund.

    e.   One Egg King ... can crack about 20,000 eggs an hour.

Since temporal NPs are semantically restricted, we could entertain the hypothesis that we can list all possible nouns that can occur in such NPs: We would have to list all week days, all months, and all time units, such as **day, week, month, year**. But this would not guarantee that we have covered all possible NPs. For example, we would have left out words like **today, tomorrow, yesterday**, but also **hour, minute** or seasons such as **summer**. Ideally, we would like to have such temporal nouns marked in the part-of-speech (POS) tagset so that we can search on the POS level. However, from the POS tagsets that we covered in section 3.3, the SUSANNE tagset is the only one that provides this information. Thus, if we have a corpus annotated with SUSANNE, we can search for all nouns with the POS tags starting in NNT. The POS tags also encode additional information, thus we have the following relevant POS tags: NNT1, NNT2, NNT1c, NNT1h, and NNT1m.

If our corpus is annotated with the PENN TREEBANK or the ICE tagset, the POS tags do not give enough information to find temporal nouns since these tagsets only distinguish between common and proper nouns. In such cases, we need syntactic annotation. In the PENN TREEBANK, for example, temporal noun phrases are annotated with the grammatical function TMP. Thus, we can search for the constituent NP-TMP.

When we search for temporal NPs in the PENN TREEBANK, we find that they have different distributions, depending on whether they modify an NP, a VP, or an S. Modifying a VP is the most typical case; there are 2,959 occurrences of this, 1,069 occurrences of an S modification, and only 636 NP modifications. A quick look at the first 20 occurrences of each case shows that **year** is the most frequent temporal noun across all three cases. In second place, we have a more varied picture: for VP modification, it is **Tuesday**; for S modification, there is a tie between **month, time, week**, and **yesterday**; and for NP modification, it is **today**. Note that this latter result is more anecdotal since the number of occurrences used is too small for a reliable investigation of the differences.

Another strategy that can be used if the temporal annotation were not present is to search for an approximation of the exact phenomenon in which we are interested. In many cases, syntactic phenomena can be approximated by sequences of POS tags. In our current example, a syntactic approximation is more effective. When we look at the examples in (1), in most cases, the temporal NP is either preceded or followed directly by another NP. Since this is one of the characteristics of a temporal NP, we can search for two consecutive NPs. We will discuss in Chapter 12 how such a query will look. For now, it will be enough to know that we can search for such a construct. However, note that this is only an approximation of the phenomenon in which we are interested. This search will both over- and undergenerate. It will overgenerate in that it will not only find sequences of NPs but also other phenomena. A quick look through the first 20 sentences in the PENN TREEBANK shows that 9 of those sentences actually contain temporal NPs. The other sentences show phenomena such as ditransitive constructions (2-a), appositions as in (2-b), fronted PPs, which contain an NP (2-c), or temporal prepositional phrases as in (2-d).

(2) a. Under the stars and moons of the Indiana Roof ballroom, nine of the hottest chefs in town fed [them] [Indiana duckling mousseline] ...

b. Newsweek, trying to keep pace with [rival] [Time Magazine] ...

c. ... and without [him] it could not be completed.

d. Separately, the Federal Energy Regulatory Commission turned down for [now] [a request] ...

The overgeneration means that we have to go through all examples and identify those that have temporal NPs. The search also undergenerates in that it does not find temporal noun phrases that are not adjacent to a noun phrase, such as the example in (1-c) in which the temporal NP is followed by a PP. Now, we could also search for the sequences of an NP and a PP. However, this search would extremely overgenerate and produce many more false positives than examples in which we are interested. For this reason, the approximations need to be chosen carefully, and we need to be aware of the fact that we may not find all occurrences of the phenomenon.

Our second example is concerned with semantic arguments and how they are realized on the syntactic level: We are interested in the sense of the verb **call** that assigns a name to a person or another entity. Examples from FRAMENET (see below) are shown in (3).

(3) a. ... he CALLS me Meldy when we're alone ...

b. it CALLS itself "the Civil War City."

c. I CALLED the various machines by masculine names ...

d. "I may CALL you by your pen name, yes?" he added.

As the examples show, there are two possibilities to use the verb in this meaning: In one construction, the verb takes two direct objects; in the other case, a direct object and **by**-phrase. We are interested in the distribution of these two constructions. If we want to search for these constructions, we have different possibilities. This is another example where it is difficult to find the whole range of examples by searching in text only since we cannot list all the possible noun phrases, and this meaning of **call** is not the most frequent meaning, so that a search for all occurrences of **call** would result in too many false positives. One possibility is to use a corpus that has annotations of semantic frames, which would allow us to search for the semantic frame that models this meaning. Such a corpus is FRAMENET (see sections 2.2.3 and 5.3.2 for a description of FRAMENET). In FRAMENET, this semantic frame is called Referring_by_name. It has 36 examples, from which 28 use two direct objects while 7 use the **by**-phrase. The remaining example, shown in (4), falls in neither category. Note that this resource offers us easy access to the examples of **call** with the required meaning, but we have to count manually how many examples fall in which category.

(4) "Progressive education" (as it was once CALLED) is far more interesting and agreeable to teachers than is disciplined instruction.

The other possibility to search for this phenomenon is to use syntactic information since we know that we are looking for the verb **call** with either two noun phrases or one noun phrase plus a **by**-PP. If we search in the PENN TREEBANK, we find 31 cases for the two direct NPs and none for the NP-PP combination. Examples of the double NPs can be found in (5-a) and (5-b). However, this query may over- and undergenerate. It can overgenerate if we do not specify the grammatical function of the second NP. In this case, we would include examples of temporal NPs, as shown in (5-c).

(5) a. But Mr. Barnum called that "a worst case" scenario.
b. Mrs. Ward says she often defended her to colleagues who called her a grandstander.
c. … Warner Brothers Production president Mark Clinton called him Oct. 19 and said Mr. Peters is "off the picture."

The query may undergenerate if we assume that the two NPs or the NP-PP combination have to follow the verb. Such an assumption excludes cases such as the ones shown in (6) (taken from FRAMENET), in which the entity is extracted from a reduced relative clause or the clause is passivized.

(6) a. In January 1997, Iran created an organization CALLED the Iranian Biotechnology Society (IBS), …
b. Establishments are no longer CALLED "Royal," …

In this section, we explored how the availability of linguistic annotation can influence which phenomena we can find and how the definition of our query can result in over- and undergeneration. In the next section, we will investigate how inconsistencies in the annotation can influence our search results.

7.2 Linguistic Annotation and Inconsistencies

When we use annotated corpora, we need to be aware of the fact that these annotations will not be perfect; they will contain errors. We need to be aware of these errors because they affect not only the reliability of the counts that we obtain from the searches but also potentially whether we can find a phenomenon at all.

Linguistic annotation can be performed in two fundamentally different ways: either by manual annotation or by automatic methods. There are hybrid methods, such as having an automatic analysis with human post-correction. While the latter may produce slightly different errors from a completely manual annotation, we will group this type under its fully manual counterpart for our discussion here. The types of errors that we can expect from manually and automatically annotated corpora are different, as already mentioned in Chapter 3.

Annotation errors by automatic methods tend to be systematic, but generally in ways that are not intuitive to the linguist. If we take POS tagging as an example (see section 3.3 for an explanation of POS tagging), typical errors that can occur when we use the PENN TREEBANK POS tagset (see section 3.3) include the following (examples are from the PENN TREEBANK, the word in question is shown with the correct and the wrong, automatically assigned, POS tag):

1. Distinguishing proper names from beginnings of sentences:

    POS taggers are generally based on statistical models and thus need to be trained on annotated training data. There are many proper names, which are not included in the training set, no matter how large it is. Proper names are often capitalized, but so is the first word in a sentence. Thus, proper names may be misrecognized as adjectives or common nouns (cf. example (7-a)), and sentence-initial common nouns may be misrecognized as proper names (cf. example (7-b)).

2. Distinguishing past participles from past tense verbs:

    Past participles and past tense verbs often have the same form. In some contexts, they can still be easily distinguished, for example, when the past participle is preceded by a form of **have**, such as in (7-c). However, in other situations, a local context of 2 words preceding the ambiguous verb may not be enough for a correct disambiguation (cf. example (7-d)). The example in (7-e) has the disambiguating context, but in this case, the word **exploded** has a strong bias towards being used as a past verb.

3. Recognizing unknown words correctly:

    For unknown words, i.e. words that do not occur in the training data, POS taggers generally estimate the correct POS label based on characteristics of the words. For example, words ending in **-ly** are most likely adverbs, and words ending in **-s** are often verbs in third person singular. However, these are heuristics and can be wrong, as shown in (7-f).

(7) a. Quebecor can put a weekly newspaper on almost any Quebec/NNP/JJ doorstep
         ...
     b. Colon/NN/NNP, lung and breast cancers are the most common and lethal forms of the disease ...
     c. he isn't eligible to be reappointed/VBN ...
     d. ... to find out what threat the Quinlan baby faced/VBD/VBN.
     e. ... which in recent months has exploded/VBN/VBD.
     f. The team used a battery of the newly developed "gene probes," snippets/NNS/ VBZ of genetic material ...

Such errors may have a considerable effect on query results if we search for POS tags that are affected by systematic errors. For this reason, it is recommended that the user of such automatically annotated corpora look for a discussion of typical errors that the annotation tool in question makes if such information is available. If this is not the case, it may make sense to look at a sample of data, to see which error types may occur. For example, if we search for uncommon plural nouns, it may make sense to also search for the same word as a third person singular verb.

In contrast to the systematic automatic errors, errors in manual annotations tend to be much more erratic. They often are produced by lapses in attention. As a consequence of their erratic nature, such errors are extremely difficult to find. One such error can be found in the PENN TREEBANK in the sentence shown in example (8): Here, the prepositional phrase **in Washington** is erroneously marked as being a temporal PP, PP-TMP while it should be a location: PP-LOC. Such errors are less harmful since they change our counts only marginally.

(8)   Last March, after attending a teaching seminar in Washington, …

However, manual annotations can also contain systematic errors or inconsistencies. This is often the case when a distinction is not intuitively clear and the guidelines used for the annotation are not explicit enough or when there is confusion about the guidelines. One example can be found in the POS annotation of the PENN TREEBANK: There are four sentences in which **yet** introduces a coordinated second clause, as in (9).

(9)   For instance, it releases Mr. Sisulu without conditions, yet his son, Zwelakhe, a newspaper editor, is restricted to his home much of the day and isn't allowed to work as a journalist.

Two of the occurrences of **yet** are annotated as adverbs, two as coordinating conjunctions. Such errors are also extremely difficult to find, but they potentially have a significant, unwanted effect on our search results. If we suspect that our query may be affected by such inconsistencies, it is useful to formulate the query less specifically, without referring to the part of the annotation that is inconsistent. However, this requires that we already know that there is an inconsistency and which parts of the annotation are affected.

7.3 Limitations of Corpus Linguistics

So far in this book, we have promoted using corpus linguistics and linguistically annotated corpora. This section is dedicated to situations in which corpus linguistics is not a good approach. As all methodologies, corpus linguistics has certain limitations. We will focus here on the two major limitations: negative evidence and rare occurrences.

One area of research that is not well served by a corpus linguistic approach is research involving negative evidence. In theoretical syntax papers, one often finds examples that violate certain constraints, and they are often ranked based on how many constraints they violate. An example of a minimal contrast between a grammatical sentence and one that violates a constraint is shown in (10). Similarly, semanticists often use negative evidence to test whether certain conditions hold.

(10) a. Jenny asked who read what.
     b. *Jenny asked what who read.

It is clear that such data cannot be extracted from a corpus since corpus data consist of language produced by humans, and are thus generally grammatical. We could argue that some of the sentences that we find in corpora are not grammatical, as shown in (11) (from the PENN TREEBANK). However, such ungrammaticalities are generally caused by lack of attention rather than a violation of a linguistic principle. Such errors are not of interest for theoretical linguists.

(11) … the debentures were snapped by up pension funds, banks, insurance companies and other institutional investors.

In such cases, psycholinguistic experiments to corroborate linguistic judgements are more suitable than corpus linguistic methods. There is only one type of negative evidence available in corpora: There exist corpora of language learners, either of children learning their native language or of adults learning a foreign language. However, errors in learner language are different from the ungrammaticalities that are interesting for theoretical linguists.

The negative evidence discussed above is a problem for general corpus linguistics, independent of whether the corpus has linguistic annotation or not. For the other type of research questions in which corpus linguistics cannot be used fruitfully, the situation is aggravated when linguistic annotation is required. This type of research questions concerns investigations where rare occurrences are needed. One such example would be the question of whether it is possible in German to front the verb complex along with parts of the middle field. German has a somewhat free word order, in which the finite verb is fixed in second position, and all other verbal elements are located at the end of a main clause. The regularities of these ordering constraints can be represented in terms of topological fields, i.e. the finite verb is in the so-called left verbal bracket, and the remaining verbal elements are in the verb complex. All intervening material is located in the middle field. Here, we use this theory to describe examples of fronting, such as in the fronted variant (13) of the canonical sentence in (12).

(12) Der Mann hat gestern   das Brot gegessen.
     The man   has yesterday the bread eaten.
(13) Das Brot gegessen hat der Mann gestern.
     The bread eaten   has the man   yesterday.

Such occurrences, if they exist in natural language, are not frequent. In such cases, an approach using corpus linguistics has to be applied with extreme care. One inherent restriction of a corpus is that it is limited in size. This means that rare phenomena may not occur in a corpus, just because of the way in which the corpus was collected. Thus, if the corpus had been extended by one more text, our phenomenon might have been present in this text, and thus would be present in the corpus as well. This also means that if we do not find a phenomenon in a corpus, it does not mean that this phenomenon does not exist in language. In other words, corpus linguistics can provide positive evidence that a phenomenon does exist, and it can provide relative evidence that one phenomenon is more frequent than another, but it cannot provide negative evidence.

As mentioned above, the problem is more pronounced in cases where we need linguistic annotation to find examples. In general, the more effort is involved in the annotation process, the smaller these corpora are. Thus, POS tagged corpora can reach a size of several million words, but syntactically annotated corpora tend to be in the range of 5,000 to 50,000 sentences. In cases where we do not find a phenomenon in a small corpus with the ideal annotation, we can extend the search to larger corpora with less costly annotation. In such cases, we may have to approximate the query, as shown for the examples in section 7.1.

To come back to our German example, in order to find such cases of fronting, we need syntactic annotations. If we use the TüBa-D/z treebank, we find 6 occurrences of such phenomena within the first 5,000 sentences. This shows how infrequent this phenomenon is, and the frequency should not be considered reliable because of the small number of occurrences. However, since we found several occurrences in the treebank, we can conclude that this is a grammatical construction in (written) German.

7.4 Summary

In this chapter, we discussed issues in corpus linguistics. We first revisited the issue of how linguistic annotation and search relate. We showed that in order to find certain phenomena, we need annotations that cover these phenomena. If such annotations are not available, we can resort to a less specific annotation and approximate the search. In this case, the search may over- or undergenerate. We further discussed the effects that errors in the annotation can have on our search results, depending on whether the annotation was carried out manually or automatically. Then, we discussed two cases in which corpus linguistics, and especially in the second case, linguistically annotated corpora cannot be used: the search for negative examples and the search for rare examples.

Further Reading

Section 7.1

FrameNet: FrameNet is documented in the following publications: Baker et al. (1998);
  Ruppenhofer et al. (2010). It is available from https://framenet.icsi.berkeley.edu/fndrupal/.
Penn Treebank: For a description of the Penn Treebank, there is an early overview paper

(Marcus et al., 1993) and a paper on predicate argument structure (Marcus et al., 1994). The bracketing guidelines (Santorini, 1991) are also freely available. The treebank is available from the Linguistic Data Consortium (LDC).[1] For more information on the PENN TREEBANK, see Chapter 4.

Section 7.3

Issues concerning linguistic data: There is a body of work that is concerned with the data situation for theoretical linguistics. Starting points are the work by Schütze (1996, 2009, 2011) and by Featherston (2007).

Learner corpora: There are several corpora available with learner language. For children learning their native language, the CHILDES Corpus (MacWhinney, 2008) is the most well-known resource. It is now part of the TALKBANK project (MacWhinney, 2007), available from http://childes.psy.cmu.edu/. One of the better-known resources for second language learner corpora is the *International Corpus of Learner English*, ICLE (Granger et al., 2009). More information is available at http://www.uclouvain.be/en-cecl-icle.html.

Topological fields: This view of German syntax was proposed, for example, by Drach (1937) and Erdmann (1886), and more recently by Höhle (1986).

TÜBA-D/Z: The TÜBA-D/Z treebank for German is documented in Hinrichs et al. (2004); Telljohann et al. (2004, 2012). It is available from http://www.sfs.uni-tuebingen.de/en/ascl/resources/corpora/tueba-dz.html. See also Chapter 4 for more information.

7.6 Exercises

1. **Searching for linguistic phenomena**: If you want to search for the following phenomena, what annotation do you need optimally/minimally?

   (a) Which expression is more frequent: **my oh my** or **boy oh boy**?

   (b) Can you extrapose relative clauses in English?

   (c) Can the verb **kill** in the sense of **overwhelm with hilarity, pleasure, or admiration**, as in (14), only take the direct object **me**, or are other objects possible, too?

   (14) a. The comedian was so funny, he was killing me!

   b. That Buffy's got his back in these cases just KILLS me.

2. **Annotation Errors**: Go to COCA http://corpus.byu.edu/coca/, search for "my [np*]" (i.e. for the word **my** followed by a proper noun), and choose the occurrences for "MY WILL." How many of the examples are erroneously POS tagged and should be common nouns instead? For more information about searching in COCA, see section 11.1.

CHAPTER 8
CORPUS LINGUISTICS USING
LINGUISTICALLY ANNOTATED CORPORA

In Part II of this book, we have provided a detailed introduction to different levels of linguistic annotation in corpora. This chapter is concerned with the actual use of annotated corpora in linguistic studies. Here, we present sample studies which show how to operationalize linguistic questions in a way that annotated corpora can be used as a resource to provide empirical evidence. In other words, we show by example how a linguistic question or hypothesis can be translated into a form that allows us to find evidence or counter-evidence in a corpus. Here, the annotations provide ways of restricting the search to interesting phenomena, but it is the task of the linguist to decide which annotations are required and how the search needs to be formulated. Some of the studies we present here are very well known in terms of how often they are cited in other publications. Others are small-scale experiments instead. We chose the latter because they give interesting examples for how to approach/use annotated corpora.

With this motivation in mind, it is important to consider the studies with regard to their replicability by readers of this book. However, replicability depends on many aspects, among them the availability of the data and their accessibility in terms of search tools and visualization of the annotation. Some of the studies made use of tools that will be introduced in Part IV of this book. However, some of the studies are hard to replicate because there are no tools that provide easy access to the data. Thus, the researchers had to program their own scripts to extract relevant examples from the corpora. There are three reasons why we think it is feasible to present these studies nevertheless. First, corpus linguistics is a quickly growing field. There is a good chance that relevant tools may become available in the future. Second, research often requires us to work in teams including people with different expertise. Thus, we often need to cooperate with colleagues from other domains, such as computer science or computational linguistics. Finally, it is always an interesting challenge to acquire some text processing and programming skills oneself (see section 8.5).

The research questions of the studies that will be introduced in this chapter are related to different levels of annotation. Some of them cannot be considered corpus-linguistic studies in the narrow sense, but they use annotated data to find empirical evidence for their analyses. The structure of the chapter loosely follows the structure of the chapters on the linguistic annotation levels. We start out with studies concerned with word-level annotation and will then proceed to syntactic annotation, to semantic annotation, and finally to discourse-level annotation. Of course, the studies do not exactly follow our structure but may take different types of levels into account, depending on which types of annotations are required to find the phenomena of interest. Thus, these studies relate to linguistic annotation across the board.

8.1 Generalizations on Parts of Speech

The first study uses an annotated corpus for finding empirical counter-evidence against the predictions of a previous analysis. This study is not a corpus-linguistic study per se: The corpus query and its results are only provided in a footnote. Culicover (2013) investigated certain relations between bound pronouns and their antecedents (for a discussion of bound pronouns see section 6.1). Culicover was interested in a particular subtype of bound pronouns, as shown in the question in (1-a), in which **his** is bound by its antecedent, the *wh*-operator **who**. The answer (1-b) illustrates how the bound pronoun is interpreted to be coreferent with the interpretation of the operator.

(1) a. [$_i$ Who] offended [$_i$ his] mother?
     b. Tom offended his – Tom's – mother. And Jerry also offended his – Jerry's – mother.

In particular, Culicover investigated unacceptable cases of so-called weak crossover, in which the bound pronoun occurs structurally between its antecedent and the derivational base position of the latter. The special property of this constellation is that the bound pronoun itself is embedded in another phrase, as in (2-a). As marked by the asterisk, it is not possible to interpret the sentence as indicated by the subscripts although we can easily think of possible answers (2-b).

(2) a. *[$_i$ Who] did [$_j$ [$_i$ his] mother] offend [$_i$ t]?
     b. Tom's mother offended Tom. And Jerry's mother offended Jerry.

The mainstream analysis rules out weak crossover cases for structural reasons. Culicover argued that this cannot be the correct explanation because there are acceptable cases of weak crossover. He suggested an explanation that is based on sentence processing instead, taking an interaction between linear order and discourse structure into account.

To empirically strengthen his argument against the mainstream analysis, Culicover searched for counter-examples in authentic language production. He used the 450

Table 8.1 Operationalization of the search for weak crossover candidates based on parts of speech patterns.

Pattern	Comment
noun pronoun$_{wh}$ pronoun$_{poss}$	relative clause
noun, pronoun$_{wh}$ pronoun$_{poss}$	(non-restrictive) relative clause
pronoun$_{wh}$ verb$_{aux}$ pronoun$_{poss}$	pronominal *wh*-question
which noun verb$_{aux}$ pronoun$_{poss}$	nominal *wh*-question
which noun pronoun$_{poss}$	embedded question

million token, part-of-speech tagged *Corpus of Contemporary American English* (coca) and the BYU search interface (see Chapter 11 for more information about the corpus and the search interface). In order to operationalize a test for weak crossover, Culicover needed to translate this phenomenon into linguistic annotations. He chose to describe the phenomenon as part-of-speech (POS) patterns that identify candidates for further manual inspection. It was crucial that the patterns consisted of a possessive determiner that was preceded by a "moved" *wh*-element. Since movement is only annotated in syntax, and since coca does not provide syntactic structure or traces, such as, for example, the PENN TREEBANK (see section 4.2), the patterns can only approximate the target phenomenon. Table 8.1 lists the patterns Culicover used in his search. He found weak crossover violations only for the first two patterns, see examples (3) and (4) (three out of 120 matches and four out of an unspecified number of matches respectively).

(3) a. ... will play on HBO later this year) presents a complex portrait of a <u>man who his</u> biographer, the Pulitzer Prize-winning political historian Samantha Power, describes in ...

   b. Have you ever thought as to why people are so vituperative about this <u>president who his</u> critics say doesn't have a philosophy – you can't call him liberal?

   c. Wojciechowski has become a symbol for Duke's revival, the gritty little <u>guy whom his</u> fellow students bark at in appreciation for his dogged defensive style.

(4) a. John, <u>Jr., whom his</u> family called John John, seldom talked with reporters about himself or his memories?

   b. The <u>farmer, whom his</u> parents had located to hide them, was a Christian.

   c. Gary has remarried, and Greg and his wife have had two <u>children, whom their</u> grandfather barely knows.

   d. It might be that a sluggish bond-servant, or an undutiful <u>child, whom his</u> parents had given over to the civil authority, was to be corrected at?

If we want to replicate Culicover's queries with the BYU search interface of coca, our findings may be different because coca is a constantly growing corpus, and texts are added at least once a year. Additionally, in addition to these differences, we can modify the search and make it more specific. Culicover's search patterns overgenerate, i.e. they are too general so that they find examples that have the sequence of POS tags but which are not part of the pattern of weak crossover. If we look at the POS tagset used for coca, the CLAWS 7 tagset, more closely, we find that we can make the search pattern more specific, and thus exclude some of the cases that are not interesting. For example, Culicover searched for a noun and a *wh*-pronoun—see the first pattern in Table 8.1. The BYU query is shown in (5). However, we can search more specifically for a common noun [nn*] and an object *wh*-pronoun [PNQO], as shown in (6). This will reduce the noise in the output. However, this more specific query would also miss some relevant cases like (3-b), in which a subject *wh*-pronoun [PNQS] is moved in a relevant way, or (4-a), in which the pattern starts with a proper name [np*].

(5) [n*] [PNQ*] [APPGE]

noun, *wh*-pronoun, possessive pronoun/pre-nominal

(6) [nn*] [PNQO] [APPGE]

common noun, object *wh*-pronoun, possessive pronoun/pre-nominal

Figure 8.1 illustrates the corpus search with the BYU search interface, and Figure 8.2 shows examples matches.

In addition to the POS pattern search in the corpus, Culicover also uses Google[1] to search for lexical patterns, such as "(N1) **who she talked with about her** (N2)" and "(N1) **who he talked with about his** (N2)" (the variables (N1) and (N2) not being part of the queries), which provided some additional cases of weak crossover violations.

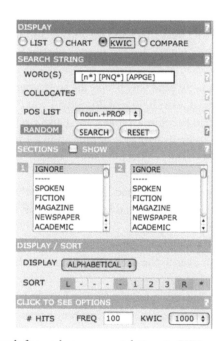

Figure 8.1 Example search for weak crossover violations in BYU search interface.

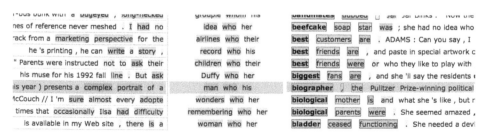

Figure 8.2 Example matches for weak crossover search in BYU search interface.

As Culicover described, the corpus matches contained only few true cases of weak crossover violation. In addition, the patterns may not have been exhaustive in the first place, in that additional true violations may have been missing from the patterns. However, for Culicover's purpose, it was only necessary to find some examples, which by their existence provide counter-evidence to the mainstream claim. Thus, frequency did not matter in his investigation.

A similar approach of identifying natural occurring examples has been applied by Gehrke and McNally (submitted), who combined a part-of-speech query with a list of lexical items that they extracted from the literature.

Their research question was a semantic one concerning frequency adjectives like **occasional, odd**, and **rare**, which can modify non-eventive nouns like **sailor** (see (7)), and provide information about the distribution of the referents (here: **sailors**) in certain kinds of situations or locations.

(7) The occasional sailor strolled by.

For the semantic argumentation, we refer to the original paper (Gehrke and McNally, submitted). We focus on the corpus-linguistic point: They needed empirical evidence to better understand the semantics of these constructions since previous analyses, they argued, were missing generalizations on the readings by not considering the full distributional pattern of these constructions.

Like Culicover in the previously introduced study, they used the 450 million token, POS tagged Corpus of CONTEMPORARY AMERICAN ENGLISH (COCA). In addition, they also employed the 100 million token BRITISH NATIONAL CORPUS (BNC) and the 155 billion GOOGLE BOOKS Corpus of American English, all available via the BYU search interface[2] (see section 11.1 for details on the search interface). Similar to Culicover, they complemented their empirical survey in the end by Google searches.

Among others, they were interested in readings in which the paraphrase in (8-a) holds, such as in the COCA example in (8-b).

(8) a. a rare visitor = one who visits rarely.
     b. Even though we were living in a Philadelphia apartment surrounded by gyms, basketball courts, and riverside bike paths, I'd become a rare visitor to any of them

The BYU search interface supported their empirical study by allowing them to specify a lexical item (or a set of lexical items or even the upload of a list of externally specified lexical items) and require it to precede or follow certain parts of speech. For our interests, it is important to point out that the interface offers the possibility of grouping search results based on the lemma annotation. This option can provide a quick overview of the results. Then one can click on a particular match and browse the actual examples in the *Key Word in Context* (KWIC) view (see section 9.1 for more information on KWIC). Figure 8.3 shows the search and examples from COCA.

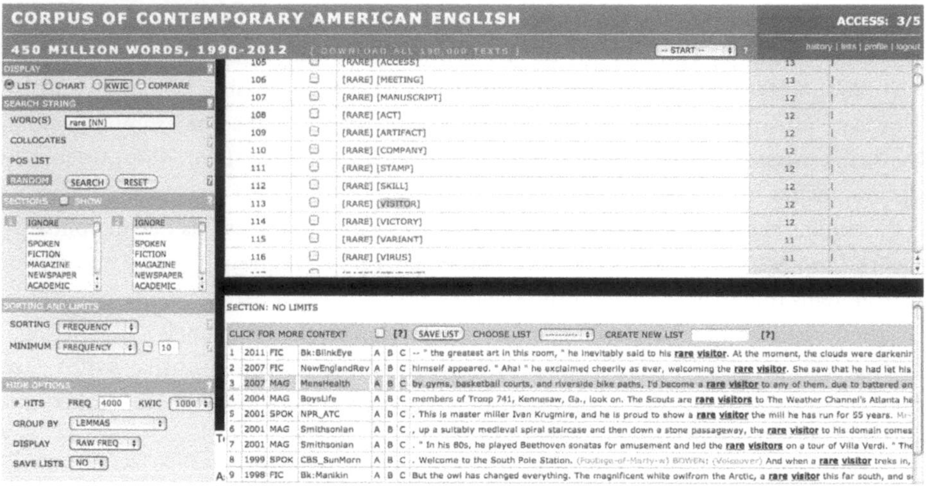

Figure 8.3 Example BYU search for the frequency adjective **rare** followed by a noun.

To summarize the corpus linguistic relevance of this study, Gehrke and McNally used large POS tagged corpora to identify different semantic readings of frequency adjectives. They filtered the adjectives by means of a list of lexical items. Tasks like theirs can greatly profit from the fact that the BYU search interface allows the search based on lemma annotation and also displays the results grouped by lemmas so that the users can efficiently browse a large number of examples. This allows them to look at a much wider range of examples than the examples generally cited in such studies. Additionally, it is possible to access examples in a systematic and more efficient way than traditional corpus browsing would do. As in the first study by Culicover, the authors were not interested in frequencies so it did not matter whether their queries were exhaustive or not.

Another study that uses part-of-speech tagged data is described by Payne et al. (2013). The authors built their analysis on an extensive study of anaphorically used **one** on the BRITISH NATIONAL CORPUS (BNC) using BNCWEB (in the CQP version, see section 11.2 for details). In addition to identifying naturally occurring examples for particular structures, they also evaluated some quantitative data.

In this study, Payne et al. (2013) challenged a long-term analysis of anaphoric **one**, as shown in the examples in (9). The analysis is based on the observation that (9-a) is less acceptable than (9-b). In the literature, the former is actually starred to be unacceptable (cf. example (10-a)).

(9)   a.   The student of chemistry was more thoroughly prepared than the one of physics.

       b.   The student with short hair is taller than the one with long hair.

The explanation of the difference in acceptability consists of the fact that the PP **of chemistry** functions as an argument of **student** whereas the PP **with long hair** is an adjunct, and that **one** can substitute for the nominal projection (Nom) but not for nominal heads (N) alone.

(10) a. *The [$_{\text{Nom}}$ [$_{\text{N}}$ student] [$_{\text{PP}}$ of chemistry]] … the [$_{\text{Nom}}$ [$_{\text{N}}$ one] [$_{\text{PP}}$ of physics]].
   b. The [$_{\text{Nom}}$ [$_{\text{Nom}}$ [$_{\text{N}}$ student]] [$_{\text{PP}}$ with short hair]] … the [$_{\text{Nom}}$ [$_{\text{Nom}}$ one] [$_{\text{PP}}$ with long hair]].

The authors pointed out that the contrast in (9) (and some additional examples) had led to the following generalizations: First, that there is a structural distinction between PP-arguments and PP-adjuncts in NPs; second, that anaphoric **one** is of category Nom and requires a Nom-antecedent accordingly (as opposed to a simple N-antecedent).

In a second step, Payne et al. (2013) distinguished three homonymous lexical readings of the word **one**: (i) Regular third person pronoun, **an arbitrary person** (genitive but no plural form); (ii) **one**$_d$ indefinite numeral determinative, 1, **some**, **a(n)**, **sole** (uninflectable); and (iii) **one**$_{ct}$ regular common count noun, anaphoric **instance thereof** (genitive and plural forms). The reading of interest here is the third reading, **one**$_{ct}$ (= anaphoric **one**).

To create an empirical basis for studying the distribution of **one**$_{ct}$, the authors operationalized the test of acceptability in terms of occurrences in the corpus, which translates into a search for potential occurrences of **one**$_{ct}$: Plural **ones** is unambiguously of type **one**$_{ct}$, no disambiguation is necessary here. The query only needed to ensure that **ones** is followed by **of**. This query is a simple query based on lexical items—see (11) for the search pattern and a sample match. To identify singular **one**$_{ct}$ in the same environment is more difficult because the determiner **one**$_d$ is very common, as in **one of the** X. Thus, the search overgenerates. To avoid having to manually look through many noisy examples, the authors restricted their search to a 'secure' context, which excluded **one**$_d$. In particular, they required that **one** is preceded by a determiner and an adjective that can be combined with common count nouns but excludes the determiner reading of **one**—see (12) for the query and a sample match. We used the CQP syntax to show the combination of words and POS tags in the search pattern (the CQP syntax query is ours).

(11) a. BNCWEB simple query: **ones of**
   b. This was hardly surprising since the differences were <u>ones of</u> style and rhetoric, not of fundamental demands.
(12) a. CQP syntax: [pos="AT0"][pos="AJ.*"][word="one"][word="of"]
   b. The issue is <u>a simple one of</u> economic competence.

The first query retrieved 136 matches in 123 texts. The authors reported that after deleting spurious items, they found 127 instances of plural **one**$_{ct}$. Performing the second query in CQP syntax (our version) returns 417 matches in 347 different texts. The authors reported that they found 408 genuine singular tokens of **one**$_{ct}$. After additional filtering of non-anaphoric occurrences in proper names and instances with oblique genitive **of**-PPs, their final empirical basis consisted of 518 instances of **one**$_{ct}$ followed by **of**.

The authors then performed a manual analysis of the semantic relations between the noun and the **of**-PP, identifying 35 coarse-grained semantic relations. For illustrative purposes, they simplified them into 24 classes in their article. Examples (13) and (14) show two example classes. Each example is followed by a summary of the semantic relation in parentheses.

(13) Object-like dependent:
   a. This interpretation is contrary to an accepted <u>one of wrestling</u> as a sport. ('wrestling' is undergoer of 'interpretation')
   b. How the printers had got hold of her photograph she did not know, but they had, and now it was being sold all over London, along with <u>ones of Lillie Langtry and other noted belles</u>. ('Lillie Langtry and other noted belles' has depiction 'photographs')
(14) Function noun:
   a. Nephrite contains a high proportion of magnesia and a considerable <u>one of lime</u>. ('proportion' is amount of 'lime')
   b. Seventy years of Byrd on record must have given us a good 50 versions of Ave verum corpus but not a single <u>one of Deus venerunt gentes</u>. ('version' is type of 'Deus venerunt gentes')

To summarize the findings of the two corpus searches of Payne et al., there are many examples in which **one**$_{ct}$ is anaphoric to a single noun (or indeed multi-word Nom) followed by an **of**-PP to which it stands in some kind of semantic relation. The corpus instances even include examples of inherently relational nouns, for which the PPs are uncontroversial complements, e.g. (13-a).

In addition to providing a syntactic and semantic analysis of **one**$_{ct}$, the authors discuss how it was possible that the original analysis of (10) had survived for decades. They assume that it is due to a frequency effect that cases like (9-a) are dispreferred. To support their assumption, the authors performed a second study on BNCWEB and extracted 100 random examples of **one**$_{ct}$ to investigate the status of post-modification in different contexts for **one**$_{ct}$. For simplicity, they extracted plural forms only, which cannot function as **one**$_d$. However, they had to exclude two instances of the plural number 1 so they ended up with 98 random instances of **one**$_{ct}$. Their analysis is shown in Table 8.2.

Payne et al. (2013) observed that only five of the post-modifiers in Table 8.2 are prepositional phrases, and of these, exactly one single example is an **of**-PP. By extrapolation, they conclude that **of**-PPs occur only in a very small proportion of occurrences of **one**$_{ct}$ in total.

However, based on further quantitative analysis of the alternation of **of**-PP and competing prenominal genitives, Payne et al. (2013) conclude that they "have found in a detailed examination of the **of**-PP dependents **one**$_{ct}$ absolutely no evidence that **one**$_{ct}$ itself has any special bearing on the frequency of occurrence of the **of**-PP, let alone its grammaticality. The frequencies which are observed are essentially those we would expect given the properties of **of**-PPs as dependents of nouns in general."

Table 8.2 Frequency of the dependents of one$_{ct}$ (in a sample of 98 examples from the BNC).

Immediately preceded by	Total examples	With post-modification
Adjective	69	10
Participle	5	0
Noun	4	1
None	4	4
the	11	10
these/those	4	3
which	1	0

In addition to the questions mentioned above, Payne et al. (2013) touch upon another important methodological point: When drawing linguistic conclusions based on corpora, there is always an issue whether the results do indeed generalize to other corpora, and to language use in general, or whether they simply provide a description of the corpus at hand. Payne et al. were concerned with a related but slightly different issue, namely whether their findings based on British English data would also generalize to corpora of American English. To this end, they compared frequencies of plural one$_{ct}$ in British English BNC data and American English data from COCA. It turned out that plural one$_{ct}$ occurs with lower overall frequencies in American English than in British English, the authors stated that the syntactic distribution and also the semantic relations in cases with **of**-prepositions did not deviate markedly in either corpus.

Finally, the authors discussed the absence of examples, such as the notorious example in (9), in the BNC data. These examples involve nouns denoting interpersonal or kin relations (e.g. **friend, brother**), role nouns (e.g. **king**), and examples of the **student of** X type. They concluded that the BNC is too small a corpus to provide proper evidence. This was indeed borne out when they extended their search to a 470 million words corpus of data from the WWW, WEBCORP, where they retrieved examples involving such nouns.

We refer the reader to the original paper for further details of their analysis. To summarize this study, it showed a pattern-based search of a 'secure' context for investigating the distribution of a particular phenomenon in a corpus. In addition to collecting examples that required further semantic analysis and manual semantic clustering, the study also used frequencies by applying a small-scale random search for estimating the general distribution of the phenomenon.

8.2 Working with Syntactic Annotation

One problem with annotated resources is that they are limited in size, which may mean that they are too small for providing sufficient relevant examples. Researchers faced with this problem often use the annotated resource as a starting point to learn more about the distribution of the phenomenon under investigation and to identify lexical features that are related with the phenomenon, which can then be used as seeds for collecting additional examples from larger, less richly annotated corpora. These examples are then manually annotated for relevant features that play a role in the investigation.

A prototypical example for such a study is the study of the dative alternation by Bresnan et al. (2007). Their research focussed on the question which linguistic factors influence the choice of expression in cases of dative alternation structures, as in (15).[3] The construction involves a ditransitive verb like **give**, which selects for two object arguments, for a theme and a recipient or goal. These arguments are either realized as two noun phrases (NPs) or as an NP and a prepositional phrase (PP). In the first case, the recipient precedes the theme (15-a); in the latter case, there is a shift of the recipient or goal argument, which is realized as the PP and has to follow the theme argument instead of preceding it ((15-b)).

(15) a.   Susan $[_V$ gave$]$ $[_{NP}$ the children$^{Recipient}]$ $[_{NP}$ toys$^{Theme}]$
b.   Susan $[_V$ gave$]$ $[_{NP}$ toys$^{Theme}]$ $[_{PP}$ to the children$^{Recipient}]$

At this point, a comment on the terminology is necessary. The construction is called dative alternation because in languages with a more elaborate case system than Modern English, verbs like **give** select for two NPs marked by two different cases: Accusative and dative, with dative being the typical case for recipients and goals, as in the German example in (16). The dative argument corresponds to the argument that shifts from NP to PP in English, which gave the dative alternation its name.

(16) Susanne gab   dem   Jungen   den   Ball
Susanne gave the$_{Dat}$ boy^{Recipient} the$_{Acc}$ ball^{Theme}
'Susanne gave the ball to the boy.'

The point that is interesting from our view concerns the fact that, at first glance, the two realization options in (15) seem interchangeable. However, there are idiomatic expressions that suggest a slight meaning difference with regard to the perspective that is taken on the situation: Causing a change of state vs causing a change of place, cf. (17).

(17) a.   That movie gave me the creeps.
[= causing a change of state (possession)]
b.   *That movie gave the creeps to me.
[= causing a change of place (movement to goal)]

The starting point of the study by Bresnan et al. (2007) is that the authors challenge the analysis that the dative alternation can be explained by this meaning difference. Bresnan et al. first discussed counter-examples found on the internet, like (18).[4]

(18) This story is designed to give the creeps to people who hate spiders, but is not true.

Then they performed an exhaustive quantitative analysis taking a variety of features into account that had been described in the literature to have an effect on the dative alternation, such as givenness or animacy of the object referents.

For their study, Bresnan et al. employed three corpora: First, the syntactically annotated SWITCHBOARD section of the PENN TREEBANK, which consists of transcribed telephone conversations and has a size of 800,000 words; second, the full SWITCHBOARD Corpus (see also section 6.2.1), which covers three million words but is unannotated and which provided them with a larger empirical basis; and third, the written *Wall Street Journal* section of the PENN TREEBANK (one million words) for a control study. We assume that they chose transcribed speech because spoken language provides better evidence for natural language than written language, which is more affected by prescriptive grammar and text type-specific patterns. Their decision to repeat the study on written data was motivated by a corpus linguistic issue, namely the problem that cross-corpus differences may undermine corpus studies, which had been brought up in the critique of using corpora for linguistic research.

Their goal was to create a representative database for naturally occurring examples of the dative alternation, such as the ones in (19).[5]

(19) a.　The airlines presented it as offering consumers more choice and better flight connections.

　　 b.　If spreads available from index arbitrage are so enormous, surely any sizable mutual-fund company could profit from offering it to small investors.

Figures 8.4 and 8.5 illustrate the partial syntax trees that were relevant for the data extraction. The subtree in Figure 8.4 contains a VP that immediately dominates two NPs. The internal structure of the dominated NPs is not relevant for the query. For example, it does not make a difference whether the NPs are simplex like **consumers** or coordinate like **more choice and better flight connections**. The last line in the figure shows a TGREP2 search pattern for this subtree (for information on TGREP2 see section 12.2).

The structure in Figure 8.5 illustrates the prepositional phrase option of the dative alternation: A VP immediately dominates an NP and a subsequent PP. In this example, the PP-label is enriched with the functional label -DTV, which explicitly marks the prepositional dative constituent. However, restricting the search pattern to this configuration would miss a number of relevant examples because the functional annotation is not exhaustive. This is why the TGREP2 query in the last line of the figure makes use of a so-called regular expression /PP(-DTV)?/, which matches strings that are

```
(VP (VBG offering)
     (NP (NNS consumers) )
     (NP
         (NP (JJR more) (NN choice) )
         (CC and)
         (NP (JJR better) (NN flight) (NNS connections) )))
```

TGREP2: VP < (NP) < (NP)

Figure 8.4 Relevant subtree of the bracketing structure of example (19-a) and a TGREP2 search pattern.

```
(VP   (VBG offering)
       (NP (PRP it) )
       (PP-DTV (TO to)
             (NP (JJ small) (NNS investors) )))
```

TGREP2: VP < (NP) < (/PP(-DTV)?/)

Figure 8.5 Relevant subtree of the bracketing structure of example (19-b) and a simplified TGREP2 search pattern.

PPs, optionally having the -DTV function. We will not go into detail where the query language is concerned but refer the reader to section 12.2. Figure 8.6 depicts the same sub-structures as graphical tree structures.[6]

To a reader with experience in syntactic queries, it is obvious that the bracketing structures in Figures 8.4 and 8.5 correspond directly to the tree structures in Figure 8.6 except for one detail: The functional label -DTV is depicted as edge label in the graphical structure instead of an extension to the PP-label. This has consequences for the query pattern in certain query languages, which we will ignore here.

Bresnan et al. extracted all verbs that appeared in either the prepositional dative structure or the double object structure in the one-million-word SWITCHBOARD section of the PENN TREEBANK. They filtered out benefactives (e.g. **buy, cook for**), those verbs for which there are three or more alternative constructions (e.g. **ask people a question, ask a question of people, ask a question to people; provide John a book, provide John with a book, provide a book to John**), and also non-alternating verbs. The latter were not identified on the basis of SWITCHBOARD because this corpus lacks the size to be conclusive in this respect. The authors used GOOGLE[7] instead by operationalizing the test for "non-alternation" as less than "five instances of a verb in each dative structure in that portion of the Internet indexed by GOOGLE." This procedure left them with 38 verbs, which they then employed in lexical searches on the full three-million-word SWITCHBOARD corpus. The extraction results were further filtered manually to exclude, for example, instances that lacked two overt objects or had

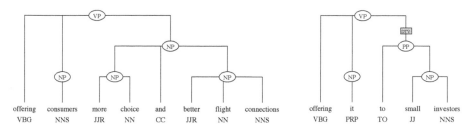

Figure 8.6 Relevant subtrees of examples (19) in graphical representation.

Table 8.3 Sample annotation of dative alternation instances.

Ex.	Verb	Recipient Realization	Recipient Length	Recipient Definiteness	Theme Length	Theme Definiteness
(19-a)	**offer**	NP	1	indefinite	6	indefinite
(19-b)	**offer**	PP	2	indefinite	1	definite

a passivized object as subject. We refer the interested reader to the original paper for further filtering details.

The resulting instances were then annotated for a number of properties that were previously discussed in the literature as having an effect on the dative alternation, such as length of the object constituents (operationalized as determining the number of words), their definiteness (definite vs indefinite), their animacy (animate vs inanimate), and accessibility (accessible vs given vs new). The reader will be familiar with these annotation labels from Part II of this book. Table 8.3 illustrates the resulting data basis, showing a simplified sample annotation of the two instances of the verb **offer** in example (19).

Using the realization of the recipient as a dependent variable, the authors derived a statistical model based on their annotated instances. This model can predict with very high accuracy whether the recipient argument was realized as NP or as PP for a given instance. We encourage the reader to consult the original paper for the statistical analysis, which is a milestone study in statistical corpus linguistics. Here, we focus on the fact that this model showed that the formal syntactic and semantic properties described above, as well as the properties of animacy and discourse accessibility, have an effect on the dative syntax. In addition, there are three empirical issues that may have distorted the empirical findings if the authors had not dealt with them in terms of appropriate statistical methodology. First, the authors took into account potential biases brought up by individual speakers of the SWITCHBOARD telephone conversations. Some speakers contributed more verb instances than others.

The second issue concerns the individual verbs, which have a very skewed distribution—see Figure 8.7. It is important to point out that the most frequent verb **give** is not

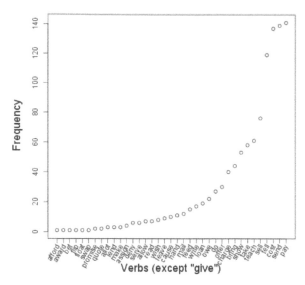

Figure 8.7 Skewed frequency distribution of dative alternation verbs in the SWITCHBOARD Corpus (the most frequent verb is not plotted). The plot is ours.

plotted at all because the inclusion of its frequency of 1,263 instances would have flattened the plot. This skewed distribution comes as no surprise. In the literature, this is described as *large number of rare events*, and refers to the fact that there are many instances with low frequencies and only few instances with high frequencies. In corpus linguistics, this type of curve is often transformed into a so-called *Zipfian* distribution, which plots items that are ranked according to their frequencies. It is always the case that there is just one most frequent item on rank 1 (here: **give**) and many items that share individual lower ranks. The most "crowded" rank normally is the last rank, which contains all items that occurred only once in the corpus (here: **afford, award, bet, flip, float, swap**).

The third empirical issue mentioned above concerns the question of how well the findings based on the corpus of the investigation generalize to other corpora, and in particular to corpora of other modalities, here written language. To answer this question, the authors extracted relevant verbs and their instances from the one-million-word Wall Street Journal section of the PENN TREEBANK and applied their original prediction model to this new data set (including a number of new verbs). The result showed that their model derived on the spoken SWITCHBOARD data very well predicted the recipient realizations of the written Wall Street Journal instances. This means that their findings on the properties that have an effect on dative syntax generalizes across written and spoken modalities.

To sum up the corpus-linguistic issues of this study: The authors made use of a syntactically annotated corpus of spoken language to identify verbs that occurred in relevant syntactic configurations. To this end, the linguistic phenomenon had to be translated into the syntactic annotation labels and their hierarchical configurations. The syntactically identified verbs were then used as seeds for extracting a large number of instances from a larger, unannotated corpus. The resulting instances were then manually annotated with semantic, syntactic, and pragmatic features to create a database for statistical tests and data modeling. Finally, the results were tested on new instances extracted from a syntactically annotated corpus of written language.

The next study that we present is also concerned with syntactic variability. More specifically, Wasow et al. (2011) investigated the optional realization of relativizers (**that** or *wh*-word) in the initial position of certain relative clauses, as illustrated in the examples in (20).[8]

(20) a. That is certainly one reason (why/that) crime has increased.
    b. I think that the last movie (which/that) I saw was *Misery*.
    c. They have all the water (that) they want.

The authors argue that dropping the relativizer cannot be completely optional because there are strong lexical preferences towards one option or the other, in terms of words occurring in the embedding NP. In the examples in (20), for example, the choice is influenced by the nouns **reason, movie, water**, the prenominal adjective **last**, and the determiners **one, the, all the**. To investigate this variance, Wasow et al. pursued a quantitative corpus analysis. Their motivation was not only to record individual lexical preferences but also to explain the reasons—in other words, how lexical choices in an NP containing a relative clause can influence whether a relativizer is used or not.

To this end, the authors used as their empirical source the syntactically annotated SWITCHBOARD section of the PENN TREEBANK (version 3), which consists of 650 transcribed telephone conversations. Considering that not all types of relative clauses show the same optionality with respect to the realization of the relativizer, the authors extracted only certain types of relative clauses as their reference set for further investigations (see below).

In the SWITCHBOARD section, relative clauses are annotated as SBAR nodes that are immediately dominated by an NP node (see also example 4.7 in section 4.1 where we gave an example of a relative clause from the written WSJ section of the PENN TREEBANK). The SWITCHBOARD data set differs from the written sections in that it includes incomplete sentences, hesitations, and other phenomena of spoken language. Example (21) and the bracketing structure in Figure 8.8 illustrate the target configuration of the study. The relative clause **that we finally had** is an SBAR dominated by the NP **nursing home**.[9] The bracketing structure shows that the WHNP phrase containing the relativizer **that** is coindexed with the trace *T* in object position, indicating that this is an object extracted relative clause.

(21) We were not really happy with, nursing home that we finally had *T*.

In Figure 8.8, -DFL- E_S marks the end of a "sentence" on the disfluency annotation level of the corpus. Figure 8.9 shows the relevant part of the sentence as a tree structure.[10]

```
( (S
   (NP-SBJ (PRP We) )
   (VP (VBD were) (RB not)
     (ADVP (RB really) )
     (ADJP-PRD (JJ happy)
       (PP (IN with)
         (, ,)
         (NP
           (NP (NN nursing) (NN home) )
           (SBAR
             (WHNP-1 (WDT that) )
             (S
               (NP-SBJ (PRP we) )
               (ADVP-TMP (RB finally) )
               (VP (VBD had)
                 (NP (-NONE- *T*-1) ))))))))
   (. .) (-DFL- E_S) ))
```

Figure 8.8 The bracketing structure of example (21).

As mentioned above, instead of extracting all relative clauses, the authors restricted their investigation to relative clause types that are not generally biased towards one of the realization forms. They excluded subject relative clauses, such as in (22-a), relative clauses involving pied piping, see (22-b), reduced subject-extracted and infinitival reduced relative clauses, see (22-c), and, finally, *wh*-relativizers, see (22-d). The exclusion of the latter was motivated by filtering non-restrictive relative clauses, in addition to avoiding noise in the data since a number of *wh*-relative clauses in the corpus are, in fact, embedded questions.

(22) a. I saw a movie *(that) offended me.
     b. A movie to *(which) we went.
     c. A movie (*that) seen by millions.
     d. *Good bye Lenin*, which /*that I enjoyed, is set in Berlin.

Since the authors did not specify how exactly they extracted the relative clauses, we provide suggestions for simplified queries, which overgenerate but give an idea of how to proceed. Figure 8.10 shows a graphical representation of the query.[11]

To the reader familiar with syntactic queries, it is obvious that the query is very unspecific—for example, it does not distinguish subject-extracted from object-extracted relative clauses, neither does it distinguish different realizations of the relativizer (**that** vs *wh*-relativizer). However, it separates relative clauses from other clausal modifiers of nouns, such as the complement clause **that the growth of the economy is leveling off** (starting with complementizer **that**) in example (23).

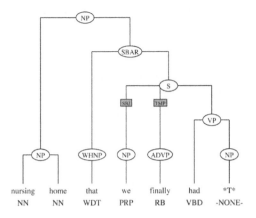

Figure 8.9: A graphical representation of non-subject extracted relative clause in the SWITCHBOARD section.

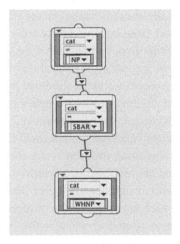

Figure 8.10: Example search for the realization of relativizer.

(23) In another reflection <u>that the growth of the economy is leveling off</u>, the government said …

Example (24) provides a corresponding search pattern in TGREP2. For further explanations of the query languages, we refer the reader to sections 12.3 and 12.2 respectively, where these search tools are introduced in detail. To avoid noise in the extraction results, further restrictions need to be added to the search patterns. We refrain from doing so here because they complicate the pattern to a complexity that is difficult to understand.

(24) NP < (SBAR) < (WHNP)

Wasow et al. report that they obtained 3,701 non-subject extracted relative clauses from the SWITCHBOARD section of the PENN TREEBANK after applying the filters described above. 1,601 (43%) of the matching relative clauses started with **that**, 2,100 (57%) had no relativizer.

In their investigation, Wasow et al. showed that the proportions of relative clauses with **that** vary strongly with the lexical realization of determiner, prenominal adjective and head noun of the embedding NP. For example, relative clauses embedded in an NP with determiner **every, all**, or **the** occurred only in 14.7 percent (10/68), 24.3 percent (50/206), and 34.2 percent (620/1,813) of their instances with **that**, much less than the average of 43 percent. In comparison, **a(n)** and **some** occurred in 74.8 percent (226/302) and 64.2 percent (43/67) of their instances with **that**, much more frequently than the average of instances suggests.

A similar picture became evident when they looked at those nominal heads that are most commonly modified by the relative clause type under investigation. The nouns **stuff, people**, and **one** occurred with relativizer **that** more often than average whereas the nouns **way, time, reason**, and **everything**, among others, strongly prefer relative clauses without relativizer. Finally, the same variation was present for different prenominal modifiers: NPs modified by **last, first, best**, and **only** seem to disprefer the realization of **that**, whereas modifiers like **little, few**, and **certain** show the opposite preference.

To explain these lexical preferences for the realization of relative clause structure, the authors looked at lexical preferences for being modified by a relative clause in the first place. Their hypothesis is that "in environments where a non-subject extracted relative clause is more predictable, relativizers are less frequent." They can show that even if NPs modified by relative clauses constitute only a small fraction of all NPs, there is a significant difference in NPs beginning with **the** versus those beginning with **a(n)** with respect to the proportions that are modified by a relative clause. The proportion of **the** NPs modified by a relative clause is significantly higher than the proportion of **a(n)** NPs modified in the same way, which correlates to the observation that **a(n)** NPs strongly prefer the realization of **that** as relativizer whereas **the** NPs disprefer it. The authors correlated the predictability of non-subject extracted relative clauses for all 35 words of their investigation (determiners, modifiers, and head nouns) against the frequency of relativizer absence, which also proved to be significant. For more details on their study and their explanation of the correlation that takes processing and production into account, we refer the interested reader to the original paper (Wasow et al., 2011). We will point out references for the statistical tests in section 8.5.

To sum up this study, Wasow et al. showed that particular choices of determiner, noun, or prenominal adjective correlate with exceptionally high or exceptionally low rates of relativizers. Their explanation hinges on the predictability of the relative clause. The more likely it is that a relative clause will occur in a particular lexical context, the more likely it is that the relativizer is dropped.

This is an exemplary study, which fully relies on the syntactic annotation of the PENN TREEBANK. The procedure includes narrowing down the relevant phenomenon by excluding cases that would distort the results for independent reasons. The operationalization of the search for the linguistic target structure required them to map the linguistic concepts on the syntactic labels and hierarchies of the PENN TREEBANK. For the investigation, two reference sets were relevant: First, the set of extracted instances of NPs modified by relative clauses, to obtain proportions of relativizer realization for individual lexical items. Second, they needed all NPs in the SWITCHBOARD section containing any of the lexical items (nouns, determiners, adjectives) under investigation, independent of whether they were modified by a relative clause or not, to obtain proportions of relative clause occurrence to determine their predictability.

8.3 On the Interaction of Coreference and Discourse Relations

In this section, we introduce a study that deals with research questions in pragmatics and takes annotation on the discourse level into account. The underlying object of investigation of this study is coherence, i.e. the effect that a text or discourse is interpreted as a coherent whole instead of a series of independent sentences (see Chapter 6 for details). In particular, the study by Louis and Nenkova (2010) investigates local coherence that describes coherence effects between adjacent sentences—more precisely, smooth transitions from one sentence to the next. From a cognitive point of view, a transition is smooth if the recipient can easily integrate the information expressed by the second sentence into the current discourse model, which is most dominantly characterized by the last sentence that has been parsed (see also Chapter 6). There are two main types of local coherence discussed in the literature: First, entity-based coherence, which requires that subsequent sentences refer to the same referents (cf. section 6.1); second, discourse relation-based coherence, which requires logical relations, such as temporal or causal relations, to hold between adjacent sentences (see section 6.3 for an introduction). Examples (25) and (26) show how a locally coherent interpretation is supported by textual means.[12]

(25) Although [$_1$ [$_2$ his] team] lost the World Series, [$_2$ [$_1$ San Francisco Giants] owner Bob Lurie] hopes to have a new home for [$_1$ them]. [$_2$ He] is an avid fan of a proposition on next week's ballot to help build a replacement for Candlestick Park.

(26) There is [an incredible pressure on [school systems] and teachers]] to raise [test scores]. [$_{Causal}$ So] [efforts to beat [the tests]] are also on the rise.

In example (25), coreferent pronouns and other noun phrases are marked by identical subscripts. One of the referents introduced in the first sentence, namely the one referred to by **San Francisco Giants owner Bob Lurie**, is mentioned again in the second sentence. The transition is smooth because of this referent. It requires little effort on the side of the recipient to add the new information provided by the second sentence to the discourse representation of this referent. In other words, the recipient knows exactly how to relate the information provided by the second sentence to that in the first sentence. We will not go into further details here, but refer the interested reader to section 8.5. In example (26), the situation is completely different. There is no overlap between the referents, which are marked in square brackets for the convenience of the reader. Instead, a smooth transition is guaranteed by the first word of the second sentence, the discourse connective **So**, which indicates a causal relation between the two sentences. This logical relation tells the recipient that the second sentence is a result of the preceding sentence (more precisely, the relation holds on the level of propositions). So, again, the recipient can easily integrate the new information into their current discourse representation.

Earlier studies have combined entity-based coherence and discourse relation-based coherence in different ways. Louis and Nenkova (2010) state that "the motivation behind such proposals have been the empirical findings that 'weak' discourse relations such as *elaboration* are the most common type of relations, and that a large percentage of adjacent sentences in fact do not have *any* entities in common. The goal of the current study was to provide empirical foundations for the distribution of factors that have an influence on local coherence."

To do so, the authors combined data from two annotated resources: The ONTONOTES Corpus (version 2.9) and the PENN DISCOURSE TREEBANK 2.0 (PDTB) (both corpora are introduced in Chapter 6), both of which share a set of 590 articles from the Wall Street Journal section of the PENN TREEBANK. The study uses coreference annotation from the ONTONOTES Corpus and discourse relations from the corresponding PDTB texts.

The PDTB includes different types of relations. For this study, both explicit and implicit discourse relations were taken into account, as well as entity-based relations (EntRel), which hold between sentences that mention the same referents directly or indirectly (for more details on the annotation see section 6.3.1). There is an overlap between the phenomena marked by EntRel in the PDTB and the coreference annotation in ONTONOTES. However, both corpora are necessary because of differences in terms of coverage and annotated phenomena: With respect to relations, ONTONOTES only marks coreference based on identity relations, whereas PDTB also uses EntRel in more indirect cases that involve bridging, such as in the examples in (27) and (28).[13]

(27) All four <u>demonstrators </u>were arrested. [EntRel] The <u>law</u>, which Bush allowed to take effect without his signature, went into force Friday.

(28) Authorities in Hawaii said the wreckage of a missing commuter plane with 20 people aboard was spotted in a remote valley on the island of Molokai. [EntRel] There wasn't any evidence of <u>survivors</u>.

With respect to coverage, EntRel has not been exhaustively annotated in the PDTB. This label was only assigned if the annotators could neither establish an explicitly marked discourse relation between two adjacent sentences nor an implicitly derived one. Only in such cases, the annotators checked whether there was an overlap in discourse referents. ONTONOTES, on the other hand, contains an exhaustive annotation of coreferent elements throughout the corpus.

Based on prior studies, Louis and Nenkova (2010) identified three hypotheses on the distribution of entity-based coherence and discourse relation-based coherence. The goal of their own study was to empirically validate these hypotheses.[14]

Hypothesis 1   Adjacent sentences that do not share entities are related by non-elaboration (i.e. "strong") discourse relations.

Hypothesis 2   Adjacent sentences joined by non-elaboration (i.e. "strong") discourse relations have lower entity coherence: Such pairs are less likely to mention the same entities.

Hypothesis 3   Almost all pairs of sentences in a coherent text either share entities or participate in non-elaboration (i.e. "strong") discourse relations.

The authors operationalized the tests for these hypotheses by grouping the relations from PDTB into two groups. Non-elaborative relations correspond to what they call "core" relations, which comprise the three topmost relations in PDTB: Temporal, Contingency, and Comparison (and all their respective sublevels—see Figure 6.8 in section 6.3 for the full set of hierarchically structured discourse relations). The second group is more heterogeneous; it comprises elaborative, "weak" relations of the general type Expansion, as well as of the type EntRel, described above. These categories allow them to test the hypotheses by comparing the occurrence and co-occurrence of what they call "weak" and "core" relations. The search for coreference relations in ONTONOTES was more straightforward than the search for discourse relations in PDTB because there are only two types of coreference annotated, identity relations (IDENT) and appositive relations (APPOS). For the current study, only the identity relation is relevant. The appositive relation marks appositive structures, which, by definition, only occur within a sentence.

To create a data set for their study, the authors decided to consider only adjacent sentence pairs within a paragraph. Paragraphs are delineated in the text formatting of the original article publication. In printed material, they are generally marked by empty lines or line breaks with indentation. The paragraph structure of the Wall Street Journal articles is provided in the original PENN TREEBANK files, and the annotation of PDTB is partly sensitive to the paragraph structure of these articles. Whereas explicit relations are annotated across paragraph boundaries, implicit relations are only marked between pairs of sentences within paragraphs. This has been a design decision to ensure consistency in the annotation, even though there are cases where an implicit relation could be inferred across paragraph boundaries.

The study by Louis and Nenkova (2010) is complicated by the fact that there are no simple query tools that allow the user to extract information as required for this investigation. This study provides an example for extracting relevant instances from annotated corpora by means of programming scripts mentioned in the introduction to the current chapter.

Table 8.4 shows extracted relations for the toy data set in (29)[15] that we set up to explain the current study. Due to space limitations, the original paper does not provide any details of this kind.

(29)   Although his team lost the World Series, San Francisco Giants owner Bob Lurie hopes to have a new home for them. He is an avid fan of a proposition on next week's ballot to help build a replacement for Candlestick Park. Small wonder, since he's asking San Francisco taxpayers to sink up to $100 million into the new

stadium. As San Francisco digs out from The Pretty Big One, opponents say the last thing the city can afford is an expensive new stadium.

A stadium craze is sweeping the country. It's fueled by the increasing profitability of major-league teams …

In the data set in Table 8.4, we provide a set of IDs to be able to distinguish different instances and also relate them to the original data: Instance ID (ID), text ID (Text), paragraph ID (Para), sentence pair ID (SentPair). Discourse relation (DiscRel) has only two values, of a non-metric type: Weak and core. In this study the distinction between explicit relations and implicit relations has been ignored. The authors report that they tested them separately and found the same tendencies as in the more general evaluation. Another option would be to be more explicit and also collect (in a separate column) the actual relation labels. Similarly, we decided to treat shared entities (SharedEnt) as having two values: Shared entities, for sentences that share entities via coreference, and no sharing. An alternative representation could have provided the count of shared entities or the proportion of shared entities with respect to all entities mentioned in the sentence pair. For the current investigation, it is sufficient to document whether there are any shared entities between the sentences.

The ID column in the table provides a unique ID for each instance in the data. Thus, each row represents a data instance—here, a pair of paragraph-internal, adjacent sentences and their properties—and each column represents a type of information for characterizing these instances. These characterizations are then employed in subsequent

Table 8.4 Fictional data set for investigating factors of local coherence in text (29) based on ONTONOTES and PDTB.

ID	Text	Para	SentPair	DiscRel	Explicit	SharedEnt
1	wsj_0126	1	s1_s2	weak	explicit	shared entities
2	wsj_0126	1	s2_s3	weak	explicit	shared entities
3	wsj_0126	1	s3_s4	core	implicit	shared entities
4	wsj_0126	2	s5_s6	weak	explicit	shared entities

…

Table 8.5 Total number (proportion) of sentence pairs in the corpus in the given categories.

	Shared entities		No sharing	
core	1,832	(21.80%)	1,580	(18.80%)
weak	2,485	(29.56%)	2,508	(29.84%)

quantitative evaluations that combine frequencies of the original data set in cross tabulations, which can then be tested for statistically significant differences or interactions.

Table 8.5 is an example of such a cross tabulation; it is adapted from the original paper (Louis and Nenkova, 2010). It provides the absolute frequencies (and proportions) of sentence pairs in the categories core relations versus weak relations, as well as shared entities versus no sharing. This presentation corresponds to a cross tabulation of the variables DiscRel and SharedEnt.

Below, we repeat Hypothesis 3 from above and rephrase it as Hypothesis 3a in such a way that it can be tested against the data. In other words, we rephrase it so that it can be falsified if its premises do not hold. To achieve this, we strengthen the prediction from "almost all pairs" to "all pairs."[16] One premise that we take for granted and do not question here is that the texts of our corpus are indeed coherent, and consequently, that also all the paragraph-internal sentence pairs in these articles are coherent.

Hypothesis 3 Almost all pairs of sentences in a coherent text either share entities or participate in non-elaboration discourse relation.
Hypothesis 3a All paragraph-internal pairs of sentences in the 590 WSJ articles either share coreferent entities or participate in core discourse relations.

Table 8.5 shows that about 30 percent of all paragraph-internal sentence pairs in the corpus are neither related by a core relation, nor do they directly share the same entities (see bottom right cell). In other words, the proportion of paragraph-internal sentence pairs that conform to the hypothesis and either share coreferent entities and/or participate in core discourse relations is approximately 70 percent (21.80% + 18.80% + 29.56%). At first glance, this seems to contradict our strong claim in Hypothesis 3a. A proportion of 70 percent is considerably smaller than the proposed 100 percent. To determine whether this deviation is indeed statistically significant, it is necessary to perform statistical tests which are beyond the scope of this book. In fact, the authors report that none of the three hypotheses is validated on the Wall Street Journal articles. We will not go into further details here and refer the interested reader to the original paper instead.

To sum up this section, the current study is special in that it combines two annotation levels from two independent corpora that (partly) share the same raw texts. It allows the authors to test discourse-related predictions that have never been validated in that way before, due to the lack of annotated resources. The authors could not use off-the-shelf tools but needed to write their own scripts to assess and relate the data instances. We used this study as an opportunity to sketch how to extract a data set from a corpus in a way that it systematically characterizes instances of the investigation in terms of relevant types of information. Such a data set can then be used as the basis for any further quantitative evaluation.

8.4 Summary

In this chapter, we have looked at linguistic studies that used corpus evidence to strengthen their linguistic argument or to falsify hypotheses. We described a set of studies using corpora with different levels of annotation, including POS annotation, lemma annotation, syntactic annotation, and coreference and discourse connective annotation. None of these studies had its main focus on the corpus-linguistic aspect; rather, the corpus was used as a tool. Our goal here was to show the reader how to translate a linguistic question into linguistic patterns that can be used in a search for phenomena. Thus, the corpus user needs to decide which types of annotations are necessary to find the phenomena of interest. We hope that we also impressed on the reader how important and useful query tools are. These will be the focus of the next part of the book.

8.5 Further Reading

Programming: Bird et al. (2009) give an introduction to the programming language Python based on the *Natural Language Toolkit* (NLTK), which provides many scripts for dealing with corpora and corpus resources (http://www.nltk.org/). Perl is another programming language widely used for processing text files. There is a considerable amount of information available online, cf. http://www.perl.org/; Schwartz et al. (2011) provides an introductory textbook.

Section 8.1

BRITISH NATIONAL CORPUS (BNC): This is a carefully sampled 100-million-word reference corpus for British English. More information is available at http://www.natcorp.ox.ac.uk/.

BYU search interface: This is an online corpus query interface of the corpus collection by Marc Davies at Brigham Young University (http://corpus.byu.edu/). It provides access to nine corpora including the BNC and COCA (see below) and other corpora in English, Spanish, and Portuguese, as well as an advanced interface to the GOOGLE BOOKS Corpus.

CLAWS: CLAWS is short for "Constituent Likelihood Automatic Word-tagging System" and describes both an automatic part-of-speech tagging program as well as the tagset used by this program. Both the POS tagger and the tagset have been developed at the University Centre for Computer Corpus Research on Language (UCREL) in Lancaster. Most notably, the BNC is tagged with CLAWS. It is important to know that there are different versions of the tagset that differ considerably (e.g. CLAWS 5 and CLAWS 7). See the webpage for documentation and comparison of the tagset versions (http://ucrel.lancs.ac.uk/claws/).

Corpus of Contemporary American English (COCA): By 2012, the corpus sampled by Marc Davies has reached a size of 450 million tokens. It is accessible via http://corpus.byu.edu/coca/; its sampling is described by Davies (2009). There is a five-minute guided tour that shows major features of the corpus (http://corpus.byu.edu/coca/help/tour_e.asp).

Using the web as corpus: Kilgarriff and Grefenstette (2003) discuss the advantages and disadvantages, and give an early overview targeting linguists and computational linguists. Hundt et al. (2007) is a collection of corpus-linguistic articles discussing different aspects of the topic. Bergh and Zanchetta (2008) provide a neat summary of the (then) state of the art. WaCky—the *Web-As-Corpus Kool Yinitiative* provides pre-processed web-based corpora that can be downloaded and queried with CQP (http://wacky.sslmit.unibo.it/doku.php?id=start). Some entries in the Language Log (http://itre.cis. upenn.edu/~myl/languagelog) discuss the use of Google for linguistic retrievals, for example, articles 000193.html and 000194.html in the archives.

Frequency adjectives: Earlier semantic analyses can be found in Bolinger (1967); Stump (1981); Larson (1988); Zimmermann (2003).

Anaphoric ONE: Its use as empirical evidence for the poverty of stimulus argument goes back to Baker (1979). Pullum and Scholz (2002) is a predecessor analysis to the one presented in the book by Payne et al. (2013).

Weak crossover: The classic references that describe this phenomenon are Postal (1971); Wasow (1972); see also Wasow (2002). In addition, we refer the reader to the related literature discussed by Culicover (2013).

WEBCORP: A linguistic web-searching tool that provides concordances as result of weblinks. WEBCORP was created by the Research and Development Unit for English Studies (RDUES) in the School of English at Birmingham City University. It can be accessed online at http://www.webcorp.org.uk/live/. More advanced searches are provided in terms of the *WebCorp Linguist's Search Engine* (http://wse1.webcorp.org.uk/home/).

Section 8.2

Dative alternation: Pinker (1989) is a classical reference for the Multiple Meaning Approach; Rappaport Hovav and Levin (2008) support the Single Meaning Approach instead. Goldberg (2013) uses this phenomenon among others in a Construction Grammar analysis.

SWITCHBOARD: The original SWITCHBOARD Corpus was published in two releases. It is available from the Linguistic Data Consortium (LDC) at http://www.ldc.upenn.edu/.

PENN TREEBANK: The syntactic annotation of treebank has been thoroughly introduced in section 4.2. The treebank is available from the Linguistic Data Consortium (LDC) at http://www.ldc.upenn.edu/.

Zipfian distribution: The distribution has originally been described with respect to social science data by Zipf (1949). Baroni (2009) gives an overview of its applications in linguistics.

Statistical/significance tests: VASSARSTATS is a website for statistical computing created by Richard Lowry, which provides interactive forms for performing significance tests among others (http://vassarstats.net/). It is accompanied by Richard Lowry's statistics textbook *Concepts and Applications of Inferential Statistics* (http://vassarstats.net/textbook/). Gries (2013) provides an introductory textbook to statistics for linguists with the language R. Baayen (2008) gives a more advanced overview on the same topic.

Section 8.3

Coherence: This term describes the fact that we experience text as a coherent whole instead of an unlinked list of sentences. The handbook articles by Andrew Kehler provide comprehensive summaries and links to further literature (Kehler, 2004, 2012).

ONTONOTES Corpus: This corpus is available free of charge from the Linguistic Data Consortium at http://www.ldc.upenn.edu/. The corpus is documented in a conference paper (Hovy et al., 2006). There is also an annotation manual for the English coreference annotation (BBN Techologies, 2004).

PENN DISCOURSE TREEBANK (PDTB): The corpus is a stand-off extension of the syntactically annotated PENN TREEBANK and is available via the LDC. The annotation of PDTB-0.2 is described in detail by Prasad et al. (2008); annotation guidelines are also available (Prasad et al., 2007).

PART IV
QUERYING LINGUISTICALLY
ANNOTATED CORPORA

CHAPTER 9
CONCORDANCES

This chapter is concerned with basic methodology for search in text. It gives a short introduction to concordances and concordancers. We will first define the basic terminology in section 9.1. Then we will look at one, freely available concordancer, AntConc, in section 9.2. Then we will look at a parallel concordancer, i.e. a concordancer which works on parallel texts: we will describe ParaConc, a commercial software with a freely available demo version, in section 9.3. There are also more powerful concordancers that allow the search in linguistically annotated corpora, especially on the word level. These will be discussed in Chapter 11.

9.1 Basic Terminology

A *concordance* is a list displaying all occurrences of a word in a text with its context in alphabetical form. A *concordancer* is a fairly simple query tool that generally allows us to search in raw text, without annotations. Concordances existed before the computer age. Then, they had to be compiled by hand and were thus only available for important texts such as the Bible, the Qur'an, or the works of Shakespeare. Outside of linguistics, concordances were often used for religious studies. Nowadays, with the availability of text in electronic form as well as the availability of concordancing software, we can load our text into a concordancer and start searching.

Concordances are generally shown in the format of *Key Word in Context* (KWIC). This means that the words that we are searching for are displayed centrally, with the left and right context displayed up to a pre-specified number of words or characters. Figure 9.1 shows the eight occurrences of the word **from**[1] in a corpus consisting of the text from the Student Blooper Collection.[2]

A *parallel concordancer* allows us to look at texts in multiple languages. This can be used, for example, for translation studies.

9.2 AntConc

AntConc is a freely available concordancer that works on all major platforms. The tool allows the user to load text files and then search in those files. Figure 9.2 shows the user interface for the standard KWIC format. The tool shows under "Corpus Files" that two texts are loaded, from the file blooper.txt,[3] the other one from the file bones.txt.[4] Under "Search Term," we enter the word(s) that we are looking for. Note that it is possible to search for sequences of words, and we can use regular expressions (see Chapter 10).

1	story" of the world from certifiably gen	blooper.txt
2	the United States, from eight grade thr	blooper.txt
3	nd Eve were created from an apple tree.	blooper.txt
4	him. Socrates died from an overdose of	blooper.txt
5	r taxis. Delegates from the original th	blooper.txt
6	ess while traveling from Washington to G	blooper.txt
7	ry large. Bach died from 1750 to the pre	blooper.txt
8	gorrilas came down from the hills and n	blooper.txt

Figure 9.1 The KWIC for the word **from** in the Student Blooper Corpus.

AntConc also has an option that allows us to determine the size of the context in terms of characters. The concordance in Figure 9.2 has a context of 20 characters, which gives us 20 characters to the left and 20 characters to the right (including the search term).

The standard setting for displaying the search results is in the order in which they appear in the text. However, AntConc also allows us to sort the results. For this, we need to choose which words it should use for sorting. This can be defined under "KWIC Sort." Under "Level 1," we choose the major sort criterion: 0 means the search term, 1R

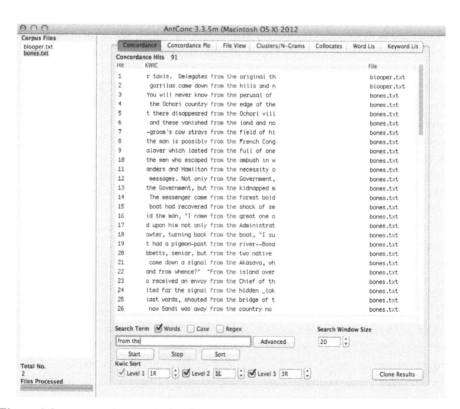

Figure 9.2 AntConc's user interface for the query for the sequence of words **from the**.

is the next word to the right, 2R the second word to the right, 1L the first word to the left, etc. In case of a tie, we can also have a second and third level of sorting. Once the sorting criterion is chosen, click "Sort."

Under the option "Advanced," we can also provide a list of words that we are looking for, i.e. we could search for the words **wife** and **she** at the same time. We can also restrict the search to cases where certain words occur in the context—for example, if we are only interested in the occurrences of **wife** if the word **his** is in the context of 5 words but not necessarily adjacent. We show the first 5 search results in (1) sorted based on the preceding word.

(1) ected of murdering *his* chief **wife**, and the only evidence ag
long time and *his* brown-eyed **wife** looked at him curiously.
great hut he had sat with *his* **wife**, a steaming dish of fish
his land and to mine, to *his* **wife** and the wives of his coun
ote "Paradise Lost." Then *his* **wife** dies and he wrote "Paradi

AntConc offers additional forms of displaying the search results. One possibility is the "Concordance Plot," a bar code representation of how the search word is distributed over the text. Figure 9.3, for example, shows the concordance plot for the word **she** in the two texts from above. The plot shows that the word was used more often in bones.txt

Figure 9.3 AntConc's concordance plot for the word **she**.

than in blooper.txt. But we can also see that there are passages in bones.txt in which **she** occurs very frequently while in others, it does not occur at all. This display is especially useful when we want to track the occurrence of a word in the story. The next option, "File View," offers the possibility of looking at the search words in the complete text, without a restriction on context size. "Clusters/N-Grams" offers the possibility to find out in which combination a word occurs in a text. This also gives the option to extract all *n*-grams from the text. *N*-grams are sequences of words of a certain length, where the *n* is a placeholder that specifies the length. For example, a *unigram* is a single word, a *bigram* a sequence of two words, a *trigram* a sequence of three words. All higher *n*-grams use numbers: 4-grams, 5-grams, etc. Figure 9.4 shows the results of a search for bigrams and trigrams.

"Word List" allows us to look at a list of words extracted from our texts, with their frequency counts, and "Keyword List" allows us to compare the word frequencies to a *reference corpus*. This gives us a statistical measure to validate hypotheses such as "the word **bones** occurs more often in the text than in a normal text." The normal text serves as our reference here. We would also expect to find the word **technology** less often in bones.txt than in a modern reference text. The option "Collocates" allows us to search for words that collocate with our search word. *Collocations* are sequences of words that occur together more often than we would expect. If we look for collocations involving the word **Robert**, the collocates are **Sir** and **Sanleigh**, since **Sir Robert Sanleigh** is one of the characters in the text.

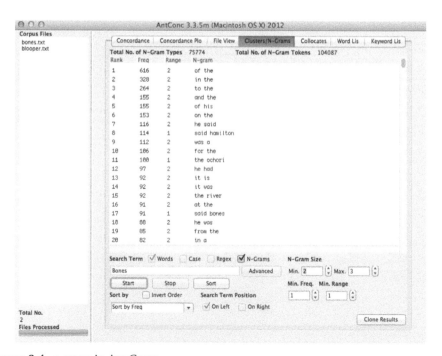

Figure 9.4 *n*-grams in AntConc.

9.3 PARACONC

PARACONC is a concordancer that can work on parallel texts in up to four languages. In order to use PARACONC, the texts have to be *aligned* on the sentence level. Alignment here means that we have to mark which sentences are translations of each other. PARACONC expects to have separate files per language. The easiest way to mark alignment is to have sentences separated into separate lines, so that translations are located on the same line in the different files. Since sometimes there is no 1:1 correspondence between sentences, it makes sense to have all sentences corresponding to one sentence in one language on this corresponding line. It would also be possible to align on the paragraph level, but this makes searching more cumbersome. Table 9.1 shows the first few lines of the English-German part of the EUROPARL Corpus, a parallel, sentence aligned corpus of the Proceedings of the European Parliament. The third line shows an example in which one English sentence was translated into two German sentences, as shown in (2).

Table 9.1 An extract of the EUROPARL English-German text.

English	German
Resumption of the session	Wiederaufnahme der Sitzungsperiode
I declare resumed the session of the European Parliament adjourned on Friday 17 December 1999, and I would like once again to wish you a happy new year in the hope that you enjoyed a pleasant festive period.	Ich erkläre die am Freitag, dem 17. Dezember unterbrochene Sitzungsperiode des Europäischen Parlaments für wiederaufgenommen, wünsche Ihnen nochmals alles Gute zum Jahreswechsel und hoffe, daß Sie schöne Ferien hatten.
Although, as you will have seen, the dreaded 'millennium bug' failed to materialise, still the people in a number of countries suffered a series of natural disasters that truly were dreadful.	Wie Sie feststellen konnten, ist der gefürchtete "Millenium-Bug" nicht eingetreten. Doch sind Bürger einiger unserer Mitgliedstaaten Opfer von schrecklichen Naturkatastrophen geworden.
You have requested a debate on this subject in the course of the next few days, during this part-session.	Im Parlament besteht der Wunsch nach einer Aussprache im Verlauf dieser Sitzungsperiode in den nächsten Tagen.
In the meantime, I should like to observe a minute's silence, as a number of Members have requested, on behalf of all the victims concerned, particularly those of the terrible storms, in the various countries of the European Union.	Heute möchte ich Sie bitten – das ist auch der Wunsch einiger Kolleginnen und Kollegen –, allen Opfern der Stürme, insbesondere in den verschiedenen Ländern der Europäischen Union, in einer Schweigeminute zu gedenken.
Please rise, then, for this minute's silence.	Ich bitte Sie, sich zu einer Schweigeminute zu erheben.
(The House rose and observed a minute's silence)	(Das Parlament erhebt sich zu einer Schweigeminute.)

(2) Although, as you will have seen, the dreaded 'millennium bug' failed to materialise, still the people in a number of countries suffered a series of natural disasters that truly were dreadful.

Wie Sie feststellen konnten, ist der gefürchtete "Millenium-Bug" nicht eingetreten. Doch sind Bürger einiger unserer Mitgliedstaaten Opfer von schrecklichen Naturkatastrophen geworden.

After loading the first 1,000 sentences per language into PARACONC, we can have a look at the alignment, by choosing "File/View Corpus Alignment," then choosing the files, and "Alignment." PARACONC also allows the correction of the alignment, by right clicking into the text field that should be corrected. A window then provides options such as splitting the sentence, merging it with the next one, or inserting an empty field.

We can now search for words, in either language, in the menu "Search." Figure 9.5 shows the search results for the word **Parlament** (Eng. **parliament**) in the German text. The English translations of the displayed German sentences are shown in the lower window. If we click on a German sentence, the corresponding English sentence moves to the top of its window.

We can also identify the English words corresponding to the German search term. To do this, we right click in the English window, and select "Hot Words." Figure 9.6 shows the window. The window lists all words that it considers possible translations for the German search term. After we choose the first one, **parliament**, the translation is highlighted (in the tool displayed in blue), as shown in Figure 9.7.

PARACONC also has an option for "Parallel Search." Here, we can search for words with a specific meaning in the other language. The word **request** or **requests** occurs 19 times in our small corpus sample. However, the translations into German vary. Figure

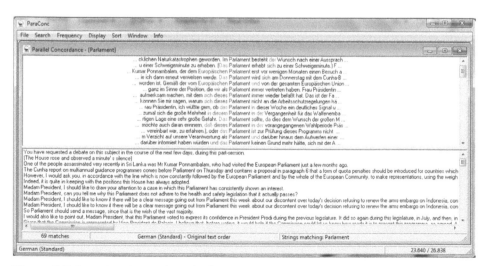

Figure 9.5 PARACONC's search results for the word **Parlament** in the German text.

Figure 9.6 Choosing a translation for the word **Parlament** in the German text.

Figure 9.7 The search results with the selected translation marked.

9.8 shows a search for the two forms of **request**[5] where the German translation does not have the word **bitten** (note that the "Not" is selected in the lower part).

Similar to AntConc, ParaConc also provides frequency counts either for an individual language, or for all languages. Figure 9.9 shows the most frequent words in our German-English sample corpus. For every word, the absolute frequency and the percentage of a word are shown. The most frequent English word, **the**, for example, occurs 2,043 times in our sample corpus, which corresponds to 7.61 percent of the words.

9.4 Summary

In this chapter, we have looked at concordances based on raw text. We looked at AntConc, a free software for monolingual concordancing, which also allows analyzing

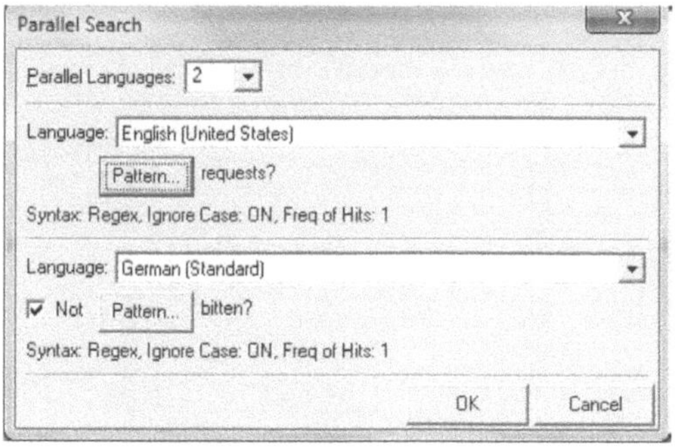

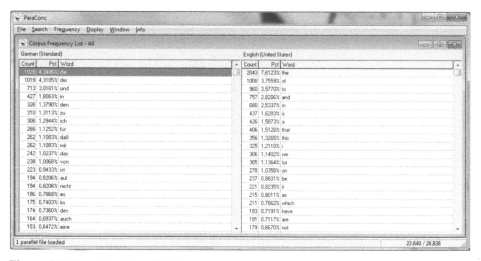

Figure 9.8 PARACONC's window for parallel search.

Figure 9.9 PARACONC's parallel frequency counts.

the text for *n*-grams and collocations. For searching in parallel text corpora, we looked at PARACONC's free demo version. This concordancer displays query results with their translations in up to 4 languages, and it also allows searches for words with specific translations.

9.5 Further Reading

Section 9.2

ANTCONC is available from http://www.antlab.sci.waseda.ac.jp/software.html. More information about different options in ANTCONC can be found in the Readme file also available from this webpage.

Beyond concordancers: For more powerful concordancers, see Chapters 10 and 11.

Other concordancers: There are several monolingual concordancers, among them MONOCONC, which is available from http://www.athel.com/mono.html, CASUALCONC, which is available from https://sites.google.com/site/casualconc/Home, and WORDSMITH, available from http://www.lexically.net/wordsmith/version6/index.html.

Section 9.3

EUROPARL: The EUROPARL CORPUS is available at http://www. statmt.org/europarl/. It is described in Koehn (2005).

Other parallel concordancers: Parallel concordancers include CASUALPCONC, available from https://sites.google.com/site/casualconc/utility-programs/casualpconc, and ANTPCONC, available from http://www.antlab.sci.waseda.ac.jp/software.html.

PARACONC is a commercial product cf. http://www.athel.com/mono.html#para. However, there is a demo version available from the same page, which is fully functional, but restricts the number of search results it displays. The manual is available from http://www.athel.com/para.html.

9.6 Exercises

1. **ANTCONC**: Download ANTCONC and your favorite text from the Project Gutenberg (http://www.gutenberg.org). Make sure that you use the plain text version of the text. Then open the text file in ANTCONC and search for the following words:
   (a) murder
   (b) thief
   (c) want
   (d) because
   (e) before
   Which word is the most frequent one? Sort the hits so that they are ordered based on the word before the word you searched for.

2. **Concordance plot**: Use ANTCONC and the text from the previous exercise to create concordance plots for all the words in the title of your book. How are they distributed? Are there words that occur more frequently at the beginning? At the end?

3. **n-grams**: Use ANTCONC and the text from the previous exercise to extract the n-grams involving the word **while**. Choose the settings so that the search term is on the right, and that only n-grams of frequency 2 or higher are displayed. How many occurrences are there of **while** as a noun, as a subordinating conjunction?

CHAPTER 10
REGULAR EXPRESSIONS

This chapter gives an introduction to regular expressions. Regular expressions are a powerful method to search in text for patterns that go beyond specifying sequences of characters. For example, we can search for all forms of the verb **begin** in a compact format without spelling out all possibilities. Regular expressions are part of many text processing software programs such as MS WORD, text editors such as NOTEPAD++, or in programming languages such as PERL or PYTHON. Note that regular expressions can also be used when searching for linguistic annotations, not only for the text itself, if the query tool that we use is equipped with a module to handle regular expressions (see Chapters 11 and 12).

We will provide motivating examples in section 10.1. Then we will discuss the inventory of regular expression operators in section 10.2, and we will return to the examples from section 10.1 and show how they are written as regular expressions in section 10.3. Finally, we will give an overview of the most important regular expression operators in frequently used editors in section 10.4.

10.1 Introduction

In many cases, looking for a single word or a sequence of consecutive words is not the best way of finding phenomena in which we are interested.

For example, let us assume that we are looking for all occurrences of the verb **begin**. If we search for this form, we will find the base form **begin**, but also **begins** and **beginning**, but we will not find the forms **began** and **begun**. We can now repeat the search with each of these forms. However, it would be much faster to search for an expression where we give all three possibilities for the second vowel: **i**, **a**, or **u**.

Searching for all forms separately is feasible for the previous example. In our next example, it is not. Let us assume we are looking for all adjectives that end in **-able** and have the negating prefix **un-**, such as in **unavoidable** or **unforgettable**. Listing all possible adjectives of this form is not only tedious, but also an onerous task, since humans find it difficult to remember more than the typical examples. Would you have remembered to include **unzippable** or **unrecoverable** in the list? Or even **un-freaking-believable**?[1] For this search, we would need to be able to say that we want the prefix and the suffix, but that it does not matter what is in between.

Our last example is from phonology. Let us assume we want to find as many two-syllable words as possible. Without syllable structure annotation, we cannot find all of them, but we can approximate English syllable structure by assuming that a syllable can consist of the following patterns of consonants (C) and vowels (V): CV, CVC, or VC. Since we are looking for two-syllable words, we want words that show any sequence of two of these patterns. However, our search program will not know what we mean by C and V (and we definitely do not want to match these literally). Thus, we have to specify what C and V mean; i.e. V would be the list of all vowels: a, e, i, o, u. And to simplify further, we can say that a C is anything that is not a V, for which we will need a concept of negation.

10.2 Regular Expression Syntax

Before we start with the regular expression syntax, a note of caution is in order. Unfortunately, there is no standard way of writing regular expressions; many programs have their own way of expressing that a character is optional, for example. For this reason, we aim at providing an introduction to the concepts available in regular expressions. In section 10.4, we will provide a table with a comparison of how to express these concepts in two text editors. But we cannot cover all regular expression modules. Thus, the reader is advised to look up the documentation of the regular expression search module that they are using.

A regular expression consists of the following types:

1. (sequences of) literal characters
2. disjunctions
3. negation
4. wildcard
5. counters

In the following, we will discuss each of them. The simplest regular expression consists of a sequence of characters that we want to find. This corresponds to a standard text search. Examples for such search terms are shown in (1).[2]

(1) a. "begin"
     b. "corpus linguistics"
     c. "A100"
     d. "correct!!!"

We can also look for *disjunctions*. We consider three types of disjunction: lists of words or characters, character classes, and ranges. If we want to find all occurrences in a text of either the word **red, blue, yellow,** or **green**, we use the | symbol (called: pipe), meaning "or," as shown in (2-a). The | operator takes wide scope, i.e. it matches all characters to its left and right. Therefore, if we want the disjunction to be on the character level, we need to use parentheses to delimit the scope. For example, to express that we want the word **family** in singular or plural, we can search for the expression in (2-b).

(2)   a.   "red|blue|yellow|green"
      b.   "famil(y|ies)"

Note that upper case characters do not match lower case ones. Also, note that we need to specify spaces and punctuation signs in the regular expressions if they may occur in the sequence—i.e. the regular expression in (3-a) would match all words that have the sequence of characters, such as **jacinthe** or **fainthearted**. If we change the expression to include a space, as in (3-b), it would match the sequence of **in**, followed by one space, followed by **the**. It would still not find examples such as in (3-c).[3]

(3)   a.   "inthe"
      b.   "in the"
      c.   ... but as doubts set in, the bottom dropped out.

We can also have *character classes*, also called *character sets*, with which we can match one of the listed characters. If we want to match the British as well as the American spelling of the color gray, we can specify the regular expression in (4). The character class is marked by square brackets. It contains the set of characters that match in this position, **e** and **a** in our example. A character class matches only one character (but see under counters), i.e. the regular expression in (4) does not match the sequences **graay** or **greay**.

(4)   "gr[ea]y"

Ranges are related to character classes; they provide an easy way to say, for example, that any lower case character, but no space or punctuation sign or digit, should be matched. Ranges allow us to specify any lower case character as in (5-a), any upper case character as in (5-b), or any digit, see (5-c). We can also list shorter ranges, such as all digits smaller than 5, see (5-d), or all characters between **k** and **p**, see (5-e). Ranges can also be combined with character classes. For example, the regular expression in (5-f) would match any digit, but also a period, an opening or closing parenthesis, a space, or a dash (-). This would match any character generally used in an American telephone number. Note that the dash is placed as the last character. This is done to avoid its interpretation as a range operator, as in the previous examples.

(5)   a.   "[a-z]"
      b.   "[A-Z]"
      c.   "[0-9]"
      d.   "[0-4]"
      e.   "[k-p]"
      f.   "[0-9.() -]"

The next type of operators in regular expressions concerns *negation*. Negation in regular expressions is generally restricted to character classes, i.e. we can match anything but the list of characters listed in the character class.[4] For example, if we want any character but a vowel, we can give a character class of (6-a) and negate it, as in (6-b). Negation is expressed by the ^ sign (say: caret) as the first symbol in the class. Thus, the expression in (6-c) would match any sequence of characters starting and ending with an **a**, with one character in the middle, which can be anything but an **a**—i.e. it would match **aba**, **aha**, **aza**, and **a;a**, but not **aaa**.

(6)   a.   "[aeiou]"
      b.   "[^aeiou]"
      c.   "a[^a]a"

Another way of requesting a character without saying exactly which character it is, is the use of the *wildcard* symbol, the period. Thus, in the regular expression in (7), the . matches exactly one character, no matter which one. This expression would match **drink**, **drank**, and **drunk**, but not **driink**.

(7)   "dr.nk"

Since the period serves as the wildcard symbol, this raises the question what to do when we actually do want to match a period in the text. For example, let us assume that we want to find preposition stranding involving the preposition **about**. An approximation of such a search would be to look for the word **about** followed by a period. However, if we use the regular expression in (8-a), the period would match one character, i.e. we would find words such as **abouts** or **about-to-be** on top of all occurrences of **about.**. In order to avoid the interpretation of the period as a wildcard, we need to *escape* it, i.e. we add a backslash (\) in front of the period, as shown in (8-b). Escaping also works for every other special character we discuss in this section if we want the literal use. For example, if we want to find the word **approximately** in parentheses, we use the expression in (8-c). Note also that characters in character classes are interpreted literally. Thus, if we want to make sure that the search for the stranded preposition includes other punctuation signs, we can use a character class, as in (8-d). Again, if we include the dash, it has to be listed as the first or the last character in the list, as shown in (8-e). This is to avoid a range interpretation.

(8)   a.   "about."
      b.   "about\."
      c.   "\(approximately\)"
      d.   "about[.!/;:]"
      e.   "about[.!/;:-]"

The last type of regular expression operators concerns *counters*. Counters allow us to say that we want to match a character or a more complex regular expression repeatedly or optionally. *Optional* parts of a regular expression need to be marked by a question mark.

Thus if we want to look for the American and the British spelling of the word **color**, we would insert an optional **u**, as in (9-a). The question mark makes the character preceding it in the regular expression optional. If we want to make longer sequences of characters, (or character classes, etc.) optional, we have to enclose the optional part in parentheses. Thus, if we want to search for the phrase **a bit** but also want to cover the variant **a little bit**, we can make **little** optional, as in (9-b). Note that the space after **little** is inside the parentheses, thus optional. Otherwise, we would require two spaces between **a** and **bit** in case the adjective is missing.

(9) a. "colou?r"
     b. "a (little)?bit"

If we want to add more occurrences of a character, we can also use the *Kleene star* (*) or the *Kleene plus* (+). * means that the character before it is matched zero, one, two, … times. + means that the character has to be matched at least once. Consequently, the expression in (10-a) will match **lot, loot, looot**, etc., but also **lt** (having zero o's). If we want to exclude **lt**, we would use the + instead, as in (10-b). Note that in combination with the wildcard, the Kleene star matches everything and anything, see (10-c).

(10) a. "lo*t"
      b. "lo+t"
      c. ".*"

Regular expression modules typically also provide support to restrict a search to the beginning or the end of a line or a word. The beginning of a line is depicted by the ^ sign, the end by the $ sign. Note that the ^ sign has two different meanings: if it is at the beginning of a character class, it serves as a negation marker; at the beginning of a regular expression, it is the marker for the beginning of a line of text. Thus, if we assume we have a file with one word per line, as shown in Figure 10.1, and want to find the word **hero** but not words like **pheromone** or **treacherous**, we can request our search string to start at the beginning of the line, as in (11-a). If we also want to exclude words such as **heroic** or **heroine**, we can add an end of line marker in the search term, as in (11-b).

(11) a. "^hero"
      b. "^hero$"

We can also match word boundaries. For that, we use an *anchor*. Anchors do not match any character at all. Instead, they match a position before, after, or between characters. For word boundaries, we use **\b**. Thus, if we want to search for **hero** in a text, we need to search for the expression in (12-a) where the first **\b** asks for a word boundary at the beginning of the word, and the second one at the end of the word. Remember that anchors do not match any character. This means that if we want to search for the

The
hero
decided
to
be
heroic
and
test
his
theory
.

Figure 10.1 An example of a file with one word per line.

sequence of words **the hero**, we have to make sure that there is a space between the two words, as in (12-b), which makes the anchors redundant.

(12) a. "\bhero\b"
 b. "\bthe\b \bhero\b."

10.3 Examples Revisited

In this section, we will go back to the examples in section 10.1 and show how these are written as regular expressions.

The first example was a search for all the forms of the verb **begin**. The simplest way to do this is to replace the vowel **i** by a wildcard sign, as in (13-a). This expression will *overgenerate* in that it matches all cases that we are looking for, but it would also match other cases such as **begwn**. A more restrictive way of formulating the query would be to restrict the second vowel to a character class of **i**, **a**, or **u**, as in (13-b). If we are only interested in the verbal use of the word, but not in words like **beginner** or **beginnings**, we can exclude them by adding information on what can follow the **n**, i.e. **-s** or **-ing**, but we have to make both optional to allow the base form. The regular expression is shown in (13-c). If we additionally want to exclude compounds, such as **beginning-level** or **intermediate/beginner**, we would add the word boundary anchors, as in (13-d).

(13) a. "beg.n"
 b. "beg[iau]n"
 c. "beg[iau]n(s|ning)?"
 d. "\bbeg[iau]n(s|ning)?\b"

In the second example, we wanted to search for all adjectives that start with **un-** and end in **-able**. This is simple now: we can replace the adjective part by a wildcard-Kleene star combination, as in (14-a), which will match all the cases shown in section 10.1. Note that this also matches the word **unable**. If we wanted to exclude the latter, we would have to change the expression to use a Kleene plus, as in (14-b). However, both expressions will also match cases such as **under considerable**, as in sentence (14-c).[5]

(14) a. "un.*able"
    b. "un.+able"
    c. Syria complied a month later, *un*der consider*able* international pressure.

In order to make sure that we stay within a single word, we can use another anchor, the one for whitespace characters, \s-, and allow anything but whitespace in the middle of the search term, as in (15).

(15) "un^\s-*able"

In the last example, we were looking for two-syllable words, and we wanted to approximate a syllable as CV, CVC, or VC, where C is a consonant, and V a vowel. In order to make the example easier to follow, we will assume we have the file in column format, as shown in Figure 10.1, which allows us to assume we only have alphabetic characters in a line. We can define a vowel in (16-a). The shortest way of defining a consonant is then the negation of a vowel, see (16-b). Thus, the CV pattern would be written as in (16-c), and the disjunction of all three possibilities for a syllable as shown in (16-d) (we inserted spaces before and after the pipes, for readability; these must be deleted in an actual search). In order to find a two-syllable word, we need to have this sequence two times, and delimit it by word boundaries, as shown in (16-e).

(16) a. "[aeiou]"
    b. "[^aeiou]"
    c. "[^aeiou][aeiou]"
    d. "[^aeiou][aeiou] | [^aeiou][aeiou][^aeiou] | [aeiou][^aeiou]"
    e. "\b([^aeiou][aeiou] | [^aeiou][aeiou][^aeiou] | [aeiou][^aeiou]) ([^aeiou] [aeiou] | [^aeiou][aeiou][^aeiou] | [aeiou][^aeiou])\b"

10.4 Overview of Regular Expression Syntax

In Table 10.1, we give an overview of the regular expression operators we have seen in the previous sections. The operators we have used so far can be used in EMACS, a text editor that is often used under LINUX or Mac OS. We also show how these can be used in MS WORD. In order to use regular expressions in MS WORD, one needs to open the "Find & Replace" menu and select "Advanced Find & Replace." There, we need the option "Use wildcards." Since the placement of these options depends on the MS WORD version, please access the MS WORD Help menu for more information.

Table 10.1 An overview of the most common regular expression operators with examples.

explanation	EMACS	examples	MS WORD	examples
disjunction	|	"my|his"		
character class	[ ]	"[aeiou]"	[ ]	"[aeiou]"
range	[a-b]	"[A-Za-z]"	[a-b]	"[A-Za-z]"
negation	[^a]	"[^aeiou]"	[!a]	"[!aeiou]"
wildcard	.	"r.n"	?	"r?n"
optionality	?	"colou?r"		
Kleene star	*	"ra*n"		
Kleene plus	+	"ra+n"	@	"ra@n"
exactly *n* occ.			{n}	fe{2}
at least *n* occ.			{n,}	fe{2,}
any no. of chars.	.*	"o.*o"	*	"o*o"
beg. of line	^	"^my"		
end of line	$	"house$"		
beg. of word	\b	"\bthe"	<	"<the"
end of word	\b	"the\b"	>	"the>"
whitespace	\s-	"\s-+"		

In general, it is mostly possible to search for phenomena in either editor. However, a closer look at the table shows that in many cases, the queries will have to use different operators. For example, while in EMACS, we have the Kleene star (*), which we can attach to any sequence of characters, character class, or any other complex regular expression; in MS WORD, the star does not attach to the previous character—instead, the star itself matches any sequence of characters. Thus, it is equivalent to ".*" in EMACS. As a consequence, if we want to find a sequence with two **the** in it, we would use the expression in (17-a) in EMACS and the expression in (17-b) in MS WORD.

(17) a. "the.*the"
    b. "the*the"

If we want to find sequences of vowels, we can use the expression in (18-a) in EMACS. Since in MS WORD, there is no Kleene plus, we have to use another operator: the curly braces allow us to specify exactly how many times we want the preceding element (e.g. {3}) or how many times at least, in which case, the number is followed by a comma, denoting an open ended range (e.g. {3,}). Thus, in MS WORD, we would use the expression in (18-b) to express that we want a sequence of one or more vowels.

(18) a. "[aeiou]+"
    b. "[aeiou]{1,}"

However, note that MS WORD does not allow the use of zero in the curly braces, i.e. we could not make the vowel optional.

10.5 Summary

In this chapter, we had a look at regular expressions. We discussed the different operators available in regular expression syntax, specifically disjunction, negation in character classes, the wildcard symbol, and counters. Then we showed how regular expressions can be used to search for three specific phenomena, which are difficult to find without regular expressions. Finally, we showed how our regular expressions differ from the ones offered in MS WORD.

10.6 Further Reading

Section 10.1

Regular expression tutorials: There are many online tutorials for regular expressions; we recommend the tutorial at http://www.regular-expressions.info/tutorial.html, or the interactive tutorial by *RegexOne* at http://regexone.com/.

Section 10.2

Regular expressions in PERL: For an overview of the treatment of regular expressions in PERL, see http://www.comp.leeds.ac.uk/Perl/matching.html. A thorough introduction to the idea of regular expressions and their realization in PERL and other programming languages is given in Friedl (2006).

Regular expressions in PYTHON: For the treatment of regular expressions in PYTHON, see Hetland (2008) or the PYTHON Standard Library documentation at http://docs.python.org/2/library/re.html.

10.7 Exercises

1. **Regular expression in MS WORD**: Take your favorite text file and open the file in MS WORD. Then open "Advanced Find" and enable "Use wildcards."
    (a) Find occurrences of **you** and **your**. Can you extend the search so that you find **yourself**, too?
    (b) Find all verbs in gerund, i.e. ending in **-ing**. Does this search overgenerate?

(c) Find occurrences of two consecutive vowels (VV).

(d) What is the maximum number of consecutive vowels in the text? For this, modify the search term consecutively to allow longer sequences. At which length do you stop finding such sequences?

(e) Find words with a CVCC pattern, where C is a consonant.

(f) Modify the previous search so that you find only complete CVCC words (such as **pick**).

(h) Find 2 non-consecutive occurrences of **for**.

(h) Modify the previous search to make sure that only complete words are matched, not sequences inside a word as in **affordable**.

(i) Find words with exactly one **w**. (Hint: all other characters are not **w**).

(j) Find occurrences of **have** and **been** separated by exactly one word.

2. **Regular expressions**: Take the third example (see (16-e)) from section 10.3 and rewrite it so that the first and second conjunct, CV and CVC, are expressed as one conjunct.

3. **More regular expressions**: The third example (see (16-e)) from section 10.3 is a simplification, in that it ignores capitalization in words and it makes the simplistic assumption that any occurrence of **y** is always a consonant. Extend this example so that it covers such cases, too.

CHAPTER 11
SEARCHING ON THE WORD LEVEL

In Chapter 3, we discussed the annotation of linguistic information on the word level. We covered lemma annotation, morphological annotation, and POS annotation. In this chapter, we will discuss how to search in corpora that include these types of annotation. We will concentrate on three different query tools: the Brigham Young University search interface (see section 11.1) to the corpora provided by this institution, the BNCWEB portal (section 11.2), and the cqp query language (section 11.3), which is used in the BNCWEB web interface as well as many other query tools, such as the IMS WORKBENCH. These query interfaces were chosen to show important concepts in searching for lexical phenomena in tools that are easily accessible via the web. In section 11.4, we will show how we can use the BNCWEB in a case study on collocations. Collocations are combinations of words that co-occur more frequently than by chance. We will show that collocations are more variably used than one would assume at first sight.

11.1 The BYU Search Interface to Corpora

Mark Davies, a corpus linguist at Brigham Young University, has been providing a web-based search interface to a list of corpora, including the British National Corpus (BNC) and the Corpus of Contemporary American English (COCA). This interface allows searching for words, lemmas, POS tags, and combinations of those with a limited support for regular expressions. In order to use the search interface, one should register, which is free. Without registration, the system limits the number of queries.

For the remainder of this section, we will use COCA to illustrate the queries. COCA currently comprises 450 million words of contemporary American English, from the years 1990–2012. The texts are taken from the following genres: spoken, fiction, popular magazines, newspapers, and academic. Figure 11.1 shows the search interface. In the upper left half, under the heading "Search String," there is a "Word(s)" field to enter our query. In the case shown in Figure 11.1, the search is for the sequence of words **in case of**. The upper half of the right half of the window shows the different strings that match the search string. In our case, this is only the exact search string, but when we use more flexible queries, there can be more than one possible string. When we click on a string that was found, the system displays all occurrences of this string in the corpus in the lower right half. The display uses the keyword in context format (KWIC) (see section 9.1 for an explanation of this format). It also provides information about the genre of the occurrence, the year, and its textual source. The search can be restricted to specific genres or time frames under "Sections." If two different genres or time frames

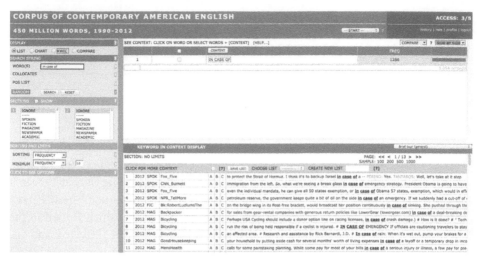

Figure 11.1 The BYU search interface to COCA.

are chosen, the upper right half will display results for both settings, in terms of absolute frequencies ("Tokens") and normalized by the numbers of words in the two settings.

Thus, if we search for the word **cool** in time frame 1990–4 and in time frame 2010–12, we find that it occurs 5,580 times in the earlier time frame and 5,187 times in the later one. However, since the earlier time frame is more than twice as large as the later one, the normalized counts are displayed as counts per million words. In our example, the normalized counts for **cool** are 53.65 for the earlier time frame and 99.93 for the later one. This shows that the word **cool** occurs more often in a million words in the later time frame. In other words, it has a chance of occurring in the later text that is almost twice as high as in the earlier time frame.

COCA is annotated for lemmas, POS tags, and for lexical semantic information (see sections 3.1, 3.3, and 5.2 for more information). The search interface allows us to integrate this information into the search. If we want to search for all forms of **cool**, we search for the lemma, which is marked by square brackets, as shown in (1). This search provides in the upper right half the list of forms that match the lemma: **cool, cooling, cooler, cooled, coolest, cools**.

(1)   [cool]

We can also search for (sequences of) POS tags. POS tags can be selected from the button "POS List" or entered directly. However, for efficiency reasons, the query tool will not display results if all of the POS tags occur more than 10 million times in the corpus. Thus, the search for an adjective followed by a noun, as shown in (2-a), will produce too many hits to display. Note that both POS tags are also marked by square brackets. The corpus is annotated with the CLAWS 7 POS tagset, which makes fine-grained distinctions similar to the ICE tagset (see section 3.3). The * signs in the POS tags mean that any subcategory of adjective or noun is matched. If we change our original query and search for adjectives in the comparative, as shown in (2-b), the search succeeds since there are fewer occurrences of the comparative adjectives in the corpus.

(2)   a.   [j*] [n*]
      b.   [jjr*] [n*]

Another way of restricting the search is to combine POS information with lexical information. If we want to know which types of **research** are mentioned in the corpus, we can search for either an adjective followed by **research,** as in (3-a), or for a noun and **research,** as in (3-b). The former will find occurrences such as **future research** or **medical research,** the latter **cell research** or **undergraduate research.**

(3)   a.   [j*] research
      b.   [n*] research

We can also search for occurrences of words for which a combination of restrictions hold. In other words, we can combine word or lemma information with POS tags for a single word—e.g. if we want to modify the search for the word **cool** to find only the adjectival use over all possible forms, we combine the search for the lemma **cool** with the information that the word has to be an adjective, as shown in (4).

(4)   [cool].[j*]

Here, the period states that both types of information concern a single word. This query over the two time periods we used above shows us that all three forms, **cool, cooler, coolest,** occur more frequently in the later time frame since the occurrences per million words for this time frame (PM2) are higher. It also shows that the comparative **cooler** gained the most in usage, it has the highest ratio of 3.52 for the second time frame. This means that the word was used more than 3 times more often in the second time frame than in the first time one.

In the POS tag queries in (2), we have used the * sign to state that we want to match all noun POS tags, not only a very specific POS tag. This is called a wildcard, or Kleene star, in regular expressions, a symbol saying "match anything" (see section 10.2 for more information). In the query interface, we can use wildcards not only for POS tags, but also for words. For example, we can search for nominalizations with the prefix **de-** and the suffix **-ation,** as in (5-a). This will find words such as **determination, detonation,** or **destabilization.** We can also use the wildcard to represent a full word, for example when we want to know which adjectives can occur in noun phrases between a determiner and the word **weather,** as in (5-b). Note that this query is more general than looking for a sequence of determiner, adjective, and **weather.** It will find occurrences such as **this bad weather** or **most inclement weather**, but also **which the weather**, in which the determiner matches **which** and the wildcard **the**.

(5) a. de*ation
     b. [d*] * weather

The BYU search interface also allows the use of the question mark as a wildcard for a single character. Thus, the query in (6) will match **sing, sang,** and **sung,** but not **siing,** since the question mark matches exactly one character. Note that it would also match **seng** if this word occurred in the corpus. This means that our search overgenerates.

Additionally, the interface allows using the | sign for disjunction. For example, we can look up whether **giving advice** is more often associated with a male or a female pronoun in the query in (7). It turns out that **him** is found in 55 cases and **her** in 35.

(6) s?ng
(7) [give] him|her advice

Since the COCA corpus is also annotated for word senses, we can extend our queries to include all synonyms of a word. The synonyms are based on WORDNET (for more information, see section 5.2). Thus, if we want to find all occurrences that involve **wasting energy**, we can search for all synonyms by having square brackets around **energy** and an = sign before the word, as shown in (8).

(8) [waste] [=energy]

This will not only find **wasting energy** but also **wastes power** and **wasting resources**.

The BYU search interface also allows us to search for collocations. (For a more through discussion of collocations, see section 11.4.) This feature is activated by clicking on "Collocates" in the "Search String" section. This creates a new text field, in which we can enter the collocation text, and the definition of the left and right context—i.e. if we want to find all collocations involving **white** and a noun, we would enter **white** in the "Word(s)" field and [n*] in "Collocations." If we then select the numbers 0 and 2, we ensure that the noun should not occur before **white**, by saying that we look at 0 words before **white**, and that the noun is within 2 words to the right of **white**.

The search for collocations can be used to search for more flexible constructions that involve intervening context. Thus, if we want to find occurrences of the phrasal verb **keep from**, we need to make sure that we also find occurrences such as **keep someone from**. We can obtain this effect by searching for the lemma **keep** and provide **from** as collocate, in a range of up to 9 words to the right and 0 to the left. The latter ensures that the preposition cannot precede the verb. This query will find the occurrences listed in (9), among others.

(9) a. … keep them from becoming …
   b. … that would have kept colleges and universities from requiring …
   c. Argentina has been kept from global capital markets …
   d. … to keep a local crisis in Greece from broadening …

11.2 BNCWEB

The BNCWEB is a search interface to the *British National Corpus* (BNC), provided by Lancaster University. The BNC is a collection of written and spoken British English from the later part of the twentieth century; it comprises approximately 100 million words. After registering for the search interface, one can use the search interface to search this specific corpus, either using the simple query, or using a more advanced language called Corpus Query Processor (CQP, see section 11.3). CQP has been used in different online query tools, such as the BNCWEB. Since access is easier via the online interface, we will use this tool to give an overview of this query language. However, before we start with CQP, we will have a quick look at the simple query mode at BNCWEB since this already covers fairly complex searches.

The BNCWEB simple query mode allows the search for sequences of words, in combination with regular expressions, as we have already seen with the BYU search interface. The following expressions can be used as wildcards: * for zero or more characters, + for one or more characters, ? for one character, and ??+ for three or more characters. Note that this is different from the standard definition of the Kleene star and plus since here, each of these symbols matches a character rather than being applied to the character before (for a more thorough discussion of these differences see Chapter 10). Thus, if we were looking for all words starting with **un-** and ending in **-able**, but excluding **unable**, we could use the query in (10-a). This query requires at least 1 character between the prefix and the suffix. However, if we wanted to exclude **unstable** as well, we could use the ??+ and require at least 3 characters, as shown in (10-b).

(10) a. un+able
   b. un??+able

There is another use of the Kleene star and plus, when they occur between spaces. In such cases, they signify complete words. Thus, if we want to search for the phrasal verb **pick up** but want exactly 2 words between the verb and the preposition, we can state the query as shown in (11-a). Note that the spaces between words and the **++** are required, otherwise, we only find hyphenated occurrences of versions of **pick-up**. The query in (11-b) allows a more flexible context of 2–5 words, the * signifying optional words.

(11) a. pick ++ up
   b. pick ++*** up

For such queries, the Key Word in Context (KWIC) option, via the button "Show KWIC View," can be very useful since it shows the matched words in bold as the focus, especially in combination with the "Sort" option (from the Menu showing "New Query"). Once we have sorted the retrieved matches, we can also specify which words should be used for sorting, and whether certain context words should have specified POS tags. The options also include "Frequency breakdown" (which shows how often each form of **pick up** occurred), "Distribution" (which shows how the occurrences distribute over different genres), and "Collocations… " (see section 11.4 for more details).

Disjunction and sets are also allowed. In sets, the alternatives are separated by commas and can be of any length. Note that here, sets are defined over words, not characters, as we have seen them used in Chapter 10—i.e. it is possible to search for **his** or **her** in certain contexts, as shown in (12) in the context of **advice**.

(12) on [his,her] advice

Additionally, the BNC is annotated for POS and lemma information. The POS tags are based on the BNC basic tagset (CLAWS 5).[1] Since the annotations are available, we can also search for them: POS tags must be preceded by an underscore, and they can attach to words. Thus, we can search for all adjectives in the superlative (AJS) that modify the word **results**, as in (13-a), or only for the modal verb readings of **can** when following the word **beer**, as in (13-b). Since we may not be familiar enough with the detailed POS tagset, the interface also provides a set of basic POS tags, which have to be written in curly braces. The example for **can** as a verb using the simplified tagset is shown in (13-c). A list of all basic and full POS tags is included in the documentation of the simple query at http://bncweb.lancs.ac.uk/bncwebXML/Simple_query_language.pdf.

(13) a. _AJS results
      b. beer can_VM0
      c. beer can_{V}

Lemmas, called *headwords* in BNCWEB terminology, are marked by curly braces. They can be combined with POS information, in which case, they are called *lemmas* in the manual. For example, we can search for all forms of **cool**, in (14-a), or for all forms of the verb **cool**, in (14-b).

(14) a. {cool}
      b. {cool/V}

The BNCWEB also offers an option to restrict the context, which is similar to the "Collocations" search that we have seen in the BYU search interface. Here, we can specify a range of words within which two words co-occur. For example, the query in (15) searches for occurrences of **buy** and **car** in a window of 4 words. Examples of sentences retrieved by this query are shown in (16). Note that in this search the order of the two words is not determined, and either one can occur first in the retrieved sentences.

(15) buy <<4>> car
(16) a. We didn't buy a car
     b. … to buy this Escort-size car …
     c. My date gets out of the car to go buy popcorn …

We can also specify that the two words need to be in the same sentence, as shown in (17). Here, the expression **<<s>>** is setting the sentence as the scope of the co-occurrence of the words.

(17) buy <<s>> car

11.3 CQP

Corpus Query Processor (CQP) is a very efficient and powerful query language, which allows us to search for all kinds of word-based phenomena. While it cannot handle syntactic annotation (see Chapter 12), it can integrate all types of annotation as long as the annotation is for individual words. This includes all types of word-based information, such as lemma, morphology, and POS information. CQP can also handle a limited set of syntactic annotation, but we will not cover this here.

CQP was initially developed for the IMS WORKBENCH at the University of Stuttgart. The IMS WORKBENCH is a query tool that can be downloaded and used with available corpora, which are annotated at the word level. Since its implementation is very efficient, it can handle large text corpora, from 10 million to 2 billion words, including the annotation. This is an order of magnitude larger than many annotated corpora available today.

The query language CQP is used as the underlying query language in the BNCWEB interface. This means that queries in the simple query mode are internally translated into CQP. As a consequence, all queries described in section 11.2 can also be used in CQP, however with a different syntax, and in many cases, they have to be much more explicit.

CQP uses the standard regular expression syntax, as described in section 10.2, with the exception of beginning and end of line and word markers and the whitespace marker. These are covered in a different way in CQP: in order to specify word boundaries, we use double quotes to delimit words. For example, if we want to search for the expression **in spite of**, the query specifies all three words, each delimited in double quotes, as shown in (18).

(18) "in" "spite" "of"

Optional words are represented as []; this can be combined with a Kleene star, in which case there is no restriction on how many words can occur in that context. We can also use a Kleene plus or a range—i.e. example (11-b) in the simple query mode of the BNCWEB interface is shown in the CQP format in (19).

(19) "pick" []{2,5} "up"

An order-independent search, such as the one shown in (15) in the simple format, is not directly possible in CQP; here, all possible orders need to be spelled out and listed as alternatives, as shown in (20). Each position in the corpus is specified by square brackets, which can match any word if no further information is provided—i.e. the [] {0, 3} allows up to 3 undefined words between **buy** and **car**. This is different from the 4 positions specified in (15), which includes one position for the second word. The two possible word orders are joined in a disjunction, in which the | symbol functions as "or."

(20) "buy" []{0,3} "car" | "car" []{0,3} "buy"

Specifying words in double quotes, as we have seen above, is a shortcut for a more explicit form. The search for **in spite of**, for which we showed the shortcut in (18), is shown in its explicit form in (21).

(21) [word="in"] [word="spite"] [word="of"]

We need this explicit form in order to look for additional information such as POS tags or lemma information. These are specified similarly. In (22), for example, we show a query for the word **search** followed by a preposition (PRP).

(22) [word="search"] [pos="PRP"]

The results of this query show that **search** can be combined with a wide range of prepositions, some of which are shown in (23).

(23) a. … fascination of the journey, of a search across hostile and uncertain spaces …
     b. … always make a bankruptcy search against your client …
     c. … she could feel his hand search behind her for the zip of her dress.
     d. The search for a theory that will combine structural explanations …
     e. In that case there will be a further preliminary search through a disk index.

Note that this query is only meaningful if the corpus is annotated and the POS tagset is based on the CLAWS 5 tagset, which uses PRP for prepositions. Example (24-a) shows a query that combines word and POS information within one word—i.e. we search for the word **can** as a verb, the same query as in (13-c) in the simple query mode.

(24) a. [word="beer"] [word="can" & pos="V.*"]
     b. [hw="beer"] [hw="can" & pos="V.*"]

If we want to make this query more general and search for the lemmas **beer** and **can**, the query is shown in (24-b). Remember that BNCWEB calls lemmas headwords (hw).

11.4 Finding Collocations

Collocations are an important concept in linguistics, and they provide one example of how the interest in the topic, the methodology to be used, as well as the definition of the concept changed with the advent of electronically accessible corpora and the introduction of corpus linguistics as a methodology. The term *collocation* was introduced by Firth (1957), who defined collocations as combinations of words that co-occur more frequently than by chance. This definition covers fixed idioms such as **go green with envy** or **call it a day** but also less formalized combinations such as **know something inside out** or **have a day off**. Firth argued that the meaning of a word can be determined by the most typical *collocates* with which it co-occurs, leading to his widely cited explanation: "You shall know a word by the company it keeps" (Firth, 1957: 179). Another definition has been proposed in the context of *phraseology*. Here, collocations are defined as combinations of words that have a semi-compositional meaning, such as in **heavy smoker**, where **heavy** is the only possible modifier for **smoker** that implies that someone smokes a lot. In this example, the adjective **heavy** has a meaning that is different from its normal use (involving weight), and specific to this noun. Choueka (1988) defines the semi-compositionality as follows: "A collocation is defined as a sequence of two or more consecutive words, [...] whose exact and unambiguous meaning cannot be derived directly from the meaning or connotation of its components." Other examples would be **white wine** or **eke out a living**. The situation is complicated further by the fact that the two definitions are neither mutually exclusive nor mutually inclusive. Thus, there are some collocations which would fall under both definitions, and others that are considered collocations only under one definition. One example of a collocation that falls under both definitions is **couch potato**, which has a high co-occurrence (see BNCWEB) and semi-compositional semantics. A **potato peeler**, by contrast, would be considered a collocation only under Firth's definition, while a **broken record** would only fall under the phraseological definition.

Firth's definition of collocations is an *empirical* one, which means it can be operationalized—i.e. we can look for all combinations of words with a higher frequency of co-occurrence than we would expect from two randomly selected words. However, such an empirical approach is only feasible given a sizable, machine-readable corpus. We would not want to manually document every occurrence of a word plus its contexts to calculate the probabilities. Thus, collocation studies have become more widespread since such corpora and query tools allowing the search for collocations have become available. Both the BYU search interface and BNCWEB provide search capabilities for finding collocations (see sections 11.1 for details on how to search for collocations with the BYU search interface). Thus, we can investigate which words co-occur most frequently, for example, with **smoker**. To search for collocations in BNCWEB, we first search for the focus word of the collocation, then we select "Collocations" from the menu "New Query." Then, the system asks whether the collocations should be calculated across sentence boundaries, whether lemma information should be used, and what the maximum window space is. After that, the words that co-occur most frequently with the original search term are displayed. There are also more options how to refine the collocation search in this window. We show the most frequent collocates for the BNC in (25) and the most frequent ones in COCA in (26).

(25) a. non-smoker
     b. cough
     c. cigarette
     d. heavy
(26) a. heavy
     b. cigarette
     c. chain
     d. former

However, we need to keep in mind that when we use these search capabilities, we rely on the statistical model that the query tool provides. The statistical models, also called *association measures*, must be fairly elaborate in order to find word combinations that occur frequently together, not only with respect to their joint occurrence but also in terms of their individual frequencies. For example, we want to exclude sequences such as **for the**, even though they are extremely frequent: the sequence **for the** occurs 159,153 times in the BNC. However, once we find out that **for** occurs 829,908 times and **the** 5,403,564, the number of joint occurrences seems less important—i.e. in terms of their individual frequencies, the number of times that they occur together is rather small.

Common association measures for collocations include statistical tests and information theoretic measures, such as *mutual information, Z-score,* the *likelihood-ratio*

Table 11.1 The four highest ranked collocates for **wine** in BNCWEB given the different association measures.

measure	1st	2nd	3rd	4th
mutual information	mulled	tastings	carafe	goblet
MI3	bottle	glass	sparkling	and
Z-score	bottle	sparkling	mulled	glass
T-score	and	of	bottle	glass
log-likelihood	bottle	glass	sparkling	red
Dice coefficient	bottle	glass	sparkling	bottles
frequency	,	of	the	and

test, or the *Dice coefficient*. We will refrain from explaining these measures here; the interested reader is referred to Manning and Schütze (1999); Evert (2008). The BNCWEB interface allows the user to select the association measure from seven options, the BYU search interface only has two. The choice of this measure has a definite effect on the search results. We show this for the BNCWEB and the word **wine**. Table 11.1 shows the four highest ranked collocates for the 7 measures. While there are words that occur with most measures, such as **bottle**, note that **red**, for example, only occurs in the list of the *log-likelihood* measure. Thus, the choice of measure is important and can have significant influence on the results.

The *phraseological* definition of collocation has the restriction of fixing at least one of the words in the collocation. For example, in the example of **white wine**, the noun is fixed and semantically unremarkable, and the adjective **white** is the focus of the investigation. Since this definition requires a lexical fixing, it is an easy, but incorrect, step to restrict this definition to completely fixed collocations, such as idioms. Grammatical combinations of words, such as the comparative clause constructions as in **the slower the better,** are often called *colligations* and treated separately from collocations. However, even if we ignore such constructions, there is a wider range of variability in collocations than generally assumed. Apart from fixed expressions such as **cut the mustard**, there are also collocations that need to be adjusted syntactically to the context. This includes adapting the verb, as in **bite the dust**. In the BNC, the following forms of **bite** are attested: **bite, biting, bit,** and **bites**. Another adaptation concerns the form of the pronoun, as in **take leave of one's senses,** for which the following pronouns are attested in the BNC: **his, her, your, their, its,** and **my**.

However, there is also variation in supposedly fixed expressions, such as in **fall asleep**. A CQP search via BNCWEB, shown in (27), returns 32 occurrences of the idiom with intervening material of up to 3 words, some of which are shown in (28).

(27) [hw="fall"] []{1,3} "asleep"
(28) a. I fell instantly asleep.
    b. … when Minton fell snoringly asleep.
    c. I realize I am too awake to fall back asleep …
    d. … from slight drowsiness to falling sound asleep.

Another example is the collocation **faint smell**, which occurs in 4 examples in the BNC with intervening material of up to 3 words (see (29)).

(29) a. … Jinny smelt the faint apricot smell they gave off.
    b. There was a faint stale smell, …
    c. The hat was so new it gave off a faint, expensive smell.
    d. … the faint but unmistakably disagreeable smell of human vomit.

These examples are easily overlooked when we restrict our queries and require the words to be adjacent. This example shows how important it is to be extremely careful in the design of the searches that we carry out to look into a specific linguistic phenomenon. Our results can only show us phenomena that we allow in the queries.

11.5 Summary

In this chapter, we have covered searching on the word level. We looked at the BYU search interface, which provides search capabilities that allow us to combine words, POS information, lemma information, and regular expression capabilities. Then we looked at the BNCWEB, an online search interface to the BNC, which uses CQP as a query language. Both search interfaces have a similar range of phenomena that can be searched. After a closer look at the query language CQP, we used the BNCWEB interface to investigate collocations.

11.6 Further Reading

Section 11.1

BYU search interface: The search interface and the corpora provided by Mark Davies at Brigham Young University can be accessed at http://corpus.byu.edu/.

CLAWS: The CLAWS tagset (Leech et al., 1994) was used to annotate the BNC. Note that there exist different versions of the tagset, and some corpora use CLAWS 5 and others CLAWS 7, which differ in some POS tags.

WORDNET: WORDNET is documented in a journal paper (Miller, 1995) and in a book (Fellbaum, 1998). It can be searched online at http://wordnetweb.princeton.edu/perl/webwn or downloaded from http://wordnet.princeton.edu/wordnet/download/. There is also an online reference manual available at http://wordnet.princeton.edu/wordnet/documentation/.

Section 11.2

BNCWEB: The BNCWEB is accessible at http://bncweb.lancs.ac.uk, the documentation of the simple query language at http://bncweb.lancs.ac.uk/bncwebXML/Simple_query_language. pdf. There is also a book available (Hoffmann et al., 2008), which provides an introduction to corpus linguistics using the BNCWEB.

Section 11.3

CQP tutorial: There is an extensive tutorial for the CQP language at http://cwb.sourceforge.net/files/CQP_Tutorial/, a condensed and very readable tutorial is available at http://bulba.sdsu.edu/cqphelp.html.

IMS WORKBENCH: The IMS WORKBENCH is available for download from http://cwb.sourceforge.net/. Online demos using a variety of corpora are listed at http://cwb.sourceforge.net/demos.php.

Online query tools: CORPUSEYE is another online query tool that uses CQP; it is available at corp.hum.sdu.dk/cqp.en.html, providing access to a wide range of corpora, many of them belonging to the genre of computer-mediated communication.

Section 11.4

Collocations: An overview of the competing definitions of collocation is provided by Bartsch (2004). A clear introduction to the Neo-Firthian approach is provided by Evert (2008). An overview of the usage of collocation in phraseology can be found in Gries (2008).

Association measures: Definitions and explanations of common association measures can be found in Manning and Schütze (1999); Evert (2008).

11.7 Exercises

1. **BYU search interface**: Go to the BYU search interface of the COCA corpus at http://corpus. byu.edu/coca/. Note that you may have to register. Search for the following phenomena:
   - (a) Which verbs co-occur with **advice** as their object?
   - (b) Search for **the X the Y**, where X and Y are comparative adjectives.
   - (c) Search for **weather** NPs, consisting of a determiner, one more word, and **weather**.
   - (d) Search for all synonyms of **white** following a copula verb, such as in **is white**.
   - (e) Which adverbs can occur between the copula and **white**?

2. **Collocations**: Look up the following collocations in BNCWEB, and check if they allow any variability. What types of variability do you find?
   - (a) bitter pill
   - (b) put one foot before the other
   - (c) call it a day
   - (d) go behind someone's back

3. **More collocations**: If you search for the collocations above in COCA, what are the differences?

CHAPTER 12
QUERYING SYNTACTIC STRUCTURES

In this chapter, we will discuss how one can search in syntactically annotated corpora, either based on constituents or on dependencies. We will assume that we have a syntactically annotated corpus (cf. Chapter 4) in which we need to search. Before we can look at individual query tools, however, we need to have a look at which logical relations hold in constituent and dependency structures (cf. section 12.1). After that, we will have a look at different query tools (sections 12.2–12.5). This is not a comprehensive list; rather, they were chosen to illustrate a variety of underlying formats, query languages, and user interfaces. We will highlight differences in the query languages of the different tools, as long as they are comparable, especially with regard to negation.

12.1 Logical Relations in Syntax Annotations

Syntactic search is one of the more complex search problems. The reason for the complexity lies in the two-dimensional structure of syntactic annotations. While most types of annotation either attach to individual words or to sequences of words, syntactic annotation also has a recursive, upward component. In constituent structure, a phrase is generally part of a larger phrase, and in dependency structure, the head of a word also has a head.

One dimension, which is the same for constituent and dependency structure, is the order of words, and of nodes (in a constituent tree). Here, we have two logical relations, *linear precedence* and *direct linear precedence*.[1] Direct linear precedence is a relation that describes adjacent words, but also adjacent syntax nodes. Thus in the constituent tree in Figure 12.1, we have a direct linear precedence between the following pairs of words: {The, $}, {$, 35.7}, ..., {a, share}, {share, .}. This relation also holds between constituent nodes, e.g. for the node pairs {NP(The ...loss), VP}[2] and {NP(86 cents), NP(a share)}. Note that for nodes, adjacency means that the second node starts at the word directly after the last word of the first node.

Linear precedence is a more general relation, in which the first member of the pair has to appear before the second one, but they are not required to be adjacent. Thus, this relation holds between all the pairs listed for direct linear precedence, but also for the word pairs such as {The, 37.7}, {The, loss}, {The, equals}, {net, cents} and for constituent node pairs such as {NP(The ...loss), NP(a share)}, {QP, VP}, or {NP(The ...loss), NP(86 cents)}. However, there is no linear precedence relation between nodes higher in the tree and ones they dominate (see below), such as for the pairs {NP(The ... loss), QP} or {S, VP}.

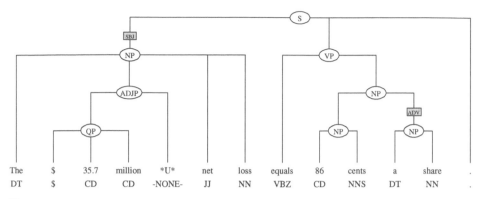

Figure 12.1 A syntactic tree from the PENN TREEBANK.

The other dimension in constituent structure concerns the *dominance* relation, which determines mother-daughter relationships between nodes in the tree. Dominance can be defined as *direct dominance*[3] or the more general form where there can be nodes between the two specified nodes. In the tree in Figure 12.1, for example, there is a direct dominance relation from the S node to the NP(**The …loss**) and between VP and NP(**86 …share**). Also there is a dominance relation from S to all nodes below it. Thus, if we are looking for an NP that contains a quantifier phrase that involves a dollar amount, the query could be stated as [NP > * QP] & [QP > $] where > * is dominance and > direct dominance.

In dependency structures, we do not have dominance relations. Instead, the dependencies by themselves are relations, and we can also look for connections between words that involve more than one dependency, i.e. connected dependencies via intermediate words, such as the connection between **has** and **The** via **brigade** in Figure 12.2. We will call this type of relation *indirect dependency relation.*[4] In the dependency structure in Figure 12.2, indirect dependencies exist, for example, between the word pairs {**has, The**}, {**has, since**}, or {**keep, case**}.

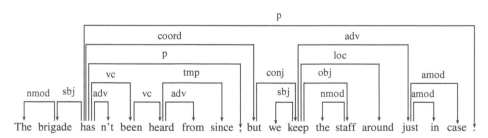

Figure 12.2 A sentence with its dependency representation.

12.2 TGREP and TGREP2

TGREP was developed for searching the PENN TREEBANK, and since it was the first available query tool, it was fairly basic, only usable under LINUX, and without any graphical user interface. TGREP2 is a reimplementation of TGREP, with many of the original limitations, but with a more complex *query language*. In our description here, we will focus on TGREP2. This description will be fairly short since by now, more powerful and more user-friendly query tools are available.

TGREP2 is called from the command line in LINUX:

tgrep2 -c ptb.t2c PATTERN

where the option -c specifies a corpus that has been prepared in advance (resulting in file "ptb.t2c"). Files have to be in the PENN TREEBANK format in order to be processed. PATTERN specifies what we are looking for in the TGREP2 query language. From now on, we will concentrate on these search patterns and ignore the rest of the command. An example of a query in TGREP2 is shown in (1).

(1)   NP < PP

This query retrieves all sentences that have a direct dominance relation between the mother node NP and a daughter PP. Note that this only finds nodes without a grammatical function. If we want to include NP nodes with grammatical functions, such as NP-SBJ or NP-TMP, we need to replace the NP symbol by a regular expression (cf. Chapter 10) allowing all labels that start with NP. This query is shown in (2). Here, the regular expression is delimited by / signs, and the ^ sign specifies that the expression is to be found at the beginning of the label.

(2)   /^NP/ < PP

TGREP2 has several options how the retrieved trees are displayed, either as indented structure as shown in Figure 12.3, as continuous bracketed structure, shown in (3-a), or just showing the words of the trees as in (3-b).

(3)   a.   ((S (NP-SBJ (NNS Investors)) (VP (VBP are) (VP (VBG appealing) (PP-CLR (TO to) (NP-1 (DT the) (NNPS Securities) (CC and) (NNP Exchange) (NNP Commission))) (S-CLR (NP-SBJ (-NONE- *-1)) (RB not) (VP (TO to) (VP (VB limit) (NP (NP (PRP$ their) (NN access)) (PP (TO to) (NP (NP (NN information)) (PP (IN about) (NP (NP (NN stock) (NNS purchases) (CC and) (NNS sales)) (PP (IN by) (NP (JJ corporate) (NNS insiders))))))))))) (. .)))

   b.   Investors are appealing to the Securities and Exchange Commission not to limit their access to information about stock purchases and sales by corporate insiders .

```
( (S
   (NP-SBJ (NNS Investors) )
   (VP (VBP are)
      (VP (VBG appealing)
         (PP-CLR (TO to)
            (NP-1 (DT the) (NNPS Securities)
               (CC and)
               (NNP Exchange) (NNP Commission) ))
         (S-CLR
            (NP-SBJ (-NONE- *-1) )
            (RB not)
            (VP (TO to)
               (VP (VB limit)
                  ( NP
                     (NP (PRP$ their) (NN access) )
                     ( PP (TO to)
                        ( NP
                           (NP (NN information) )
                           ( PP (IN about)
                              ( NP
                                 (NP (NN stock) (NNS purchases)
                                 (CC and)
                                 (NNS sales) )
                              ( PP (IN by)
                                 (NP (JJ corporate) (NNS insiders) )))))))))))))
   (. .) ))
```

Figure 12.3 A tree with 3 NP-PP direct dominance relations (marked in bold).

Searching in TGREP2 can become complex and difficult to read. In (4), we show a query looking for an NP with three or more adjectives.

(4)   /^NP/ <2 /^JJ/ <3 /^JJ/ <4 /^JJ/ <5 /^JJ/

In this query, every node is specified as a regular expression, thus also finding NPs with grammatical functions as well as adjectives in comparative or superlative (JJR or JJS). The numbers behind the direct dominance determine which daughter we are looking for. Thus the first JJ is daughter no. 2 of the NP, which means that there should be one, unspecified, word before the first adjective.

Since the queries quickly become unreadable, we refrain from giving more details with regard to the query language. The interested reader is referred to the TGREP2 manual.

12.3 TigerSearch

TigerSearch is a query tool for syntactically annotated corpora, with a focus on constituent annotation. The query tool offers a graphical user interface, which allows the user to draw partial tree structures, and the tool will retrieve all the trees that contain this structure. In order to search in syntactically annotated corpora using TigerSearch, these corpora first have to be loaded into the tool. For this, a separate tool called TigerRegistry is provided in the distribution. TigerRegistry can read a range of different file formats, including the Penn Treebank format (cf. section 4.2) or the susanne format. Thus, corpora in the most commonly used formats can be imported without any prior conversion to a specific data format, which generally involves programming. The internal format in which corpora are stored in TigerSearch is *TigerXML*, which has become a quasi-standard for the XML representation of syntactically annotated corpora. TigerRegistry is distributed with a manual, which explains step by step how to import corpora.

One of the main advantages of TigerSearch is the graphical search interface, which allows the user to build queries without knowing the query language. Figure 12.4 shows an example of the graphical search, showing a query for a coordinated NP that has one daughter which is not an NP in the Penn Treebank. In order to find coordinated structures, we assume a word node with the POS tag CC (coordinating conjunction), and for the non-NP daughter, we specify a node where the equal sign is crossed out, which then

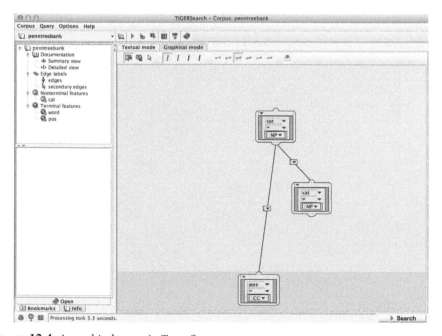

Figure 12.4 A graphical query in TigerSearch.

reads as "is not." Note that we do not specify the order between the conjunction and the non-NP conjunct. Thus, either one could precede the other.

In the graphical search, TIGERSEARCH distinguishes between word nodes and syntax nodes. The former have to be located in the dark gray area, cf. the node for the POS CC in Figure 12.4. The latter are located in the lighter gray area, such as the NP node. For word nodes, one can either choose to search for a word or a POS; for syntax nodes, we can specify the category (cat) of the constituent. The arcs between nodes represent direct dominance; a dashed arc would mean dominance. The type of relation can be chosen by clicking on the triangle. When direct dominance is chosen, one can additionally select the grammatical function of the dominance relation. Linear precedence is represented by arcs between the sides of two nodes. Figure 12.5 shows a query involving a grammatical function and direct linear precedence. This example searches for sentences that have an NP dominating an adverbial phrase (ADVP) immediately followed by a temporal NP (TMP). This query would find sentences with NPs such as **a report out last week** or **strong dividends again next year**.

TIGERSEARCH provides the number of sentences in which the search structure was found, but also the number of subgraphs. For example, if a structure we search for occurs twice in one sentence, it would count once towards the sentence count, but twice towards the subgraph count. The user can browse through all the hits in TIGERSEARCH and also save a list of all sentences containing this phenomenon, in different formats. In TIGERSEARCH, the matched nodes are highlighted in bright red;

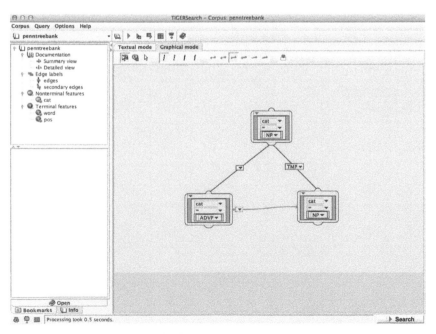

Figure 12.5 A more complex graphical query in TIGERSEARCH.

all nodes dominated by the root node of the query are marked in dark red. An example is shown in Figure 12.6.

The graphical user interface is a way to allow users easy search capabilities without having to learn a complete query language. However, internally, TigerSearch translates the graphical queries into its query language. Proficient users can enter the query directly in the query language itself. The queries shown graphically in Figures 12.4 and 12.5 are shown in (5) in the query language.[5]

(5) a. #n1:[cat="NP"] > [pos="CC"] & #n1 > [cat!="NP"]
   b. #n1:[cat="NP"] > #n2:[cat="ADVP"] & #n1 >TMP #n3:[cat="NP"] & #n2 . #n3

A node is represented in square brackets: [cat="NP"] is a syntax node of type NP, [pos="CC"] is a word with POS tag CC. Direct dominance is represented by the > sign,[6] i.e. [cat="NP"] > [pos="CC"] specifies that the NP directly dominates the CC. The more general dominance is written as >*. Nodes can also be assigned names, which is necessary if they enter into different relations. In (5-a), the root NP node has dominance relations to two nodes, which must be stated separately. Thus, we give the node a name, #n1. All names have to start with the # sign; the following part of the name is chosen by the user. We decided to call it "n1" (for node 1). Names are separated from the node definition by a colon. Then, we can use this name to specify the second relation: #n1 > [cat!="NP"], saying that the mother NP called #n1 dominates the non-NP node. The negation in the non-NP is written as !: [cat!="NP"]. In (5-b), we also have direct linear precedence, #n2 . #n3, and the use of the grammatical function TMP, which is attached to the dominance relation: >TMP.

TigerSearch also permits the use of "and" and "or" connections within nodes or for values, accessible by clicking in the gray area on the side of the node or next to the value. Figure 12.7 shows a query for an NP or an NX[7] with a daughter **advertised**, which has the POS tag VBN. There is only one occurrence in the Penn Treebank: **GMAC's**

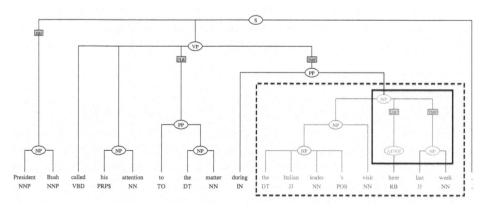

Figure 12.6 A sentence that matches the query in Figure 12.5.

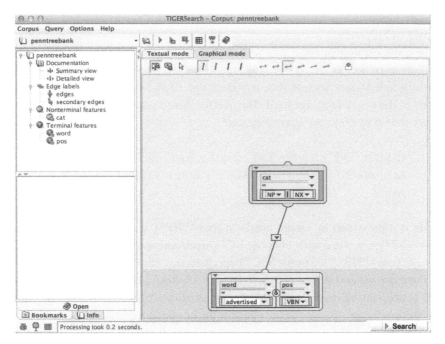

Figure 12.7 A graphical query involving logical relations.

advertised finance rates. Note than an "and" relation is only useful if two different types of information are combined (here: word and POS) since a single word cannot have two POS tags and a syntax node cannot have two different categories.

Sometimes, we need to search for nodes that have a specific grammatical function. For this, TIGERSEARCH requires us to create the mother and the daughter node involved in the grammatical function. Since we do not necessarily want to specify the type of the mother node, we can create a node without entering any information. In the query language, empty syntax nodes are entered as "[NT]," empty word nodes as "[T]". Thus, if we want to search for a temporal NP, we need to specify the empty mother, which has an NP daughter, and there is a direct dominance from the empty node to the NP; then, the dominance relation can be set to be temporal (TMP). The query is shown in (6).

(6)   [NT] >TMP [cat="NP"]

In the example in Figure 12.4, we have seen the use of negation. What we have not explained yet is where negation can be used, and what exactly this means. We can negate within the node, e.g. [cat!="NP"], and we can negate both types of dominance and linear precedence relations: #n1 !> #n2 for dominance and #n1 !. #n2 for linear precedence. Additionally, we can negate a value, e.g. [cat=(!"NP")]. But what exactly the negation means is not obvious. Let us assume we are looking for an NP which does not have an internal ADJP. The most intuitive way of saying this would be the one in (7).

(7)   [cat="NP"] !> [cat="ADJP"]

However, what (7) really means in TIGERSEARCH is "I am looking for an NP and an ADJP, such that there is no direct dominance relation between the two"—i.e. this query would find all sentences with at least one NP and at least one ADJP, where the NP is either sister node to the ADJP, its daughter, or somewhere else in the tree, just not the direct mother node. The reason for this behavior of TIGERSEARCH is that in its query language, nodes are existentially bound, which is a fancy way of saying that we can only look for nodes which are actually there, but we cannot say: "Find a tree that does *not* have such a node." This means that we cannot search for ellipsis or for grammatical phenomena that are characterized by features that are not present if these phenomena are not explicitly encoded in the annotation. The PENN TREEBANK, for example, encodes certain types of ellipsis by null elements. In such cases, we can search for these null elements. The reason for the restriction to existing nodes in TIGERSEARCH is that such queries are computationally very intensive. If the tool allowed queries for trees that do not have certain nodes or relations, the tool would have to search many more possibilities, which would increase query times exponentially in many cases, and the tool would not be efficient.

This section here only describes the most important features of TIGERSEARCH. A complete list of its features can be found in the user manual (see section 12.7).

12.4 FANGORN

FANGORN is a query tool for constituent trees. It is very efficient, and it allows the user to build queries based on paths in trees. FANGORN's query language is similar to *XPath*, a well-known query language for XML documents. The basic principle for this query language is that everything needs to be specified in paths. For example, we could look for a VP containing an NP with the word **loss**; the expression is shown in (8-a). // represents dominance, and / direct dominance. Note that we generally start each query with the dominance operator, saying that the first node in the search path can be anywhere in the tree. Only in cases where we require this node to be the root node of the tree, we start with /. Thus, the example in (8-b) is looking for a question (SQ) having a coordination conjunction (CC) as a daughter. Note also that, in contrast to TIGERSEARCH, the POS tag of the word, NN in example (8-a), is considered a separate node in the tree.

(8)   a.   //VP/NP/NN/loss
      b.   /SQ/CC

In FANGORN, we can also search for linear precedence. It distinguishes between preceding and following siblings. (9) shows an example in which we search for occurrences of the expression **in spite of**, where -> specifies that we are looking for: **in**, followed by **spite**, which is then followed by **of**.

(9) //in->spite->of

So far, we have seen queries in which we had one path going through two or more nodes/words. However, this does not work if we want to specify a node and more than one daughter, for example, if we want to look for an NP with a PP and a word with POS tag CC as daughters. In order to search for such coordinated NPs in FANGORN, we need to use a construct called *filter*. A filter is attached to a node label and consists of square brackets in which two partial paths are combined with an AND or an OR relation.

(10) //NP[/PP AND /CC]

The query for the coordinated NP is shown in (10). Here, we specify in the filter that the mother NP needs to have two paths: one leading to the daughter NP, the other to the CC. We can also combine different types of paths in the filter, as shown in (11).

(11) //NP[/ADVP AND ->NP-SBJ]

This query is for an NP that has an adverbial phrase (ADVP) as daughter, and is immediately followed by a subject NP (NP-SUBJ). Note that in FANGORN's query language, grammatical functions are attached to the syntactic category; they are not a feature of the arc like in TIGERSEARCH. Such combinations of syntactic category and grammatical function are considered an inseparable symbol. Thus, the query in (12-a) will only match sentences where there is an NP without grammatical function label between the VP and **week**. In order to find cases with temporal NPs, we need the query in (12-b).

(12) a. //VP/NP//week
      b. //VP/NP-TMP//week

Note also that the query in (11) is not similar in structure to the TIGERSEARCH query shown in Figure 12.5, since here, the subject NP is a sibling of the first NP, not a daughter. In the PENN TREEBANK, it matches one sentence, shown in (13).

(13) Michael Basham, deputy assistant secretary for federal finance, said 0 the Treasury may wait until [NP late Monday or [$_{ADVP}$ even] early Tuesday] [$_{NP-SBJ}$ *-2] to announce whether the auctions are *-1 to be rescheduled *-106.

The TIGERSEARCH query in Figure 12.5 translated into FANGORN's language is shown in (14). Note that FANGORN has a separate relation, =>, which means direct following sibling, thus requiring that both nodes are daughters of the same node.

(14) //NP[/ADVP=>NP-TMP]

FANGORN also has a form of negation, which needs to be specified in a filter. (15) shows a query looking for a word with POS tag VBG, which **is** directly preceded by the word **is** and directly succeeded by a pronoun (POS tag: PRP), and which does not have a clause as its immediate sibling.

(15) //VBG[<-is AND ->PRP AND NOT =>S]

This query will find sentences such as the one in (16-a) but not the one in (16-b).

(16) a. But although he thinks that it [$_{VP}$ [$_{VBZ}$ is] [$_{VBG}$ hurting] [$_{NP}$ [$_{PRP}$ him]]], he doubts 0 it could be stopped *-1.

b. "Just a blind fear of the unknown [$_{VBZ}$ is] [$_{VBG}$ causing] [$_{S}$ [$_{NP-SUBJ}$ them] to beg the regulators for protection]."

Note that negation in FANGORN is different from negation in TIGERSEARCH: while in TIGERSEARCH, the negated part is subject to existential binding; in FANGORN, it is not—i.e. the query in (17-a) will return all PPs that do *not* contain any prepositions marked with IN. In TIGERSEARCH, in contrast, the corresponding query, shown in (17-b), will return all PPs that have at least one word that is not an IN.

(17) a. //PP[NOT /IN]

b. [cat="PP"] > [pos!="IN"]

Admittedly, there is a large overlap in the search results, namely all PPs with the prepositions **to** (POS tag: TO), **including**, or **according**. The latter two words are assigned the POS tag of an **-ing** verb (VBG), but they function as prepositions, thus the mother node is a PP. However, the query in TIGERSEARCH will also find PPs with an IN but additionally with another word that is not an IN as direct daughters. Examples of such sentences are shown in (18).

(18) a. ... the smooth, needle-like fibers [$_{PP}$ such/JJ as/IN crocidolite] ...

b. ... used [$_{PP}$ in/IN "/" very modest amounts "/"] ...

c. ... report a profit $19.3 million for the first half of 1989 [$_{PP}$ rather/RB than/IN the $5.9 million it posted].

d. ... [$_{PP}$ because/RB of/IN the potential ...]

As a consequence, the TIGERSEARCH query in (19-a) is meaningful in that it searches for an IN and a non-IN on the word level, which are directly dominated by a PP, while the FANGORN query in (19-b) has a valid syntax but will never retrieve any examples because it searches for a PP which has an IN and at the same time has only daughters that are not IN.

(19) a. #n1:[cat="PP"] > [pos="IN"] & #n1 > [pos!="IN"]

b. //PP[/IN AND NOT /IN]

One major difference between TIGERSEARCH and FANGORN is that we need to know the query language of FANGORN, while the graphical user interface of TIGERSEARCH allows us to perform a search without actually knowing the language behind. However, we still need to be familiar with the annotation scheme in order to know how the phenomenon is annotated—i.e. if we want to look for coordinated NPs with unlike conjuncts (cf. section 2.3), we need to know that in the PENN TREEBANK the mother node of such a coordination of unlike constituents is a UCP. FANGORN offers the possibility of building a query from a tree, which allows us an indirect way of searching without actually knowing the annotation scheme. To look for our coordination of unlikes, we could start out by looking for an adjective (JJ), followed by a conjunction (CC) and a determiner (DT), as a first approximation of a coordinated NP with an adjectival phrase and an NP daughter. One of the trees that are listed as a result is shown in Figure 12.8.

Now, we can click the button saying "Build query from tree" and then modify the tree so that we include the UCP and the NP, but delete the too specific JJ and DT. This results in the query in (20). The \ specifies that the UCP is the direct mother of CC, and NP is a direct daughter of UCP.

(20) //CC\UCP/NP

This query retrieves sentences such as the one shown in (21).

(21) a. Rudolph Agnew, [$_{ADJP}$ 55 years old] and [$_{NP}$ former chairman of Consolidated Gold Fields PLC], ...
  b. Compound yields assume [$_{NP}$ reinvestment of dividends] and [$_{SBAR}$ that the current yield continues for a year].
  c. ITC officials said 0 final Commerce Department and ITC rulings won't come until [$_{NP}$ next March] or [$_{ADVP}$ later].

< Match 1 of 1 >

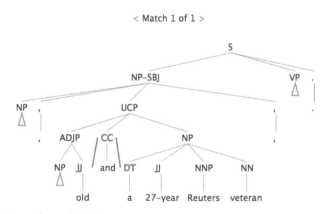

Figure 12.8 A search result in FANGORN.

12.5 NETGRAPH

NETGRAPH is a query tool for dependency annotation (cf. section 4.6). More specifically, it was developed for the PRAGUE DEPENDENCY TREEBANK (PTB), but it can be used to query other dependency treebanks if they can be converted into the format underlying the tool. NETGRAPH uses a client-server architecture. This means that a server needs to be installed, which can be accessed by client programs installed on different computers. We will concentrate here on the client that is provided by the developers, which allows access to the PTB, with its server set up in Prague.

The query tool has a graphical user interface, similar to TIGERSEARCH, in which one can create a query by a combination of clicking and typing. The first step in NETGRAPH is the choice of files on which to perform our queries. For the following discussion, we assume that we have selected all available files and copied them to the panel "Custom subcorpus selection" by clicking on the ">>" button; then, we choose "use the custom selection for searching."

We switch to query mode by choosing "Query" in the lower menu. Figure 12.9 shows the graphical interface in query mode.

NETGRAPH regards a dependency graph as a tree structure, in which the heads are located high and its dependents on the next lower level. In order to search for a phenomenon, we again create a partial tree representing our phenomenon. In the "factory" panel of the tool, we can construct the basic structure by clicking. The button "new query" will give us a single node, "subtree" will add a dependent to an existing node, "brother" another node that is a co-dependent of the head of the current node. The query is shown as a term in NETGRAPH's query language, and at the same time as

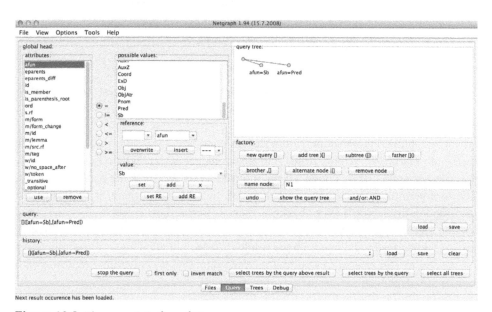

Figure 12.9 The query interface of NETGRAPH.

a graph in the field. Here, the node labeled "afun=Pred" is in a sibling relation (called "brother") to the node labeled "afun=Sb." Note that while linguists in the Western world tend to use female forms, such as mother or daughter, to refer to nodes in a tree, Eastern Europe has a tradition of using male terms instead. In NETGRAPH's query language, the tree is displayed in a similar fashion to the bracketing formats presented in Chapter 4. The query shown in Figure 12.9 is repeated in (22).

(22) [ ]([afun=Sb]),[afun=Pred])

Each node is represented by square brackets, and parentheses mark the dependents. This query says that we have a node that is not defined further, [ ], which has two dependents: [ ]([ ], [ ]). Dependency labels are called analytical functions in the PTB, and even though they are shown on the dependent, they define the relation to the head. The first dependent has the analytical function subject (Sb), the second dependent is a predicate (Pred). The information about a node must be entered via the keyboard, but the panel "attributes" allows us to choose the type of information that we want to represent in a node, for example the analytical function. The panel "possible values" then displays all values for the type of information. A double click copies these into the query.

If the query is complete, we click on "select trees by the query." In order to look at the results of the query, we select "Trees" from the lower menu. Figure 12.10 shows a dependency tree found by the query in (22). The Czech sentence, cf. (23), is displayed in the upper part.

(23) Jak konstatoval premiér   Václav Klaus, vláda
As said   Prime Minister Václav Klaus, the government
nevidí žádné důvody k umělému urychlování či zpomalování
sees no   reason to artificially accelerating or decelerating
bankrotů.
bankruptcy.
"As noted by Prime Minister Vaclav Klaus, the government sees no reason to artificially accelerate or decelerate bankruptcy."

In the graphical representation of the dependency tree, the nodes mentioned in the query are marked in yellow (head) and green (dependents). Yellow is used to show the selected node. For this node, all the information is shown in the panel on the left. The tool permits the selection of other nodes, by clicking on them, if we want their information displayed. If we go back to "Query," we can now create a new query, and we can run this query on the sentences already selected by the first one, by clicking on "select queries by the query above result." This would allow us to make our query more specific—for example, by adding the constraint that we only want predicates with exactly two dependents. This query is shown in (24).

(24) [afun=Pred,_#sons=2]

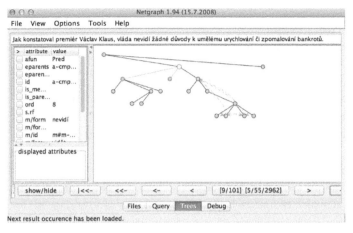

Figure 12.10 A search result in NETGRAPH.

Note that there are no spaces allowed in the query. The second type of information we require, that the predicate only has two dependents, is a *meta attribute*. Such attributes allow us to specify information that is not related to one specific node. Apart from restricting the number of dependents, we can also specify the number of all descendants, i.e. the number of nodes in the complete subtree, or the number of siblings, i.e. nodes with the same head as the current node. Or we can mark a node as optional, or specify that a node must not be a direct dependent, but an indirect one, as defined in section 12.1. A full list of meta attributes can be found in the manual.

NETGRAPH also allows the use of logical and/or relations on different levels. They can be used to have alternative values within a node, as in (25-a), where we take care of potential capitalization of words, or to specify alternative nodes, as in (25-b), where we search for the lemma **prezident**, but with different POS tags, and with the (analytic) function subject in the first case.

(25) a. [w/token=Prezident|prezident]

b. [m/lemma=prezident,m/tag=NNMS1—-A—-
,w/token=Prezident,afun=Sb]|[m/lemma=prezident,m/tag=NNMP5—
-A—-]|[m/lemma=prezident,m/tag=NNMS6—-A—-]

We can also combine complete trees with and/or. This can be achieved by the button "and/or:AND." By clicking on the button, we can switch between AND and OR. A query for a tree with two predicates, one with 3 left siblings and one with exactly 4 indirect dependents, is shown in (26). Here the AND specifies that both of the following subtrees have to be found in one sentence. The same query, but using OR, would look for sentences that either have a predicate with 3 left siblings, or with 4 indirect dependents. A sentence that matches the query using AND is shown in Figure 12.11; the matched sentence is shown in (27).

(26) AND
[afun=Pred,_#lbrothers=3]
[afun=Pred,_#descendants=4]

(27) Jde   o   subjektivní rozhodnutí věřitele,   a   je
     It concerns about subjective   decision   of the client, and is
     proto logický postoj bank,   které zvažují, zda   se
     why   logical attitude of banks, that   estimate, whether REFL
     jim   bankrot   vyplatí nebo ne.
     to them bankruptcy benefits or   not.
     'It is about the subjective decision of the client and that is why the attitude of banks
     is logical, which estimate whether the bankruptcy is advantageous to them or not.'

NETGRAPH also has a limited type of negation. It allows the negation of the complete
query, by selecting the button "invert match." This displays all the trees that do *not*
match the query—i.e. for the query in (26), we would see all trees that do not have the
two predicates as specified. The results would contain all the sentences that have either
one or the other predicate, or none at all.

12.6 Summary

In this chapter, we have looked at the different relations that hold in constituent trees
as well as in dependency graphs. We discussed linear precedence, dominance, and
dependency, both in the direct and the indirect form. Then, we had a look at three
query tools for constituent search, TGREP2, TIGERSEARCH, and FANGORN, as well as

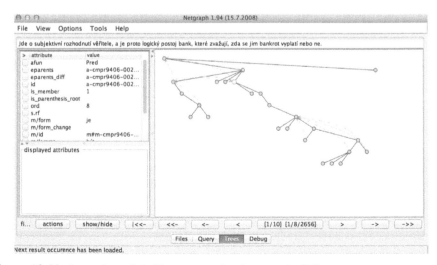

Figure 12.11 A search result in NETGRAPH using the query in (26).

Netgraph for dependencies. We showed the main features for each query tool, and gave an introduction to the graphical interface and to their individual query languages. We also showed differences in the query languages with regard to negation. Since all tools use different symbols for similarly defined relations, we provide an overview of the most important relations in Table 12.1. We still need to say a word about saving search results for further processing or analysis. Tgrep2 prints the results on the screen, and in linux, such an output can easily be redirected into a file. Both TigerSearch and Netgraph provide the possibility to save search results in different formats via a menu option. In Fangorn, there is no such option, but it is possible to copy and paste the displayed trees into a file. Another option to save individual trees in graphical form would be to take a screen shot of the tree as it is displayed in the tool. Since methods for taking screen shots differ widely between operating systems, we suggest that the interested reader look up the instructions in the manuals.

12.7 Further Reading

Section 12.2

Tgrep2 (including the manual) is available from http://tedlab.mit.edu/~dr/Tgrep2/.

Section 12.3

TigerSearch is available from http://www.ims.uni-stuttgart.de/forschung/ressourcen/ werkzeuge/tigersearch.en.html, and it works under most platforms. A slightly outdated version that may work better with certain operating systems is available at http://www.hum. uit.no/a/gerstenberger/tigersearch.html. The TigerSearch manual is available at http:// www.ims.uni-stuttgart.de/forschung/ressourcen/werkzeuge/TIGERSearch/manual.html.

TigerXML: For a description of *TigerXML*, we refer the reader to Chapter V in the TigerSearch User Manual by König et al. (2003, Ch. 4), available at http://www.ims. uni-stuttgart.de/forschung/ressourcen/werkzeuge/TIGERSearch/manual.html.

Table 12.1 The most central search relations, in comparison between Tgrep2, TigerSearch, Fangorn, and Netgraph.

relation	TGREP2	TigerSearch	Fangorn	Netgraph
direct linear precedence	.	.	->	[],[]
linear precedence	..	.*	- ->	
direct dominance/dependency	<	>	/	[]([])
dominance/dependency	<<	> *	//	_transitive=true
not	!	!	NOT	"invert match"
and, or	&, |	&, |	AND, OR	&,|, AND, OR

Section 12.4

FANGORN: The code for a local installation is available at http://code.google.com/p/fangorn/. A description of the query language can be found at http://code.google.com/p/fangorn/wiki/Query_Language.

XPATH: An XPATH tutorial is available at http://www.w3schools.com/xpath/.

Section 12.5

For **NETGRAPH**, the client download is available at http://quest.ms.mff.cuni.cz/netgraph/install.html, the client manual at http://quest.ms.mff.cuni.cz/netgraph/doc/netgraph_manual.html.

Other query tools: ICARUS is a search and visualization tool that primarily targets dependency trees. The tool is available from http://www.ims.uni-stuttgart.de/forschung/ressourcen/werkzeuge/icarus.en.html. INESS is an online tool that allows querying constituent and dependency structure of treebanks that have been uploaded by the owners, cf. http://iness.uib.no/iness/main-page; TÜNDRA is an online query tool for constituent and dependency structures available at http://weblicht.sfs.uni-tuebingen.de/weblichtwiki/index.php/Tundra. There is a query tool that is based on the philosophy that users should be able to type in a sentence, which is then analyzed syntactically by the tool, and the user can choose the part of the tree that models the intended phenomenon to search for more sentences (as described for FANGORN): the *Linguist's Search Engine* (LSE). Descriptions of the tool can be found in Resnik and Elkiss (2005); Resnik et al. (2005). A reimplementation of the original tool is available at http://www.linguistics.ruhr-uni-bochum.de/resources/else. ANNIS (http://www.sfb632.uni-potsdam.de/d1/annis/) is a more general search and visualization tool, which can search in different levels of annotation, including syntactic annotations. ANNIS will be introduced in section 13.4.

12.8 Exercises

1. **TIGERSEARCH**: What are the following queries searching for?

   (a)

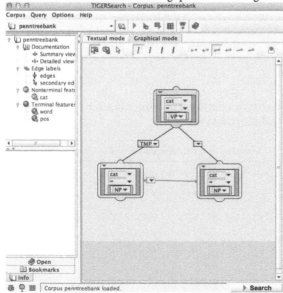

(b)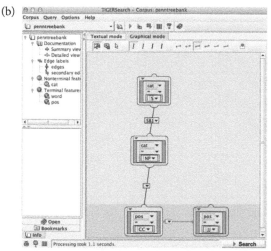

2. **FANGORN**: Go to the FANGORN download page at http://code.google.com/p/fangorn/, download the tool and start it (information can be found in the installation instructions on the web page under wiki or in the README file). Once FANGORN is running, open http://localhost:9090 in your browser. This will show the start page. Unfortunately, the implementation only works for MAC OS and LINUX. WINDOWS users will have to install a LINUX emulation, such as CYGWIN, first. Then, search for the following phenomena:
   (a) an NP that has an adverbial phrase and a prepositional phrase as daughters
   (b) an NP that has an adverbial phrase, followed by a prepositional phrase
   (c) an NP that has a noun phrase and a temporal noun phrase as daughters
   (d) an NP that is coordinated with an ADJP; how can you make sure that they are conjuncts, not just adjacent?
   (e) the sequence of words **in the fourth quarter**; then make it more general so that you find any **quarter**
   (f) the sequence **in the X quarter** that is part of an NP
   (g) the sequence **in the X quarter** followed by a VP that has an NP-ADV

3. **More FANGORN**: Install and start FANGORN (see above) and search for the following phenomenon: **the X to S** where **X** is a noun and **S** a clause. Start by finding a sequence of words where the first noun is **right**. Then click on "Build query from tree" and modify the query so that it covers the NP and the to. Can you delete the first noun and replace it by its POS tag?

4. **Search dependencies**: Download the NETGRAPH client from http://quest.ms.mff.cuni.cz/ netgraph/install.html and start it. Instructions how to start it can be found on the following webpage: http://quest.ms.mff.cuni.cz/netgraph/index.html. Select port 2100 in the second text field. Select the all files till no. 28 and click on ">>." Then, create queries that search for the following phenomena:
   (a) a node with two dependents
   (b) a node with exactly two dependents
   (c) a node with the following two dependents: a subject (Sb) and a direct object (Obj)
   (d) a node that does not have a subject and a direct object dependent
   (e) a node that is a subordinating conjunction and is the head of a deleted element
   (f) a sentence where the subject is head of a subordinating conjunction
   (g) a sentence where the subject is head of a subordinating conjunction and where the direct object also is the head of a subordinating conjunction

A list of analytic functions and their description can be found at http://ufal.mff.cuni.cz/ pdt2.0/doc/manuals/en/a-layer/html/ch03.html#s1-list-anal-func.

CHAPTER 13
SEARCHING FOR SEMANTIC AND DISCOURSE PHENOMENA

As we have seen in Chapters 5 and 6, semantic and pragmatic annotation is more diverse in structure than syntactic annotation. Additionally, there are only a few specialized tools available. We therefore restrict this chapter to the introduction of just a few individual tools and interfaces for searching semantic and pragmatic information in resources introduced in previous chapters: The TIMEBANK browser in section 13.1; the PDTB browser, the RSTTOOL plus an online interface to the RST SPANISH TREEBANK in section 13.3; and finally ANNIS, a general-purpose tool for multi-layered annotated data, in section 13.4.

13.1 Accessing Fully Annotated Texts in FRAMENET

FRAMENET is a semantic resource in which the annotation of semantic roles is based on semantic frames. This resource has been introduced in section 5.3.2. In order to have access to the fully annotated texts in FRAMENET, the user can either request the download of the annotated data in stand-off XML format (which is not particularly user-friendly) or browse the texts online in the FRAMENET browser. Given that the text collection is small, there is no specialized tool for browsing the English fully annotated texts. The user has to click through the list of subcorpora and then the individual text titles. After clicking on one title, the text is displayed in the upper part of the browser window with all frame-evoking elements printed in underlined bold letters (see Figure 13.1), which includes an example that we have introduced in section 5.3.2 in detail (cf. example (27) in section 5.3.2, repeated here as (1)). The light gray highlighted words in the text are automatically identified named entities and temporal expressions, for example **Venetian**, which we will not cover in the following description.

(1)   ..., but the Cyclades remained in Venetian hands for another generation or more

The frame-evoking elements are annotated with their frame label as subscript—for example, **remained** in (1) is an instantiation of the frame State_continue. The user can display the frame elements that belong to such an individual frame-evoking element by clicking on the element in the text. The sentence is then displayed in the lower part of the window with color-coded marking of the frame elements. The lower part of Figure 13.1, for example, shows the frame set for the verb remained. There is also an option of displaying the frame element labels in bracketed form (option "Turn colors off").

Corpus Linguistics and Linguistically Annotated Corpora

HOME   FRAMENET   FRAMENET DATA   BIBLIOGRAPHY   ACCOUNT

Home

FrameNet Data

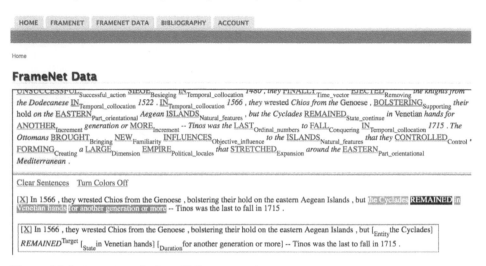

Figure 13.1 FRAMENET display of fully annotated text.

The reason why we mention the FRAMENET browser is that the text display is supplemented by online lexical tools, which are helpful to understand the annotation and make full use of the information provided by FRAMENET. First of all, there are the *Frame Index* and the corresponding *Lexical Unit Index,* which list all frame concepts and all lexical units respectively, along with the annotated sentences that use those concepts or lexical units. For our example, the user will find more information on the frame State_continue in the Frame Index and more information on the verb **remain** in the Lexical Unit Index respectively, including lists of annotated example sentences. A small drawback is that the example sentences do not link back into the corpus itself. In addition to these main indices, there is FRAMESQL, a browser for searching the FrameNet data for specific combinations of frame elements, grammatical functions, and syntactic phrase types. The tool also allows for cross-linguistic comparisons of frames (English (BFN), German (SALSA), Japanese (JFN), Spanish (SFN)). Figure 13.2 shows an example search that filters all examples of the frame State_continue that contain a frame element of the phrase type "sentence introduced by **whether**" (swhether). Note that for this frame, the only cross-linguistic option is the Japanese FrameNet (JFN).

Finally, the FRAMEGRAPHER visualizes how concepts are related to each other by means of semantic relations. For example, the frame State_continue is used by the frame Continued_state_of_affairs (see the upper image of Figure 13.3). 'Using' means that the child frame presupposes the parent frame as background, but—in contrast to Inheritance, which is an ISA relation—not all parent frame elements need to be bound to child frame elements. The Continued_state_of_affairs frame is evoked by the following set of non-verbal lexical units **as yet, as of yet, so far, still, to date, up to** (see example (2) for an illustration).

252

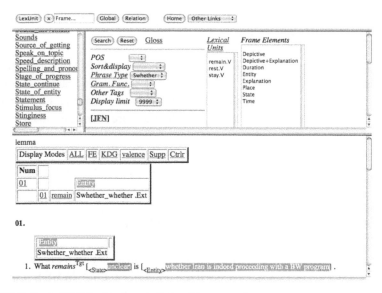

Figure 13.2 FrameSQL tool to search FrameNet examples.

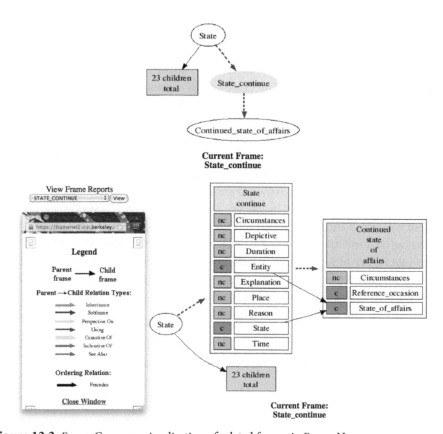

Figure 13.3 FrameGrapher visualization of related frames in FrameNet.

(2) PBGC guarantees the benefit [$_\text{State\_of\_affairs}$ that you had earned] up to^{Target} [$_\text{reference\_occasion}$ the date of plan termination].

After clicking (exactly) on a frame relation arrow head, FRAMEGRAPHER reveals which frame elements correspond to each other in the related frames, see the lower image of Figure 13.3, which illustrates how the core elements Entity and State of the (parent) frame State_continue relate to the core elements of its child state Continued_state_of_affairs.

Employing these additional tools can be very useful when browsing the fully annotated FRAMENET texts since they visualize important factors of the annotation.

13.2 Browsing Temporal Information in TimeBank

TimeBank is a corpus annotated with temporal information that we have described in detail in section 5.4. The project developed the online TimeBank browser originally for its annotators to support the evaluation of their annotation. This browser can now be used for independent exploration of the annotated corpus. To understand the properties of the browser, it is helpful to know that the annotators of TimeBank annotated the sentences by type. This means, they annotated all occurrences of one type, instead of annotating adjacent corpus sentences one after the other, for all the types they contained. The annotators needed to check whether their annotation was accurate and complete. This is the reason why the browser tool supports different ways of accessing the data and their annotation. In particular, it supports both list-based and search-based options (see the summary in Table 13.1).

The article-based access leads the user to a full text view of the chosen article, in which events, TIMEXes, and signals are clickable. For an explanation of these types of annotation, see section 5.4. For example, we can choose text wsj_0778.tml (a Wall Street Journal article), from which we extracted example (38) in section 5.4. Figure 13.4 shows the full text view with clickable instances.[1] Events, signals and TIMEXes are coded in different colors and are distinguished by different subscripts.

Clicking on **soon** opens an exhaustive list of all the occurrences of this TIMEX in the corpus (see Figure 13.5). The box on top of the page offers links that will open another window. For instance, clicking on "all links" will open a second window with a tabular display of all links that are annotated in the current text.

Table 13.1: Access types provided by the TimeBank browser.

Search type	Access
List-based	articles, events, TIMEXes, signals
Search-based	ALinks, SLinks, TLinks, simple Query

wsj_0778.tml

Show: events I timexes I all links I alinks I slinks I tlinks
Selected link:

CREATION_TIME: ^{t232}

0   WSJ891027-0117
      = 891027
    891027-0117. Law: @ U.S. Threats to Seize Fees @ Scare Lawyers From Cases @
    ---- @ By Laurie P. Cohen @ Staff Reporter of The Wall Street Journal
        10/27/89$_{t232}$
    WALL STREET JOURNAL (J) CRZYQ LAW AND LEGAL AFFAIRS (LAW)
    BANKRUPTCIES (BCY) JUSTICE DEPARTMENT (JUS) SECURITIES AND
    EXCHANGE COMMISSION (SEC)

1   The government is sharpening$_{e1}$ its newest weapon against white-collar defendants:
    the power$_{e200}$ to prevent$_{e4}$ them from paying$_{e6}$ their legal bills.

2   And defense lawyers are warning$_{e8}$ that they wo n't stick$_{e9}$ around if$_{s11}$ they do n't
    get paid$_{e14}$.

...

9   Mr. Antar is being investigated$_{e73}$ by a federal grand jury in Newark , where
    prosecutors have told$_{e74}$ him that they may soon$_{t234}$ seek$_{e75}$ an indictment$_{e77}$ on
    racketeering and securities fraud charges.

Figure 13.4 Interactive full text display in the TimeBank browser.

The search-based access to TimeBank offers many filter options, which originally
allowed the annotators to efficiently find very specific sets of examples for comparison
with their current annotation. For the linguistic user, it is sufficient to specify only some
of the filter options to retrieve interesting classes of examples. For example, we want to
investigate reporting events that report about some other event of the type occurrence,
which only takes place after the reporting itself. In other words, we are interested in
reporting events that are related to an occurrence event by a TLink of the type BEFORE.
To obtain relevant examples, we make use of the *tlinks* option in the top menu of the
TimeBank browser. This opens the page *Find TLinks* with a number of filter options.
Figure 13.6 shows the filter options we used. We only minimally restricted the search
options for both event classes and the relation type. A user does not need to know the
options by heart. Except for the token and value fields, all other fields offer drop-down
lists with valid values to choose from.

The result page first summarizes the search pattern (here {REPORTING} {BEFORE}
{OCCURRENCE}) and provides the number of matches (here 8). Then, it lists up to 250
matches for the query. Each match starts with an icon that links to the full text display
of the matching instance. Figure 13.7 shows, for example, the eighth match of our query,
which belongs to the example text that we also used above (text wsj_0778). Each match is
headed by its particular instantiation of the search pattern. In our case, this instantiation
includes the specification of the event token, its class (which was predefined in the query),

TimeBank 1.2 Timex — soon

📄 22 The likelihood that the federal budget will soon$_{t214}$ move$_{e107}$ from deficit into surplus has further improved$_{e109}$ the outlook.

📄 1 Control Data Corp. , which just months ago$_{t204}$ was hemorrhaging$_{e1}$ financially , thinks$_{e2}$ it will be healthy$_{e2438}$ enough soon$_{t206}$ to consider$_{e3}$ repurchasing$_{e4}$ public debt.

📄 12 Kellogg is so anxious$_{e206}$ to turn$_{e32}$ around Corn Flakes sales that it soon$_{t207}$ will begin$_{e33}$ selling$_{e34}$ boxes for as little as 99 cents , trade sources say$_{e35}$.

📄 9 Mr. Antar is being investigated$_{e73}$ by a federal grand jury in Newark , where prosecutors have told$_{e74}$ him that they may soon$_{t234}$ seek$_{e75}$ an indictment$_{e77}$ on racketeering and securities fraud charges.

📄 16 Westinghouse also expects$_{e79}$ its international sales to soon$_{t147}$ grow$_{e81}$ to 25%')">25%$_{e469}$ of total corporate sales from$_{s149}$ 20%')">20%$_{e152}$ last year$_{t150}$.

Figure 13.5 Exhaustive list of TIMEX **soon** in the TimeBank browser.

and its values for tense and aspect. Example (3) shows two specifications. (3-a) is the specification used in the example in Figure 13.7, where the reporting event is expressed in sentence 12 and the occurrence event in sentence 11. (3-b) is another example instantiation in which the aspect feature has an actual value PERFECTIVE_PROG.

(3) a. BEFORE {told REPORTING PAST NONE} {issued OCCURRENCE PAST NONE}

    b. BEFORE {telling REPORTING PAST PERFECTIVE_PROG} {announcement OCCURRENCE NONE NONE}

Finally there is the search option *queries* in the top menu. It overlaps with the link search options but provides a different display of the results. It first requires the user to filter for the types of elements to be related. A drop-down list allows us to choose from queries on entity-entity relations (qE-E), TIMEX-entity (qT-E) and entity-TIMEX (qE-T) respectively. It also allows us to explicitly query for relation types that relate to specified events (qR-E-E). A qE-E query for the event **told** results in the summary display in Figure 13.8 (note that there is no lemmatization available, and each word form determines its own event). In the white panel of **after**, we find an instance of the event **issued**, which brings us back to our old example shown in Figure 13.7.

13.3 Working with Discourse Relations

13.3.1 *PDTB Browser*

In section 6.3, we introduced two resources that contain annotation of discourse relations: the PENN DISCOURSE TREEBANK and the DISCOURSE RELATIONS REFERENCE CORPUS. In this section, we will briefly describe how these annotations can be accessed.

Find TLinks

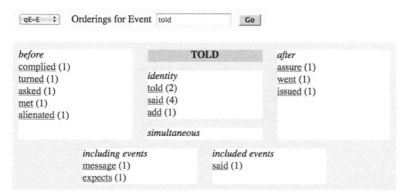

Figure 13.6 TIMEBANK browser search window for TLinks.

BEFORE { told REPORTING PAST NONE } { issued OCCURRENCE PAST NONE }

11 According$_{e208}$ to individuals familiar with Mr. Antar 's case, prosecutors issued$_{e93}$ their warning this week$_{t235}$ after$_{s209}$ one of Mr. Antar 's attorneys asked$_{e95}$ whether legal fees might be subject$_{e210}$ to seizure$_{e98}$.

12 In a letter, prosecutors told$_{e100}$ Mr. Antar 's lawyers that because of the recent$_{t236}$ Supreme Court rulings$_{e214}$, they could expect$_{e101}$ that any fees collected from Mr. Antar may be seized$_{e104}$.

Figure 13.7 TIMEBANK browser example result for a TLinks search.

Query TimeBank

qE–E ◆	Orderings for Event	told		Go

before	**TOLD**	*after*
complied (1)		assure (1)
turned (1)	*identity*	went (1)
asked (1)	told (2)	issued (1)
met (1)	said (4)	
alienated (1)	add (1)	
	simultaneous	

	including events	*included events*
	message (1)	said (1)
	expects (1)	

Figure 13.8 TIMEBANK browser example summary for an event-event query.

The PENN DISCOURSE TREEBANK, which was also used as an empirical basis in section 8.3, is distributed with a browser to access the annotation: the PDTB browser. To use this tool, the user needs to have local copies of the discourse annotation files as well as of the syntactically annotated PENN TREEBANK (version II) files. The latter is necessary because the discourse annotation is distributed as a stand-off annotation layer to the syntactically annotated treebank, which means that it does not include the text tokens itself but refers to them in terms of index pointers. The browser then combines the information provided by both resources, making them accessible together, and visualizes them.

If both resources are installed locally, one can use the PDTB browser for browsing and querying the annotations. Figure 13.9 shows the browser interface, which is organized in three panels: The syntactic parse trees are on top, the actual discourse annotation at the bottom left, and the raw text at the bottom right. The discourse annotation is color-coded both in the parse tree panel as well as in the raw text view: Arg1 is highlighted in yellow (here: light gray); Arg2, which includes the discourse connective if it is explicit in the text, is marked in blue (here: dark gray); and the connective itself is highlighted in red (here: first word of the example). The discourse annotation panel provides a list of the relations of the current text. Each relation is either represented by its explicit or implicit connective, for example **Although**, an alternative lexicalization of the discourse relation (AltLex), or it is marked as an entity relation (EntRel). The panel provides the discourse features associated with the connective in tabular form. Table 13.2 shows the annotation of **Although** in the sentence in (4), which is also shown in the browser view in Figure 13.9.[2]

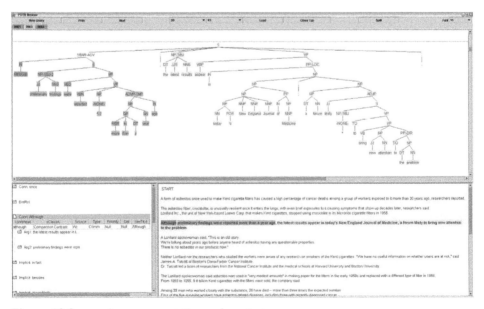

Figure 13.9 PDTB browser annotation and raw text.

Table 13.2 Discourse features displayed in the PDTB browser.

Conn: Although

connHead	sClassA	Source	Type	Polarity	Det
although	Comparison.Contrast	Wr	Comm	Null	Null

Arg1: the latest results appear in t...
Arg2: preliminary findings were repo...

(4) Although preliminary findings were reported more than a year ago, the latest results appear in today's New England Journal of Medicine, a forum likely to bring new attention to the problem.

The head of the connective (connHead) is trivial here because **although** is a one-word connective. sClassA is an abbreviation for the semantic class of the discourse connective. There is also an optional sClassB for cases of ambiguity, which is not the case in our example. In the example, there is only one class label assigned, Comparison of type Contrast; see Figure 6.8 (p. 143) for the complete hierarchy used in the PDTB. The subsequent features Source, Type, Polarity, and Det do not directly characterize the discourse relation but the speaker's or author's attribution, which characterizes, for example, whether the speaker knows or believes that their assertions hold true, or whether they simply report what others had claimed or even convey their own doubts. The feature Source distinguishes between different types of agents; in the example, it is *Wr* for 'writer'. The feature Type encodes the nature of the relationship between the agents and what they express by the arguments of the connective, also reflecting their factuality; the type Comm marks the relation that is conveyed by standard verbs of communication. (Scopal) polarity, which is related to negation, and Det (erminacy) are both set to *Null* in the example table. Determinacy is set to *Indet* in cases where it is not possible to assign an attribution to anyone in particular. Arg1 and Arg2 are also annotated with the attribution features Source, Type, Polarity, and Det.

The PDTB browser is supported by a graphical search interface (see Figure 13.10). This interface refers to the same set of features as introduced above. The user can compose a query by specifying the types of the features in the corresponding fields of the Query window. The browser's query language is based on XPath, a well-known query language for XML documents. The full query string is automatically converted into an XPath query, shown in the Full Query String field at the bottom of the window. The options panel on the right-hand side of the window illustrates the hierarchy of semantic class labels by indentation.

13.3.2 RSTTool

For the second resource annotated with discourse relations, the DISCOURSE RELATIONS REFERENCE CORPUS, which we have introduced in section 6.3.2, there is no genuine

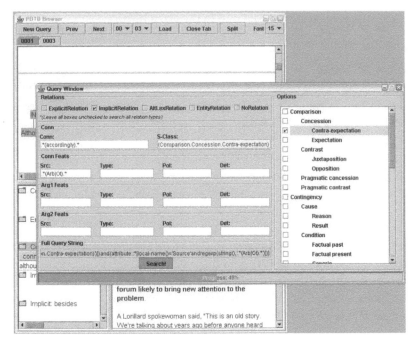

Figure 13.10 PDTB browser query interface.

query tool (but see ANNIS in section 13.4 below). However, we will briefly introduce RSTTOOL, which was originally created as an annotation tool but is also very useful for browsing annotated texts—for example, the annotated text distributed in the DISCOURSE RELATIONS REFERENCE CORPUS. The tool can be installed on all major platforms.[3] It can import raw texts files for annotation, but it can also import different versions of annotated RST files (.rst, .rs2, .rs3), as well as a representation of discourse relations in terms of labeled parenthesis (.lisp), reminiscent of the programming language LISP.

Figure 13.11 illustrates a sample display of a short text from the DISCOURSE RELATIONS REFERENCE CORPUS. Figure 13.12, finally, shows the statistics of this text, which the system creates at the click of the button "Statistics." In particular, the statistics table provides absolute frequencies and proportions of individual discourse relations in the text. In Figure 13.11, for instance, Elaboration occurs 7 times in this text, which makes up 28 percent of all discourse relations annotated in this text if multi-nuclei relations are only counted once (the latter is the default of an option). In addition, the table provides for all mono-nucleus relations the proportion of occurrences in which the satellite preceded its nucleus (S^N) or vice versa (N^S). In the case of Elaboration, this relation is 0:7, i.e. the nucleus precedes the satellite in all Elaboration instances in this text.

Before we continue in the next section with a multi-purpose search and visualization tool that also includes an option for querying RST-annotated texts, we would like to point the reader to an online interface for the RST SPANISH TREEBANK. While this is a

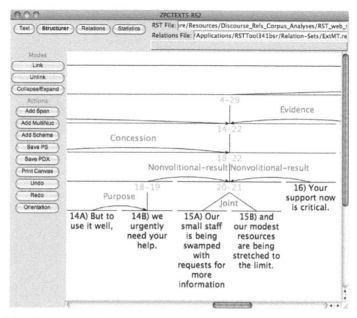

Figure 13.11 RSTTOOL tree browser (and annotator).

resource that is of limited usability, it shows that search tools for these phenomena are possible. Also it can potentially be adapted to be usable with other corpora.

The interface is available in Spanish, English, and French. The data set, of course, consists of a collection of Spanish texts. Similar to the GRONINGEN MEANING BANK (cf. section 5.5), the RST SPANISH TREEBANK relies on collaborative annotation. This means that everyone can contribute data to the corpus. The website provides a download option for the whole corpus, as well as three different query options: RST_stats_EDUs provides a statistical analysis of elementary discourse units (EDUs); RST_stats_rel provides the same information for discourse relations; finally, RST_extract allows the user to extract text passages corresponding to particular discourse elements—for example, all strings that correspond to Purpose relations, as the one shown in Figure 13.11 for English.

13.4 ANNIS: Multi-Purpose Search and Visualization

The last tool that we will introduce in this chapter is ANNIS—or more precisely, its third version, ANNIS3. ANNIS is different from other tools that we have introduced so far in that it is not specific to a particular type of annotation or annotation format. Instead, it can capture different types of annotation, thus allowing the user to relate diverse linguistic information provided by richly annotated, multi-layered corpora in one search query. ANNIS was originally designed with a focus on information structure: ANNIS is an acronym for *ANNotation of Information Structure*. However, it is the nature

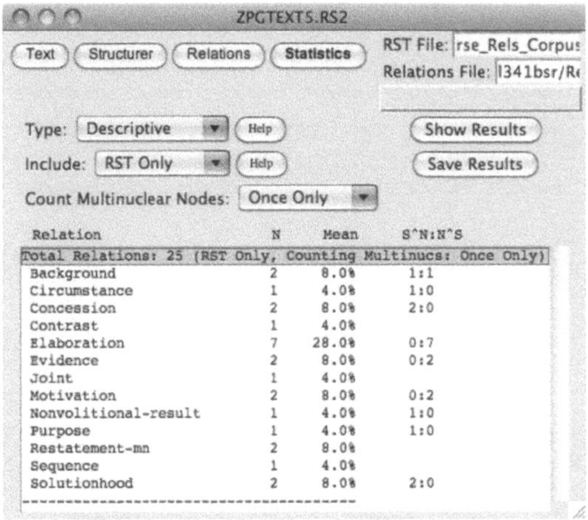

Figure 13.12 RSTTool statistics of the text in Figure 13.11.

of information structure that it interacts with different levels of linguistic description (see also section 6.2 for a brief introduction). This means that other types of annotation, such as for coreference and for syntax, have to be included in order to provide a full picture. Before we introduce the search tool itself, we want to motivate its use by introducing one information structural annotation example in detail. In the example in (5), **Die Jugendlichen in Zossen** is the *aboutness topic*, which captures "what the sentence is about".[4]

(5) Die Jugendlichen in Zossen wollen ein Musikcafé.
     the young_people in Zossen want   a   music cafe.
     'Zossen's youth want a music cafe.'

One test to identify an aboutness topic is provided in (6).[5]

(6) An NP X is the aboutness topic of a sentence S containing X if S would be a natural continuation to the announcement *Let me tell you something about X*.

It is interesting to evaluate empirically to what extent this type of category correlates, for example, with the grammatical function, syntactic category, and information status of the NP. Figure 13.13 shows the results panel of ANNIS, which provides this information for the sentence in (5) in one window. The aboutness topic functions as the subject (Sbj), as specified in the dependency graph. The NPs of the aboutness topic (ab) are both assigned the information status new, cf. the information structure grid. Finally, the constituent tree models the NP structure explicitly while it is encoded only implicitly in the dependency tree. The constituent annotation conforms to the TIGER Corpus guidelines (cf. section 4.5).

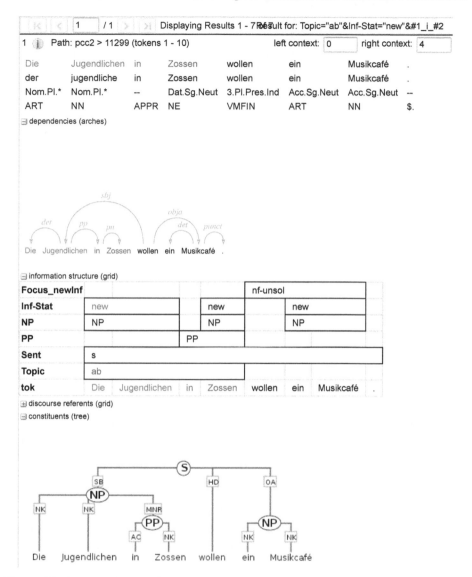

Figure 13.13 ANNIS display of morphosyntactic, dependency, information structural, and constituent annotation of example (5).

ANNIS is available in three versions. There is an online version available with pre-installed corpora. In addition, it can be freely downloaded from the project webpage and installed locally on all major operating systems, either for private use or as a server version. The download versions have special system requirements; consequently, for most users, it will not be sufficient to download the tool—they will have to install a specific database program before being able to use ANNIS. More specifically, ANNIS

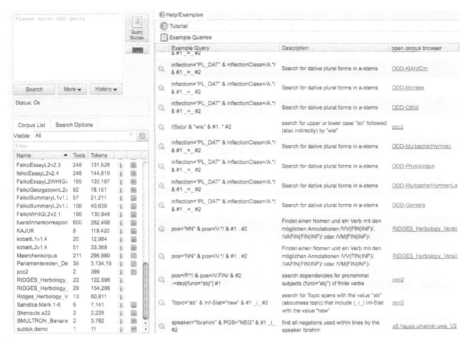

Figure 13.14 Annis start window.

requires a PostgreSQL database; the server version has additional requirements. We will not go into further details here but refer the user to the detailed description provided in the Annis documentation (see section 13.6). Instead, we will concentrate on the query options that Annis offers independent of its installation type.

The Annis online interface first shows the start screen, as in Figure 13.14. We will first briefly describe the different panels before we focus on the query options themselves.

The top left panel is the search form, in which experienced users can type in search queries in terms of the query language *AnnisQL*, which is related to the query languages used in CQP and TigerSearch (cf. sections 11.3 and 12.3 respectively). Below this search form, there is the "Search" button. The "Status" panel gives feedback on the wellformedness of queries and if a query was successful, the number of matching instances and documents. Before the first query, the status is Ok.

Next to the search form, there is the "Query Builder" button, which will open a search canvas for graphical query building, similar to the one in TigerSearch (see below for more information). Below, the button with the small keyboard icon opens a panel for typing in characters that go beyond simple ASCII format—for example, umlauts in the German script. It allows the user to type queries in many non-Latin scripts even if their own keyboard does not support them. However, for some character sets to be displayed properly, the encoding settings of the browser may need to be adjusted.

Since Annis allows access to a large number of resources at the same time, the menu item "Corpus List" provides a list of all the available corpora. The corpus information is presented as a five-column table, listing all available corpora as well as the number of their texts and tokens. The fourth column provides an important link to information about the annotation, which we will describe below in more detail. The fifth and final column is a link to the corpus browser that provides a full text view of all texts of the corpus.

Moving to the right half of the screen, the start screen shows a panel with example queries for different corpora and a general help page for querying corpora. There is also a "Tutorial." The tutorial uses the POTSDAM COMMENTARY CORPUS (PCC), a small sample of which we will also use for illustrating the search of discourse annotation with ANNIS below. The PCC is a German corpus of 176 newspaper texts annotated with multiple layers of linguistic description (see Chapter 6). Other panels that are displayed on the right half of the screen when activated are the graphical Query Builder and also the panel with query results. One can switch between these different panels by clicking on the tabs in the upper part of the window.

As mentioned above, we will use the PCC for explaining which types of queries are possible in ANNIS. A demo sample of two texts is available in the online version. We will demonstrate the basic use of the graphical search by a simple syntactic query based on the syntactic annotation level of PCC, which conforms to the TIGERCORPUS guidelines. Figure 13.15 shows a query for an NP that dominates a determiner and a non-NP category, in which the boxes and their connections represent nodes and edges of the constituent tree. Note that ANNIS does not distinguish terminal and non-terminal nodes, as TIGERSEARCH does (cf. section 12.3).

To create the query in Figure 13.15, we first need to choose PCC in the Corpus List (bottom left of the panel) and then activate the Query Builder (top), which we use in

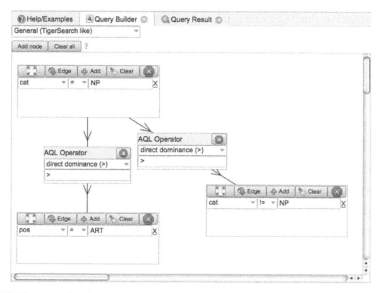

Figure 13.15 A graphical syntactic query in ANNIS

the *General (TigerSearch like)* mode. Nodes can be added to the canvas by clicking on the "add node" tab on top. An empty node box is a placeholder for any terminal (e.g. word) or non-terminal node (e.g. NP) in the corpus. For our query, we need to create an NP node that has a non-NP daughter and dominates a determiner (ART, such as **der** 'the'). To do so, we need to create three nodes first. We want to have the nodes in an arrangement as depicted in the figure. Our top node needs to be of the syntactic category NP. Thus, we click on "+Add," which adds a node condition in the box. The default setting is that of a condition on the token (tok). For our query, we edit this via the drop-down list, which presents us with all possible features that we can use to describe the node, and choose "cat" (for category). The list of available features depends on the annotation layers available for a corpus. For PCC, the drop-down list offers the features tok, Focus_newInf, Inf-stat, etc. All in all, there are 21 such features in PCC.

Now that we have the node restricted to a non-terminal node in syntactic terms, we need to restrict it further to an NP by typing in the value "NP" to the right of the equal sign. Here we are not offered a drop-down list of possible values. The user has to look up a corpus description—for example, the annotation guidelines of the corpus—to discover which values are valid. Next, we need to relate the right-hand-side daughter node to the NP node. To do so, we need to click on the ↓*Edge* button of the NP node (at the top of the node box). Clicking on an Edge tab of one box activates receptive *Dock* tabs on all other boxes on the canvas. Clicking on one of them will insert an edge between the two boxes. Note that edges in ANNIS are always labeled as *direct (linear) precedence* by default. We need to change the setting to *direct dominance* (for an explanation of these relations, see section 12.1). Then, we change the daughter node to match any non-terminal node except for an NP. Instead of the default equal sign, we choose the negated equation (!=). For the second daughter, we need a condition on the part of speech (POS) annotation, which we set to the value of a determiner (ART). After finishing building the query, the status information should be checked for any inconsistencies in the query.

Then, we click on the "Search" button for starting the search. This query results in six matches in the two texts of PCC including **Die Jugendlichen in Zossen** shown in example (5) above. The results can be browsed in the Results window to the right. They can also be downloaded by using the "Export" function, which is hidden under the "More" button on the left. As of now, ANNIS offers five different export options, including the export of plain text.

To summarize the process of building a query in ANNIS, we list the seven steps:

1. Corpus List: Choose one or more corpora.
2. Corpus information: Familiarize yourself with the annotation features and values.
3. Query Builder: Insert nodes, edges, and conditions on them.
4. Status: Check for warnings on inconsistencies of the query.
5. Search button: Start the search.
6. Query Results: Browse the results.
7. More button: Export the results.

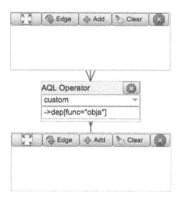

Figure 13.16 A graphical dependency query in ANNIS.

ANNIS is very versatile and allows queries for a wide range of phenomena. In addition to searching for syntactic constituents, we can also query syntactic dependencies, which are encoded as (labeled) directed edges. Here, the condition "->dep" must be selected for the edge. Figure 13.16 shows a query for two nodes that are related by a dependency relation labeled as accusative object (obja) as provided, e.g., in the example in Figure 13.13.

Information structure is annotated in terms of spans instead of trees in PCC. This means that the relations between nodes we have seen so far in the queries do not hold. Instead, there are relations of identity (_=_), inclusion (_i_), overlap (_o_), left-align (_l_), and right-align (_r_). The leftmost query in Figure 13.17 shows a query for topic and information status (Inf-Stat) requiring that the information status span is included in the topic span. One match for this query is, for example, **Die Jugendlichen in Zossen** from example (5) above.

Coreference relations are queried in terms of labeled edge similar to dependencies. In particular, they are marked by ->anaphor_antecedent in PCC (cf. the middle query in

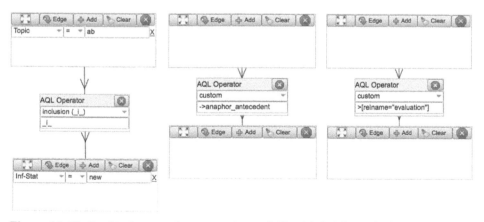

Figure 13.17 Graphical queries for a span relation (left), a labeled directed edge (mid), and a labeled dominance relation (right) in ANNIS.

Figure 13.17). *Rhetorical relations* differ from this because they are annotated as edges in a hierarchical tree structure. Consequently, they are represented in queries, similar to edges in constituent trees, by labeled dominance relations, e.g. >[relname="evaluation"] for a rhetorical relation of type evaluation, cf. the rightmost query in Figure 13.17.

The results of queries on coreference annotation are displayed in a textual view with coreference chains being coded in a different color. Each occurrence of a particular entity is underlined in the same color (see Figure 13.18). We have already shown the display of RST trees in ANNIS in Figure 13.13 above.

We provide an overview of the query options in ANNIS in Table 13.3. For a full summary of all operator options, we refer the reader to the ANNIS manual (see section 13.6).

Before we conclude this section, there are some specifics of the ANNIS system that we need to clarify. First, note that the label NP, for example, occurs in different positions in the query options as well as in the results display. For instance, it is a feature in the drop-down list of node conditions but it is also a value for the feature cat in the same drop-down list. In Figure 13.13, the label NP occurs as feature as well as value in the information structure grid in the middle, and it is a node label in the constituent tree at the bottom. This is due to the fact that the label NP has different functions in the tool and in the annotation. Internally, these different functions of NP cannot be confused, since all features are organized in so-called *name spaces*. This means that instead of the feature NP on the level of information structure, the system encodes the feature *exmaralda:NP*, which adds *exmaralda* as name space to NP.[6] Table 13.4 summarizes the uses of the label NP. With respect to the node category, the name space is *tiger*, i.e. the explicit reference to this feature is *tiger:cat*, and the feature value is NP. Using name spaces helps to keep feature names unique, which is a necessary condition for a general search tool, since it is unknown which types of annotation are available in a corpus to be used with the tool. This uniqueness condition does not hold for names of values. Thus, it does not matter that the features tiger:cat and exmaralda:NP can both be instantiated by a value NP, since these values are completely dependent on the features. We can

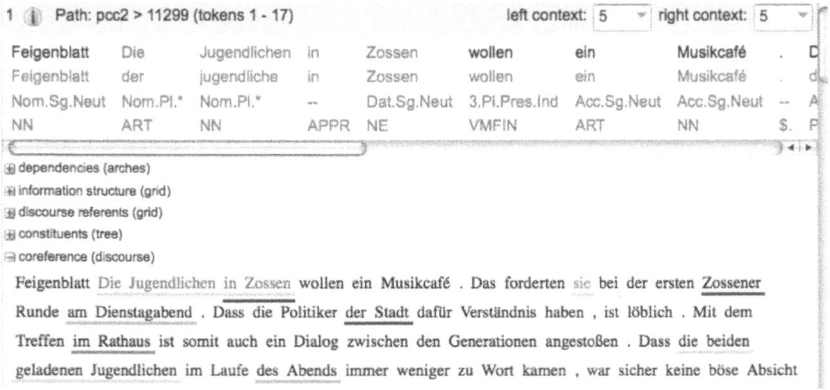

Figure 13.18 Results for a query of anaphoric relations in ANNIS.

Table 13.3 Summary of ANNIS operators used in this section.

Operator	Explanation	Level of application
.	Direct precedence	Default linear relation
.*	Indirect precedence	
_=_	Identical coverage	Spans; applicable to all levels of annotation
_i_	Inclusion	
_o_	Overlap	
_l_	Left align	
_r_	Right align	
>LABEL	Direct dominance	Hierarchical trees (box-in-box); constituency, RST
>LABEL *	Dominance	(transitive closure)
->LABEL	Directed edge	Directed graphs; dependencies, coreference
->LABEL *	Edge	(transitive closure)

Table 13.4 Different NP labels in PCC.

Level	Name space	Feature	Value	Comment
Constituent tree	tiger	cat	NP	displayed in constituent tree
Information structure	exmaralda	NP	NP	displayed in grid view

find information about existing features and their name space in the corpus-specific information on its annotation (cf. the information link in the Corpus List). Figure 13.19 shows the corpus information for the PCC. More specifically, this provides a summary of the metadata on the left-hand side including a link (URL) to corpus-related material, such as a project webpage or annotation guidelines, if available. On the right-hand side, it lists all features and relation labels used in the corpus, organized in four subsections: Node Annotations, Edge Annotations, Edge Types, and Meta Annotations.

Figure 13.19 shows the features of the metadata. To search for them, we always need to add their name space. A graphical query would require, for example, "meta::Genre" in a node condition and "Sport" as the value. Queries for meta annotation also require the specification of a second node in order to be well-formed. However, this second node can be a dummy node without any conditions or any other further specification.

To conclude this section, ANNIS is a very versatile search and visualization tool, which can display results in terms of token-based lemma and POS annotation, annotation grids, constituent trees, dependency graphs, text with color-coded unlined entities, and RST trees. It has not been developed for one particular corpus with specific annotation levels, but was planned as a multi-purpose tool from the beginning. There is a trade-off between this flexibility in use and the complexity of feature names and search queries. ANNIS solved this problem by using name spaces for features and by offering the option to omit the name spaces for feature names in queries if they are unique in a corpus. This is why the user does

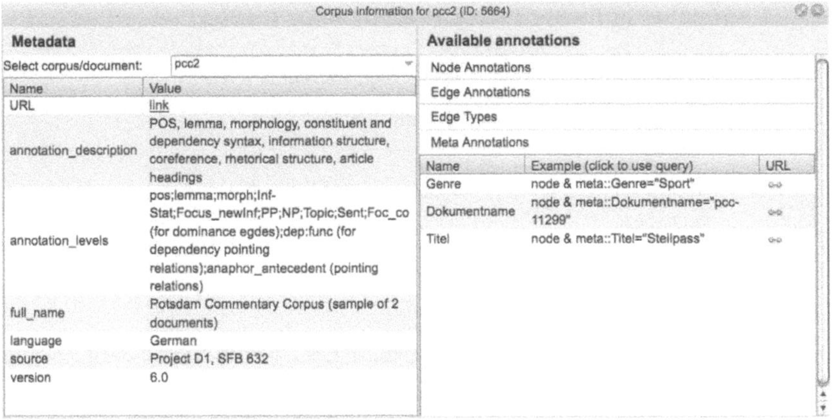

Figure 13.19 Corpus Information for PCC in ANNIS.

not see name spaces added to the feature names in the drop-down list of the PCC node conditions. In addition, the interface offers a large number of example queries for the user to adapt to their own needs. A final remark on efficiency: ANNIS has been optimized for richly annotated corpora, which are normally (semi-)automatically annotated and, hence, only of a limited size. ANNIS is not the tool of choice for large, automatically created, mega-corpora. For such cases, more focused tools, such as CQP, are a better choice.

13.5 Conclusion

In this chapter, we introduced query tools that give access to semantic and discourse annotation. In contrast to syntactic annotation, semantic and discourse annotation is more diverse in nature, which also has an effect on annotation structures and query tools respectively. First, we introduced the online access to the fully annotated texts in FRAMENET and the supporting lexical search and browsing tools, which help to interpret the frame annotation properly. Next, we looked into options to browse temporal information in TIMEBANK, by means of its online browsing tool. For other semantic resources introduced in Chapter 5 which we did not cover here, we provided access options in the further reading section of earlier chapters. For accessing discourse annotation, we introduced three tools: First the RSTTOOL, which is not a search tool proper but rather a tool for creating and visualizing individual discourse trees spanning whole texts according to the framework of Rhetorical Structure Theory. We also introduced the online interface to the SPANISH RST CORPUS, which includes a search function. Then, we gave an introduction to the PDTB browser, which gives access to discourse relation annotation of the PENN DISCOURSE TREEBANK. Finally, we rounded off the chapter by providing an overview of ANNIS, a multi-purpose search and visualization tool that captures syntactic annotation as well as coreference and discourse annotation.

13.5 Further Reading

Section 13.1

Frame Index: The index of semantic frames is accessible at https://framenet.icsi.berkeley. edu/fndrupal/index.php?q= frameIndex. The FrameNet book (Ruppenhofer et al., 2010) describes the content provided in the individual entries in detail.

Lexical Unit Index: This index complements the Frame Index above by providing access to frames via lexical items. It is accessible at https://framenet.icsi.berkeley.edu/fndrupal/index. php?q=luIndex.

FRAMESQL: This is a tool for searching the FRAMENET online database. It is documented by Sato (2008) and is accessible at https://framenet2.icsi.berkeley.edu/frameSQL/fn2_15/notes/.

FRAMEGRAPHER: This is a tool for visualizing relations between frame elements of related frames, accessible at https://framenet.icsi.berkeley.edu/fndrupal/FrameGrapher.

Section 13.2

TIMEBANK browser: The current version is the TIMEBANK 1.2 browser, accessible via http:// timeml.org/site/timebank/browser_1.2/index.php.

Section 13.3

PDTB browser: This browser is freely available at http://www.seas.upenn.edu/~pdtb/tools. shtml#browser. It requires the raw text files of the PENN TREEBANK and the stand-off annotation of the PENN DISCOURSE TREEBANK in a particular folder structure, described in Prasad et al. (2007, Ch. 6).

RSTTool: This tool can be downloaded from http://www.wagsoft.com/RSTTool/. The download includes a detailed manual, which can also be called from the tool menu "Help." The tool also provides an FAQ, which is very helpful for the beginner user.

RST SPANISH TREEBANK: The project relies on collaborative data creation. The corpus is accessible via an online search interface at http://corpus.iingen.unam.mx/rst/.

Section 13.4

ANNIS: The tool was developed in the context of the Berlin/Potsdam-based collaborative research centre *Information Structure: The Linguistic Means for Structuring Utterances, Sentences and Texts*. Documentation, download, and online access are available via http:// www.sfb632.uni-potsdam.de/Annis/. There is a manual by Zeldes (2013). ANNIS is accompanied by different conversion tools for converting annotation layers into its native relANNIS format (http://www.sfb632.uni-potsdam.de/annis/tools.html), most notable SALTNPEPPER (cf. https://korpling. german.hu-berlin.de/p/projects/saltnpepper/wiki/).

POSTGRESQL: This is a freely available open source database program, available from http:// www.postgresql.org/.

POTSDAM COMMENTARY CORPUS (PCC): This is a German corpus of 176 newspaper texts annotated with multiple layers including connectives and their arguments in spirit of the PENN DISCOURSE TREEBANK and relations according to Rhetorical Structure Theory (Stede, 2004). Stede (2008) discusses problems that arise in the annotation of hierarchical discourse relations. The PCC is available upon request from Manfred Stede at the University of Potsdam, Germany http://www.ling.uni-potsdam.de/acl-lab/Forsch/pcc/pcc.html

Corpus Linguistics and Linguistically Annotated Corpora

EXMARaLDA: EXMARaLDA is a grid-based tool that was originally developed for multi-level annotation of transcribed spoken and multi-modal corpora. It is available at http://www.exmaralda.org/en_index.html. The tool only offers rudimentary search functions but it is complemented by the query tool EXAKT (http://www.exmaralda.org/en_exakt.html) for full-fledged search capabilities.

Other query tools: There are other tools that can be used for browsing and querying semantic and discourse-related annotation. One tool worth mentioning is ICARUS, which was briefly introduced in context of dependency annotation at the end of Chapter 12. As of spring 2014, it also includes a query and visualization option for coreference annotation (http://www.ims.uni-stuttgart.de/forschung/ressourcen/werkzeuge/icarus.html). There are two very well-known tools for coreference annotation, which also allow the user to browse the annotation: PALinkA (http://clg.wlv.ac.uk/projects/PALinkA/, http://clg.wlv.ac.uk/trac/palinka/wiki/WikiStart) and MMAX2 (http://mmax2.sourceforge.net/). Finally, there is the ONTONOTES DB TOOL, which was briefly mentioned in Chapter 6. It is freely distributed with the corpus via the *Linguistic Data Consortium* (LDC). We did not introduce it in detail because it has special system requirements for its installation, and the query language XPATH is only suitable for experienced users.

13.7 Exercises

1. **FRAMENET tools**:
   (a) Look up the entry for the Communication frame in the *Frame Index* at https://framenet.icsi.berkeley.edu/fndrupal/index.php?q=frameIndex. How is the frame defined? What are its core frame elements? What are its non-core frame elements? Which lexical units instantiate this frame? What kind of metaphorical usage do many words of this frame allow?
   (b) Then, switch the perspective and look up the Lexical Unit say.v in the *Lexical Unit Index* at https://framenet.icsi.berkeley.edu/fndrupal/index.php?q=luIndex. How many readings in terms of semantic frames does say.v have? Are they related?
   (c) What does the FRAMESQL query shown below search for (https://framenet2.icsi.berkeley.edu/frameSQL/fn2_15/notes/)? An example result is: **As a result, the merchants were forced to limit their salvoes to one a day – and from then on, they signaled the noon hour daily [**$_{Addressee}$**for all] to hear.**

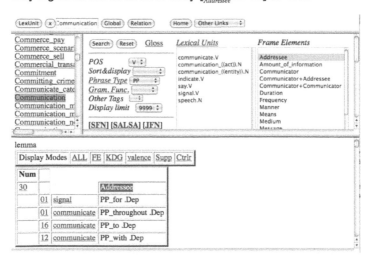

2. **RSTTOOL**: Go to the RSTTOOL download page (http://www. wagsoft.com/RSTTool/). Install the tool and load the RST file *America-mt.rs2* from folder *Analyses*.
   (a) Browse the text first (Text). What did the Anglo-American Cattle Company establish near Powder River?
   (b) Then, browse the tree (Structurer). Which kind of discourse relation relates span 1 and spans 2–8?
   (c) Look for multi-nuclei relations. Which ones do you find?
3. **More RSTTOOL**: Go to the web page of the DISCOURSE RELATIONS REFERENCE CORPUS at http://www.sfu.ca/rst/06tools/discourse_relations_corpus.html (see section 6.3 for an explanation of the annotation) and download *Corpus, zipped analysis files (300 Kb)*.
   (a) From the *RST_web_site* folder, load RST file *LETGO7.RS2* in the RSTTool. Ignore the pop up warning on the relations definitions (click "yes"). Read the text (Text) and browse the discourse tree (Structurer).
   (b) Click on the statistics button. Choose Type: "Descriptive," Include: "RST only," and then click "Show results." What are the three most common relations in this text? Did you expect this?
   (c) Go back to the tree view (Structurer). Look for an antithesis relation. Click on "Save PS" in the menu on the left and then click on the green span ids above the relation and create a PS image of this subtree.

APPENDIX A
PENN TREEBANK POS TAGSET

Tag	Description
CC	Coordinating conjunction
CD	Cardinal number
DT	Determiner
EX	Existential **there**
FW	Foreign word
IN	Preposition or subordinating conjunction
JJ	Adjective
JJR	Adjective, comparative
JJS	Adjective, superlative
LS	List item marker
MD	Modal
NN	Noun, singular or mass
NNP	Proper noun, singular
NNPS	Proper noun, plural
NNS	Noun, plural
PDT	Predeterminer
POS	Possessive ending
PRP	Personal pronoun
PRP$	Possessive pronoun
RB	Adverb
RBR	Adverb, comparative
RBS	Adverb, superlative
RP	Particle
SYM	Symbol
TO	**to**
UH	Interjection
VB	Verb, base form

Penn Treebank POS Tagset

Tag	Description
VBD	Verb, past tense
VBG	Verb, gerund / present participle
VBN	Verb, past participle
VBP	Verb, non-3rd person, singular, present tense
VBZ	Verb, 3rd person, singular, present tense
WDT	Wh-determiner
WP	Wh-pronoun
WP	Possessive wh-pronoun
WRB	Wh-adverb
$	$
.	Sentence-final punctuation
,	Comma
- -	dash
:	colon or ellipsis
"	opening quotation mark
"	closing quotation mark
(	opening parenthesis
)	closing parenthesis

APPENDIX B
ICE POS TAGSET[1]

Tag	Description	Examples
ADJ	adjective, uninflected	honorary tiny possible
ADJ(comp)	adjective, comparative	greater lesser cheaper
ADJ(edp)	adjective, -ed participle	renewed worried used
ADJ(ingp)	adjective, -ing participle	uncaring amazing depressing
ADJ(sup)	adjective, superlative	boldest scariest fiercest
ADV(add)	adverb, additive	also too even
ADV(excl)	adverb, exclusive adjective	just merely only
ADV(ge)	adverb, general	any recently not
ADV(ge,comp)	adverb, general, comparative	less earlier more
ADV(ge,sup)	adverb, general, superlative	best least
ADV(inten)	adverb, intensifier	as all so
ADV(inten,comp)	adverb, intensifier, comparative	more or less
ADV(inten,sup)	adverb, intensifier, superlative	most
ADV(partic)	adverb, particulariser	especially at least particularly
ADV(phras)	adverb, phrasal	on away out
ADV(rel)	adverb, relative	where when
ADV(wh)	adverb, WH-word	whenever when where
ANTIT	anticipatory it	it
ART(def)	article, definite	the ye
ART(indef)	article, indefinite	an a
AUX(do,imp)	auxiliary, verb 'to do', imperative	do
AUX(do,imp,neg)	auxiliary, verb 'to do', imperative, negative	don't
AUX(do,past)	auxiliary, verb 'to do', past tense	did
AUX(do,past,neg)	auxiliary, verb 'to do', past tense, negative	didn't
AUX(do,pres)	auxiliary, verb 'to do', present tense	do does doth
AUX(do,pres,neg)	auxiliary, verb 'to do', present tense, negative	doesn't don't
AUX(do,pres,procl)	auxiliary, verb 'to do', present tense, proclitic	d'
AUX(let, imp)	auxiliary, verb 'to let', imperative	let
AUX(modal,past)	auxiliary, modal	could might should
AUX(modal,past,encl)	auxiliary, modal, enclitic	'd

ICE POS Tagset

Tag	Description	Examples
AUX(modal,past,neg)	auxiliary, modal, negative	wouldn't couldn't shouldn't
AUX(modal,pres)	auxiliary, modal, present tense	will can may
AUX(modal,pres,encl)	auxiliary, modal, present tense, enclitic	'll
AUX(modal,pres,neg)	auxiliary, modal, present tense, negative	won't can't cannot
AUX(pass,edp)	auxiliary, passive, -ed participle	been
AUX(pass,infin)	auxiliary, passive, infinitive	be get
AUX(pass,ingp)	auxiliary, passive, -ing participle	being getting
AUX(pass,past)	auxiliary, passive, past tense	was were
AUX(pass,past,neg)	auxiliary, passive, past tense, negative	wasn't weren't
AUX(pass,pres)	auxiliary, passive, present tense	are is get
AUX(pass,pres,encl)	auxiliary, passive, present tense, enclitic	's 're 'm
AUX(pass,pres,neg)	auxiliary, passive, present tense, negative	isn't
AUX(pass,subjun)	auxiliary, passive, subjunctive	were
AUX(perf,infin)	auxiliary, perfect, infinitive	have
AUX(perf,ingp)	auxiliary, perfect, -ing participle	having
AUX(perf,past)	auxiliary, perfect, past tense	had haven't was
AUX(perf,past,encl)	auxiliary, perfect, past tense, enclitic	'd
AUX(perf,past,neg)	auxiliary, perfect, past tense, negative	hadn't
AUX(perf,pres)	auxiliary, perfect, present tense	have has
AUX(perf,pres,encl)	auxiliary, perfect, present tense, enclitic	's 've
AUX(perf,pres,neg)	auxiliary, perfect, present tense, negative	haven't hasn't
AUX(perf,subj)	auxiliary, perfect, subjunctive	had
AUX(prog,edp)	auxiliary, progressive, -ed participle	been
AUX(prog,infin)	auxiliary, progressive, infinitive	be
AUX(prog,past)	auxiliary, progressive, past tense	was were
AUX(prog,past,neg)	auxiliary, progressive, negative	weren't wasn't
AUX(prog,pres)	auxiliary, progressive, present tense	is are am were
AUX(prog,pres,encl)	auxiliary, progressive, present tense, enclitic	's 're 'm
AUX(prog,subjun)	auxiliary, progressive, subjunctive	were
AUX(semi,edp)	auxiliary, semi, -ed participle	seemed to begun failed
AUX(semi,infin)	auxiliary, semi, infinitive	be expected to have continue
AUX(semi,ingp)	auxiliary, semi, -ing participle	beginning to failing having
AUX(semi,past)	auxiliary, semi-auxiliary, past tense	had to were failed
AUX(semi,past,disc)	auxiliary, semi, past tense, discontinuous	was going to
AUX(semi,past,encl)	auxiliary, semi, past tense, enclitic	'd
AUX(semi,pres)	auxiliary, semi, present tense	seems to seem have is allowed

Tag	Description	Examples
AUX(semi,pres,disc)	auxiliary, semi, present tense, discontinuous	are going to also
AUX(semi,pres,encl)	auxiliary, semi, present tense, enclitic	'm 're 's
AUX(semi,pres,encl, disc)	auxiliary, semi, present tense, enclitic, discontinuous	're going to
AUX(semi,pres,neg)	auxiliary, semi, present tense, negative	aren't likely to
AUX(semi,subjun)	auxiliary, semi, subjunctive	were going to
AUX(semip,edp)	auxiliary, semi followed by -ing participle, -ed participle	stopped finished
AUX(semip,imp)	auxiliary, semi followed by -ing participle, imperative	stop
AUX(semip,infin)	auxiliary, semi followed by -ing participle, infinitive	keep
AUX(semip,past)	auxiliary, semi followed by -ing participle, past tense	began to stopped finished
CLEFTIT	cleft it	it
CONJUNC(coord)	conjunction, coordinating	and or but
CONJUNC(subord)	conjunction, subordinating	though that when
CONNEC(appos)	connective, appositive	for example in particular that is
CONNEC(ge)	connective, general	however for instance
EXTHERE	existential there	there
FRM	formulaic expression	good morning please thank you
GENM	genitive marker	's '
INTERJEC	interjection	pooh oh eh
N(com,plu)	noun, common, plural	Protestant ministers Protestants immigrati
N(com,sing)	noun, common, singular	news founder jail
N(prop,plu)	noun, proper, plural	Christians Free Churches Anglicans
N(prop,sing)	noun, proper, singular	Reverend Sun Myung Moon Unification Church
NADJ(comp,plu)	nominal adjective, comparative, plural	longer
NADJ(edp,plu)	nominal adjective, -ed participle, plural	fallen oppressed deprived
NADJ(ingp,plu)	nominal adjective, -ing participle, plural	suffering
NADJ(plu)	nominal adjective, plural	injured everyday persistent
NADJ(prop)	nominal adjective, proper	American fundamental
NADJ(sing)	nominal adjective, singular	usual unusual new
NADJ(sup,plu)	nominal adjective, superlative, plural	slightest laxest tightest
NADJ(sup,sing)	nominal adjective, superlative, singular	worst best fairest
NUM(card,plu)	numeral, cardinal, plural	sixties thousands billions
NUM(card,sing)	numeral, cardinal, singular	nine five thousand

Tag	Description	Examples
NUM(frac,sing)	numeral, fraction, singular	a third one fifteenth half
NUM(hyph)	numeral, hyphenated pair	1973-4 1979-80 2-0
NUM(mult)	numeral, multiplier	once twice thrice
NUM(ord)	numeral, ordinal	last other previous
NUM(ord,plu)	numeral, ordinal, plural	others
NUM(ord,sing)	numeral, ordinal, singular	another
PREP(ge)	preposition, general	about of
PREP(phras)	preposition, phrasal	as across over
PROFM(conjoin)	proform, conjoin	so on et cetera
PROFM(one,plu)	proform, one, plural	ones
PROFM(one,sing)	proform, one, singular	one
PROFM(so,claus)	proform, so, clausal	not so
PROFM(so,phr)	proform, so, phrasal	so
PRON(ass)	pronoun, assertive	some
PRON(ass,sing)	pronoun, assertive, singular	something someone somebody
PRON(dem)	pronoun, demonstrative	such
PRON(dem,plu)	pronoun, demonstrative, plural	those these
PRON(dem,sing)	pronoun, demonstrative, singular	this that
PRON(exclam)	pronoun, exclamatory	what
PRON(inter)	pronoun, interrogative	what who which
PRON(neg)	pronoun, negative	none no
PRON(neg,sing)	pronoun, negative, singular	nobody no one nothing
PRON(nom)	pronoun, nominal relative	what whatever who
PRON(nonass)	pronoun, nonassertive	any
PRON(nonass,sing)	pronoun, nonassertive, singular	anything anyone anybody
PRON(pers)	pronoun, personal	you
PRON(pers,plu)	pronoun, personal, plural	they we us
PRON(pers,plu,encl)	pronoun, personal, plural, enclitic	's
PRON(pers,sing)	pronoun, personal, singular	he it I
PRON(poss)	pronoun, possessive	your thy yours
PRON(poss,plu)	pronoun, possessive, plural	our their theirs
PRON(poss,sing)	pronoun, possessive, singular	its my his
PRON(quant)	pronoun, quantifying	most more enough
PRON(quant,plu)	pronoun, quantifying, plural	few many several
PRON(quant,sing)	pronoun, quantifying, singular	much a lot single
PRON(recip)	pronoun, reciprocal	one another each other

Tag	Description	Examples
PRON(ref,plu)	pronoun, reflexive, plural	themselves ourselves
PRON(ref,sing)	pronoun, reflexive, singular	himself itself herself
PRON(rel)	pronoun, relative	who that which
PRON(univ)	pronoun, universal	all
PRON(univ,plu)	pronoun, universal, plural	both
PRON(univ,sing)	pronoun, universal, singular	every each everyone
PROPIT	prop it	it
PRTCL(for)	particle, for	in order for
PRTCL(to)	particle, to	in order to so much as
PRTCL(with)	particle, with	with without
PUNC(cbrack)	closing parenthesis	)]
PUNC(col)	colon	:
PUNC(com)	comma	,
PUNC(cquo)	closing quotation mark	' "
PUNC(dash)	dash	- ‐
PUNC(ellip)	ellipsis	...
PUNC(exm)	exclamation mark	!
PUNC(obrack)	opening parenthesis	([
PUNC(oquo)	opening quotation mark	' "
PUNC(per)	period	.
PUNC(qm)	question mark	?
PUNC(scol)	semicolon	; ;
REACT	reaction signal	yes of course why
V(cop,edp)	lexical verb, copular, -ed participle	been appeared become
V(cop,imp)	lexical verb, copular, imperative	be
V(cop,infin)	lexical verb, copular, infinitive	be seem get
V(cop,ingp)	lexical verb, copular, -ing participle	becoming getting turning
V(cop,past)	lexical verb, copular, past tense	was looked became
V(cop,past,neg)	lexical verb, copular, past tense, negative	wasn't weren't
V(cop,pres)	lexical verb, copular, present tense	are is get
V(cop,pres,encl)	lexical verb, copular, present tense, enclitic	's 're 'm
V(cop,pres,neg)	lexical verb, copular, present tense, negative	isn't aren't doesn't
V(cop,subjun)	lexical verb, copular, subjunctive	were
V(cxtr,edp)	lexical verb, complex-transitive, -ed participle	meant called regarded
V(cxtr,imp)	lexical verb, complex-transitive, imperative	make put keep
V(cxtr,infin)	lexical verb, complex-transitive, infinitive	see call expect

ICE POS Tagset

Tag	Description	Examples
V(cxtr,ingp)	lexical verb, complex-transitive, -ing participle	defining seeing leaving
V(cxtr,past)	lexical verb, complex-transitive, past tense	described had put
V(cxtr,pres)	lexical verb, complex-transitive, present tense	call find makes
V(dimontr,imp)	lexical verb, complex-ditransitive, imperative	guide
V(dimontr,infin)	lexical verb, complex-ditransitive, infinitive	tell
V(dimontr,past)	lexical verb, complex-ditransitive, past tense	asked
V(ditr,edp)	lexical verb, ditransitive, -ed participle	awarded given shown
V(ditr,imp)	lexical verb, ditransitive, imperative	grant charge give
V(ditr,infin)	lexical verb, ditransitive, infinitive	have tell give
V(ditr,ingp)	lexical verb, ditransitive, -ing participle	telling offering
V(ditr,past)	lexical verb, ditransitive, past tense	had told explained
V(ditr,pres)	lexical verb, ditransitive, present tense	ask gives offer
V(intr,edp)	lexical verb, intransitive, -ed participle	opened said increased
V(intr,imp)	lexical verb, intransitive, imperative	carry turn live
V(intr,infin)	lexical verb, intransitive, infinitive	confer fade believe
V(intr,ingp)	lexical verb, intransitive, -ing participle	subsiding continuing leaning
V(intr,past)	lexical verb, intransitive, past tense	was happened departed
V(intr,past,neg)	lexical verb, intransitive, past tense, negative	didn't wasn't
V(intr,pres)	lexical verb, intransitive, present tense	talk go asks
V(intr,pres,encl)	lexical verb, intransitive, present tense, enclitic	's
V(intr,pres,neg)	lexical verb, intransitive, present tense, negative	isn't haven't don't
V(intr,subj)	lexical verb, intransitive, subjunctive	come be
V(montr,edp)	lexical verb, monotransitive, -ed participle	had described convened
V(montr,imp)	lexical verb, monotransitive	take pass suppose
V(montr,infin)	lexical verb, monotransitive, infinitive	get recall know
V(montr,ingp)	lexical verb, monotransitive, -ing participle	announcing following including
V(montr,past)	lexical verb, monotransitive, past tense	shared had thought
V(montr,pres)	lexical verb, monotransitive, present tense	visits feel wants
V(montr,pres,encl)	lexical verb, monotransitive, present tense, enclitic	've
V(trans,edp)	lexical verb, transitive, -ed participle	allowed witnessed said
V(trans,imp)	lexical verb, transitive, imperative	let help teach
V(trans,infin)	lexical verb, transitive, infinitive	allow hear help
V(trans,ingp)	lexical verb, transitive, -ing participle	leaving forcing sending
V(trans,past)	lexical verb, transitive, past tense	asked wanted insisted
V(trans,pres)	lexical verb, transitive, present tense	want has find

NOTES

Chapter 1

1. Example (2) is taken from the PENN TREEBANK, a syntactically annotated corpus, see section 4.2.
2. We will mark examples in running text by using typewriter font throughout.
3. Example (4-a) is taken from the PENN TREEBANK.
4. Formatting can capture sentence segmentation, for example, by keeping sentences apart by empty lines.
5. The focus on size is one definition of a balanced sample. Another understanding is to include texts samples from different sources and different genres to the extent that the sample sizes mirror the influence of the genre in the language which is modeled in the corpus.
6. The example is taken from the NPS CHAT CORPUS which is part of the *Natural Language Toolkit* (NLTK).
7. These numbers were retrieved from the PENN TREEBANK (see section 2.1).
8. http://www.google.com/search?hl=en&ie=ISO-8859-1&q=\%22give+the+creeps-+to\%22&btnG=Google+Search (cached)
9. http://www.nltk.org/

Chapter 2

1. This sentence is taken from the Student Blooper collection at http://www.cse.unsw. edu. au/~norman/Jokes-file/StudentBloopers.htm.
2. Copied from http://www.ldc.upenn.edu/annotation/
3. Computational linguistics is also called natural language processing (NLP).
4. Taken from the Student Blooper collection.
5. The examples are copied from Saurí et al. (2006: 3).
6. Both sentences are adapted from Pustejovsky et al. (2003: 8–9).
7. Both sentences are adapted from Pustejovsky et al. (2003: 8–9).
8. The examples are taken from the online version of FRAMENET at https://framenet. icsi. berkeley.edu/fndrupal/.
9. The examples are taken from the online version of FRAMENET.
10. The example is copied from Prasad et al. (2008), ex. (6).
11. Note that XML tags are different from POS tags.
12. The example is copied from the TEI guidelines at http://www.tei-c.org/release/doc/tei-p5-doc/en/html/TS.html.

Notes

13. The example is copied from the Corpus Encoding Documentation at http://www.cs. vassar. edu/CES/CES1.Annex9.html.

14. This example is copied from Farrar and Langendoen (2003: 99).

Chapter 3

1. This sentence is taken from the Student Blooper collection at http://www.cse.unsw. edu. au/~norman/Jokes-file/StudentBloopers.htm.

2. http://corpus2.byu.edu/coca/

3. We use a transliteration of Arabic characters into Roman characters to make the differences between words more visible. This transliteration is traditionally called Buckwalter transliteration since it was developed by Tim Buckwalter.

4. Taken from the Student Blooper collection.

5. Taken from the Student Blooper collection.

6. Adapted from the Student Blooper collection.

7. Taken from the Student Blooper collection.

Chapter 4

1. This sentence is taken from the Student Blooper collection at http://www.cse.unsw.edu. au/~norman/Jokes-file/StudentBloopers.htm.

2. Adapted from the Student Blooper collection.

3. Retrieved from TiGerSearch, cf. Chapter 12.

4. For an explanation of the null category *, see below.

5. Both corpora are freely available from Geoffrey Sampson's webpage: http://www. grsampson. net.

6. http://ice-corpora.net/ice/index.htm

7. These data are not meant for human consumption. The corpus is accompanied by a query tool, icecup, which allows browsing through the sentences and searching for specific phenomena via a graphical interface.

8. CoNLL: Conference on Natural Language Learning

9. From http://ufal.mff.cuni.cz/pdt2.0/doc/manuals/en/a-layer/html/ch03s02.html

Chapter 5

1. Named entity class annotation is available in an enhanced version of TüBa-d/z starting from release 7 in 2012.

2. English translation of the play by David Spencer: "Jamaica."

3. Source: Weischedel et al. (2012).

4. Source: OntoNotes.

5. ONTONOTES Normal Form view can be found in text files of type **.onf**; it is also the output format of the ONTONOTES DB TOOL.

6. Source: ONTONOTES.

7. All definitions and examples are taken from WordNet 3.1: http://wordnet.princeton.edu/.

8. The example from SEMCOR originally belongs to a BROWN Corpus sample from *Stranger in a Strange Land* by Robert A. Heinlein.

9. Found in COCA, at http://corpus.byu.edu/coca/.

10. This example is taken from the PropBank Guidelines.

11. PROPBANK was annotated on top of PENN TREEBANK 2.

12. Example (20) is copied from Palmer et al. (2005).

13. Example (22) is copied from Palmer et al. (2005).

14. See https://verbs.colorado.edu/propbank/framesets-english/.

15. This example is taken from the ONTONOTES Corpus. ONTONOTES includes actual PROPBANK data as well as additional material annotated according to the PROPBANK guidelines.

16. Question answering is a sub-area of computational linguistics in which automatic methods are investigated to find the answers to questions in text.

17. The example is taken from the subcorpus *American National Corpus Texts – Berlitz History of Greece*, https://framenet.icsi.berkeley.edu/fndrupal/index.php?q=framenet_request_data.

18. This definition is copied from the *Linguistic Units Index*: https://framenet.icsi.berkeley.edu/fndrupal/index.php?q=luIndex.

19. This example is taken from the FRAMENET Corpus, and more specifically from the PROPBANK Wall Street Journal Text – Bell Ringing.

20. The examples are copied from Ruppenhofer et al. (2010) and the MASC data respectively.

21. This sentence is from TIMEBANK (version 1.2).

22. It would have been interesting to compare TIMEBANK and ONTONOTES annotation on the basis of their PROPBANK WSJ material. Unfortunately, the corpora contain disjunct subsets of the PROPBANK data.

23. Examples are taken from TIMEBANK.

24. The example is taken from Saurí et al. (2006).

25. The example is taken from Saurí et al. (2006).

26. Verb senses are taken from VERBNET (see the Further Reading section).

27. *Amazon Mechanical Turk*: https://www.mturk.com

28. *Wordrobe*: http://wordrobe.housing.rug.nl

Chapter 6

1. The example was taken from the ONTONOTES Corpus. For details on the corpus, see below.

2. Note that we use our own numbering in the examples in this section.

3. The annotation of singletons is ours.

4. This example, as well as the examples in (8), are copied from the MUC annotation guidelines.

Notes

5. Both examples are copied from the OntoNotes annotation manual.

6. These examples are copied from Markert and Nissim (2005).

7. These examples are copied from Markert et al. (2012).

8. These examples are copied from Nedoluzhko and Mírovský (2011).

9. These examples are taken from the annotation guidelines of the NP4E Corpus (see below for details).

10. Source: http://groups.inf.ed.ac.uk/switchboard/infotags.html.

11. Source: http://groups.inf.ed.ac.uk/switchboard/structure.html.

12. The example is taken from Riester and Baumann (2013).

13. This example is also copied from Riester and Baumann (2013).

14. Another example copied from Riester and Baumann (2013).

15. Source: http://groups.inf.ed.ac.uk/switchboard/kontrasttags.html.

16. There is a more fine-grained annotation, which we do not cover here; the interested reader is referred to Götze et al. (2009).

17. In this section, the examples are taken from the PDTB guidelines (Prasad et al., 2007) if not indicated otherwise.

18. The table is copied from Prasad et al. (2007).

19. The example is copied from Prasad et al. (2008).

20. Both examples are taken from Sanders (1997).

21. The example is taken from Prasad et al. (2010).

22. The table is adapted from Prasad et al. (2008).

23. The Darwin Text belongs to the "unpublished analyses" of the RST website subcorpus.

24. The corpus distribution actually contains all 15 texts from the RST website but one of them lacks the analysis part (file DISKAD.RS2). On the website itself, all analyses are available.

25. The image is from Mann and Thompson (1988) as used in Taboada and Stede (2009).

26. The following examples are all taken from the RST website subcorpus. Subtrees were printed with RSTTool.

Chapter 7

1. http://www.ldc.upenn.edu/

Chapter 8

1. www.google.com

2. corpus.byu.edu

3. The example is taken from Bresnan et al. (2007).

4. The example is copied from Bresnan et al. (2007).

5. The examples are extracted from the written Wall Street Journal section of the Penn Treebank.

6. The trees were generated in TigerSearch (see section 12.3).

7. www.google.com

8. The examples are copied from Wasow et al. (2011).

9. The example is taken from the Switchboard corpus.

10. The graphical representation was created in TigerSearch (see section 12.3).

11. The query is shown in TigerSearch (see section 12.3).

12. Example (25) is taken from the OntoNotes Corpus, example (26) from Louis and Nenkova (2010).

13. Both examples are taken from Louis and Nenkova (2010).The underlining of the heads of referents was added by us for didactic reasons.

14. The hypotheses are slightly adapted from Louis and Nenkova (2010). For didactic reasons, we paraphrase "non-elaboration" as "strong." In the original paper these relations are called "core" (see below). See section 8.5 for further references.

15. The text is the beginning of article wsj_0126 from OntoNotes.

16. We use Hypothesis 3a for didactic reasons. It is not part of the original paper by Louis and Nenkova (2010).

Chapter 9

1. Based on AntConc.

2. http://www.cse.unsw.edu.au/~norman/Jokes-file/StudentBloopers.htm

3. Taken from the Student Blooper collection at http://www.cse.unsw.edu.au/~norman/Jokes-file/StudentBloopers.htm.

4. Title: Bones, Being Further Adventures in Mr. Commissioner Sanders' Country, author: Edgar Wallace, Project Gutenberg, http://www.gutenberg.org/cache/epub/24450/pg24450.txt.

5. This is a regular expression in which the ? means the preceding character is optional. For more information on regular expressions cf. Chapter 10.

Chapter 10

1. This form is attested once in the Corpus of Contemporary American English (coca), http://corpus.byu.edu/coca/.

2. We put all regular expressions in double quotes to show their exact boundaries. This should not be done when copying these examples into a search field.

3. Found in coca.

4. Programming languages such as perl or python provide another type of negation, which allows the negation of strings. This is done via a *negative lookahead assertion*. We will not discuss this here since most regular expression modules do not allow this. More information can be found in the Python Standard Library documentation at http://docs.python.org/2/library/re.html.

5. Found in coca.

Notes

Chapter 11

1. A list of the CLAWS 5 POS tags is available at http://www.natcorp.ox.ac.uk/docs/c5spec.html or from the BNC menu.

Chapter 12

1. We will see in the next sections that every query tool uses its own symbols to represent the logical relations we discuss here. While the variance may be discouraging, the concepts behind the notion change only to a much smaller degree.
2. We provide the range of words that a node covers if the node label alone would be ambiguous.
3. Direct dominance is also called *immediate dominance*. We will consistently use direct dominance throughout the chapter, even though some of the query tools use immediate dominance.
4. In mathematical terms, this is the *transitive closure* of the dependency relation.
5. It is also possible to draw the partial tree, as shown before, and have the system translate the query, by using the appropriate button (see the TIGERSEARCH User Manual).
6. Note that this sign is the mirror image of the one used by TGREP.
7. An NX is a noun phrase conjunct in a complex, coordinated noun phrase, as in [$_{NP}$ the [$_{NX}$ smart dog] and [$_{NX}$ rude cat]].

Chapter 13

1. The example is part of the TIMEBANK Corpus.
2. The example is from the Wall Street Journal section of the PENN TREEBANK.
3. In MAC OS X, the tool needs to be called from wish (Windowing Shell).
4. The example is taken from the POTSDAM COMMENTARY CORPUS.
5. This test and others are specified in the annotation guidelines by Götze et al. (2007).
6. EXMARALDA is the tool that had been used for annotating the level of information structure in the first place.

Appendix B

1. Adapted from http://www.comp.leeds.ac.uk/ccalas/tagsets/ice.html

BIBLIOGRAPHY

Adger, David (2003), *Core Syntax: A Minimalist Approach*, Oxford: Oxford University Press.

Asher, Nicholas and Alex Lascarides (2003), *Logics of Conversation*, Studies in Natural Language Processing, Cambridge: Cambridge University Press.

Atkins, Sue, Jeremy Clear and Nick Ostler (1992), "Corpus design criteria," *Literary and Linguistic Computing* 7(1), pp. 1–16.

Baayen, Harald (2008), *Analyzing Linguistic Data: A Practical Introduction to Statistics*, Cambridge: Cambridge University Press.

Babko-Malaya, Olga (2005), *Propbank Annotation Guidelines*. http://verbs.colorado. edu/~mpalmer/projects/ace/PBguidelines.pdf

Bader, Markus and Jana Häussler (2010), "Toward a model of grammaticality judgments," *Journal of Linguistics* 46(02), pp. 273–330.

Baker, Carl L. (1979), "Syntactic theory and the projection problem," *Linguistic Inquiry* 10, pp. 533–82.

Baker, Collin, Charles Fillmore and John Lowe (1998), "The Berkeley FrameNet project," in "Proceedings of the 36th Annual Meeting of the Association for Computational Linguistics and 17th International Conference on Computational Linguistics (COLING-ACL)," Montréal, Canada, pp. 86–90.

Baroni, Marco (2009), "Distributions in text," in A. Lüdeling and M. Kytö (eds), *Corpus Linguistics: An International Handbook*, Vol. 2, Berlin: Mouton de Gruyter, pp. 803–21.

Bartsch, Sabine (2004), *Structural and Functional Properties of Collocations in English*, Tübingen, Narr.

Basile, Valerio, Johan Bos, Kilian Evang and Noortje Venhuizen (2012), "Developing a large semantically annotated corpus," in "Proceedings of the Eighth International Conference on Language Resources and Evaluation (LREC)," Istanbul, Turkey, pp. 3196–200.

Baumann, Stefan and Arndt Riester (2012), "Lexical and referential givenness: Semantic, prosodic and cognitive aspects," in G. Elordieta and P. Prieto (eds), "Prosody and Meaning," Vol. 25 of *Interface Explorations*, Berlin: Mouton de Gruyter, pp. 119–62.

BBN Technologies (2004), *Co-reference Guidelines for English OntoNotes. Annotation guidelines.* http://catalog.ldc.upenn.edu/docs/LDC2007T21/coreference/english-coref.pdf

Beesley, Kenneth and Lauri Karttunen (2003), *Finite-State Morphology*, Palo Alto CA: CSLI Publications.

Bentivogli, Luisa and Emanuele Pianta (2005), "Exploiting parallel texts in the creation of multilingual semantically annotated resources: the Multi-SemCor Corpus," *Natural Language Engineering, Special Issue on Parallel Texts* 11(3), pp. 247–61.

Bergh, Gunnar and Eros Zanchetta (2008), "Web linguistics," in A. Lüdeling and M. Kytö (eds), *Corpus Linguistics: An International Handbook, Vol.1*, Berlin: Mouton de Gruyter, pp. 309–27.

Biber, Douglas (1993), "Representativeness in corpus design," *Literary and Linguistic Computing* 8, pp. 243–57.

Biber, Douglas, Susan Conrad and Randi Reppen (1998), *Corpus Linguistics: Investigating Language Structure and Use*, Cambridge: Cambridge University Press.

Bird, Steven, Ewan Klein and Edward Loper (2009), *Natural Language Processing with Python — Analyzing Text with the Natural Language Toolkit*, O'Reilly Media.

Blair-Goldensohn, Sasha, Kathleen McKeown and Owen Rambow (2007), "Building and refining rhetorical-semantic relation models," in "Human Language Technologies 2007: The Conference of the North American Chapter of the Association for Computational Linguistics," Rochester, NY, pp. 428–35.

Bolinger, Dwight (1967), "Adjectives in English: Attribution and predication," *Lingua* 18, pp. 1–34.

Brants, Sabine, Stefanie Dipper, Peter Eisenberg, Silvia Hansen, Esther König, Wolfgang Lezius, Christian Rohrer, George Smith and Hans Uszkoreit (2004), "TIGER: Linguistic interpretation of a German corpus," *Research on Language and Computation* 2(4), Special Issue on Treebanks and Linguistic Theories, pp. 597–620.

Brants, Sabine, Stefanie Dipper, Silvia Hansen, Wolfgang Lezius and George Smith (2002), "The TIGER treebank," in "Proceedings of the First Workshop on Treebanks and Linguistic Theories (TLT)," Sozopol, Bulgaria, pp. 24–41.

Brants, Thorsten (1998), *TnT – A Statistical Part-of-Speech Tagger*, Universität des Saarlandes, Computational Linguistics, Saarbrücken, Germany. http://www.coli.uni-sb.de/~thorsten/tnt/

—(2000), "TnT – a statistical part-of-speech tagger," in "Proceedings of the 1st Conference of the North American Chapter of the Association for Computational Linguistics and the 6th Conference on Applied Natural Language Processing (ANLP/NAACL)," Seattle, WA, pp. 224–31.

Bresnan, Joan (2000), *Lexical-Functional Syntax*, Oxford: Blackwell.

—(2006), "Is knowledge of syntax probabilistic? Experiments with the English dative alternation," in S. Featherston and W. Sternefeld (eds), *Roots: Linguistics in Search of Its Evidential Base*, Berlin: Mouton de Gruyter, pp. 77–96.

Bresnan, Joan, Anna Cueni, Tatiana Nikitina and Harald Baayen (2007), "Predicting the dative alternation," in G. Bouma, I. Kraemer and J. Zwarts (eds), *Cognitive Foundations of Interpretation*, Royal Netherlands Academy of Arts and Sciences, pp. 69–94.

Burchardt, Aljoscha, Katrin Erk, Anette Frank, Andrea Kowalski, Sebastian Pado and Manfred Pinkal (2006), "The SALSA Corpus: A German corpus resource for lexical semantics," in "Proceedings of the 5th International Conference on Language Resources and Evaluation (LREC)," Genoa, Italy, pp. 969–74.

Byron, Donna (2002), "Resolving pronominal reference to abstract entities," in "Proceedings of 40th Annual Meeting of the Association for Computational Linguistics (ACL)," Philadelphia PA, pp. 80–7.

—(2003), *Annotation of Pronouns and their Antecedents: A Comparison of Two Domains*, Technical Report 703, Department of Computer Science, University of Rochester.

Calhoun, Sasha, Jean Carletta, Jason Brenier, Neil Mayo, Dan Jurafsky, Mark Steedman and David Beaver (2010), "NXT-format Switchboard Corpus: a rich resource for investigating the syntax, semantics, pragmatics and prosody of dialogue," *Language Resources and Evaluation* 44(4), pp. 387–419.

Carlson, Lynn and Daniel Marcu (2001), *Discourse Tagging Manual*, Technical Report ISI Tech Report ISI-TR-545, Information Science Institute, University of Southern California.

Carnie, Andrew (2002), *Syntax: A Generative Introduction*, Oxford: Blackwell.

Chafe, Wallace L. (1994), *Discourse, Consciousness, and Time*, Chicago IL: University of Chicago Press.

Chanev, Atanas, Kiril Simov, Petya Osenova and Svetoslav Marinov (2007), "The BulTreeBank: Parsing and conversion," in "Proceedings of the International Conference on Recent Advances in Natural Language Processing (RANLP)," Borovets, Bulgaria, pp. 114–20.

Choueka, Yaacov (1988), "Looking for needles in a haystack," in "Proceedings of RIAO "88," Cambridge MA, pp. 609–24.

Clark, Herbert H. (1977), "Bridging," in P. N. Johnson-Laird and P. C. Wason (eds), *Thinking: Readings in Cognitive Science*, Cambridge: Cambridge University Press, pp. 411–20.

Čmejrek, Martin, Jan Cuřín, Jiří Havelka, Jan Hajič and Vladislav Kuboň (2004), "Prague Czech-English Dependency Treebank: Syntactically annotated resources for machine translation," in "Proceedings of the 4th International Conference on Language Resources and Evaluation (LREC)," Lisbon, Portugal, pp. 2191–4.

Culicover, Peter W. (2013), "The role of linear order in the computation of referential dependencies," *Lingua* 136, pp. 125–44.

da Cunha, Iria, Juan-Manuel Torres-Moreno and Gerardo Sierra (2011), "On the development of the RST Spanish Treebank," in "Proceedings of the 5th Linguistic Annotation Workshop (LAW)," Portland OR, pp. 1–10.

Daelemans, Walter, Jakub Zavrel, Peter Berck and Steven Gillis (1996), "MBT: A memory-based part of speech tagger-generator," in "Proceedings of the 4th Workshop on Very Large Corpora," Copenhagen, Denmark, pp. 14–27.

Davies, Mark (2009), "The 385+ million word Corpus of Contemporary American English (1990–2008+): Design, architecture, and linguistic insights," *International Journal of Corpus Linguistics* 14(2), pp. 159–90.

Debusmann, Ralph, Denys Duchier and Geert-Jan Kruijff (2004), "Extensible Dependency Grammar: A new methodology," in "Proceedings of the COLING-2004 Workshop on Recent Advances in Dependency Grammar," Geneva, Switzerland, pp. 78–85.

Doddington, George, Alexis Mitchell, Mark Przybocki, Lance Ramshaw, Stephanie Strassel and Ralph Weischedel (2004), "The Automatic Content Extraction (ACE) program: Tasks, data, and evaluation," in "Proceedings of the Fourth International Conference on Language Resources and Evaluation (LREC)," Lisbon, Portugal, pp. 837–40.

Dowty, David R. (1991), "Thematic proto-roles and argument selection," *Language* 67(3), pp. 547–619.

Drach, Erich (1937), *Grundgedanken der Deutschen Satzlehre*, Frankfurt/M.: Diesterweg.

Duchier, Denys and Ralph Debusmann (2001), "Topological dependency trees: A constraint-based account of linear precedence," in "Proceedings of the 39th Annual Meeting of the Association for Computational Linguistics (ACL) and the 10th Conference of the European Chapter of the ACL (EACL)," Toulouse, France, pp. 180–7.

Eckart, Kerstin, Arndt Riester and Katrin Schweitzer (2012), "A discourse information radio news database for linguistic analysis," in C. Chiarcos, S. Nordhoff and S. Hellmann (eds), *Linked Data in Linguistics. Representing and Connecting Language Data and Language Metadata*, Berlin/Heidelberg: Springer, pp. 65–75.

Erdmann, Oskar (1886), *Grundzüge der deutschen Syntax nach ihrer geschichtlichen Entwicklung dargestellt*, Stuttgart: Verlag der Cotta'schen Buchhandlung. Erste Abteilung.

Evert, Stefan (2006), "How random is a corpus? The library metaphor," *Zeitschrift für Anglistik und Amerikanistik* 54(2), pp. 177–90.

—(2008), "Corpora and Collocations," in A. Lüdeling and M. Kytö (eds), *Corpus Linguistics: An International Handbook, Vol. 2*, Berlin: Mouton de Gruyter, pp. 1212–48.

Farrar, Scott and D. Terence Langendoen (2003), "A linguistic ontology for the semantic web," *GLOT International* 7(3), pp. 97–100.

Featherston, Sam (2007), "Data in generative grammar: The stick and the carrot," *Theoretical Linguistics* 33(3), pp. 269–318.

Fellbaum, Christiane (ed.) (1998), *WordNet: An Electronic Lexical Database*, Cambridge MA: MIT Press.

Fillmore, Charles J. (1976), "Frame semantics and the nature of language," *Annals of the New York Academy of Sciences: Conference on the Origin and Development of Language and Speech* 280(1), pp. 20–32.

Firth, John (1957), "A Synopsis of linguistic theory 1930–55," in *Studies in Linguistic Analysis*, Oxford: The Philological Society, pp. 1–32.

Bibliography

Forsyth, Eric N. and Craig H. Martell (2007), "Lexical and discourse analysis of online chat dialog," in "Proceedings of the First IEEE International Conference on Semantic Computing (ICSC 2007)," Irvine CA, pp. 19–26.

Francis, W. Nelson and Henry Kučera (1967), *Computational Analysis of Present-Day American English*, Providence RI: Brown University Press.

—(1979), *Brown Corpus Manual*. Brown University.

Friedl, Jeffrey E. (2006), *Mastering Regular Expressions*, 3rd edn, Sebastopol CA: O'Reilly.

Fromkin, Victoria, Robert Rodman and Nina Hyams (2013), *An Introduction to Language*, 10th edn, Boston MA: Wadsworth Cengage Learning.

Garside, Roger, Geoffrey Leech and Anthony McEnery (eds) (1997), *Corpus Annotation*, London: Longman.

Gehrke, Berit and Louise McNally (submitted), "Distributional modification: The case of frequency adjectives." Note: This is a heavily revised version of a manuscript previously circulated under the title "Frequency adjectives as distributional modifiers."

Geurts, Bart and David I. Beaver (2011), "Discourse representation theory," in E. N. Zalta (ed.), *The Stanford Encyclopedia of Philosophy*, Fall 2011 edn. http://plato.stanford.edu/archives/fall2011/entries/discourse-representation-theory/

Giménez, Jesús and Lluís Màrquez (2004), "SVMTool: A general POS tagger generator based on Support Vector Machines," in "Proceedings of the 4th International Conference on Language Resources and Evaluation (LREC)," Lisbon, Portugal, pp. 43–6.

Godfrey, John, Edward Holliman and J. McDaniel (1992), "SWITCHBOARD: Telephone speech corpus for research and development," in "Proceedings of the IEEE Conference on Acoustics, Speech, and Signal Processing (ICASSP)," San Francisco CA, pp. 517–20.

Goldberg, Adele E. (2013), "Argument structure constructions versus lexical rules or derivational verb templates," *Mind & Language* 28(4), pp. 435–65.

Götze, Michael, Cornelia Endriss, Stefan Hinterwimmer, Ines Fiedler, Svetlana Petrova, Anne Schwarz, Stavros Skopeteas, Ruben Stoel and Thomas Weskott (2007), "Information structure," in S. Dipper, M. Götze and S. Skopeteas (eds), *Information Structure in Crosslinguistic Corpora: Annotation Guidelines for Phonology, Morphology, Syntax, Semantics, and Information Structure*, "Working Papers of the CRC 632, Interdisciplinary Studies on Information Structure (ISIS)," no. 7, pp. 147–87.

Götze, Michael, Thomas Weskott, Cornelia Endriss, Ines Fiedler, Stefan Hinterwimmer, Svetlana Petrova, Anne Schwarz, Stavros Skopeteas and Ruben Stoel (2009), *Information Structure*, Technical Report, University of Potsdam and Humboldt University Berlin.

Granger, Sylviane, Estelle Dagneaux, Fanny Meunier and Magali Paquot (2009), *International Corpus of Learner English v2*, Louvain: Presses universitaires de Louvain.

Gries, Stefan (2008), "Phraseology and linguistic theory: A brief survey," in S. Granger and F. Meunier (eds), *Phraseology: An Interdisciplinary Perspective*, Amsterdam: John Benjamins, pp. 3–25.

—(2013), *Statistics for Linguistics with R: A Practical Introduction*, 2nd edn, Berlin/Boston: de Gruyter.

Grishman, Ralph and Beth Sundheim (1996), "Message Understanding Conference – 6: A brief history," in "Proceedings of the 16th International Conference on Computational Linguistics (COLING)," Copenhagen, Denmark, pp. 466–71.

Habash, Nizar (2010), *Arabic Natural Language Processing*, Morgan & Claypool Publishers.

Hajičová, Eva (2009), "Information structure from the point of view of the relation of function and form," in *The Prague School and Theories of Structure*, Göttingen: V&R Unipress, pp. 107–27.

Hajič, Jan, Alena Böhmová, Eva Hajičová and Barbora Vidová-Hladká (2003), "The Prague Dependency Treebank: A three-level annotation scenario," in A. Abeillé (ed.), *Treebanks:*

Building and Using Parsed Corpora, Dordrecht/Boston/London: Kluwer Academic Publishers, pp. 103–27.

Halliday, Michael A. K. (1967), "Notes on transitivity and theme in English (part 2)," *Journal of Linguistics* 3, pp. 199–244.

Hasler, Laura, Karin Naumann and Constantin Orăsan (2006a), *2006 Guidelines for annotation of within-document event coreference*. University of Wolverhampton. http://clg.wlv.ac.uk/projects/NP4E/event_guidelines_2006.pdf

—(2006b), *2006 Guidelines for annotation of within-document NP coreference*. University of Wolverhampton. http://clg.wlv.ac.uk/projects/NP4E/NP_guidelines_2006.pdf

Hasler, Laura, Constantin Orăsan and Karin Naumann (2006), "Towards cross-document event annotation," in "Proceedings of the Fifth International Conference on Language Resources and Evaluation (LREC)," Genoa, Italy, pp. 1167–72.

Hellwig, Peter (2003), "Dependency Unification Grammar," in V. Agel, L. M. Eichinger, H.-W. Eroms, P. Hellwig, H. J. Heringer and H. Lobin (eds), *Dependency and Valency*, Berlin/New York: Walter de Gruyter, pp. 593–635.

Hemphill, Charles, John Godfrey and George Doddington (1990), "The ATIS Spoken Language Systems Pilot Corpus," in "Proceedings of the DARPA Speech and Natural Language Workshop," Hidden Valley PA, pp. 96–101.

Hetland, Magnus Lie (2008), *Beginning Python*, New York: APress.

Hinrichs, Erhard, Julia Bartels, Yasuhiro Kawata, Valia Kordoni and Heike Telljohann (2000a), "The Tübingen treebanks for spoken German, English, and Japanese," in W. Wahlster (ed.), *Verbmobil: Foundations of Speech-to-Speech Translation*, Berlin: Springer, pp. 550–74.

—(2000b), "The Verbmobil treebanks," in "Proceedings of KONVENS 2000, 5. Konferenz zur Verarbeitung natürlicher Sprache," Ilmenau, Germany, pp. 107–12.

Hinrichs, Erhard, Sandra Kübler, Karin Naumann, Heike Telljohann and Julia Trushkina (2004), "Recent developments in linguistic annotations of the TüBa-D/Z treebank," in "Proceedings of the Third Workshop on Treebanks and Linguistic Theories (TLT)," Tübingen, Germany, pp. 51–62.

Hirschman, Lynette and Nancy Chinchor (1997), "MUC-7 coreference task definition," in "Message Understanding Conference Proceedings." http://www-nlpir.nist.gov/related_projects/muc/proceedings/co_task.html

Hoffmann, Sebastian, Stefan Evert, Nicholas Smith, David Lee and Ylva Berglund Prytz (2008), *Corpus Linguistics with BNCweb – A Practical Guide*, Frankfurt am Main: Peter Lang.

Höhle, Tilman (1986), "Der Begriff 'Mittelfeld,' Anmerkungen über die Theorie der topologischen Felder," in "Akten des Siebten Internationalen Germanistenkongresses 1985," Göttingen, Germany, pp. 329–40.

Hou, Yufang, Katja Markert and Michael Strube (2013), "Global inference for bridging anaphora resolution," in "Proceedings of the 2013 Conference of the North American Chapter of the Association for Computational Linguistics: Human Language Technologies," Atlanta GA, pp. 907–17.

Hovy, Eduard, Mitchell Marcus, Martha Palmer, Lance Ramshaw and Ralph Weischedel (2006), "OntoNotes: The 90% solution," in "Proceedings of the Human Language Technology Conference of the NAACL," New York NY, pp. 57–60.

Hudson, Richard (1990), *English Word Grammar*, Oxford: Blackwell.

—(2007), *Language Networks: The New Word Grammar*, Oxford: Oxford University Press.

Hundt, Marianne, Nadja Nesselhauf and Carolin Biewer (2007), *Corpus Linguistics and the Web (Language and Computers. Studies in Practical Linguistics* no. 59), Amsterdam: Rodopi.

Ide, Nancy, Collin Baker, Christiane Fellbaum, Charles Fillmore and Rebecca Passonneau

(2008), "MASC: The manually annotated sub-corpus of American English," in "Proceedings of the Sixth Language Resources and Evaluation Conference (LREC)," Marrakech, Morocco, pp. 2455–60.

Ide, Nancy, Collin Baker, Christiane Fellbaum and Rebecca Passonneau (2010), "The manually annotated sub-corpus: A community resource for and by the people," in "Proceedings of the ACL 2010 Conference Short Papers," Uppsala, Sweden, pp. 68–73.

Ide, Nancy and Keith Suderman (2004), "The American National Corpus first release," in "Proceedings of the Fourth Language Resources and Evaluation Conference (LREC)," Lisbon, Portugal, pp. 1681–4.

Järvinen, Timo and Pasi Tapanainen (1998), "Towards an implementable dependency grammar," in "Proceedings of the Joint COLING/ACL Workshop: Processing of Dependency-Based Grammars," Montreal, Canada, pp. 1–10.

Johansson, Richard and Pierre Nugues (2007), "Extended constituent-to-dependency conversion for English," in "Proceedings of NODALIDA 2007," Tartu, Estonia, pp. 105–12.

Johnson, Keith (2008), *Quantitative Methods in Linguistics*, Malden, Oxford and Victoria: Blackwell Publishing.

Joshi, Aravind (1987), "An introduction to Tree Adjoining Grammars," in A. Manaster-Ramer (ed.), *Mathematics of Language*, Amsterdam: John Benjamins, pp. 87–115.

Kaeding, Friedrich Wilhelm (1897), *Häufigkeitswörterbuch der deutschen Sprache*, privately published, Steglitz.

Kamp, Hans and Uwe Reyle (1993), *From Discourse to Logic*, Dordrecht/Boston/London: Kluwer Academic Publishers.

Karlsson, Fred (1990), "Constraint grammar as a framework for parsing running text," in "Proceedings of the 13th International Conference on Computational Linguistics (COLING)," Helsinki, Finland, pp. 168–73.

Karlsson, Fred, Atro Voutilainen, J. Heikkilä and Atro Anttila (eds) (1995), *Constraint Grammar: A Language-Independent System for Parsing Unrestricted Text*, Berlin: Mouton de Gruyter.

Karttunen, Lauri and Kenneth Beesley (1992), *Two-level Rule Compiler*, Technical Report ISTL-92-2, Xerox PARC.

Kehler, Andrew (2004), "Discourse coherence," in L. Horn and G. Ward (eds), *Handbook of Pragmatics*, Oxford: Basil Blackwell.

—(2012), "Cohesion and coherence," in C. Maienborn, K. Heusinger and P. Portner (eds), *Semantics: An International Handbook of Natural Language Meaning*, Berlin/Boston: Walter de Gruyter, ch. 74.

Kilgarriff, Adam (1998), "SENSEVAL: An exercise in evaluating word sense disambiguation programs," in "Proceedings of the International Conference on Language Resources and Evaluation (LREC)," Granada, Spain, pp. 581–8.

Kilgarriff, Adam and Gregory Grefenstette (2003), "Introduction to the special issue on the web as corpus," *Computational Linguistics* 29(3), pp. 333–47.

Kipper, Karin, Hoa Trang Dang and Martha Palmer (2000), "Class-based construction of a verb lexicon," in "Proceedings of the 17th National Conference on Artificial Intelligence," Austin TX, pp. 691–6.

Kipper Schuler, Karin (2005), *VerbNet: A Broad-Coverage, Comprehensive Verb Lexicon*, PhD thesis, University of Pennsylvania.

Koehn, Philipp (2005), "Europarl: A parallel corpus for statistical machine translation," in "Proceedings of the 10th Machine Translation Summit," Phuket, Thailand, pp. 79–86.

König, Esther, Wolfgang Lezius and Holger Voormann (2003), *Tigersearch 2.1 User's Manual*, Technical Report, IMS, University of Stuttgart.

Krifka, Manfred (2008), "Basic notions of information structure," *Acta Linguistica Hungarica* 55(3), pp. 243–76.

Larson, Richard (1988), "Events and modification in nominals," in D. Strolovitch and A. Lawson (eds), "Proceedings of the 8th Semantics and Linguistic Theory Conference (SALT)," Massachusetts Institute of Technology, pp. 145–68.

Leech, Geoffrey (1997), "Introducing corpus annotation," in R. Garside, G. Leech and A. McEnery (eds), *Corpus Annotation*, London: Longman, pp. 1–18.

Leech, Geoffrey, Roger Garside and M. Bryant (1994), "CLAWS4: The tagging of the British National Corpus," in "Proceedings of the 15th International Conference on Computational Linguistics (COLING)," Kyoto, Japan, pp. 622–8.

Lemnitzer, Lothar and Heike Zinsmeister (2010), *Korpuslinguistik — Eine Einführung*, 2nd edn, Tübingen: Gunter Narr.

Levin, Beth (1993), *English Verb Classes and Alternations*, 1st edn, Chicago: University of Chicago Press.

Löbner, Sebastian (1985), "Definites," *Journal of Semantics* 4, pp. 279–326.

—(2011), "Concept types and determination," *Journal of Semantics* 28, pp. 279–333.

Louis, Annie and Ani Nenkova (2010), "Creating local coherence: An empirical assessment," in "Human Language Technologies: The 2010 Annual Conference of the North American Chapter of the Association for Computational Linguistics," Los Angeles CA, pp. 313–16.

MacWhinney, Brian (2007), "The TalkBank project," in J. Beal, K. Corrigan and H. Moisl (eds), *Creating and Digitizing Language Corpora: Synchronic Databases*, Basingstoke: Palgrave-Macmillan, pp.163–80.

—(2008), "Enriching CHILDES for morphosyntactic analysis," in H. Behrens (ed.), *Trends in Corpus Research: Finding Structure in Data*, Amsterdam: John Benjamins, pp. 165–98.

Mann, William C. and Sandra A. Thompson (1988), "Rhetorical structure theory: Toward a functional theory of text organization," *Text* 8(3), pp. 243–81.

Manning, Chris (2003), "Probabilistic syntax," in R. Bod, J. Hay and S. Jannedy (eds), *Probabilistic Linguistics*, Cambridge MA: MIT Press, pp. 289–341.

Manning, Christopher and Hinrich Schütze (1999), *Foundations of Statistical Natural Language Processing*, Cambridge MA: MIT Press.

Marcu, Daniel and Abdessamad Echihabi (2002), "An unsupervised approach to recognizing discourse relations," in "Proceedings of the 40th Annual Meeting of the Association for Computational Linguistics," Philadelphia PA, pp. 368–75.

Marcus, Mitchell, Grace Kim, Mary Ann Marcinkiewicz, Robert MacIntyre, Ann Bies, Mark Ferguson, Karen Katz and Britta Schasberger (1994), "The Penn Treebank: Annotating predicate argument structure," in "Proceedings of the ARPA Human Language Technology Workshop, HLT 94," Plainsboro NJ, pp. 114–19.

Marcus, Mitchell, Beatrice Santorini and Mary Ann Marcinkiewicz (1993), "Building a large annotated corpus of English: the Penn Treebank," *Computational Linguistics* 19(2), pp. 313–30.

Markert, Katja, Yufang Hou and Michael Strube (2012), "Collective classification for fine-grained information status," in "Proceedings of the 50th Annual Meeting of the Association for Computational Linguistics (ACL)," Jeju Island, Korea, pp. 795–804.

Markert, Katja and Malvina Nissim (2005), "Comparing knowledge sources for nominal anaphora resolution," *Computational Linguistics* 31(3), pp. 368–401.

Maruyama, Hiroshi (1990), "Structural disambiguation with constraint propagation," in "Proceedings of the 28th Meeting of the ACL," Pittsburgh PA, pp. 31–88.

McEnery, Tony and Andrew Hardie (2012), *Corpus Linguistics: Method, Theory and Practice*, Cambridge: Cambridge University Press.

McEnery, Tony and Andrew Wilson (2001), *Corpus Linguistics: An Introduction*, Edinburgh: Edinburgh University Press.

McEnery, Tony, Richard Xiao and Yukio Tono (2005), *Corpus Based Language Studies*, London/New York: Routledge.

Bibliography

McGregor, William (2009), *Linguistics: An Introduction*, London/New York: Continuum International.

Mel'čuk, Igor A. (1988), *Dependency Syntax: Theory and Practise*, SUNY Series in Linguistics, Albany, NY: State University of New York Press.

Menzel, Wolfgang and Ingo Schröder (1998), "Decision procedures for dependency parsing using graded constraints," in "Proceedings of the Joint COLING/ACL Workshop: Processing of Dependency-Based Grammars," Montréal, Canada, pp. 78–86.

Meyer, Charles F. (2008), "Pre-electronic corpora," in A. Lüdeling and M. Kytö (eds), *Corpus Linguistics: An International Handbook*, Vol. 1, Berlin: Mouton de Gruyter, pp. 1–14.

Meyers, Adam, Ruth Reeves, Catherine Macleod, Rachel Szekely, Veronika Zielinska, Brian Young and Ralph Grishman (2004), "The NomBank project: An interim report," in "Proceedings of the HLT-NAACL Workshop: Frontiers in Corpus Annotation," Boston MA, pp. 24–31.

Miller, George A. (1995), "WordNet: A lexical database for English," *Communications of the ACM* 38(11), pp. 39–41.

Miller, George A., Martin Chodorow, Shari Landes, Claudia Leacock and Robert G. Thomas (1994), "Using a semantic concordance for sense identification," in "Proceedings of ARPA Human Language Technology Workshop," Plainsboro NJ, pp. 240–3.

Miller, George A., Claudia Leacock, Randee Tengi and Ross T. Bunker (1993), "A semantic concordance," in "Proceedings of the Third DARPA Workshop on Human Language Technology," Plainsboro NJ, pp. 303–8.

Naumann, Karin (2007), *Manual for the Annotation of In-document Referential Relations*. Universität Tübingen. http://www.sfs.uni-tuebingen.de/resources/tuebadz-coreference-manual-2007.pdf

Navaretta, Costanza (2008), "Pronominal types and abstract reference in the Danish and Italian DAD corpora," in "Proceedings of the Second Workshop on Anaphora Resolution (WAR II)," Bergen, Norway, pp. 63–71.

Navaretta, Costanza and Sussi Olsen (2008), "Annotating abstract pronominal anaphora in the DAD project," in "Proceedings of the Sixth International Conference on Language Resources and Evaluation (LREC)," Marrakesh, Morocco, pp. 2046–52.

Navigli, Roberto and Simone Paolo Ponzetto (2010), "Babelnet: Building a very large multilingual semantic network," in "Proceedings of the 48th Annual Meeting of the Association for Computational Linguistics (ACL)," Uppsala, Sweden, pp. 216–25.

Nedoluzhko, Anna and Jiří Mírovský (2011), *Annotating Extended Textual Coreference and Bridging Relations*, in "Prague Dependency Treebank, Technical Report", Prague University.

Nedoluzhko, Anna, Jiří Mírovský, Radek Ocelák and Jiří Pergler (2009), "Extended coreferential relations and bridging anaphora in the Prague Dependency Treebank," in "Proceedings of Discourse Anaphora and Anaphor Resolution Colloquium (DAARC)," Goa, India, pp. 1–16.

Nelson, Gerald, Sean Wallis and Bas Aarts (2002), *Exploring Natural Language: Working with the British Component of the International Corpus of English*, Amsterdam: John Benjamins.

Nissim, Malvina, Shipra Dingare, Jean Carletta and Mark Steedman (2004), "An annotation scheme for information status in dialogue," in "Proceedings of the 4th Conference on Language Resources and Evaluation (LREC)," Lisbon, Portugal, pp. 1023–6.

O'Grady, William, John Archibald, Mark Aronoff and Janie Rees-Miller (2009), *Contemporary Linguistics: An Introduction*, 6th edn, Bedford: St. Martin's.

Ohara, Kyoko (2012), "Semantic annotations in Japanese FrameNet: Comparing frames in Japanese and English," in "Proceedings of the Eighth International Conference on Language Resources and Evaluation (LREC)," Istanbul, Turkey, pp. 1559–62.

Palmer, Martha (2009), "Semlink: Linking PropBank, VerbNet and FrameNet," in "Proceedings of the Generative Lexicon Conference," Pisa, Italy, pp. 9–15.

Palmer, Martha, Dan Gildea and Paul Kingsbury (2005), "The Proposition Bank: A corpus annotated with semantic roles," *Computational Linguistics* 31(1), pp. 71–106.

Passonneau, Rebecca (2004), "Computing reliability for coreference annotation," in "Proceedings of the Fourth International Conference on Language Resources and Evaluation (LREC)," Lisbon, Portugal, pp. 1503–6.

Payne, John, Geoffrey K. Pullum, Barbara C. Scholz and Eva Berlage (2013), "Anaphoric 'one' and its implications," *Language* 89(4), pp. 794–829.

Pianta, Emanuele, Luisa Bentivogli and Christian Girardi (2002), "MultiWordNet: Developing an aligned multilingual database," in "Proceedings of the First International Conference on Global WordNet," Mysore, India, pp. 93–302.

Pinker, Steven (1989), "The learnability and acquisition of the dative alternation in English," *Language* 65(2), pp. 203–57.

Poesio, Massimo (2000), *The Gnome Annotation Scheme Manual.* University of Essex.

Poesio, Massimo, Florence Bruneseaux and Laurent Romary (1999), "The MATE meta-scheme for coreference in dialogues in multiple languages," in "Proceedings of the ACL Workshop on Standards for Discourse Tagging," College Park MD, pp. 65–74.

Pollard, Carl and Ivan Sag (1994), *Head-Driven Phrase Structure Grammar*, Studies in Contemporary Linguistics, Chicago IL: University of Chicago Press.

Postal, Paul M. (1971), *Crossover Phenomena*, New York, NY: Holt, Rinehart and Winston.

Pradhan, Sameer and Jeff Kaufman (2012), *OntoNotes DB Tool Documentation. Release 0.999b*, BBN Technologies.

Prasad, Rashmi, Nikhil Dinesh, Alan Lee, Eleni Miltsakaki, Livio Robaldo, Aravind Joshi and Bonnie Webber (2008), "The Penn Discourse Treebank 2.0," in "Proceedings of the 6th International Conference on Language Resources and Evaluation (LREC)," Marrakech, Morocco, pp. 2962–8.

Prasad, Rashmi, Aravind Joshi and Bonnie Webber (2010), "Realization of discourse relations by other means: Alternative lexicalization," in "Proceedings of the 23rd International Conference on Computational Linguistics (COLING)," Beijing, China, pp. 1023–31.

Prasad, Rashmi, Eleni Miltsakaki, Nikhil Dinesh, Alan Lee, Aravind Joshi, Livio Robaldo and Bonnie Webber (2007), *The Penn Discourse Treebank 2.0 Annotation Manual.* University of Pennsylvania.

Prince, Ellen F. (1981), "Toward a taxonomy of given-new information," in P. Cole (ed.), *Radical Pragmatics*, New York, NY: Academic Press, pp. 223–55.

—(1992), "The ZPG Letter: Subjects, definiteness, and information-status," in S. Thompson and W. Mann (eds), *Discourse Description: Diverse Analyses of a Fund Raising Text*, Philadelphia/ Amsterdam: John Benjamins, pp. 295–325.

Pullum, Geoffrey K. and Barbara C. Scholz (2002), "Empirical assessment of stimulus poverty arguments," *The Linguistic Review* 19, pp. 9–50.

Pustejovsky, James, José Castaño, Robert Ingria, Roser Saurí, Robert Gaizauskas, Andrea Setzer and Graham Katz (2003), "TimeML: Robust specification of event and temporal expressions in text," in "Proceedings of the fifth international workshop on computational semantics," Tilburg, The Netherlands, pp. 1–11.

Pustejovsky, James and Amber Stubbs (2013), *Natural Language Annotation*, Sebastopol CA: O'Reilly.

Quirk, Randolph, Sidney Greenbaum, Geoffrey Leech and Jan Svartvik (1985), *A Comprehensive Grammar of the English Language*, London: Longman.

Radford, Andrew (2004), *Minimalist Syntax: Exploring the Structure of English*, Cambridge: Cambridge University Press.

Rappaport Hovav, Malka and Beth Levin (2008), "The English dative alternation: The case for verb sensitivity," *Journal of Linguistics* 44(1), p. 129–67.

Bibliography

Renkema, Jan (2004), *Introduction to Discourse Studies*, Amsterdam: John Benjamins.

Resnik, Philip and Aaron Elkiss (2005), "The Linguist's Search Engine: An overview," in "Proceedings of the ACL Interactive Poster and Demonstration Sessions," Ann Arbor MI, pp. 33–6.

Resnik, Philip, Aaron Elkiss, Ellen Lau and Heather Taylor (2005), "The web in theoretical linguistic research: Two case studies using the Linguist's Search Engine," in "Proceedings of the 31st Meeting of the Berkeley Linguistics Society, BLS-31," Berkeley CA, pp. 265–76.

Riester, Arndt and Stefan Baumann (2013), "Focus triggers and focus types from a corpus perspective," *Dialogue & Discourse* 4(2), pp. 215–48. Special issue on "Beyond Semantics: The Challenges of Annotating Pragmatic and Discourse Phenomena."

Rösner, Dietmar and Manfred Stede (1992), "Customizing RST for the automatic production of technical manuals," in R. Dale, E. Hovy, D. Rösner and O. Stock (eds), *Aspects of Automated Natural Language Generation*, vol. 587 of *Lecture Notes in Computer Science*, Berlin and Heidelberg: Springer, pp. 199–214.

Ruppenhofer, Josef, Michael Ellsworth, Miriam R. L. Petruck, Christopher R. Johnson and Jan Scheffczyk (2010), *FrameNet II: Extended Theory and Practice*, International Computer Science Institute.

Salgueiro Pardo, Thiago Alexandre and Eloize Rossi Marques Seno (2005), "Rhetalho: Um corpus de referência anotado retoricamente," in "Anais do V Encontro de Corpora," São Carlos-SP, Brazil.

Sampson, Geoffrey (1993), "The SUSANNE corpus," *ICAME Journal* 17, pp. 125–7.

—(1995), *English for the Computer*, Oxford: Clarendon Press.

—(2003), "The structure of children's writing: Moving from spoken to adult written norms," in S. Granger and S. Petch-Tyson (eds), *Language and Computers: Extending the Scope of Corpus-Based Research: New Applications, New Challenges*, Amsterdam: Rodopi, pp. 177–93.

—(2007), "Grammar without grammaticality," *Corpus Linguistics and Linguistic Theory* 3(1), pp. 1–32.

Sampson, Geoffrey and Diana McCarthy (eds) (2004), *Corpus Linguistics: Readings in a Widening Discipline*, London and New York: Continuum International.

Samuelsson, Yvonne and Martin Volk (2005), "Presentation and representation of parallel treebanks," in "Proceedings of the NODALIDA Workshop on Treebanks," Joensuu, Finland, pp. 147–59.

—(2006), "Phrase alignment in parallel treebanks," in "Proceedings of the 5th Workshop on Treebanks and Linguistic Theories (TLT)," Prague, Czech Republic, pp. 91–102.

Sanders, Ted (1997), "Semantic and pragmatic sources of coherence: On the categorization of coherence relations in context," *Discourse Processes* 24, pp. 119–47.

Santorini, Beatrice (1990), *Part-of-speech tagging guidelines for the Penn Treebank Project*. Department of Computer and Information Science, University of Pennsylvania, 3rd Revision, 2nd Printing. ftp://ftp.cis.upenn.edu/pub/treebank/doc/tagguide.ps.gz

—(1991), "Bracketing guidelines for the Penn Treebank Project." Department of Computer and Information Science, University of Pennsylvania. ftp://ftp.cis.upenn.edu/pub/treebank/doc/old-bktguide.ps.gz

Santorini, Beatrice and Anthony Kroch (2007), *The Syntax of Natural Language: An Online Introduction using the Trees Program*. http://www.ling.upenn.edu/~beatrice/syntax-textbook/.

Sato, Hiroaki (2008), *New functions of FrameSQL for multilingual FrameNets*, in "Proceedings of the Sixth International Conference on Language Resources and Evaluation (LREC)," Marrakech, Morocco, pp. 758–62.

Saurí, Roser, Jessica Littman, Bob Knippen, Robert Gaizauskas, Andrea Setzer and James Pustejovsky (2006), *TimeML Annotation Guidelines*. http://www.timeml.org/site/publications/specs.html

Schauer, Holger (2000), "From elementary discourse units to complex ones," in "Proceedings of the 1st SIGdial Workshop on Discourse and Dialogue," Hong Kong, pp. 46–55.

Schmid, Helmut (1994), "Probabilistic part-of-speech tagging using decision trees," in "Proceedings of the International Conference on New Methods in Language Processing," Manchester, Great Britain, pp. 44–9.

—(1995), "Improvements in part-of-speech tagging with an application to German," in "Proceedings of the ACL SIGDAT-Workshop," Dublin, Ireland, pp. 47–50.

Schröder, Ingo (2002), *Natural Language Parsing with Graded Constraints*, PhD thesis, Hamburg University.

Schütze, Carson (1996), *The Empirical Base of Linguistics: Grammaticality Judgments and Linguistic Methodology*, Chicago: University of Chicago Press.

—(2009), "Web searches should supplement judgements, not supplant them," *Zeitschrift für Sprachwissenschaft* 28(1), pp. 151–6.

—(2011), "Linguistic evidence and grammatical theory," *Wiley Interdisciplinary Reviews: Cognitive Science* 2(2), pp. 206–21.

Schwartz, Randal L., Brian D. Foy and Tom Phoenix (2011), *Learning Perl*, 6th edn, Sebastopol, CA: O'Reilly Media.

Scrivner, Olga and Sandra Kübler (2012), "Building an Old Occitan corpus via cross-language transfer," in "Proceedings of the First International Workshop on Language Technology for Historical Text(s)," Vienna, Austria, pp. 392–400.

Scrivner, Olga, Sandra Kübler, Barbara Vance and Eric Beuerlein (2013), "Le Roman de Flamenca: An annotated corpus of Old Occitan," in "Proceedings of the Third Workshop on Annotation of Corpora for Research in the Humanities," Sofia, Bulgaria, pp. 85–96.

Sgall, Petr, Eva Hajičová and Jarmila Panevová (1986), *The Meaning of the Sentence in Its Pragmatic Aspects*, Dordrecht: Reidel.

Skut, Wojciech, Thorsten Brants, Brigitte Krenn and Hans Uszkoreit (1998), "A linguistically interpreted corpus of German newspaper texts," in "ESS-LLI Workshop on Recent Advances in Corpus Annotation," Saarbrücken, Germany, pp. 12–25.

Skut, Wojciech, Brigitte Krenn, Thorsten Brants and Hans Uszkoreit (1997), "An annotation scheme for free word order languages," in "Proceedings of the Fifth Conference on Applied Natural Language Processing (ANLP)," Washington, DC.

Sorace, Antonella and Frank Keller (2005), "Gradience in linguistic data," *Lingua* 11, pp. 1497–524.

Sporleder, Caroline and Alex Lascarides (2008), "Using automatically labelled examples to classify rhetorical relations: An assessment," *Natural Language Engineering* 14(3), pp. 369–416.

Stede, Manfred (2004), "The Potsdam Commentary Corpus," in "Proceedings of the ACL Workshop on Discourse Annotation," Barcelona, Spain, pp. 96–102.

—(2008), "RST revisited: Disentangling nuclearity," in C. Fabricius-Hansen and W. Ramm (eds), *"Subordination" versus "Coordination" in Sentence and Text – A Cross-Linguistic Perspective*, Studies in Language Companion Series, Amsterdam: John Benjamins, pp. 33–58.

Steedman, Mark (2000), *The Syntactic Process*, Cambridge MA: MIT Press.

Stegmann, Rosmary, Heike Telljohann and Erhard W. Hinrichs (2000), *Stylebook for the German Treebank in VERBMOBIL*, Technical Report 239, Verbmobil. http://www.sfs.uni-tuebingen.de/fileadmin/static/ascl/resources/stylebook_vm_ger.pdf

Stump, Gregory T. (1981), "The interpretation of frequency adjectives," *Linguistics and Philosophy* 4, pp. 221–57.

Taboada, Maite (2009), "Implicit and explicit coherence relations," in J. Renkema (ed.), *Discourse, of Course*, Amsterdam: John Benjamins, pp. 127–40.

Taboada, Maite, Caroline Anthony and Kimberley Voll (2006), "Methods for creating semantic orientation dictionaries," in "Proceedings of the 5th International Conference on Language Resources and Evaluation (LREC)," Genoa, Italy, pp. 427–32.

Taboada, Maite and Jan Renkema (2008), *Discourse relations reference corpus*. http://www.sfu.ca/rst/06tools/discourse_ relations_corpus.html

Taboada, Maite and Manfred Stede (2009), "Introduction to RST – Rhetorical Structure Theory." Slides: http://www.sfu.ca/rst/06tools/index.html

Taboada, Maite and William C. Mann (2006), "Rhetorical Structure Theory: Looking back and moving ahead," *Discourse Studies* 8(3), pp. 423–59.

Tapanainen, Pasi and Timo Järvinen (1997), "A Non-projective dependency parser," in "Proceedings of the 5th Conference on Applied Natural Language Processing (ANLP)," Washington DC, pp. 64–71.

Tapanainen, Pasi and Atro Voutilainen (1994), "Tagging accurately – Don't guess if you know," in "Proceedings of the Fourth Conference on Applied Natural Language Processing (ANLP)," Stuttgart, Germany, pp. 47–52.

Telljohann, Heike, Erhard Hinrichs and Sandra Kübler (2004), "The TüBa-D/Z treebank: Annotating German with a context-free backbone," in "Proceedings of the Fourth International Conference on Language Resources and Evaluation (LREC)," Lisbon, Portugal, pp. 2229–35.

Telljohann, Heike, Erhard Hinrichs, Sandra Kübler, Heike Zinsmeister and Kathrin Beck (2012), *Stylebook for the Tübingen Treebank of Written German (TüBa-D/Z)*, Seminar für Sprachwissenschaft, Universität Tübingen, Germany. http://www.sfs.uni-tuebingen.de/fileadmin/static/ascl/resources/tuebadz-stylebook-1201.pdf

Tesnière, Lucien (1959), *Éléments de syntaxe structurale*, Paris: Editions Klincksieck.

Teubert, Wolfgang (2005), "My version of corpus linguistics," *International Journal of Corpus Linguistics* 10(1), pp. 1–13.

Tiedemann, Jörg (2012), "Parallel data, tools and interfaces in OPUS," in "Proceedings of the 8th International Conference on Language Resources and Evaluation (LREC)," Istanbul, Turkey, pp. 2214–8.

Torabi Asr, Fatemeh and Vera Demberg (2012), "Implicitness of discourse relations," in "Proceedings of COLING 2012," Mumbai, India, pp. 2669–84.

Toutanova, Kristina and Christopher D. Manning (2000), "Enriching the knowledge sources used in a maximum entropy part-of-speech tagger," in "Proceedings of the Joint SIGDAT Conference on Empirical Methods in Natural Language Processing and Very Large Corpora (EMNLP/VLC)," Hong Kong, pp. 63–70.

Toutanova, Kristina, Dan Klein, Christopher Manning and Yoram Singer (2003), "Feature-rich part-of-speech tagging with a cyclic dependency network," in "Proceedings of HLT-NAACL 2003," Edmonton, Canada, pp. 252–9.

Vallduví, Enric and Elisabet Engdahl (1996), "The linguistic realisation of information packaging," *Linguistics* 34, pp. 459–519.

Versley, Yannick and Anna Gastel (2013), "Linguistic tests for discourse relations," *Dialogue & Discourse* 4(2), pp. 142–73. Special issue on "Beyond Semantics: The Challenges of Annotating Pragmatic and Discourse Phenomena."

Wahlster, Wolfgang (ed.) (2000), *Verbmobil: Foundations of Speech-to-Speech Translation*, Berlin: Springer.

Wallis, Sean and Gerald Nelson (2006), "The British Component of the International Corpus of English," Release 2. CD-ROM. London: Survey of English Usage, UCL.

Wasow, Thomas (1972), *Anaphoric Relations in English*, PhD thesis, MIT, Cambridge, MA. Unpublished doctoral dissertation.

—(2002), *Postverbial Behavior*, Stanford CA: CSLI Publications.

Wasow, Thomas, T. Florian Jaeger and David Orr (2011), "Lexical variation in relativizer frequency," in H. Simon and H. Wiese (eds), *Expecting the Unexpected: Exceptions in Grammar*, Berlin: Walter de Gruyter, pp. 175–96.

Webber, Bonnie (2004), "D-LTAG: Extending lexicalized TAG to discourse," *Cognitive Science* 28, pp. 751–79.

Weischedel, Ralph, Martha Palmer, Mitchell Marcus, Eduard Hovy, Sameer Pradhan, Lance Ramshaw, Nianwen Xue, Ann Taylor, Jeff Kaufman, Michelle Franchini, Mohammed El-Bachouti, Robert Belvin and Ann Houston (2012), *OntoNotes Release 5.0 with OntoNotes DB Tool v0.999 beta*, Linguistic Data Consortium.

Wolf, Florian and Edward Gibson (2006), *Coherence in Natural Language*, Cambridge MA: MIT Press.

Wolf, Florian, Edward Gibson, Amy Fisher and Meredith Knight (2004), *Discourse Graphbank*, Linguistic Data Consortium.

Wynne, Martin (ed.) (2005), *Developing Linguistic Corpora: A Guide to Good Practice*, Oxbow Books. http://www.ahds.ac.uk/creating/guides/linguistic-corpora/

Zeldes, Amir (2013), *ANNIS. User Guide 1.0.0 (ANNIS version 3.0.1)*, SFB 632 Information Structure/D1 Linguistic Database. Humboldt-Universität zu Berlin/Universität Potsdam.

Zeyrek, Deniz, Işın Demirşahin, Ayışığı Sevdik Callı and Ruket Cakıcı (2013), "Turkish Discourse Bank: Porting a discourse annotation style to a morphologically rich language," *Dialogue & Discourse* 4(2), pp. 174–84. Special issue on "Beyond Semantics: The Challenges of Annotating Pragmatic and Discourse Phenomena."

Zimmermann, Malte (2003), "Pluractionality and complex quantifier formation," *Natural Language Semantics* 11, pp. 249–87.

Zinsmeister, Heike, Erhard Hinrichs, Sandra Kübler and Andreas Witt (2009), "Linguistically annotated corpora: Quality assurance, reusability and sustainability," in A. Lüdeling and M. Kytö (eds), *Corpus Linguistics: An International Handbook*, Vol. 1, Berlin: Mouton de Gruyter, pp. 759–76.

Zipf, G. K. (1949), *Human Behaviour and the Principle of Least Effort*, Cambridge MA: Addison-Wesley.

INDEX

Index

Index

Index

Index

Index

9 781441 116758